P9-DWT-058

VENICE

VENICE

A NEW HISTORY

THOMAS F. MADDEN

VIKING

VIKING
Published by the Penguin Group
Penguin Group (USA) Inc., 375 Hudson Street, New York, New York 10014, U.S.A. •
Penguin Group (Canada), 90 Eglinton Avenue East, Suite 700, Toronto, Ontario, Canada
M4P 2Y3 (a division of Pearson Penguin Canada Inc.) • Penguin Books Ltd, 80 Strand,
London WC2R 0RL, England • Penguin Ireland, 25 St Stephen's Green, Dublin 2, Ireland
(a division of Penguin Books Ltd) • Penguin Group (Australia), 707 Collins St., Melbourne,
Victoria 3008, Australia (a division of Pearson Australia Group Pty Ltd) • Penguin Books
India Pvt Ltd, 11 Community Centre, Panchsheel Park, New Delhi – 110 017, India •
Penguin Group (NZ), 67 Apollo Drive, Rosedale, Auckland 0632, New Zealand (a division
of Pearson New Zealand Ltd) • Penguin Books, Rosebank Office Park, 181 Jan Smuts
Avenue, Parktown North 2193, South Africa • Penguin China, B7 Jaiming Center, 27 East
Third Ring Road North, Chaoyang District, Beijing 100020, China

Penguin Books Ltd, Registered Offices:
80 Strand, London WC2R 0RL, England

First published in 2012 by Viking Penguin,
a member of Penguin Group (USA) Inc.

1   3   5   7   9   10   8   6   4   2

Map illustrations by Meighan Cavanaugh

Library of Congress Cataloging-in-Publication Data

Madden, Thomas F.
Venice : islands of honor and profit : a new history / Thomas F. Madden.
p.   cm.
Includes bibliographical references and index.
ISBN 978-0-670-02542-8 (alk. paper)
1. Venice (Italy)—History. I. Title.
DG676.M33 2012
945'.311—dc23   2012005304

Printed in the United States of America
Set in Diverda Serif with Medium Roman
Designed by Daniel Lagin

For Page, Helena, and Melinda

CONTENTS

Contents

ACKNOWLEDGMENTS

Because I have, in one form or another, been working on this book for more than two decades, I have accrued so many debts that to list them all would require almost another chapter. There are, nonetheless, a few whom I must not fail to thank.

First and foremost I am grateful to my friend and mentor, the late Professor Donald E. Queller. It was he who first introduced me to the rich history of Venice and, despite my occasional protests, persuaded me to devote my efforts to its study. Near the end of his life Don Queller had begun a new book on the history and culture of Venice. Unfortunately, he did not live to finish it. I have no idea what became of his notes, but I am certain that had he lived a few years longer, there would have been no need for this book. I am also grateful to Don's old classmate, the late Professor Louise Buenger Robbert, who was always a source of guidance and support for my work in Venice. As with any scholar, I have benefited enormously from the suggestions, advice, and kindnesses of my colleagues in the field. I offer my special thanks to Alfred J. Andrea (University of Vermont), Andrea Berto (Western Michigan University), Patricia

Fortini Brown (Princeton University), Michela Dal Borgo (Archivio di Stato di Venezia), Robert C. Davis (Ohio State University), Blake de Maria (Santa Clara University), Ronnie Ellenblum (Hebrew University), M. Cecilia Gaposchkin (Dartmouth College), Benjamin Z. Kedar (Hebrew University), Bianca Lanfranchi (Archivio di Stato di Venezia), Serban Marin (National Archives of Romania), Sally McKee (University of California, Davis), Christopher Pastore (University of Pennsylvania), Jonathan Riley-Smith (Cambridge University), Juergen Schulz (Brown University), Alan M. Stahl (Princeton University), Diana Gilliland Wright (Independent Scholar), and all of the staff at the Biblioteca Nazionale Marciana, the Museo Correr, and the Archivio di Stato di Venezia.

Because Venice is an expensive city, no foreign scholar could afford to live and work there without significant support. I am, therefore, grateful to all of my financial benefactors, especially the Mellon Faculty Development Fund and the Gladys Krieble Delmas Foundation. My editor, Kevin Doughton, deserves special thanks for the extraordinary care he took with this project. His expert eye and inspired suggestions helped to bring out more of the human story behind the leaves of history. As always, I am deeply grateful to my agent, John F. Thornton, for his enthusiastic and unfailing support. My warm thanks also to Michele and Carla Gradenigo and their daughters, Marta and Giulia, who have always welcomed me and my family to Venice with a kindness and generosity that is truly Venetian.

Last, I thank my family. My wife, Page, got more than she bargained for when she married a historian who later whisked her and her infant and toddler off to live in Venice. Far from the romantic gondola rides, she experienced the joys of hanging laundry in freezing weather, daily shopping with wriggling children, and persistent plumbing problems. She bore it with poise and good humor, and even came to love Venice despite it all. It has been among my greatest pleasures to watch my

ACKNOWLEDGMENTS

daughters, Helena and Melinda, grow up against the backdrop of our stays in Venice. My fondest memories there are not of historical discoveries in the archives, but of my children riding tricycles in the *campo* or playing joyfully in the Giardini. It is impossible for me to imagine the city without them. Words can never express my love, gratitude, and admiration for these three remarkable women.

Po River

Milan

Verona

Trieste

Venice

Genoa

Ravenna

Zara

Florence

Ancona

Ragusa

Danube River

CORSICA

Rome

Durazzo

Naples

Bari

Thessalonica

Taranto

SARDINIA

CORFU

SICILY

Modon

Coron

Mediterranean

Tripoli

The Venetian World

Tana

Caffa

Black Sea

Bosporus

Trebizond

Constantinople

*egean
Sea*

Athens

Antioch

Famagusta

Tripoli

Tyre

CYPRUS

Acre

CRETE

Jerusalem

Sea

Alexandria

Cairo

Territory controlled by
the Venetian Empire

© 2012 Meighan Cavanaugh

VENICE AND THE LAGOON

Piave

Brenta

• Treviso

Altino

HERACLEA

JESOLO

CAORL

TORCELLO

• Vicenza

VENICE

Padua

LIDO (SAN NICOLÒ)

MALAMOCCO

PELLESTRINA

CHIOGGIA

Adige

N

W   E

S

Po

Areas of land after 600 A.D.

© 2012 Meighan Cavanaugh

Aquileia

GRADO

Trieste

Adriatic Sea

ISTRIA

CITY OF VENICE

CANNAREGIO

SANTA CROCE

SS. Giovanni e Paolo

SAN POLO   Rialto   CASTELLO

Santa Maria
Gloriosa dei   *Grand Canal*   Church of   Arsenale
Frari   SAN MARCO   San Marco

DORSODURO   Piazza   San Zaccaria
San Marco   Palace of the Doge   San Pietro
di Castello

Bacino di San Marco

Giudecca Canal

GUIDECCA   San Giorgio
Maggiore

Venice in 1500

VENICE

INTRODUCTION

We will consider, attend to, and work for the honor and profit
of the people of Venice in good faith and without fraud.

—From the doge of Venice's oath of office, 1192

In the year 452 the world was ending.

The Roman Empire, which for centuries had dispensed prosperity, power, and security to its citizens, was crumbling. Once,
long ago, the roads of the empire had bustled with merchants, soldiers,
and citizens making their way across a landscape of peace and plenty.
Now those roads were the avenues of invasion for barbarians and conquerors.

At the head of the Adriatic Sea, the lush plains and hills of the Veneto
were especially hard hit, for they stood at the crossroads of the eastern
and western halves of the broken empire. In the old days of the Pax Ro-
mana this area had been one of great beauty and wealth. Patavium
(modern Padua) had boasted of its affluent citizens who reaped rich

profits from the wool and wine afforded by the verdant countryside. Noble Aquileia, the "eagle city," was a place of opulence with heavily fortified walls surrounding magnificent forums, palaces, monuments, and harbors. Its markets and homes spilled over with every luxury and delicacy that a vast empire could afford.

But in 452 Attila the Hun came to Aquileia. Abandoned by their empire, the citizens of the great city manned the walls and defied the Asian conqueror and his fearful hordes. The Aquileians were a determined people, and they fought with great courage. Three months later Attila was still frustrated in his ambition, still unable to take the city—and his men were grumbling. One morning, while considering his next move, Attila took a walk around the fortifications and noticed something unusual.

The storks were restless.

Beyond the walls, on the roofs of Aquileia hundreds of white storks had been nesting for months, but this morning there was something different about them. They no longer lounged serenely, looking contemptuously from their perches down onto the Huns. Instead, they were busily picking up their young and flying off toward the horizon. Attila knew an omen when he saw one. At once he ordered his men to storm the walls. The storks proved prescient. Great Aquileia fell that day. The Huns quickly reduced the city to a smoldering, corpse-strewn ruin. Soon they would do the same at Patavium, and Concordia, and Altinum, and every other Roman city in Attila's path.

The few survivors of this devastation searched for refuge but found none. Where could one flee when even Rome itself was in danger? With no secure retreat on the mainland, ragged bands of refugees made their way to the marshes of the nearby lagoon, a brackish hideaway between the land and the Adriatic Sea. They loaded their families and what possessions they could scrounge onto boats and rowed out to the sandy islands of a new watery world. There they found safety from the barbarians. There, they hoped, they could survive the end of their world.

Although they could never have known it, the desperate men, women, and children in those lonely boats were the founders of one of history's most remarkable cities. From an archipelago of sand, trees, and marsh they would bring forth the extraordinary beauty that is Venice—a city unlike any other. It did not happen all at once or easily. For centuries the lagoon remained a collection of small island communities. Even after settlements began to cluster around Rialto, Venice was still a place of wood and mud. But that, too, would change. By the thirteenth century Venice was no longer simply a town built on the water, it had become western Europe's second-largest city with a maritime empire that stretched across the Mediterranean Sea. Venice and wealth would become kindred concepts. And with that wealth the Venetians built a magnificent city—a stunning composition of stone and waves that still evokes wonder today.

Venice and its history have always fascinated people from all walks of life. It is a place of contradictions—a city without land, an empire without borders. Everyone knows what Venice is, but fewer know *why* it is or *how* it came to be. It is not simply a work of art, but a birthplace of modern capitalism. The medieval market stalls of Rialto were the nerve center for a complex commercial network that stretched thousands of miles, in which bond markets, liability insurance, and banking (among other things) developed. While the rest of medieval Europe groaned under kings and landed magnates, the Venetians formed a free republic—one that would last for a thousand years.

In the last quarter century there has been a tremendous flowering of historical scholarship on the city of Venice. One can visit the hushed reading rooms of the Archivio di Stato or the Biblioteca Marciana in

Venice any time of the year and find dozens of professional scholars from around the world closely studying the manuscripts and documents of past ages. The fruits of all that research have been presented in thousands of journal articles and scholarly monographs. As a result, we now know much more about Venice than we have ever known before. By their nature, however, these studies are technical and difficult to comprehend without extensive background knowledge. And, of course, only a minority are in English.

As a professional historian, I have spent my share of hours in Venice's archives and libraries and penned my share of scholarly studies. At some point, though, it seems to me that someone must draw from that wealth of scholarship to produce a new history of Venice accessible to anyone with a desire to know about it. That is the purpose of this book.

Writing the history of Venice is a proud, ancient tradition in itself, yet one that has often involved taking a certain license with the facts. The Biblioteca Marciana holds hundreds of centuries-old manuscripts, containing in their yellowed parchment pages a wealth of histories of Venice written in Latin or the Venetian dialect. These are, for the most part, a fascinating hodgepodge of local legend, cherished traditions, and pure fabrication. Occasionally there were attempts at real accuracy, such as Doge Andrea Dandolo's fourteenth-century *Chronica*, based on solid archival documentation and a sincere desire to tell a true tale. But the vast storehouse of Venice's state archives was not available to just anyone. Indeed, the archives were open to virtually no one. That changed after 1797 when the Republic of Venice fell and its archives were packed away into the Frari monastery, where they still remain today. Modern history writing can perhaps be traced to Pierre Darù's multivolume *Histoire de la République de Venise*, published in 1819. Drawing extensively from Venetian archival documents, Darù, who had been one of Napoleon's assistants, painted a generally unflattering picture of the Republic of Venice. Venetian scholars quickly fired back with their own larger, more comprehensive, and better reasoned histories based on careful studies in the archives and manuscript collections. The greatest of these was Samuele Romanin's *Storia documentata di Venezia,* published between 1853 and 1861. It is difficult to overstate the importance of this work, which ran to ten volumes and for the first time brought together an extensive historical narrative with edited archival documents to support it. Romanin's book was the basis for dozens, perhaps hundreds, of shorter histories written in English, French, and German for popular audiences during the nineteenth and twentieth centuries.

Since 1900, though, comprehensive histories of Venice based on independent research have been relatively rare. Among the best are Heinrich Kretschmayr's *Geschichte von Venedig* (1905–34), Roberto Cessi's *Storia della Repubblica di Venezia* (1944–46), and Frederic C. Lane's *Venice: A Maritime Republic* (1973). None of them, however, are what one might call an easy read. For that, the twentieth century served up a cornucopia of histories of Venice written by a variety of popular authors, including Gore Vidal, Jan Morris, Peter Ackroyd, and John Julius Norwich. Yet professional historians have been slow to take up the challenge of producing a new comprehensive history of Venice based on the best available research. Elizabeth Horodowich's *A Brief History of Venice* (2009) makes a good start. This present book, however, aims to tell the story of Venice more completely with an emphasis on the people and events that shaped its unique history. It is impossible to talk about Venice without speaking of the artistic and cultural treasures that it produced—and those are certainly here. But it is the overriding aim of this book to set Venice within its own times, to follow its people, both common and noble, and to examine the challenges that they faced. The artists and musicians are here—but so, too, are the doges, the sailors, the priests, and the prostitutes.

The people of Venice have always been among the most fascinating in the world. During more than two decades of research, I have had the privilege of reading thousands of their personal documents from the Middle Ages and forming close friendships with Venetians of our own time. I have learned over those years that Venetians are not a people who can be boiled down to a myth or a trope, as some histories and guidebooks have unfortunately done. This is particularly true when we look to the medieval and Renaissance history of Venice. Venetians from that millennium are often branded disdainfully with the mark of Shylock, Shakespeare's Venetian moneylender who insists upon his "pound of flesh." Perhaps, as the great historian of Venice, Donald E. Queller, once remarked, it is simply that intellectuals and academics are uncomfortable around businessmen. The Venetians, who were businessmen through and through, often appear in modern histories as the equivalent of snake-oil salesmen: crafty, conniving, greedy, and on the make. I respectfully disagree with that assessment. Norwich, for example, goes too far when he writes, "There spoke the authentic voice of Venice. The state might come first, but enlightened self-interest was never far behind." Similarly, Donald M. Nicol was wrong, I believe, when he summed up the Venetian character saying, "They were Venetians first, and Christians afterwards." Over the decades I have held in my hands too many medieval Venetian parchments containing wills, reports, and writs of charitable donations to believe that so diverse a people can be dismissed with such stereotypes. Capitalism and idealism are not incompatible concepts. Like all peoples, the Venetians were a complex tapestry of good and wicked, selfless and selfish, honorable and shameful. They cannot be pressed between the leaves of a stale morality tale.

It is my hope, then, that this book will open a door for its reader to a clear and fascinating history of the city and republic of Venice. Of course, no single volume could ever encompass so vast a subject. But the high and low points are all here, as well as the battles, triumphs, tears, and tragedies along the way. It is a remarkable tale, and one that deserves to be told.

· · ·

Fifteen centuries ago the families who loaded their simple boats and fled the Huns were escaping one world and building a bridge to another. While Europe was becoming a feudal battleground, Venice established a republic of free citizens. That republic would survive across the centuries, just long enough to inspire new generations who likewise sought to escape a crumbling world. They included the Founding Fathers of the United States of America. John Adams, for example, carefully researched the history of Venice, setting some of it down in his work *A Defence of the Constitutions of Government of the United States of America* (1787). But by then time was running out for aged Venice. Although the world's newest republic sought formal relations with the world's oldest, the histories of America and Venice would overlap for only two decades before the latter was no more.

And yet, before the storks again took wing, the achievements of the city on the water were carefully passed on to a new age.

CHAPTER 1

REFUGEES ON THE LAGOON:
The Origins of Venice

No one forgets a first glimpse of Venice. Whether arriving by plane, boat, train, or car, there is that startling moment when one looks across the waves and finds what should not be there—stone towers, rich churches, and packed buildings rising up out of the sea. The extraordinary beauty of Venice only adds to its improbability. How does such a city exist? Who were the people who built it and why did they think it worth such unyielding efforts?

Of course, no one with options would willingly build a city on a group of marshy islands set in the middle of a brackish lagoon. Venice was a child of necessity, built by the survivors of an ancient world that was quickly passing away. They did not choose to construct a shimmering jewel in the sea and they could not have imagined that their refuge would one day serve as a tourist playground. They chose merely to live free, and found that to do so they had to make a home in the water. In those early years important elements of the Venetian character were being forged. The Venetians were a determined people: determined to resist the changes that swept Europe, determined to remain loyal to

their state and to one another, determined to remain Catholics in communion with the pope in Rome, and determined to fight the sea itself to achieve those goals.

The earliest Venetians were Romans, citizens of an empire that had long ago brought unprecedented peace and prosperity to the Western world. Unfortunately for them, by the fifth century AD the peace was sporadic and the prosperity rapidly disappearing. The Roman economy had experienced a steep decline since the third century, when the empire was plagued by political corruption and civil war. The path to imperial power in those days was the military. Every Roman general entertained the idea that the next emperor might be found in his own shaving mirror. Emperors in the third century held on to power only so long as they kept their troops happy and watched their rivals closely.

As the empire crumbled from within, it was attacked from without. Waves of barbarian invasions swept across the western half of the empire in the fourth and fifth centuries, leaving devastation and suffering in their wake. Particularly hard hit were the Italian lands at the northern end of the Adriatic Sea (what is today the Veneto and Friuli Venezia Giulia regions of Italy). The main thoroughfare between the eastern and western empire was a Roman road known as the Via Postumia, which crossed directly through this region. The cities along this Roman road were prosperous trading centers. Some, like Patavium and Aquileia, were among the wealthiest in the empire. But Rome could no longer defend them. It could not even defend itself. Where once carts laden with merchandise and legions of Roman soldiers had traveled, in the fifth century barbarian warriors rushed from prey to prey.

In happier days the Venetian lagoon just off the coast had been a haunt of fishermen and wharf workers, as well as an occasional vacation home of the well-to-do. It was one of a string of lagoons that stretched from Ravenna to Aquileia, each connected by Roman navigational channels. The lagoons were the offspring of the Alps. Each winter when the Alpine snow melts, the rivers of northern Italy swell with rushing waters bearing the rock and silt of their mountain passage. This debris makes its way down the mountains and across the plains until at last it empties into the Adriatic. Yet not all of it is swept away. Currents and tides in the Adriatic cause some of the sediment to form banks of sand and dirt parallel to the shore, called *lidi*. Water trapped behind these long, sandy islands forms shallow lagoons, where the water is naturally less agitated than the sea, making it an ideal harbor for vessels. Since water flows out at low tide through breaks in the lidi, there is more time for sediment to deposit in the lagoon, resulting in islands, bars, and canals through which the water drains. Left to its own devices, a lagoon like this eventually silts up completely, becoming part of the mainland. Indeed, this is what happened to most of the lagoons from the Roman era. The city of Ravenna, for example, where the western Roman fleet once docked, is now several miles from the sea. The largest of the region's rivers, the Po, once had a delta that stretched from Ravenna to Altinum (Altino). Along that delta Romans navigated through canal-linked lagoons strung together like pearls.

In those days the few people who lived in the lagoons of the Adriatic were mostly fishermen, who kept temporary houses on a few islands. Since water depth in the lagoons was so variable, navigation was often by means of flat-bottomed boats that could glide over almost any submerged obstacle. On mainland Veneto, prosperous cities established wharves in the nearby lagoon where large vessels could anchor and unload their goods. But conditions did not encourage permanent residence. While the fish were plentiful, the water was brackish, the soil poor, and the mosquitoes ferocious.

The lagoon of Venice, which stretched from Chioggia to Grado, was well known to the inhabitants of the ancient Veneto region, and it was ultimately this familiarity that would lead to the city's foundation. The Veneto people were industrious, and their main cities, such as Patavium,

Altinum, Concordia, Tarvisium (Treviso), and the provincial capital, Aquileia, were crisscrossed by Roman roads bearing merchandise to the region's markets and factories. Culturally, the Veneto was a melting pot, with a healthy mixture of native Veneti and Roman colonial cultures, seasoned liberally with Greek and Levantine elements. As a people between Constantinople in the East and Rome in the West, they were not only at home in a far-reaching cosmopolitan empire, they depended on it. That dependence was soon to be shattered. In AD 402 the first of the major barbarian invaders, the Goths, descended on the region. Full of fear and with no hope of resistance, the people of the cities along the Veneto's roads fled to the safety of the nearby lagoon. Taking what they could carry and hiding the rest, they boarded their small vessels and rowed out to the inhospitable islands dotting the waterscape. From there they watched the smoke of their burning homes and prayed that the crisis would pass. It did not. The Goths under their chieftain Alaric pressed on to Rome itself, which they conquered and sacked in 410. The empire was not yet fallen, but the old world was dying—that much was plain. The Roman Empire that the barbarians joyfully dismembered was a Christian state, so it was natural for many Romans to see in the fall of the Eternal City the passing away of all earthly things.

When the Goths finally departed, the lagoon refugees returned to their ruined cities and began rebuilding. And yet, some must have remained on the islands. After all, during the months of exile, they had put considerable effort into building wooden houses on stilts, digging fishing holes, and learning the natural channels. For those with little to return to on the mainland, the lagoon offered some consolation. Most importantly, it offered safety. Although the Goths had gone for the moment, they remained a potent force in the western empire. Instability and invasion meant that armies, both Roman and barbarian, continued to march along the Roman roads, bringing more carnage and more flames. The citizens of Padua, Altino, and the other nearby towns there-fore found themselves running for the shelter of the lagoons with some regularity in the first half of the fifth century. We can imagine that with each such flight more and more of them chose the safety of the water to the ever-present danger at home. These lagoon people—for so they had become—were experts on the channels, islands, and the flat-bottomed boats used to navigate through them. No Gothic commander would venture into that forbidding domain.

Because Venice would one day become the opulent capital of a mar-itime empire, it is not surprising that its citizens later developed a con-stellation of foundation stories. The earliest held that the Roman government in Padua sent three "consuls" to an island group known as Rivoalto, or "high bank." It was here that a natural channel made its ser-pentine way through an archipelago of marshy islands, some of which were submerged during high tide. The high bank was probably an island at a bend in the channel that withstood the tides. Rivoalto is today's Rialto, and the winding channel, the Grand Canal. The consuls were sent, we are told, to establish a trading post, which suggests that some settlers could be found in the area. It is said that the three officials founded the city of Venice there at Rialto on the Feast of the Annuncia-tion, March 25, 421.

Like many origin stories, this one offers dubious particulars. The earliest surviving versions of it are from the fourteenth century, and dif-ferent medieval chronicles provide different names for the three con-suls. Still, the tale may preserve a germ of truth. Based on subsequent events, it appears that the Rialtine islands located in the center of the lagoon were not much favored as places to settle. Instead, the first refu-gees preferred the higher, wooded islands on the lagoon's periphery. But the combination of a deep channel and a high bank would lend itself to shipping, so there may well have been a trading post and a scattered village of sorts at Rialto in the fifth century. It would, in any case, have been quite small. One can still today get a feel for this embryonic Venice by taking the vaporetto (Venice's water bus) on the short ride from Burano to Torcello. There, from the deck of the churning vessel, one can see the low, marshy islands of the lagoon, covered in grasses and populated by birds. It is a stunning reminder of just how improbable the city of Venice really is.

In 452 Attila the Hun, known to Roman Christians as the Scourge of God, besieged the once-proud city of Aquileia. Set at a major crossroads, Aquileia was a cosmopolitan and influential urban center. It boasted one of the oldest Christian communities in western Europe, second only to Rome. Indeed, its bishop bore the title Patriarch, something no other bishop in the West save the pope could claim. Though battered by the storms of previous invasions, Aquileia still managed to hold out against Attila and his powerful armies. According to the historian Jordanes, writing a century later, Attila launched his final attack when he noticed the storks that nested in the city picking up their young and flying away. Aquileia fell that day, and those citizens who could not escape were sold into slavery or put to the sword. The rest fled to the nearby island of Grado. Like Alaric before him, Attila was headed for Rome, but along the way the Scourge of God met the successor of St. Peter, Pope Leo I, who persuaded him to abandon his plan. Within the year Attila was dead— probably at the hand of his new, young wife—and the threat of the Huns died with him. Yet Aquileia had already been reduced to rubble, and though many of its citizens likely returned, the city would never again be more than a village. Even today it remains a sleepy town set in a broad landscape of ancient ruins. For most tourists it is simply one more quaint hamlet on the way to the beach resorts of Grado. Yet in the magnificent cathedral of Aquileia one can still experience the opulent sophistication of that lost city by simply looking downward to the stunning fourth-century mosaic floor.

Venetians long remembered the part that Attila the Hun played in the birth of their city. For the destruction of the provincial capital had driven refugees not only to Grado but also to islands and towns across the length of the Venetian lagoon. And although many people did return home, the population of the lagoon continued to rise with each new attack. Later Venetian chroniclers recorded that in 466 the people of the lagoon elected three tribunes to act as their government. In those days a tribune was a Roman official with primary responsibility over the local military, but also with governing authority answerable to the emperor in Rome. In truth, though, Rome was by then so unsafe that the emperors ruled from Ravenna, when they ruled at all. Precisely how this early Venetian government functioned is unclear. Because the lagoon dwellers were grouped into small island communities scattered across the region, there was a fair amount of discord and violence between them. Theoretically, the tribunes would have dealt with this problem. In practice, they appear to have participated in it. These were lawless, chaotic times with little for a Roman to cling to in the way of legitimate authority.

But cling the Venetians did. They were a tenacious people who refused to cooperate with the times. In the late third century the Roman Empire had been divided into two halves by the emperor Diocletian. The Veneto was situated in the western half, and thereby subject to the emperors in Rome. In 330 the first Christian emperor, Constantine I, founded a new capital for the eastern half of the empire, which came to be called Constantinople (modern Istanbul). In 476 the Gothic warlord Odoacer deposed Romulus Augustulus, the last Roman emperor in the West. No one, Odoacer least of all, thought that this constituted the end of the Roman Empire. Instead, the Gothic leader claimed to rule Italy in the name of the emperor in Constantinople. Rather than start a fight, Emperor Zeno in the East obligingly appointed Odoacer to rule the West as his governor. This was, however, merely a pleasant fiction. Odoacer ruled because he commanded his Gothic forces, not because Zeno sent him a richly decorated parchment. Nevertheless, the gesture was important. Civilization is a difficult habit to break. Although they had been battered by invasions and civil wars for decades, the Romans in the West could only conceive of legitimate authority as deriving from the Roman government. The Germanic barbarians, who spoke the Roman tongue and worshipped the Roman God (Jesus Christ), felt much the same way—even as they dismembered the Roman empire.

As for the early Venetians, they accepted the authority of Odoacer in Italy, but only insofar as it was derived from the emperor in Constantinople. Although this probably had little practical effect in the fifth century, it did help to forge an enduring element in Venetian identity. The Venetians were a people suspended between two worlds. Loyal to the government at Constantinople, they nonetheless lived in the West and were beholden to western authorities—whether imperial appointments over their government or Roman popes over their Church. From its very beginning, then, Venice was shaped by the twin poles of power that lay east and west.

In 488 a new Gothic leader, Theodoric, marched into Italy with his armies under the orders of Emperor Zeno, who wished to overthrow Odoacer. In part he was responding to Odoacer's treatment of native Romans, but he also hoped to remove the troublesome Goths from the eastern half of the empire. Theodoric captured Ravenna in 493 and subsequently signed a treaty with Odoacer that the two would rule jointly. At the dinner party to celebrate the peace, Theodoric assassinated Odoacer with his own hands. Despite the poor table manners, Theodoric considered himself to be a cultured barbarian. Raised in the imperial court at Constantinople, he had a good idea how to govern a Roman state. Although, like most Germanic invaders, Theodoric was an Arian Christian who believed that Christ was less than God, he nonetheless practiced toleration of the native Catholics in Italy. By all accounts, the years of his reign (493–526) were a golden age in Italy, a time when the city of Rome was rebuilt and order restored.

No such rebuilding occurred in the lagoon, of course. Yet the restoration of order in Rome and Ravenna did mean closer communications and, therefore, more requests from the mainland for aid to support the central government. One of those requests was sent by Cassiodorus, Theodoric's prefect of Ravenna. The letter was addressed to the "maritime tribunes" of "Venetia." It survives purely by accident—simply because it was copied into Cassiodorus's *Variae*, a collection of documents meant to serve as models for government officials. By modern standards it is a grossly overwritten letter, so filled with puffery and tortured prose that it almost forgets to get to the point—a simple request for help transporting oil and wine across the lagoon from Istria to Ravenna. Nevertheless, Cassiodorus's wordiness is a boon for historians. In the thickets of his verbiage he provides a rich description of life among the small Venetian communities of 523. Describing their homes, he says:

> Venetia, the praiseworthy, once full of the dwellings of the nobility, stretches from Ravenna and the Po on the south, while on the east it enjoys the delightful Ionian shore, where the alternating tide reveals and then conceals the face of the fields by its ebb and flow. Here, like the water birds, you have made your home. He, who was previously on the mainland, finds himself on an island, so that you might imagine yourself in the Cyclades from the sudden alterations in the appearance of the shore. Amid the wide expanse of the waters can be seen your scattered homes, not the product of nature, but built by the care of man into a firm foundation. For by a twisted and knotted osier-work the earth there collected is turned into a solid mass, and without fear you use so fragile a bulwark to oppose the waves of the sea, since the

waters are unable to sweep away the shallow shore, because the water is not deep enough to give them power.

In these rustic quarters, the first Venetians lived simply. According to Cassiodorus:

> The inhabitants have only one concept of plenty: that of filling their bellies with fish. Poverty and wealth, therefore, are on equal terms. One kind of food sustains everyone. The same kind of dwelling shelters all. No one can envy his neighbor's home; and living in this moderate style they escape that vice [of envy] to which the rest of the world is susceptible.

Unless the laws of human nature were somehow suspended in the lagoon, we can assume that Cassiodorus is exercising poetic license when describing the equality and amity among its residents. And since he was asking the Venetians to transport commodities for the provincial government without cost, a little flattery of their generous nature would certainly not go amiss. Nonetheless, Cassiodorus's description makes it plain that, compared with Ravenna, the people of Venice did not have much.

If fish provided the food for the early Venetians, it was salt that provided their income. Cassiodorus writes:

> All of your attention is focused on your salt-works. Instead of driving the plow or wielding the sickle, you roll your cylinders. From there comes your whole crop. You find there a product that you did not manufacture. And there is your money coined. Every wave is the servant of your art. One might tire of searching for gold. But salt is something that everyone hopes to find. And rightly so, since every kind of meat owes its flavor to it.

It is often said that Venice grew rich on the "spice trade." This is true—yet that spice was not exotic cloves or cardamom, but simple salt. Aside from fish, the lagoon does not offer much in the way of foodstuffs. Throughout its long history, Venice has always had to import its food, which requires money. The earliest Venetians built saltworks that allowed lagoon water to flow during high tide into wide basins, where it was trapped and left to evaporate in the sun. They then used heavy cylinders to roll over the salt, breaking it up into pieces that could be loaded aboard boats for export. It fetched a tidy sum—crucial for the tiny, but growing, economy of early Venice, and indeed for many centuries to come. It is often said that Venetians left salt production behind when international trade and commerce became their path to riches. That is simply untrue. Medieval and Renaissance commercial documents bear strong witness to the continued importance of the salt trade. Indeed, the Venetian government established its own Salt Office, which would grow to become one of the most powerful organs of the state.

Whether or not life in the lagoon was as sublime as Cassiodorus suggests, it was at least stable and reasonably safe. That was about to change. After Theodoric's death in 526, relations between the native Catholic Romans and their Arian barbarian masters degenerated rapidly. The golden age had expired. In 533 the emperor in Constantinople, Justinian I, decided to roll back the Germanic invasions and restore the Roman Empire in the West. His general, Belisarius, sailed to North Africa, where he ejected the Vandals and reclaimed the entire region. Two years later, Belisarius landed in Italy, thus beginning the long and bitter Gothic War (535–54). For almost two decades the Romans and the Goths clashed, bringing yet more destruction and chaos to an already battered peninsula. For the early Venetians, there was never any doubt about which side they would support. Requests for aid came from Constantinople, and the men of the lagoon dutifully armed themselves, boarded their war vessels, and assisted Belisarius with the conquest of Ravenna in

539. According to one medieval chronicle, the *Chronicon Altinate*, in gratitude for their assistance the emperor granted Venetian sailors the right to trade in ports across the Roman Empire.

By 555 the Romans had finally won the war in Italy—but at great cost. The city of Rome, having changed hands several times, was in ruins. There was much talk of restoring the city to its former glory, but until it could be rebuilt, it was hardly a fit place for an emperor. Justinian simply made Italy a province, placing Rome under the authority of an "exarch," or governor, based in Ravenna. Exarch is a Greek title, which reveals much about the changing nature of the Roman Empire. Cut off from Rome itself, the government in Constantinople had increasingly adopted the Greek language, which dominated high culture in the East. Indeed, Justinian was the last emperor to speak Latin as his native tongue. The passing away of Latin in the East and the increasingly Oriental character of the imperial court in Constantinople have led modern historians to refer to the empire from this period forward as the Byzantine Empire. We shall do so here as well. However, it is important to remember that the term is a modern one. Although he might speak Greek, every citizen in the eastern empire called himself a Roman. For Venetians, therefore, the emperor in Constantinople was not Byzantine, but Roman. And so were they—at least in those early days. Throughout their histories, the underlying foundation that bound Venice and Constantinople together was that shared Roman heritage.

The new exarch of Ravenna had jurisdiction over the Venetian lagoon, and thereby over the tribunes there. Once again the Roman Empire spanned the Mediterranean world. On his deathbed in 565 Justinian could realistically conclude that the tide of history had turned—that the empire was on its way back. But it was not to be. Already a devastating plague had swept across the empire, killing millions. Worse, a new Germanic barbarian tribe, the Longobards (Long Beards), or Lombards, were on the move and headed for Italy. Like the Goths before them, they were warlike Arian Christians who needed a home. Italy, where Byzantine forces were weakened, seemed perfect.

It would take nearly two centuries for the Lombards to expel the Byzantines from their provincial capital at Ravenna, but they had conquered much of Italy long before that. The Lombard invasions so devastated the Veneto region that they are literally responsible for a second founding of Venice. Beginning in 568 Lombard armies systematically captured all the main cities in the Veneto and extended their conquests westward to Milan. Unlike the Goths and Huns, though, the Lombards had come to stay. They took over the cities, claimed the countryside, and even established a new capital at Pavia. Theirs was a kingdom that would endure. Even today the region is known as Lombardy. For the citizens of the cities in the Veneto, this was a story that they had lived before, but now with a very different ending. It was no longer possible to flee to the lagoon, wait out the conquest, and return home when the barbarians had left for greener pastures. The Lombards, with their own laws, customs, and form of Christianity, were not leaving. This time, the flight to the lagoon would be permanent.

The collapse of the Roman government in western Europe left a profound power vacuum in the rapidly shrinking cities there. Simple tasks like repairing walls, clearing the streets, caring for the poor, and mustering troops were increasingly left to local initiative. The only institution that still had the organization to undertake such activities was the Catholic Church, and since virtually all Romans were Catholics, it is not surprising that they looked to their spiritual leaders when political leaders failed them. As a result, bishops and archbishops in the West began to assume more and more authority during the fifth and sixth centuries. The pope in Rome or the archbishop in Milan often found himself saddled with a host of responsibilities that had nothing at all to do with the shepherding of souls.

When the people of the Veneto heard of the Lombard invasion, they, too, naturally looked to their religious leaders. Membership in the Church defined these communities. If they were to transplant themselves, they must also transplant their church, its holy relics, its clergy, and its ecclesiastical leader. The bishops would be the ones to lead their people to new homes in the Venetian lagoon. City by city, the mainlanders took up their journey into the lagoon. The people of Aquileia fled to Grado. Those in Concordia settled at Caorle. The Paduans moved to Malamocco, on the end of the island known today as the Lido, while the citizens of Treviso made their new home at Chioggia. These were the last of the exiles. In each case, the people brought all that was dear to them in order to build new lives in a new world.

The most important group of refugees were those from the prosperous town of Altinum (Altino), which was very close to the Venetian lagoon—only a dozen or so miles northwest of modern Venice. Today the city is largely lost, although the ghostlike image of it can still be seen beneath the fields and farms by means of aerial photography. The medieval *Chronicon Altinate* tells a story with elements suspiciously similar to those surrounding the fall of Aquileia. It finds the citizens of Altino bravely preparing to defend their homes against the Lombards, only to notice nesting birds fleeing the city, and quickly choosing to follow their sage example. Some, we are told, left the region altogether, heading to Ravenna, Istria, or Rimini. But the majority of citizens agreed to follow Bishop Paul of Altino wherever he would lead them. According to the *Chronicon*, Paul and his flock heard a heavenly voice telling them to climb the city's tower and seek the stars. When the bishop reached the top of the stone steps and looked across to the south, he saw the islands of the lagoon spread out before him like the stars of the sky.

With no plans to return, the refugees from Altino brought with them everything that could be carried. Even the stone lintels, pavement, and wall reliefs were pried from the buildings and piled into boats. These stray bits of ancient Rome would remain a powerful reminder for the

exiles of just who they were and from whence they had come. Undoubtedly refugees from other Roman towns brought similar items, but all
these preserved artifacts were classified by later generations as *altinelle*,
small pieces of Altino. (In time this would come to mean any small bricks
that resembled those used in the ancient city.) But the most important
cargo—in some ways more important than the people themselves—was
the church of Altino and the body of their heavenly patron, St. Heliodorus, their ancient bishop. His richly adorned body was carefully
placed into a boat and rowed out to its new home on the island of Torcello. There Bishop Paul, with the financial assistance of Emperor Heraclius in Constantinople and Exarch Isaac in Ravenna, built a new
cathedral: the church of Santa Maria Assunta, completed in 639. Much
of that first church is lost, although the ruins of the baptistery are still
visible. The church of Santa Maria Assunta that now stands in Torcello is
a later construction, dating primarily from projects in 864 and 1004. But
the original dedicatory inscription still survives and can be seen today
in the sanctuary.

To visit Torcello is to step back into a Venice that has long since
passed away. Although medieval Torcello would grow to become a bustling city of some fifty thousand people, by the thirteenth century it had
been eclipsed by Venice proper and thereafter quickly declined. Today
the buildings and wharves that once hummed with activity across Torcello are gone, replaced by orchards and wild grass. But Santa Maria
Assunta survives. From its rich mosaics to its ancient stonework, it is a
patchwork of materials fused together to create a thing of rare beauty.
Beneath the high altar and behind an ancient grate one can even glimpse
the casket of St. Heliodorus—still safe, just as his people hoped when
they lovingly brought him here fourteen centuries ago.

Not all refugees from Altino settled at Torcello. Some began building
on the nearby islands of Burano (now famous for its lace) and Mazzorbo.
It is not surprising that these islands were quickly snapped up by the

desperate citizens. On high ground, they are protected from the tides. They also have the advantage of being the first islands one comes upon when rowing south from Altino. With only five miles between Torcello and Altino, it is no wonder that after the Lombards had destroyed their city and settled in nearby Padua that the people frequently visited the old ruins to gather more building materials. Other refugees from Altino settled on islands a bit farther from home: Murano (now famous for its glass), Ammiana, and Constantiaca (now lost). It was said that these six islands were named for the six gates of Altino. According to various accounts, Torcello was named either for a gate that was near a tower in the old city or for the tower that Bishop Paul ascended or perhaps both.

Over on the northeastern edge of the lagoon, the refugees from Aquileia followed their own spiritual leader, Patriarch Paulinus, who relocated from his magnificent cathedral to the modest church of Sant'Eufemia on the nearby island of Grado. There they joined the descendants of those who had fled Aquileia after the sack of Attila two centuries before. The very fact of a patriarch at Aquileia gives insight into the proud character of the future Venetians. According to ancient traditions, St. Peter had sent his disciple, St. Mark the Evangelist, to Aquileia to spread Christianity in the region. After building a sizable community of Christian converts there, St. Mark assigned an "overseer" (*episcopus*) as its leader, a common practice in early Christian communities. The English word for *episcopus* is "bishop," but not all bishops were created equal. From the earliest decades of Christianity, bishops in major governmental centers, called metropolitans (or archbishops), exercised authority over other bishops in their region. It was said that St. Mark established Aquileia as a metropolitan "see" (the home city of a bishop) before sailing away to Alexandria and leaving behind his own disciple, St. Hermagoras, as the metropolitan bishop.

By the third century the three principal sees of the Catholic Church were Rome, Antioch, and Alexandria. The first two were founded by

St. Peter, the last by St. Mark. Bishops in those cities, as successors to St. Peter, were generally afforded more authority than other bishops, since Peter was the apostle on whom Christ had bestowed the keys of the kingdom of God and the authority of binding and loosing (Matthew 16:19). These three were called the patriarchal sees—a distinction codified during the Council of Nicaea in 325. Aquileia, while a large city, was not in the same league as Rome, Antioch, and Alexandria. While it was a metropolitan see with jurisdiction over other bishops in its province, it was not set apart by the fathers at Nicaea like the big three. This must have been a sore point for Aquileians, who were proud of a succession from St. Mark no different from that of Alexandria. Perhaps because of this, bishops of Aquileia began to use the patriarchal title anyway. Although it was not strictly official, over time it stuck. The ecclesiastical authority of the patriarch of Aquileia extended into Istria and across the upper Adriatic, including all the churches of the Venetian lagoon. He was no different canonically from any other metropolitan bishop, but he did have an impressive (if misleading) title.

Unlike the humble churchmen ministering to the simple fishermen of Venice, the patriarch of Aquileia was a player in the imperial and ecclesiastical politics of the Roman Empire. During the complex (and not overly important) Schism of the Three Chapters, which rocked much of the empire in the mid-sixth century, Patriarch Macedonius of Aquileia removed himself and his see from Roman obedience, thus earning him a papal excommunication in 554. The Church in Aquileia was still estranged from the pope in 568 when Patriarch Paulinus collected the relics, gathered his flock, and fled to Grado before the Lombard invasion. On that beautiful island, the bishop and people founded "New Aquileia," a name that never quite caught on. And so, just as the episcopate of Altino had been transplanted to Torcello, so the metropolitan see of Aquileia was transferred to Grado. Ironically, although the Lombards who settled in ruined Aquileia possessed the great cathedral church, they nevertheless recognized the authority of the patriarchs just across the water in Grado, since they were the bishops of Aquileia in exile.

This unusual ecclesiastical relationship between Grado and Aquileia was about to become even more unusual. In 607 a newly elected patriarch of Aquileia in Grado formally ended the Schism of the Three Chapters there, and returned the entire congregation to obedience to the pope in Rome. No longer was the successor of St. Mark a schismatic. But the decision did not sit well with the Lombards in Aquileia, who were in a near constant war with the Roman and Byzantine authorities in Italy. As long as the patriarch in Grado was separated by schism from those authorities, they were willing to accept him. But they would not abide a patriarch who owed obedience to their enemy. So the Lombards elected their own patriarch of Aquileia, who was installed in the old cathedral church in the city. Thus, within a few miles of each other were two patriarchs of Aquileia, both claiming jurisdiction over the entire metropolitan see. Naturally, the pope in Rome and the emperor in Constantinople recognized only the patriarch in Grado. But that was of little interest to the Lombards, who kept their patriarch of Aquileia anyway. He ruled over the churches in the region that the Lombards controlled. As for the patriarch of Grado, he was left with the lagoon.

Almost a century passed before the Lombards finally relented and accepted full communion with the pope in Rome. Yet they were unwilling to give up their own patriarch in Aquileia, or to allow the patriarchs in Grado, many of whom were Venetians or Greeks, to govern churches in Lombard lands. To put an end to the problem, Pope Sergius I was willing to overlook the rather obvious problem that the Catholic Church had two patriarchs of Aquileia, each claiming the same jurisdiction, the same title, and the same succession from St. Mark. For the next five centuries these two bishops would square off against each other in the papal curia, the canon law courts, and even on the battlefield. The intricacies of these struggles are not important here. What is important is that the Church in Venice was locally governed by the patriarch of Grado, whose authority waxed and waned with that of the military might of Venice. In other words, Grado was the mother church of Venice and all she controlled. The patriarch of Aquileia, on the other hand, was the ecclesiastical authority on the terra firma, and thereby a creature of the powers there—first the Lombards and later the Franks. And the two patriarchs, each jealous of the other's possessions and privileges, were forever at odds.

Although later Venetian authors tried to clean up the details, Venice was nonetheless a child of chaos, uncertainty, and fear. Yet it was also the product of courage, defiance, and resolve. The first Venetians were Romans, proudly refusing to cooperate with a world in collapse, and clinging to a glorious past that had no hope of return. That proud, conservative outlook tempered with a pious devotion to God and his Church was woven deeply into the Venetian character from its earliest years.

CHAPTER 2

ST. MARK'S REST:
The Birth of the City
of Venice, 697–836

In 810 King Pepin of Italy paused his invasion of the lagoon to have a conversation with an elderly Venetian woman. Having fought his way across the long, sandy island of Pellestrina during a sweltering Venetian summer, Pepin and his Frankish warriors had reached the unimpressive town of Malamocco on the Lido. Although it resembled a large fishing village (which it was), Malamocco was actually the capital of the Venetian lagoon. The Venetian people, scattered across islands, separated by waters, and divided by fierce rivalries, had tried to forge a unified government there, but found a capital without a common identity a shallow thing. It was Pepin who would unify them, although that was never his intention. Faced with his powerful invasion, the Venetians put aside their differences to fight the common foe. They did so valiantly and with extraordinary resolve, yet they could not save Malamocco.

The victorious king entered the rustic capital only to find that its sole remaining resident was an old woman. When the king asked where the people of Venice had gone, the woman stretched out her arm, pointing to the center of the lagoon, to the islands of Rivoalto across the waves. There, she said, the Venetians were hiding, fearful of the greatness of Pepin. To save themselves they had left behind their capital—and her—and she advised Pepin not to let them escape his might. The Franks, she insisted, should build a wooden bridge to span the short distance to the central islands, where they could trap the Venetians in their own refuge. Pepin eagerly took the woman's advice, completing the light bridge in a short time. Yet as the Frankish cavalry rode across it, their horses were dazzled by the sunlight on the dancing waves and frightened by the rocking planks of the bridge. One after another the horses reared and leaped into the water, leading to such chaos among the rest of the army that the bridge itself began to collapse. Like Pharaoh's army, the might of the Franks was vanquished by God and the sea. The clever woman, who watched the mayhem from the shores of the old capital, chuckled softly to herself as she looked across the water to the new capital of the Venetian people—the true city of Venice.

The story of the tricky old crone was told with pride by generations of Venetians. The woman, as might be suspected, is a fiction, but the Frankish invasion, as we shall see, certainly was not. Still, the myth captured a foundational element in Venetian history. Venice, the collection of fiercely independent refugees, had been fused together by blood and cunning into one people with one capital and one heavenly patron behind the impregnable wall of the sea.

Although the Venetian lagoon was a busy place in the seventh century, there was as yet no city of Venice. Torcello remained the largest settlement, with perhaps as many as five thousand people living on the island. There were many other towns and villages, too, linked by a few large vessels and swarms of flat-bottomed boats. More people in the lagoon meant more economic activity and, therefore, more to fight about. The Byzantine provincial government in Ravenna appointed additional tribunes for the Venetians to oversee their far-flung settlements, but that did little to stem the growing disagreements. Violence was becoming a significant problem. The Catholic Church also responded to the growing population by establishing new dioceses with new bishops. All the lagoon's bishops remained subordinate to the patriarch of Grado, who oversaw the Venetian Church, but the fledgling Venetian state had no such unifying figure.

According to John the Deacon, a Venetian chronicler writing some four centuries later, it was Patriarch Christopher of Grado who first suggested that the scattered lagoon dwellers elect a leader to help bring peace and unity to the region. In 697, we are told, the twelve tribunes elected a *dux* (leader), which in the Venetian dialect is *doge*. Depending on the tradition one accepts, that first doge was either Paoluccio Anafesto or Orso Ipato. The last names of both men suggest Italian versions of Greek words. "Ipato" is probably a version of the Greek *hypatus*, a Byzantine title meaning "consul." In other words, the doge was a Byzantine (that is, Roman) official. And so the Venetians had a leader—the first of 118 doges that would govern the city-state—but they remained citizens of the Roman Empire. Indeed, some of the subsequent doges were appointed directly from the provincial capital at Ravenna. The Venetian doge, however, was no duke (as the same title came to be known elsewhere in Europe). He presided over the tribunes, but he did not replace them. Instead, the doge's office was evidence of the growing realization that the scattered island communities of the lagoon were slowly becoming one entity.

And that entity was increasingly independent. This was not a conscious decision, but rather the gradual result of a neglectful Byzantine government. The seventh century had not been kind to the eastern empire. Largely spared the Germanic invasions that had crushed the west, the eastern Roman Empire was now invaded by powerful Asian empires. First came the Persians, who conquered Syria, the Holy Land, and even laid siege to Constantinople itself. After more than two decades of devastating warfare, Emperor Heraclius managed to defeat the Persians and eject them from the empire. Yet no sooner had the victories been celebrated than Arab armies, professing the new religion of Islam, rose to take their place. Wielding the sword of jihad, the Muslims had conquered all of Syria, Palestine, and Egypt by 642. By 711 they had conquered North Africa, and then went on to capture Spain. The emperor in Constantinople was left with Greece, Asia Minor, and dwindling portions of Italy. In short, the Byzantines had their hands full. Although their provincial government in Italy held on by a thread, it had little time to bother with the merchants and fishermen of the Venetian lagoon.

In 742 the new Venetian capital was established at Malamocco, on the southern end of the Lido. Nevertheless, a good deal of warfare between the islands continued, making leadership an unenviable duty. Doge Orso was killed in one such battle. His son, Teodato (742, 744–56), also died violently. Upon his death, a rival doge, Galla Gaulo, was elected, but was just as quickly deposed, blinded, and sent to a monastery (in what was the Byzantine fashion at the time for toppled emperors). His successor, Domenico Monegaurio (756–65), met with much the same fate. These were lawless times, made worse by the fact that Venetian doges were not rulers in any real sense. Legally, the ruler of the lagoon was the emperor in Constantinople. The doge was, at best, a governor. Medieval kings and Byzantine emperors derived their authority from God. Venetian doges did not. Instead, their power flowed directly from the people they governed. Although they had significant powers, early doges were nonetheless beholden to the Venetian people and the tribunes. During times of crisis, the people could form a great assembly known as the *arengo*. No power in the lagoon, save perhaps the faraway emperor, could trump the arengo.

And so it was that within this troubled medieval lagoon a republic, founded on the authority of the "people of Venice," was born. It was the only one left in the world—and it would last for a thousand years. It grew and thrived uniquely there because Venice itself was unique. Land was scarce in that watery world. Status and wealth, therefore, were based not on a landed aristocracy, but on entrepreneurial skill. Venetians produced little food, but they did an increasingly large amount of business in Italy and the East. Venetian merchants sailed their vessels down the Adriatic and up the Italian rivers, buying and selling in the growing markets there. Many of the commodities they purchased ended up back in the lagoon, which was becoming an emporium of considerable importance. This system, based on liquid rather than landed wealth, created shifting constituencies of power that tended to reject privilege and insist on equality. Venetians were capitalists and, as such, fiercely individualistic. They prized freedom and distrusted concentrated power. That is why their doges were elected by the people. It is also why they were allergic to the concept of a ducal dynasty, though many doges tried in vain to establish one.

Doge Maurizio Galbaio (765–87), for example, was determined that his family should retain permanent hold on the dogeship. Decisive, perceptive, and strong, he was just the sort of man who usually founds royal dynasties. He responded to the increasing settlement in and around the little lagoon island of Olivolo (probably named for an olive grove) by helping to establish a new bishop there to oversee the parishes of the central lagoon. In 775 a small wooden church on Olivolo dedicated to Saints Sergius and Bacchus was consecrated as the new cathedral church of San Pietro. Because a fortification was subsequently built on the island, it was later renamed Castello (castle), by which it is still known today. San Pietro di Castello would remain the cathedral for the city of Venice for a millennium. Following a common Byzantine practice, Doge Maurizio used his clout to have his son, Giovanni, elected co-doge with him. Then, when Maurizio died in 787, Giovanni repeated the practice by having his own son, Maurizio II, elected co-doge. In this way the Galbaio family hoped to establish their dynasty.

But the world was changing rapidly in the late eighth century. In 751 Ravenna had finally succumbed to the warlike Lombards, leaving Pope Zachary in Rome nearly defenseless against a people who now dominated the Italian mainland. With no help to be had from distant and distracted Constantinople, the pope turned to another Germanic tribe, the Franks. Fierce in battle, the Franks had conquered and settled Gaul, or what is today France (named, of course, for them). Unlike the other barbarians who had invaded the West, the Franks were Catholic. In return for the pope's support of his bid for the Frankish crown, Pepin the Short led his armies across the Alps and into Italy. Not only did Pepin neutralize the Lombard threat, but he gave to the popes in perpetuity the city of Rome and the lands around it. This they would henceforth rule as their own kingdom, known as the Patrimony of St. Peter or simply the Papal States. These lands, which stretched across the midsection of Italy from Rome to Ravenna, provided security and income for the papacy in an age when money and loyalty were scarce commodities. The popes would rule this state until 1870.

Pepin's achievements were impressive, but dwarfed by those of his more famous son, Charlemagne. His fame is certainly warranted. Charlemagne oversaw a small intellectual revival in Europe, ordered the reform of the monasteries that dotted the landscape, and paid close attention to the doctrinal and liturgical uniformity of the Catholic Church in Europe. But most of all, he was a good warrior, endlessly hungry for conquest. Almost every season he mustered the troops owed to him by feudal obligation and marched on one of his neighbors. Sometimes it was the pagan Saxons in the north German forests, sometimes the Muslim powers in Spain, and sometimes the troublesome Lombards in northern Italy. The last were so thoroughly defeated that Charlemagne established a new government in the region, adding "King of the Lombards" to his growing list of titles. As a result of all this warfare, Charlemagne had cobbled together a mighty kingdom that included what is today France, Germany, and northern Italy. It almost seemed as if the days of the Roman Empire, with one ruler and some measure of peace, had been restored.

Indeed, that is just what Pope Leo III thought. On Christmas Day 800 during a visit to Rome, Charlemagne knelt before the pope to receive his blessing. Leo produced a crown, which he placed on Charlemagne's head, proclaiming him "emperor of the Romans." Although Charlemagne later insisted that he knew nothing of the pope's plans, he made no attempt to reject the title. Quite the contrary—he spent the rest of his life trying to live up to it. The coronation of Charlemagne was a bold statement from a recovering West. It asserted that the Roman Empire was once again restored in Europe, only this time by means of the papacy and one very successful Germanic warlord.

Naturally, the real Roman government in Constantinople took a dim view of the ceremony in Rome. Charlemagne was a Frank, a barbarian, a descendant of those Germans who had dismembered the Roman Empire. The true emperor (or, in 800, empress) was the divinely ordained ruler in Constantinople, bedecked in jewels and holding court in the sumptuous palaces of the largest city in the known world. Roman emperors were not, in the opinion of the Romans of the East, illiterate barbarians who could not eat with a fork without prior instruction. But scoffing at the spectacle was about all that the Byzantines could do in response. For his part, Charlemagne eagerly sought their approval, even offering to marry Empress Irene, a proposal that was swiftly rejected.

Charlemagne's rise to power and his new imperial title raised interesting questions in the Venetian lagoon, where the inhabitants still claimed to be subjects of the Roman Empire. The power of Charlemagne's family (known today as the Carolingians) was truly impressive. Indeed, it extended across Lombardy and the Veneto, having completely displaced the old Lombard masters. The confederation of towns and villages in the Venetian lagoon could profit mightily from Carolingian friendship. It was for this reason that a powerful minority of Venetians, led by Patriarch John of Grado, urged closer ties with Charlemagne and the Franks. This, of course, would mean turning away from Venice's traditional allegiance to Constantinople. It appears that most Venetians, including the doge and his son, opposed this course of action. They were, after all, a people set apart—in western Europe, but not of it. Why should they bow to this Frankish king? The economic, cultural, and emotional ties between Venice and Constantinople could not so easily be sundered.

The political dispute came to blows in 797 when the bishop of Olivolo died. As was the custom, the doge nominated his successor. He chose a Greek, who was probably from Constantinople. Although this was no doubt meant to score a victory against the pro-Frankish minority, the fact that the Greek in question was only sixteen years old allowed Patriarch John of Grado to refuse to ordain him. Doge Giovanni sent his son, Maurizio II, with a squadron of ships to Grado to force the issue. In the ensuing battle the patriarch himself was badly wounded. Perhaps overzealously, the doge's men picked up the battered patriarch, carried him to the high tower of his church, and tossed him down. This shocked even the lagoon dwellers, who were not unaccustomed to a little blood in their politics, and turned many of them against the doge. News of Charlemagne's coronation as Roman emperor in 800 may have further swayed some Venetians to the pro-Frankish side. The murdered Patriarch John was succeeded by his nephew, Fortunatus, who quickly recruited the tribune of Malamocco, Obelerio, to the pro-Frankish side. Joined by other leading Venetians, the two men traveled to nearby Frankish-controlled Treviso, where they plotted the overthrow of the doge.

In 802 their plans bore fruit. The conspirators successfully incited an uprising in the lagoon that forced Doges Maurizio and Giovanni to flee, ending the Galbaio clan's hopes for a long-lasting dynasty.

Obelerio's subsequent elevation to the dogeship was a complete victory for the pro-Frankish party, or so it seemed. A large number of Venetians still could not bring themselves to repudiate loyalty to Constantinople. Owners of merchant vessels were especially unwilling to do anything that might jeopardize their access to the rich markets of the Byzantine Empire. In an attempt to hold the lagoon, the imperial government in Constantinople sent rich gifts and vaunted titles to the new doge, hoping to sway him from the Franks. In 808 they sent something more—a full squadron of warships that spent the winter in the lagoon. As the pendulum of public opinion began to swing back to Constantinople, Obelerio had his brother, Beato, elected co-doge. Perhaps Beato was pro-Byzantine, and if so, this may have been a compromise of sorts. In the spring, the Byzantine fleet sailed out of the lagoon to launch an attack on Frankish Comacchio, not far from Ravenna. Although a military failure, the Byzantine strike launched from the Venetian lagoon captured the attention of Charlemagne's son, Pepin, who ruled from Ravenna as "King of the Lombards." Pepin came to the conclusion that Doge Obelerio either had switched to the Byzantine side or was simply too weak to keep Byzantine warships out of Venetian waters. Either way, Pepin decided to end the problem of Venetian independence once and for all.

Pepin's invasion began in 810, and it would be one of the greatest challenges Venice ever faced. The Frankish king's resources were vast, and he was determined to use them to bring the lagoon dwellers to heel. From his perspective, the Carolingian empire included all of central Europe—no exceptions. The Venetians naturally had a different perspective. No barbarian army had ever conquered their lagoon. Their ancestors had fled the invasions that crushed the ancient empire in order to preserve their lives, faith, and culture. They were Rome unfallen. Of course, it was one thing to hold those high principles and quite another to prove them against a formidable foe. The Venetians employed every defense against the Franks that their watery fortress could offer. They rowed old vessels into the main channel entrances and sank them so as to bar the way. They removed the buoy markers, which guided large transport vessels along the deep channels and away from the sandy shoals just below the water. These actions alone made it impossible for Pepin's forces to penetrate the interior of the lagoon. Instead, Pepin concentrated on the periphery, where most of the people and property were located. To the east his armies conquered Jesolo and Grado. From the south he captured Chioggia and then marched along the narrow lido of Pellestrina that separated the lagoon from the Adriatic Sea. Here the Venetians were forced to make their stand, fighting bravely. For at the end of this lido was their capital, Malamocco. Venetian factional divisions evaporated. Obelerio and his party had no choice now but to condemn the Frankish invasion and join the common defense, although the sincerity of their conversion was much suspected. In an attempt to destroy the Venetians, Pepin had managed to fuse them into one people, determined to protect their shared home.

It was out of this determination that the city of Venice was born. As the Frankish forces pressed on toward Malamocco, Venetian women and children boarded their boats and fled to the center of the lagoon—to the marshy archipelago of islands around Rialto, not far from Castello. This was the least habitable part of the lagoon, which is the reason that it had never attracted more than a handful of residents. But it was safe, at least for the moment. As the summer of 810 dragged on, the fighting on Pellestrina bogged down in the stifling heat and humidity. Soon disease struck the Frankish army, forcing Pepin to face the realization that the Franks might actually fail in their conquest. Even the capture and destruction of Malamocco did not end the struggle, for the retreating Venetians simply boarded their vessels and crossed over to the safety of the Rialto islands. In a fit of desperate anger, Pepin demanded that the Venetians surrender at once. "You are under my hand and my providence," he thundered, "since you belong to my land and to my dominions." The Venetians responded cleverly, proclaiming both their loyalty to the emperor in Constantinople and their rejection of the imperial title of Pepin's father. Their short reply read simply, "We wish to be the subjects of the Roman emperor, and not of you."

Faced with the collapse of his campaign, Pepin was eager to salvage what victory he could. He agreed to withdraw from the lagoon in return for a Venetian promise to render an annual tribute. This settlement allowed him to maintain the fiction that the lagoon did indeed belong to him. The problem of Venice's unique status, however, was not resolved and it would only be ironed out between Charlemagne and the Byzantines two years later. As he grew older, Charlemagne became obsessed with a desire to have Constantinople recognize him as the western Roman emperor. Rather than face more wars in Italy and Istria, the emperor in Constantinople agreed to send a delegation to the tiny Frankish capital at Aachen to hail Charlemagne as emperor. As part of the deal, Charlemagne confirmed that the Venetian lagoon was under the jurisdiction of the eastern emperor, and therefore not part of the Carolingian empire. It was, in other words, subject to the Roman emperor, and not to him.

As the Franks marched out of the ruined towns that they had invaded, the Venetian people reflected on how much damage had been done and how many lives had been lost. Doge Obelerio, who had been the face of the pro-Frankish faction, was immediately overthrown, along with his brother, Beato. The people turned instead to Agnello Partecipazio (811–27), who had distinguished himself in the war against Pepin. The Partecipazios were a family of some importance and antiquity in the lagoon. Originally from Pavia, they had settled first at Eraclea and then later moved to Rialto. Agnello's home was built in an open marshy area, almost precisely where the Ducal Palace (or Palace of the Doges) stands today. Doge Agnello argued that the capital should be moved from Malamocco to Rialto. The Frankish invasion had demonstrated just how vulnerable the Venetians really were, and the new doge was determined to reorganize and strengthen the lagoon.

What later became the city of Venice looked nothing at all like a city in 811. It was a loose collection of largely uninhabited islands scattered around the Grand Canal and Rialto. On some of these islands families like the Partecipazios had built compounds of wooden houses, shelters, and workshops. There they tended their animals, grew some grapes, and loaded and unloaded their vessels. The Rialto area was, like much of the lagoon, a place to do business. As the commercial wealth of various families grew, they naturally expanded their compounds, sometimes by filling in channels between islands or constructing simple bridges. Essential to a compound of any size was a church and an open field known as a *campo*. Families of means financed their island church and developed strong loyalties to their various patron saints. They also funded monasteries, which could be found in abundance throughout the lagoon. Remnants of this early Venice can still be seen today in the more than fifty parish churches that dot the Venetian landscape, each with its own campo. Most of these churches were at one time the foundation of a small island compound.

Building a new capital at Rialto was no small task, but the Venetians had help. Their determination in resisting Pepin and their loyalty to the emperor in Constantinople did not go unnoticed in the East. Emperor Leo V sent craftsmen and artisans from Constantinople as well as significant amounts of money to help with the move. Doge Agnello appointed a commission of three men to oversee all operations. One was authorized to strengthen the lidi of the lagoon, building them up and fortifying them to better resist the battering sea and foreign invasion. Another commission member oversaw the physical improvement of the muddy islands of Rialto. Earth was piled onto and around them to raise and expand the ground level. Deeper canals were dug to allow easier communication and travel between the islands. Finally, the third member, the future doge Pietro Tradonico, took up the task of new public constructions. Among the most important of these were the wells. Because the water of the lagoon is brackish (a mixture of salt water and freshwater), it is unfit for consumption, and digging a conventional well on the sandy lagoon islands would simply provide more brackish water. Instead, the Venetians developed wells that were actually elaborate rainwater collectors. The main campo was excavated and a clay cistern placed at its lowest point. Then channels were extended up to various locations on the campo and a wellhead positioned over the whole thing. Then the cistern was covered over. When it rained, freshwater would collect on the campo, flow through the collection grates (many of which can still be seen throughout the city), and run through a layer of sand for filtration. The water would then collect in the cistern and be lifted up and out via buckets at the wellhead (*pozzo*). These wellheads, although capped and usually of later construction, are still found everywhere in Venice.

Emperor Leo V also sent to the Venetians the body of St. Zacharias, the father of St. John the Baptist, as well as funds to construct a new women's monastery to house the relic. In time, San Zaccaria would become the wealthiest and most powerful religious house in Venice. The original Byzantine structure no longer survives, replaced by the Renaissance building that stands there today. But one can get the flavor of the first San Zaccaria by visiting the somber, serene, and often-flooded twelfth-century crypt of the church. Nearby, at what is today the tourist-thronged Piazza San Marco, were two grassy islands with a few orchards and a river running between them. There the Byzantines also built a new wooden church dedicated to the fourth-century Greek martyr St. Theodore of Amasea, who was famous for slaying a demon-possessed crocodile in Egypt. Theodore was to be the patron saint of Venice, signified by the construction of a new doge's palace very close to the church. Although St. Theodore would later lose that distinction, his statue, complete with crocodile, still watches over the Piazzetta San Marco from the top of one of the two columns of the Molo. The new palace replaced the private residence of Doge Agnello. It was a stone structure, built directly on the waterfront at about the same location as the current Ducal Palace. Given the perils of the times, the first palace was a fortress. Later chronicles refer to the palace's defensive nature, and the oldest surviving map of Venice, from the fourteenth century, depicts it as a crenellated castle.

St. Theodore enjoyed only a few years as Venice's patron saint. The means of his replacement, though, would remain a story of supreme importance to Venetians for centuries. Its origins are found in the ongoing dispute between the patriarch of Grado, who had ecclesiastical jurisdiction over the Venetian lagoon, and the patriarch of Aquileia, whose jurisdiction extended to the mainland churches. Both claimed to be the true patriarch of Aquileia, and therefore each of them maintained that he alone was the legitimate successor of St. Mark. With the election of the pro-Frankish pope Eugenius II (824–27), the patriarch of Aquileia seized the opportunity to deal with the Grado problem once and for all. Eugenius called both patriarchs to a synod in Mantua in 827 so that the issue could be resolved. There the patriarch of Aquileia laid out a detailed case against Grado, arguing that it was a mere parish that had usurped apostolic authority. The successor of St. Mark, he contended, was the patriarch of Aquileia, not a minor priest on a nearby island. The patriarch of Grado had no response, largely because he declined to attend. Likely he expected nothing good from Eugenius and so hoped to put off the problem. But the synod and the pope ruled promptly against Grado, decreeing that the patriarchate of Aquileia was to be restored to its former authority. Grado and the bishops of the lagoon were placed under Aquileia's jurisdiction.

This situation was intolerable to the Venetians. They had not spilled blood defending their homes from Pepin and the Franks only to have their Church given over to the enemy. In the Middle Ages a church was not simply a building one visited on Sundays. It was the foundation of one's life, the hope for salvation, and the comforter along the way. It was also a major property owner. Aside from more than a hundred parish churches and monasteries in the Venetian lagoon, there were the numerous saltworks, vineyards, and farmlands that the churches and monasteries owned on the islands and terra firma. The Venetians would not allow a Frankish patriarch of Aquileia to acquire control over all of that.

But how to resist? The initial strategy, as evidenced by the patriarch's absence at Mantua, was to ignore the whole thing. Since the pope died shortly after the synod, there was some hope that a new pope might reverse it. But there was no denying that it would be a difficult case to make. The patriarch of Grado was forced to claim succession from the ancient patriarchs of Aquileia, while the current patriarch of Aquileia vehemently denied it. St. Mark, after all, had founded the patriarchal see in Aquileia, not Grado. Venice simply had no answer to that.

But it soon would.

In 829—only two years after the decision at Mantua—two Venetian merchants, Buono, the tribune of Malamocco, and Rustico of Torcello, were conducting some illegal business in Alexandria. All business in Egypt was technically illegal, since Emperor Leo V had forbidden his subjects to conduct trade with Muslims. Much of what happened during their visit is shrouded in legend, but the essentials are probably correct. Buono and Rustico, we are told, visited the church of St. Mark in Alexandria, where they prayed and venerated the sacred body of the Evangelist. Afterward, they happened to strike up a conversation with Stauracius, a Greek monk, and Theodorus, a Greek priest, both on staff at the church. The two complained to the Venetians about recent persecutions of Christians at the hands of the Muslim authorities. They were particularly worried about a plan to rob the Christian churches in

Alexandria of their marble. Buono and Rustico had a radical solution. They suggested that the two Greeks take the body of St. Mark and come back with them to Venice, where they would be joyfully welcomed. Stauracius and Theodorus were intrigued, but afraid to offend the saint by moving his body to a strange land. St. Mark, after all, had been bishop of Alexandria and had died there. The Venetians responded that Venice was not a strange land at all, for St. Mark had been to the lagoon on his way to Aquileia, where he had established the metropolitan see. That seemed reasonable enough, so it was decided that the four would steal the body and smuggle it onto a waiting Venetian ship.

To the modern mind, stealing a holy object may seem perverse, but it was not so in the Middle Ages. For medieval Christians the relic of the saint was a conduit between the holy person and the world. Saints were made manifest in their relics. They rewarded those who honored them and punished those who disgraced or abused them. *Furta sacra* (holy theft) was not a robbery but a rescue. A saint, it was believed, could only be moved if he or she wished it—either because proper devotion was not shown at the present location or because the new location was the home of those with greater devotion. Since this sort of rescue happened often during the Middle Ages, an entire genre of literature developed, known as *translatio*, to describe and validate a transfer. There is much of that literary genre in this legend.

The four men secretly went to the tomb of St. Mark and removed its stone cover. There they found the Evangelist's body wrapped in a silk cloth with many seals affixed to the front to prevent tampering. Undeterred, they rotated the saint onto his stomach, cut the silk at the back, and carefully removed the body. Then they inserted another body, that of St. Claudian, into the silk shroud, sewed it back up, and rotated the replacement with the intact seals faceup. The perfect crime. Or almost.

In the Middle Ages, relics of great sanctity were said to give off a powerful sweet aroma, known as the holy odor in *translatio* texts.

St. Mark, of course, gave off a great deal. As soon as the four men carried the hidden body into the main church, the worshippers and other clergy knew that something was up. Word spread quickly that the body of St. Mark had been stolen, although a subsequent less-than-thorough inspection of the seals convinced some that it was not. Buono and Rustico managed to get the saint's body onto their vessel, but the Muslim authorities, who had been alerted to the danger, demanded to inspect the ship's cargo. To avoid detection, the Venetian merchants cleverly hid the Evangelist in a large basket, which they filled with raw pork. When the Muslim officials opened the container and saw the unclean meat, they shut it with horror and fled the ship. And so it was that St. Mark left Alexandria and sailed to Venice.

As in all *translatio* stories, the authenticity of the relic was further validated by various storms at sea and other dangers from which the saint miraculously delivered the travelers after suitable supplications. At last the Venetians returned to Istria, where they sent word to the doge that if he would pardon them for trading in Alexandria, they would render to him the body of St. Mark. He readily agreed. A grand ceremony then took place with Doge Giustiniano Partecipazio (the son of the recently deceased Agnello), the patriarch of Grado, all the bishops, and many of the Venetian people in attendance to welcome the saint's arrival. The importance of this relic for the Venetians cannot be overstated. In the near term it added a powerful argument to the patriarch of Grado's claim to be the successor of St. Mark. After all, had not the saint himself chosen to rest in Venice, rather than Aquileia? In the long term, though, it served as a nexus around which Venetian national identity would form.

Astonishingly, the body of St. Mark was not handed over to the patriarch of Grado or even to the bishop of Castello, as would have been the case anywhere else in Europe. The island of Grado was rejected immediately, probably because it was so close to Aquileia and so distant from the fleets of Venice that could protect it. According to John the Deacon, the original plan was to transfer the body to the cathedral of San Pietro di Castello once the building was complete. Until then, it was kept at the Ducal Palace. However, at some point the saint made it clear that he much preferred the company of the doge. And so the original plan was abandoned. Doge Giustiniano ordered a small chapel to be built to permanently house the saint. This simple structure, completed in 832, was the first church of San Marco, built on the site of the current one. But it was not, strictly speaking, a church at all—just a household chapel attached (as it still is today) to the Ducal Palace. Since the members of the Partecipazio family were attempting to establish themselves as a ducal dynasty in Venice, the decision to keep the relic was probably meant to associate the saint with the family, just as other saints around Venice were associated with those families who had built churches in their honor.

But it did not work out that way. Only four years after the completion of the first chapel, Doge Giovanni Partecipazio was overthrown—a victim of the factional violence that was again disturbing the city. Members of the rival Mastalici family waylaid the doge as he was walking home from church at the cathedral of San Pietro. They shaved off his hair and beard and forced him to take clerical vows. He lived the remainder of his days as a monk on Grado. The election of a new doge, Pietro Tradonico, firmly established the principle that the palace and its chapel belonged to the people of Venice and not to any particular family. Henceforth, St. Mark was the special patron of the doge and, by extension, the Republic of Venice. St. Theodore had been replaced. Yet the building that housed St. Mark's body, even when it was later rebuilt on a grand scale, remained a ducal chapel. It was not a cathedral. It was not even a parish church. It was part of the Ducal Palace and, therefore, the property of the people of Venice. St. Mark belonged to them all.

Of course, one might question whether Buono and Rustico had

been altogether forthright with the Greeks when they persuaded them to take away the relic. After all, according to tradition St. Mark had lived in Aquileia, so it could hardly be said that his relocation to Venice was a return home. There was, after all, no Venice in St. Mark's day. But the Venetians found a way around that problem, too. They claimed that when St. Mark traveled between Rome and Aquileia, he had docked his boat at Rialto to rest. There an angel came down from heaven and proclaimed to him, "*Pax tibi, Marce, evangelista meus. Hic requiescat corpus tuum*" (Peace be with you, Mark, my Evangelist. Here shall your body rest). Thus was it divinely ordained that St. Mark should remain forever in Venice. This point was further underscored by the new symbol of Venice. For centuries the Venetians have depicted the winged lion, the ancient iconography of St. Mark and his Gospel, with one paw resting on an open book and the words of the angel's greeting plainly visible.

In time, the association between St. Mark and the Venetian republic would become so firm as to be inseparable. The story of his first visit to Rialto and his exciting trip from Alexandria to Venice would become a foundational element in Venetian history and identity. Even today, one can see a depiction of the bamboozled Muslim inspectors on the facade of San Marco and a full mosaic cycle of his *translatio* on the inside walls of the church. Then, as now, the lion of St. Mark was on every banner. Venice had become the Republic of St. Mark.

CHAPTER 3

COMING OF AGE:
INDEPENDENCE, EXPANSION,
AND POWER, 836–1094

F inding two merchants in Muslim Alexandria in the ninth century pilfering the body of a saint is good evidence that Venetians were conducting trade across the Mediterranean Sea at
that time. Their overall business model was a simple one: Buy low, sell
high. The ninth-century markets on the island of Torcello teemed with
activity, just as they would at Rialto in the late tenth century. Venetian
businessmen paid handsomely for a wide range of commodities, many
of which were grown or produced in Europe and then transported overland or by river to the lagoon. These included foodstuffs, timber, and, of
course, the locally produced salt. These goods were then loaded aboard
a sailing vessel by an enterprising merchant, who would head out of the
lagoon, down the Adriatic, and into the wide Mediterranean in search
of profit. Invariably, he turned left, as Venetians did virtually all their
overseas trade in the eastern Mediterranean—primarily in the Byzantine Empire. The markets there were larger than anything in Europe
and the goods they offered were in high demand back home. This cycle

of buying and selling, with Venice the nexus between Europe and Byzantium, brought wealth to a growing number of Venetian families.

Venice's success as a commercial center was based in large part
on its location at the head of the Adriatic Sea. It was a convenient
place from which to move goods to and from other European markets,
while also providing plenty of commercial docks and local markets
for overseas shipping. In short, Venice was a medieval businessman's
paradise—a place where fortunes were made (and presumably lost).
More commerce in the ninth and tenth centuries meant more wealth,
more people, and more power concentrated in the Venetian lagoon. Crucial to this trade, however, was the safety of shipping in the Adriatic.
When Byzantine fleets policed those waters, all was well. Yet, by the
ninth century, as the empire continued to lose territories to the Arabs in
the East and the government was rocked by a series of scandals and palace coups, Constantinople could no longer maintain regular patrols. As
a result, during the 830s conditions in the Adriatic became intolerable.
Slavic pirates raided coastal towns and plundered Venetian vessels at
will. Even worse, Muslim armies were wresting control of Sicily from
the Byzantine Empire. Twice in the 840s the Venetians outfitted fleets
to help the Byzantines battle the Muslims, but with little success. As
for the Adriatic, the Venetians came reluctantly to the conclusion that
they would simply have to police it themselves. The stability and safety
of shipping there was so important to them that it soon became known
as the Sea of Venice. It had become their waterway, the long blue entrance to the ballroom of Venice.

The Venetians were blessed during those years with some stability
in leadership. Doge Pietro Tradonico (836–64) reigned longer than anyone who had previously held the office. Like his predecessors, the Gal-
baios, he made his son co-doge in an attempt to keep the position in the
family. However, his son died in 863, weakening his support and providing an opening for those who opposed his dogeship. On what seemed a

quiet evening one year later, the aged doge was attending vespers at the nearby convent of San Zaccaria. As he left the church to walk home, eight conspirators surrounded and killed him. Fearing a coup, his body-guard and servants fled to the fortified Ducal Palace, locking it up tight. As word of the murder spread, the city descended into mayhem, with various factions clashing violently. The details are not altogether clear, but it seems that the conspirators and their sympathizers resented the attempt of one man to monopolize the dogeship for his family. As indi-vidual wealth had risen in Venice, newly prosperous families aspired to their own political power, and they naturally opposed those who excluded them from it. This potent dynamic would continue to drive events in Venice for centuries.

In all ages, privilege and economic mobility are enemies. Compli-cating this picture was the essentially conservative nature of the Vene-tians. Resisting concentrated power was, they believed, praiseworthy. But many of them wondered if it justified the cold-blooded murder of an elderly doge. As days passed, popular sentiment in Venice turned against the conspirators. At last, they were rounded up and executed or exiled. The arengo, which consisted of little more than a throng of men gathering noisily in the open field that would one day be the Piazza San Marco, elected another member of the previous ducal family, Orso I Partecipazio (864–81). This may have been a reaction against the reaction—in other words, a return to an established clan so as to deny the conspirators their victory. Whatever the reason, it is interesting (although baffling) that at about this time the Partecipazio family changed its surname to Badoer, a name that would echo across the history of medieval Venice.

The new doge brought much-needed stability to the lagoon, at a time when the world outside was anything but stable. Muslim raiders continued to make incursions into the Adriatic, preying on towns and Venetian shipping. Just as bad were the Slavic pirates working from their bases in the crannied coasts of Croatia. And all across Europe the Vikings were raiding and pillaging at will, although they do not seem to have bothered with Venice, which could defend itself on the sea. The doge was kept busy responding to these external threats. Despite the opposition such practice had previously engendered, Orso took his son, Giovanni, as his colleague in the dogeship. He also took part in what would become a long-standing custom, having his daughter elected abbess of San Zaccaria. Because of the prestige and wealth of this religious house, the position of its abbess was highly coveted. There is some evidence that Orso also did away with the old tribunes, replacing them with judges. The latter were officials, probably elected, who served in the court of the doge. The earliest surviving charters make plain that judges were present at all official events and signed all acts, so they probably still served as a check on the doge's power. However, unlike elsewhere in Europe, churchmen did not serve in Venice's ducal court. The church and state were separate in Venice in a way that they were not elsewhere.

Doge Giovanni Badoer (881–88) maintained a steady hand on the Venetian ship of state until his health failed in 887, when he abdicated. The people replaced him with Pietro Candiano (887), a vigorous man who promised to deal personally with the pirates along the Dalmatian coast. This he did with vigor, although he was killed in the war, thus forcing Badoer to once again take up the dogeship. Pietro Candiano probably settled the problem of Adriatic piracy, since we hear no more of it for some time. However, a new and much greater danger was on its way from the East.

The Magyars, a warlike nomadic people, had migrated from southwest Asia into southeastern Europe and settled in what is today Hungary. From there they launched devastating raids across central Europe and Italy. Like the other invaders pouring into Europe at this time, the

Magyars were neither Christian nor Romanized. Like the Huns centuries earlier, they tore into the shattered West with unparalleled ferocity. Indeed, many Europeans believed that they *were* Huns, which may explain the origin of their name "Hungarian."

By 899 the Magyars covered the mainland of northern Italy. The Venetian lagoon was not spared. Once again the towns on the periphery were the first to fall. The Magyars captured Eraclea and Equilo as well as Lombard towns on the mainland such as Altino, Treviso, and Padua. Having surrounded the lagoon, they quickly conquered Chioggia in the south and began marching north toward the city along the lido of Pellestrina—in other words, moving precisely in King Pepin's footsteps. Yet like Pepin's, the Magyars' assault stalled at Malamocco. There the new fortifications stopped the invasion and the Venetians rallied, forcing the Magyars to retreat. It was a tremendous victory. The powerful Magyars, who had defeated even the Carolingian king, were unable to threaten seriously the new Venetian capital at Rialto. The foresight of Doge Agnello Partecipazio had paid rich dividends. Venice was secure from the most awesome foe of its day, and would remain so for centuries.

It is perhaps not surprising that in the aftermath of the frightening Magyar attacks, the Venetians decided to further strengthen their defenses. The doge, we are told, ordered the construction of a long wall along the shoreline of the city facing the lidi. It stretched from the modern Riva degli Schiavoni—today packed with hotels, restaurants, and trinket sellers—to the church of Santa Maria Zobenigo (del Giglio), west of San Marco. Needless to say, it ruined the view. In addition, a heavy chain was suspended across the Grand Canal entrance, and secured at the church of San Gregorio, very near the present location of Santa Maria della Salute. Given the continued effectiveness of the waves in shielding Venice, it is uncertain how long the Venetians maintained these new constructions. The oldest surviving map of Venice, drawn in the fourteenth century, depicts no such wall or chain, although it does clearly indicate that the Ducal Palace remained fortified.

The decades after the Magyar invasion were prosperous and relatively peaceful for Venice. The dogeship alternated between the Badoer and Candiano families with little strife. This was a time of building, when Venetian entrepreneurs, fully supported by their pro-business government, were establishing trade agreements on the mainland and in ports across the eastern Mediterranean. Venetian fleets not only beat back the threat of piracy in the Adriatic, but also deployed patrols to make certain that cargo from all vessels, whether Venetian or not, was unloaded at the markets in Venice, where the government naturally took its share of taxes.

With Venice's gaze fixed on the rich emporia of the East, it is surprising that the feudal West made so abrupt an entry into Venetian life in the mid-tenth century. The doorway was Pietro IV Candiano (959–76), the son of Doge Pietro III Candiano (942–59). Although Pietro III had taken his son as co-doge, that was unsatisfactory to the latter, who apparently did not want to wait for his father's death to seize power. The young Pietro was part of a faction with ties to feudal barons in northern Italy and Germany. In its most basic form, feudalism was a means by which lands were worked to produce surplus in order to raise and maintain medieval armies. Vassals, who managed the lands, owed military service and fealty to their lords, who, in turn, either owned the lands or owed similar service to their own lords. Although feudalism was—in one form or another—practiced across western Europe, it was nonexistent in Venice, which lacked the territories to support it. In other words, feudalism required land, something noticeably rare in Venice. The Venetians were capitalists who dealt above all in liquid assets. They purchased food from mainland feudal estates, but generated their own income from business transactions, chief of which involved commercial shipping. Venetians had no need of a medieval army—only an effective navy, which their state organized using the rich tax revenues of a vibrant economy. In this, too, Venice was out of step with its age.

Perhaps the young Pietro was seduced by the evolving romanticism of martial prowess or the ways of the increasingly independent barons of the mainland. Or perhaps it was simply a matter of power, for this was the age of King Otto I of Germany, who had successfully imposed his authority north of the Alps and was preparing to do the same in Italy. Whatever the case, Pietro staged a coup against his father in 950, a coup that failed spectacularly. Once again the Venetians had been asked to choose between the new order of feudal lords in Europe and their centuries-long loyalty to the Byzantine (or Roman) Empire in the East. And once again they repeated the choice that had given birth to their state. They refused to join what their ancestors had fled.

Pietro should have been executed for treason, yet his aged father begged for his life and the people reluctantly granted it. The young man fled the lagoon to his noble friends on the mainland and soon found his calling as a warrior, leading armies in the service of King Berengar of Italy. In gratitude, the king allowed Pietro to wage his own war of piracy against Venice, capturing merchant vessels on the Po River and the Adriatic Sea. If that were not bad enough, a disease of some sort hit the city of Venice causing widespread deaths, including that of the heart-broken doge. For reasons that are not altogether clear, when the people assembled to elect their new doge, they chose young Pietro, the treasonous pirate lord. He was, after all, the son of the doge and his election had the practical benefit of ending the attacks on Venetian shipping.

But the Pietro who moved into the Ducal Palace was not at all like the impetuous rebel who had left. In clothing, manner, and even language he resembled a feudal baron, not a Venetian doge. Almost immediately he leveraged his new title to propose marriage to Waldrada, the

sister of the Marquis of Tuscany and a kinswoman of Emperor Otto himself. The fact that Doge Pietro IV already had a wife and a grown son was
no impediment. He simply sent his wife to the cloister at San Zaccaria
and his son, now forcibly tonsured, to a monastery. The new German
wife brought to the doge her rich lands in The Marches, Treviso, Friuli,
and elsewhere. She also brought armed retainers, who garrisoned the
Ducal Palace and accompanied the ducal family everywhere. It seemed
to many Venetians that the Germans had taken by marriage what they
had failed to capture by force. Discontent spread rapidly in the lagoon
and an opposition party soon sprang up, led by the Morosini family. A
rival family, the Coloprinis, supported the doge.

Matters came to a head in 976, when a war between the factions
broke out in the streets and canals of Venice. The Morosinis and their
supporters won the day, pursuing their enemies all the way to the Ducal
Palace. There they set fire to houses built around the fortified structure.
The fire grew into a mighty blaze that cut across the San Marco area. Not
only was the palace consumed, but so also was the wooden chapel of
San Marco, the old church of St. Theodore, and some three hundred
other buildings. The body of St. Mark, so carefully purloined from Alexandria and installed in the newborn Venice, was lost in the flames.
When the doge's family and servants rushed to escape the burning palace, their enemies barred the way. Pietro begged for mercy, promising
to grant their every wish, but to no avail. He was run through with a
sword while trying to force his way out. His infant son, born of his new
German wife, was pierced with a spear while resting in his nurse's arms.
Only Waldrada survived, perhaps because the rebels feared retribution
from her family or perhaps because she was simply absent from Venice
at the time.

As the last of the fires was extinguished, the Venetians began to see
the rebellion differently. Once again a popular groundswell of violence

became bitterly unpopular in the cold light of day. This recurring phenomenon in their history—violent defiance followed by remorse and sorrow—was the product of strong individualism mixed with a businessman's natural desire for security, stability, and order. On the one hand, Venetians distrusted concentrated power and reacted passionately when they believed that a doge or anyone else was trying to acquire it. On the other hand, they were merchants and shopkeepers who relied on a peaceful and predictable marketplace and government. And there was also the matter of the destruction of the body of the Evangelist. To lose one's spiritual patron and protector was no small thing to medieval men and women. Thus, while the ashes of the government buildings still smoldered, the people of Venice sought a new doge to bring healing to their state.

They settled on an inspired choice. Pietro Orseolo (976–78) was an aged man well respected for his wisdom, piety, and service to the state. Since at least 968 he had been planning to enter a monastery. One tradition even records that Orseolo and his wife took a holy vow of celibacy, living as brother and sister since the birth of their only son. On August 12, 976, the people of Venice gathered at the bishop's church, San Pietro di Castello. There they persuaded old Orseolo to take on the dogeship, although he did so reluctantly and with a grim determination to complete his task quickly.

Doge Orseolo's first priority was establishing peace with Germany. The distant successor to Charlemagne, Otto II, had been crowned Holy Roman emperor by Pope John XIII in 967. He was beside himself with rage over the treatment of Waldrada and her family. To smooth things over, the doge agreed to make restitution payments to Waldrada that were so large a special tax had to be imposed on the Venetians to raise it. Additional taxes were levied to fund the rebuilding effort in Venice, although Orseolo financed the reconstruction of the Ducal Palace himself. The entire San Marco area was soon echoing with the hammers and saws of workers. Venice was again building. Optimism for the future returned.

With that Doge Orseolo judged that his work was done. On the evening of September 1, 978, he packed what little belongings he still possessed and fled the city under cover of darkness. Unlike his predecessor, Orseolo was not seeking foreign allies, but eternal salvation. He traveled westward until he arrived at the new monastery of St. Michael of Cuxa in the Pyrenees. There he joyfully took up the coarse Benedictine habit, leaving aside the rich garments of the doge. For the next nine years he lived, worked, and prayed in that stone refuge—a building that has since been transported to New York City, where one can visit it in The Cloisters museum. Almost immediately after his death in 987 miracles were reported at his tomb. In time the Catholic Church recognized Pietro Orseolo as a saint—the only doge to attain that distinction in the long history of Venice.

Yet Orseolo's project had not brought an end to the rivalry between the Morosinis and the Coloprinis, largely because the question of whether Venice should embrace the German empire in Italy remained unanswered. The new doge, Tribuno Menio (979–91), remained neutral enough to persuade both families to put their name to a very important document. In 982 Venice donated the Island of Cypresses, south of the Ducal Palace, to Abbot Giovanni Morosini for the foundation of a new Benedictine monastery dedicated to St. George. This island and its institution, San Giorgio Maggiore, would henceforward hold a special place for Venetians. Its proximity to the governmental center and its picturesque location still make it one of the most recognizable features of the city. The document, dated December 20, 982, was signed by the doge, three bishops, and 131 other leading citizens. First among the signers were the leaders of the two factions, Stefano Coloprini and Domenico Morosini.

This parchment, which still survives in the Venetian archives, provides a rare snapshot of the power structure in Venice at this crucial period. The number of new families, indeed the sheer number of families new or old, that appear on the signature list suggests that the factional struggle was expanding the base of participating citizens as both sides scrambled for support among wealthy men. Henceforth, this body of "good men" or "faithful ones," as they were interchangeably called in documents, would become a permanent part of the doge's court. Because of their new wealth, these elites had the interest and the time to concern themselves with matters of government. Initially they represented the "people of Venice," who were too busy with their own affairs to be present for the increasing duties of the growing Venetian government. Yet these elites soon became a new political force carving out their own place between the doge and people. From this loose, ad hoc group would later evolve the Great Council of Venice.

The Europe of the new millennium was a changed place. The Germanic barbarian invasions were long since finished, their peoples settled across the landscape. The new invasions of Magyars from the east, Muslims from the south, and Vikings from everywhere had subsided and would soon cease altogether. After centuries of chaos, Europeans were at last able to lift their heads and survey their battered world. In some places they even began rebuilding. The Holy Roman emperors in Germany had once again established themselves as the preeminent power in the West, although they no longer ruled all of Charlemagne's great empire. Carved out of it to the west was the kingdom of France, now led by the Capetian monarchs, whose dynasty would last throughout the Middle Ages. Other states were soon planted by the Normans, the Catholic descendants of the marauding Norsemen. From their base in Normandy they would capture England in 1066 under their leader, William the Conqueror, thus ushering in a new era in the history of that kingdom. They would also invade Sicily and southern Italy, cobbling together a kingdom that displaced the warring Arabs and Byzantines there.

The Church, too, was rebuilding. The tumult of the preceding centuries had taken a hard toll on an institution that relied on communication and discipline to ensure that clergy were seeing to the spiritual needs of the faithful. Because bishops and abbots were powerful men with lands and wealth, their offices were often sold to the highest bidder by the lay lord to whom they owed feudal service. It was an intolerable situation, for it meant that the shepherds themselves were little more than wolves. By 1000, though, the reform movement centered at the French monastery of Cluny was spreading quickly across Europe, changing minds, hearts, and not a few abbots. By the mid-eleventh century the reformers had captured the papacy, leading to an extraordinary rebirth of the Catholic Church almost everywhere. In time, this reinvigorated Church would find itself at odds with the restored German emperors, yet that church-state struggle was itself uniquely European. In other words, as the new millennium dawned, Europe was becoming something new, what we today call the West.

Like much of Europe, the Republic of Venice's fortunes changed dramatically in the eleventh century. Factional strife withered under Doge Pietro II Orseolo (991–1008), a man who cultivated close relations with both German and Byzantine emperors. Otto III of Germany was Orseolo's personal friend. The German ruler even visited Venice in 1001 as the doge's special guest. For his part, the Byzantine emperor Basil II issued a chrysobull, or imperial edict, in 992 that defined Venetian merchants' rights and privileges and reduced the tolls and tariffs they paid while doing business in eastern ports. In this important document, one can see the changing relationship between Venice and the Byzantine Empire. Slowly over centuries, Venice had become an independent entity. It was no longer a province or client of Constantinople. And yet, neither was it completely foreign. Instead, the Byzantine emperor referred to the Venetians as *extraneos* (outsiders), who, by regularly aiding imperial operations in Italian waters, had proved themselves to be steadfast allies of the Roman Empire.

And, indeed, they were. In 1000 Doge Orseolo led a war fleet against Croatian pirates based in Dalmatia, the lands along the eastern shore of the Adriatic Sea. In short order the Venetians not only suppressed the privateers but extracted oaths of loyalty from all the Dalmatian towns. Orseolo promptly added to his title *dux Dalmatiae* (doge of Dalmatia), a designation that was later confirmed by the emperor in Constantinople. Whether by coincidence or design, this Venetian military action assisted Basil II in his war against the Bulgarians by weakening their allies, the Serbs and Croats. Four years later, the doge personally led Venetian warships to Bari on the southern Adriatic, where they broke the Arab siege of the Byzantine city.

Yet Venetian intervention could do little to arrest the decline of Byzantium, which continued to be battered by foes from every side. In 1071 the Normans conquered Bari, the last Byzantine outpost in Italy, and though they posed no direct threat to the city of Venice, they were a serious threat to Venetian control of the Adriatic Sea. In the same year a powerful Turkish invasion army met Byzantine forces at the Battle of Manzikert in Asia Minor (modern Turkey). The Muslim warriors scattered the Christians, quickly capturing the central region known as Anatolia. Within a few years the Turks had established a new state, the sultanate of Rum (Rome) with its capital at Nicaea. All that remained of the battered Byzantine Empire was the city of Constantinople, now within sight of the Turkish empire, and Greece.

In desperate need, Emperor Alexius I Comnenus sent an appeal to Pope Gregory VII asking for Western troops to help push back the Turkish conquests. Although Gregory was willing to help (indeed, he even considered leading an army himself to Constantinople), his ecclesiastical reforms soon led him into an intractable struggle with the German emperor, Henry IV, that would consume the papacy's attention for the next three decades.

Venetians were not much affected by this struggle between church and state—at least not in the eleventh century—but a persistent weakened Byzantine Empire spelled economic trouble for them. Venice's prosperity was built on a peaceful Adriatic and profitable trade in the East. The former was essential for the latter. The emboldened Norman leader in Italy, Robert Guiscard, threatened both. Like William the Conqueror, Robert longed for a grand conquest of a new kingdom, and his attention was naturally drawn to the wounded and weak Byzantine Empire. The seat of imperial power and the richest city in the Western world, Constantinople seemed like the burial goods of a dying world. For Robert, the way was clear. From Bari he would head due east across the Adriatic and capture the Byzantine coastal city of Durazzo (modern Durrës). From there the ancient Roman road, the Via Egnatia, stretched some five hundred miles to the capital itself.

Venetians looked on the coming Norman invasion of Byzantium with dread. Normans were wild and warlike—in other words, bad for business. It was not long before Norman freebooters were actively disrupting Venetian shipping in the Adriatic. In 1074 the Norman count Amico of Giovinazzo even attacked Dalmatian cities under Venetian control. Doge Domenico Silvio (1070–85) immediately led a war fleet against Amico, defeated him, and reasserted Venetian dominance in the area. Reeling from external attacks and torn by internal unrest, the Byzantines, however, could no longer project any effective force into the Adriatic. The authoritative force of Doge Silvio's campaign made clear that control of that sea had passed from Byzantium to Venice.

The Venetian war fleet, though already formidable, was not yet in the eleventh and twelfth centuries the well-oiled naval juggernaut it would eventually become. At the time of Doge Silvio's campaign, it was composed of a mixture of public and private vessels organized on an ad hoc basis to deal with specific missions. Two main types of vessels dominated its ranks. The first were merchant ships pressed into service as transports to carry men, supplies, and siege weapons. These round-hull vessels could generally carry 350 tons, but there were some larger varieties that could move twice that. They were powered by two and sometimes three lateen sails, each on its own mast, and were maneuvered by steering oars on either side of the stern rather than by single sternpost rudders as in modern ships. On average, six hundred men could fit on their two or three levels. The lateen sails allowed the vessels to tack reasonably well into the wind, yet they were unwieldy to manage and therefore required large crews.

The other vessel was the rowed galley, designed for naval warfare, repelling enemies and protecting the transports. Venetian galleys in the Middle Ages were long, sleek boats that carried one mast with a single lateen sail. At the bow they had a beak—a hinged plank with an iron spike designed to be lowered onto enemy vessels. The oarsmen were seated in a single bank with two oarsmen per bench, each rowing a separate oar. The galley was designed to be swift and nimble, no matter the weather. When it closed upon a vessel, the beak could be used either to damage it sufficiently to sink it, or as a bridge so that the marines could run across and fight hand to hand.

These vessels were built in shipyards scattered across the city. Several of these are mentioned in medieval documents at places along the Grand Canal or on nearby islands. These were the days before the great Arsenale, when shipbuilding was still farmed out to private entrepreneurs. Because ships were important to Venice, so, too, was the lumber necessary to build those ships. Indeed, the Venetians were obsessed by the constant need for fine timber, and their intervention in Dalmatia was in large measure predicated on the rich forests that could be found there. In later centuries, when the Venetians were established on the Italian mainland, they practiced an exacting sort of forestry, keeping meticulous records of every tree and imposing harsh fines on those who poached in the state groves.

Robert Guiscard launched his much-anticipated attack against Durazzo in the summer of 1081. Emperor Alexius I Comnenus dispatched envoys to Venice, promising rich rewards in return for military aid, but Doge Silvio needed little convincing. If Robert was successful at Durazzo, he would hold strong points on both sides of the mouth of the Adriatic. From there he could cripple or halt altogether Venetian overseas trade—the very lifeline of Venice's prosperity. The Venetians quickly assembled an impressive war fleet and Doge Silvio again took command. In the late summer or autumn of 1081 the fleet reached Durazzo, where it found the Normans already besieging the Byzantine city. Silvio ordered his countrymen to attack the Norman fleet, which outnumbered the Venetians by a considerable margin. Nonetheless, the expert Venetian sailors destroyed the Norman navy in short order. Once in control of the port, the Venetians supplied the people inside Durazzo and assisted with their defense. But the Normans did not give up. With additional men and ships they continued to besiege Durazzo. Finally, on October 15, Emperor Alexius arrived from the east with a large mercenary army. He tried to break the Norman siege, but failed miserably. Robert's men scattered the Byzantine forces and even managed to wound Alexius in the melee. Thus chastened by this show of strength, the emperor returned home, leaving the defense of Durazzo to Venice.

The Norman siege continued throughout the winter of 1081–82. It ended with treachery. In February the Normans bribed a Venetian renegade to open a gate while the citizens slept. With bloody fury, the Normans stormed the city, killing or capturing hundreds of Venetians. After securing Durazzo, Robert Guiscard began his march into the heart of the Byzantine Empire. Yet events in Rome intervened. The German emperor, Henry IV, was moving south through Italy, bent on capturing his enemy, Pope Gregory VII. At the pope's summons, Robert returned to Italy to defend the Church, leaving his son Bohemond behind to prosecute the war against Byzantium. In Robert's absence, Venetian and Byzantine forces rallied and in fierce battles erased most of the Norman victories. In the fall of 1083 a new Venetian fleet attacked Durazzo and recaptured the city, although the citadel, manned by a few Normans, tenaciously held out. After wintering there, the Venetians set sail to the south for the island of Corfu, which they also soon captured. The tables had turned. Venice now held the southeastern coast of the Adriatic.

But the Norman threat had not yet passed. After settling matters in Italy, Robert Guiscard assembled another large fleet. Bad weather delayed his departure, so it was not until November 1084 that his vessels set sail for Corfu. Well informed of the danger, Emperor Alexius again summoned Venice to muster an armada in defense of the Byzantine Empire, and once again, Doge Silvio complied, sending a fleet south where it joined with Alexius's own makeshift navy. Learning of the defenders' movements, Robert changed course, heading instead to Cassiopi in northeast Corfu. There one of the largest naval engagements of the Middle Ages took place. The allied fleet twice defeated the Normans, who took heavy casualties. It seemed to everyone, Robert included, that the great Norman offensive was over. The Venetians sent messengers home to herald their great victory. Hearing of the jubilant celebrations among his enemies, Robert sank into a deep despair.

Weeks later, though, the Norman leader shook off his depression and made plans for a bold counteroffensive. In January 1085, a time of year in which medieval ships never sailed, the Norman fleet appeared suddenly off Corfu. The Venetian and Byzantine commanders, amazed at Robert's courage and audacity, scrambled to their vessels. But this time the Normans had caught the Venetians by surprise. After long and bloody fighting, the Normans defeated the allied fleet. According to the daughter of the emperor, Anna Comnena, thirteen thousand Venetians were killed in the battle and many more taken prisoner. Captured Venetians were cruelly mutilated and then ransomed back to their relatives. Robert hoped to use these prisoners as spokesmen for peace with Venice, but they openly defied him, swearing loyalty to the Byzantine emperor.

This devastating naval defeat was Venice's worst yet. Back home the people exploded in outrage when news of glorious victory was followed by tales of humiliating defeat. Blaming their doge, they overthrew Domenico Silvio and replaced him with Vitale Falier (1085–96). But more amazing news was yet to come. Wintering in Greece, the victorious Norman forces were decimated by plague. In July 1085 Robert Guiscard himself contracted the disease and died, and with him his war against Byzantium. After so much strife and bloodshed, the Norman danger had miraculously evaporated.

Emperor Alexius I had promised great rewards for Venetian aid, and he made good on that promise. In a chrysobull he conceded the high imperial title of *protosebastos* to the doge, annual stipends for the doge and patriarch of Grado, annual tithes for Venetian churches, a church in Durazzo, and substantial buildings and properties in Constantinople. The latter would form the nucleus of the city's new Venetian Quarter. This city within a city, located directly on Constantinople's commercial docks, quickly became a cornerstone of Venetian overseas trade. The emperor also granted Venetian merchants the right to conduct trade in all Byzantine ports completely tax free. A few years later Alexius also gave the doge titled jurisdiction over the lands of Dalmatia and Croatia. Henceforth, all Venetian doges referred to themselves as "doge of Venice, Dalmatia and Croatia and also imperial *protosebastos*." It was quite a mouthful.

The chrysobull of Alexius I forever changed relations between Venice and the Byzantine Empire. Most important was the tax exemption, which gave Venetian merchants a sizable advantage over their Genoese, Pisan, and even Greek competitors. In effect, Venetian wharves in Byzantine ports became duty-free zones. Merchants from Venice flocked to the eastern empire to take advantage of their privileged status, and in short order, many of them grew rich. Alexius could not see it then, but the new and conspicuous wealth of Venetian merchants and residents in Constantinople and other Greek ports would transform attitudes toward Venice among Byzantines from gratitude into envy and resentment. From the Byzantine perspective, the Venetians had always been poor cousins of the empire: not quite barbarians, but almost as crude and ill-mannered as the rest of western Europe. Now, as nouveaux riches, the Venetians were boorish as well. It was galling to see these rough sailors flaunting their wealth in the streets of Constantinople—wealth that had come to them from the generosity of the emperor and at the expense of the Byzantine people. These festering resentments would drive a wedge between the two peoples, fueling centuries of rancor.

By the late eleventh century Venice had become a city that scarcely resembled the muddy archipelago of islands to which Doge Agnello Partecipazio had led his people in 811. It now teemed with a population of some fifty thousand souls, making it the second-largest city in western Europe. Within a century it would double again in size. To sustain that kind of growth in a lagoon, additional land was a necessity. As rivers were filled in, marshes drained, and bridges built, parish boundaries in Venice came to separate neighborhoods rather than independent island communities. Although Venetians retained their parish identities, their various patron saints, once a sign of prestige and independence, were now displaced by devotion to St. Mark, the patron of the doge and the state. It is not surprising, then, that the Venetians decided to build a new church of San Marco, one that would better reflect the wealth and prestige of their vibrant community.

To construct a new San Marco—the third and final version of the doge's great chapel—a battery of builders, craftsmen, and artists were hired in Constantinople during the reign of Doge Domenico Contarini (1043–70). The Greek architects modeled the new stone structure on the Church of the Holy Apostles in Constantinople—a now-lost building that had served as the burial site for emperors since the time of Constantine the Great. San Marco was probably the first stone church to be built in Venice, and it was certainly the grandest to be found anywhere in the region, perhaps in the entire West. We can only imagine the difficulties of building so large a structure on a smallish island of sand. Undoubtedly there were false starts and mishaps. However, it is clear that the basic structure was nearing completion by 1070, when Doge Contarini died. His successor, Domenico Silvio, was crowned in the new, although still unfinished, church. Silvio ordered all Venetian merchants bound for eastern ports to purchase marbles or other decorative stone to beautify the building. He is also credited with beginning the mosaic program that would one day cover the length and breadth of the sanctuary.

The date of San Marco's completion is not clear, probably because it would always remain a work in progress. The usual date given for its dedication is 1094, during the dogeship of Vitale Falier, who is buried in its atrium. The glorious new church, which still draws thousands of visitors daily, was both a gift to the patron saint of the republic and a declaration of independence from Byzantium. Venice was no longer a community of refugees, but had become a great power in its own right. The enormous edifice of San Marco made that statement eloquently enough to both friend and foe.

While stunning, the new San Marco conspicuously lacked the body of St. Mark, lost in the fire that destroyed the first church in 976. An insurmountable problem to the modern mind, perhaps, but it was nothing of the sort in the Middle Ages. If God wished to preserve the body of St. Mark, he could very well do so. After all, had he not sent his angel to foretell that the Evangelist would one day rest in Venice? A variety of

stories soon developed to explain the rediscovery of St. Mark's body
after the dedication of his new church. In most of them, the doge, patriarch, and citizens prayed fervently to have the relic restored, now that a
suitable temple had been built to house it. The body was then miraculously revealed by the falling away of plaster or stone from a wall or (in
most versions) a column in the new church. Behind the broken material
could be seen either the arm or the whole body of the patron saint. During the thirteenth century, the story was even rendered in mosaics on
the west wall of the south transept of the church, where it can still be
seen. This mosaic is one of the earliest depictions of Venetians, including women and children. In the *Preghiera Sancti Marci* the people and
doge are shown attending a Mass to beseech God for the return of the
holy relic. In the adjoining *Apparitio Sancti Marci* the doge, clergy, and
people watch as the column opens and the miracle is complete.

Just as the magnificent edifice of San Marco rose from the ashes, so,
too, the beloved St. Mark had at last returned to his people, at a moment
when they were poised to expand their already considerable power to
the farther reaches of this world.

CHAPTER 4

A MERCHANT REPUBLIC
IN A FEUDAL AGE:
ECCLESIASTICAL AND POLITICAL
REFORM, 1095–1172

I n November 1095 medieval Europe groaned and gave birth to something genuinely new—something that would claim Venetian attention for centuries. On a wide, grassy plain in France, Pope Urban II addressed a great assembly of nobles and knights who had traveled to the Council of Clermont to receive his blessing. He told them a heartbreaking story of recent Turkish conquests, both in Asia and the Holy Land, and of the Turks' brutal persecutions of Christians living in the East and attacks on European pilgrims traveling to Jerusalem. It was a tale oft-told in the Middle Ages. For more than four centuries the armies of Islam had overrun the old Christian world, capturing two-thirds of it by 1050. In 1071 the Turks had defeated Byzantine armies at the Battle of Manzikert and subsequently claimed all of Asia Minor. Out of options, Constantinople pleaded with the popes for military assistance against the Muslim invaders. For decades the struggle between the German emperor and the papacy had kept the pope from fulfilling Alexius I Comnenus's desperate request for assistance. By the 1090s, though, the popes had gained the upper hand in that struggle, and were at last in a position to do something about the dramatic decline of the Christian world.

On that French plain in 1095, Urban II delivered a sermon that has passed from history into legend. He implored the knights and nobles of Europe to do penance for their sins by joining a grand expedition to aid their brothers and sisters in Christ, who were even then suffering under the cruel oppression of the Turks. He urged them to march to the East and expel the Muslims from the lands that they had wrongfully conquered, restoring them to Christianity once more. With God's help they would not only right these wrongs, but could even press on to Jerusalem itself, returning it at last to Christendom.

The response to Urban's speech was tremendous. *"Deus vult!"* (God wills it!), the warriors cried with piety and passion. The same shouts echoed all across Europe as the First Crusade was preached everywhere. It was a phenomenon like no other in world history. Thousands of Christians spent extraordinary sums and left behind family and lands in a fervent desire to serve Christ by aiding the least of his brethren—the subjugated Eastern Christians. And by helping them, the crusader also helped himself—for he knew well his sins and the penalty for them. This expedition was not only an act of charity but a means of salvation. Waves of pious enthusiasm swept through a vigorously recharged Europe. Something new, something utterly unprecedented, was in the air.

The Italian merchant cities were not immune to these sentiments. Indeed, they shared them, just as they shared their Catholic faith with their northern neighbors. The main army of the First Crusade soldiered forth from Europe in 1096 and the next year Genoese merchants sent off a small fleet of thirteen vessels to catch up with it. Venice and Pisa, though, had grander visions. They were the only two states in Europe to collectively take up the crusader's cross. In France, Great Britain, and Germany, monarchs stood aloof from the seemingly impossible project, while their vassals prepared for departure. By contrast, the governments in Venice and Pisa poured enormous resources into the Crusade from the start.

By the time word reached Venice of Pope Urban's call to arms, Doge Vitale Falier was close to death. Infirmity may have kept him from embracing the Crusade, or he may simply have shared the skepticism of his royal counterparts. But in December 1096, as the various armies of the First Crusade were beginning to depart, Doge Falier died. When the Venetians assembled to choose a new doge, they turned to Vitale Michiel (1096–1101), a strong proponent of Venetian participation in the Crusade. Immediately after he was crowned in San Marco, Michiel sent word to the towns on the Dalmatian coast to prepare for a glorious enterprise to free the lands of Jesus Christ. In the lagoon, shipwrights began work on war galleys, cutting and bending the wooden planks, crafting oared vessels both swift and deadly. At Rialto the government issued orders to merchants, pressing their great roundships into service as supply transports. It was a large, expensive, and time-consuming task. One year later, when Pisa launched its fleet, Venice was still preparing its own. In the spring of 1099, though, it was finally ready: a mighty armada of some two hundred vessels—the largest single contribution to the First Crusade.

Doge Vitale Michiel called together the citizens of Venice and, much like Urban at Clermont, exhorted them to leave their families and country behind to take up the cross of Christ. As he spoke of the great spiritual and material benefits they could win in this holy mission, the Venetians cheered mightily; thousands of them took the cross that very day. The bishop of Castello, Enrico Contarini, was made the spiritual head of the Crusade, while Giovanni Michiel, the doge's son, took command of the fleet. In an emotional ceremony, the patriarch of Grado, Pietro Badoer, gave to Bishop Contarini a banner emblazoned with a large cross. The doge then gave his son the banner of St. Mark to carry into battle against the Muslims. In July 1099, with some nine thousand

Venetian crusaders on board, the fleet sailed out of the lagoon and into the Adriatic Sea.

Thus began a tradition imprinted powerfully on the Venetian civic character—one of grand expeditions in the service of the faith. This voyage would be replayed frequently in later years: during the Venetian Crusade of 1122, the Fourth Crusade of 1202, and a host of other expeditions and wars. In this case, however, although the Venetians could not have known it at the time, within a few days or weeks of their departure the grand prize of the Crusade, Jerusalem, had fallen into Christian hands. The First Crusade, against all odds, had succeeded.

The Venetian Crusade fleet sailed first to the Greek island of Rhodes, home of the famed Colossus of antiquity, where it spent the winter. Shortly after its arrival the Venetians received a surprising message from Alexius I, warning that if they persisted in sailing east to join the Crusade, he would revoke Venetian commercial privileges in the empire. Although the emperor had for years begged for Crusades, now he was forcefully admonishing the Venetians to stay away. From Alexius's perspective, the whole expedition had gone off the rails, though it had started splendidly. With the crusaders' assistance, Alexius had reclaimed from the Turks the city of Nicaea, the site of the First Ecumenical Council where the ancient Church fathers had forged the Nicene Creed. But the rest of the expedition had not gone as well. While Alexius returned to Constantinople to tie up loose ends, the First Crusade had marched across Anatolia, making its way to Antioch, one of the ancient patriarchates of the Church where the name "Christian" was first coined. There the crusaders met their gravest challenge. Famine, starvation, and renewed Turkish attacks conspired against them. But somehow they persevered and captured Antioch. Desperate for reinforcements, they put their hopes in Alexius I, who was due to arrive with a powerful Byzantine army. But the emperor never came. Having received faulty intelligence that the crusaders were destroyed at

Antioch, he had returned to Constantinople. When the crusaders learned of Alexius's betrayal, they disclaimed their oaths to restore the Crusade's conquests to the Byzantine Empire, and instead kept Antioch for themselves. From Alexius's perspective, therefore, the crusaders had become almost as dangerous as the Turks.

This is the strange turn of events that led Alexius to warn off the Venetians, and his message contained not just a threat but a promise: If the Venetians abandoned the expedition, he would furnish rich rewards. Bishop Contarini warned his countrymen that if they turned their backs on the cross for worldly gains, they risked not only shame before men but also the wrath of God. And so, the Venetians remained true to their crusader vows.

As the blossoms of spring emerged in 1100, the Venetian crusaders set sail from Rhodes for the Holy Land, making one very important stop along the way. On May 27 they landed at the Byzantine coastal town of Myra (modern Demre), made holy by the life of its famous bishop and the patron of sailors, St. Nicholas. Thirteen years earlier the Venetians, who were of course sailors, had made plans to steal the body of St. Nicholas from its church in Myra. In preparation, they built a new church and monastery for the saint on the Lido, close to the channel from which Venetians left the lagoon and began their sea voyages. Unfortunately for them, the sailors of Bari had the same idea—and they got there first, carrying away Nicholas's bones in 1087. Losing this race remained a sore point for the Venetians, who now had a church with a conspicuously vacant altar.

The Venetian crusaders decided to stop at Myra and investigate the situation for themselves, just to be certain. The local Greek clergy insisted, even under torture, that the body of St. Nicholas had already been taken by the men of Bari. In an attempt to appease the Venetians, though, the priests suggested that they take the body of the saint's uncle and namesake. It was not as good as the real St. Nicholas, but it was something. While the Venetians were taking the bones of the uncle, they smelled the sweet aroma that emanated from relics of great sanctity. Following the scent, the Venetians discovered yet another group of bones, which they concluded must be the "true" body of St. Nicholas. Either the men of Bari had been duped into taking the wrong body or they did not collect it all. Joyously, the Venetians loaded both relics aboard ship. They were later deposited and revered at the church of San Nicolò on the Lido, where they still remain. For centuries afterward, Venetian sailors implored the aid of the saintly bishop as they sailed past his church on their way to the wide world. The Bariense, who had their own St. Nicholas, naturally disputed the authenticity of the one on the Lido. A modern study of both sets of relics has concluded, remarkably, that they were both right. Although the Bari relic consists of larger pieces, both cities have what amounts to a collection of bone fragments. Investigators concluded that the sailors from Bari had seized the larger pieces, but left many broken bits, which the Venetians later claimed. Although a difficult jumble, the thousands of pieces do appear to have come from the skeleton of one man.

With St. Nicholas on board, the Venetian Crusade fleet sailed east, arriving at Jaffa in June 1100. There the Venetians met the remnants of the First Crusade. After capturing Jerusalem, most of the crusaders had returned home, leaving a small number of westerners to consolidate the gains and attempt to create a new Christian state in an otherwise Muslim Middle East. The crusaders' leader, Godfrey of Bouillon, praised God for the Venetians' arrival, for he commanded only a thousand men, while the crusaders from the lagoon numbered nine times that figure. Along the eastern coast of the Mediterranean, the Christians held only Jaffa, but they hoped to conquer the rest. Heavily defended Acre was the key. In return for commercial rights in the captured city, the Venetians agreed to assist Godfrey with a large-scale siege. But Godfrey's subsequent death changed their plans. Instead of Acre, Doge Michiel helped

Tancred, the regent of Antioch, to capture nearby Haifa. The siege lasted more than a month, but the city fell on August 20, 1100. Unfortunately, Haifa was no Acre, lacking the population, wealth, ports, and markets of its much larger neighbor. Instead of property and riches, the Venetians returned home with almost nothing. Like most crusaders, they had hoped for salvation and wealth, but were disappointed in the latter.

The success of the First Crusade would nevertheless be an economic boon to Venice, for it not only opened new eastern ports but also provided new sources of revenue by transporting pilgrims to the Holy Land. During the following decades smaller Crusades or bands of armed pilgrims made their way to the East to assist those few Europeans (mostly French and therefore referred to collectively as "Franks") who chose to live there permanently. Although the Muslims surrounding the crusader states were victims of their own disunity, they nonetheless posed a serious risk to the small Christian outposts.

In 1119 King Baldwin II of Jerusalem wrote to the pope and to Venice begging for assistance against his Muslim enemies. Pope Calixtus II passed the request on to the Republic of St. Mark, which had already proved itself capable of mustering the necessary force. In 1120 ten papal legates arrived in the lagoon with a letter from the pope imploring the Venetians to come to the aid of the Holy Land. Doge Domenico Michiel (1118–29) accompanied the papal legates to San Marco, where he summoned the people to hear the pontiff's letter, and followed with a stirring speech of his own. In the ominous glow of a thousand candles and beneath the gaze of dozens of mosaic saints, the words of the doge echoed through the vast church.

Venetians, what splendid renown and immortal glory will you receive through this? What rewards will you receive from God? You will earn the admiration of Europe and Asia; the standard of St. Mark will fly triumphantly over those distant lands: new profits, new sources of greatness will come to this most noble country.... Enflamed with the holy zeal of religion, moved by the suffering of your brethren, excited by the example of all Europe, prepare your arms, think on the honors, think on your triumphs, and be guided to the blessings of heaven.

The response was tremendous. With the excited acclamation of the people, the doge himself took the cross, leaving his son Leachim and another kinsman, also named Domenico, as vice-doges. The pattern established in 1099 was followed once again. Venice was on Crusade.

The Venetian shipworks sprang back to life, and the city's industries spent the remainder of 1120 and part of 1121 building and outfitting the large crusading fleet. Michiel ordered all Venetians engaged in overseas commerce to return home and assist with the effort. The forces of the Venetian Crusade consisted of a fleet of approximately 120 vessels and more than fifteen thousand men. Doge Domenico Michiel, though, planned to make use of these forces to advance state interests along the way. During the first year of Michiel's dogeship the aged emperor Alexius I Comnenus had died and was succeeded by his eldest son, John II Comnenus (1118–43). The new emperor had been born two years after the war with Robert Guiscard, too late to remember Venice's great service to Byzantium at Durazzo. But he had seen the effects of Venice's tax reward, and his generation had stewed in resentment at what they saw as Venetian arrogance borne of the spoils. Indeed, by virtue of Alexius's chrysobull of 1082, Venetians had become richer and more numerous in the eastern empire than ever before. They were contemptuous of Byzantine officials, many of whom, because of the chrysobull, had no power over them anyway. The freedom that some Venetians felt in flouting Byzantine law is evident enough in their cavalier thefts of the relics of St. Nicholas from Myra and St. Stephen from Constantinople. Behind all this Venetian impetuousness, John believed, was his father's chrysobull. He refused to renew it.

From the Venetian perspective, John's decision was the height of ingratitude. Yet at the time, aside from sending ambassadors with complaints, there was little that Doge Michiel could do. Now as he looked across the Bacino San Marco at the brightly colored war fleet at his command, a fleet not unlike the one Domenico Silvio had led to Byzantium's defense in 1081, the doge saw a new and more persuasive instrument of diplomacy. The memory of the Venetian dead in the war against Robert Guiscard and the Normans was still powerful in the lagoon, for they had fought long and hard, and paid a heavy price to protect the Byzantine Empire. They would not now be dismissed out of hand by this young emperor. If John II would not honor his father's promises, then let him lose Corfu, purchased for him with the blood of Venetians. The doge and his council made plans to capture the island on their way to the Holy Land.

John II was not the only one with something to fear from the Venetian crusading fleet. Dalmatian rebels could also expect swift punishment. Farther south, the citizens of Bari, too, remained wary. There was, after all, that delicate matter of the body of St. Nicholas. The Venetians might well be tempted to use their Crusade fleet as they had at Myra, forcing their way into the city of Bari and capturing another body of the saint to accompany them on their journey. That would certainly put an end to the competing claims. But the doge did not want to provoke Bari. If the Bariense believed they were in danger, their ships could pose a threat to the Venetian fleet and its operations at Corfu. Therefore, in May 1122, three months before the fleet's departure, the doge issued a solemn oath that no Venetian would harm the property, life, or limb of the citizens of Bari. The document, which survives, was signed by the doge as well as by 372 of the greater men of Venice who had taken the cross.

It is a fascinating document, providing a roll call of the leading Venetians who left family and home to serve God and St. Mark.

The fleet set sail on August 8, 1122. After receiving supplies and men from the Dalmatian towns, Doge Michiel led the armada to Corfu, where it besieged the Byzantine citadel. Although one often imagines medieval warfare as a violent clashing of great armies, in truth the most effective tactic was a siege. Fortifications, like that of the citadel at Corfu, were designed to withstand powerful assaults. As a result, most medieval warfare consisted of doing nothing at all. The besiegers surrounded a fortification and attempted to starve out the defenders before they were forced to leave themselves. At Corfu, the siege lasted all winter. In early spring 1123, messengers from the kingdom of Jerusalem finally persuaded the doge to leave aside his quarrel with the emperor and sail immediately to aid the Holy Land. When the Venetians arrived at Acre in May, they discovered a desperate situation. The Arab navy from Egypt had blockaded Jaffa on the coast in an attempt to cut Jerusalem off from its closest access to the sea. Perhaps hearing of the arrival of the Venetian fleet, the Arab commanders decided to return the navy to its base at Ascalon. Swiftly the doge ordered a small group of Venetian merchant vessels to lure the Egyptians into battle. Once the engagement began, the republic's warships surrounded and destroyed the Muslim vessels. Michiel, we are told, led his own galley against the opposing Egyptian flagship and sank it. The victory was total: Hardly a Muslim vessel survived the engagement. The next year the doge led the Venetians against the Muslim-controlled city of Tyre, assisting a Frankish attack. After a difficult siege, it fell in July 1124, upon which the grateful king Baldwin II amply rewarded the Venetians. In every city in the kingdom of Jerusalem the republic received a street, bakery, bath, and church, freedom from all tolls and customs, and the right to use its own weights and measures. It also received one-third of Tyre as its own Venetian Quarter there. With great celebration, the Venetians raised their sails and headed back home. On the way, they received even more good news. Rather than endure additional attacks on his empire, Emperor John II agreed to renew his father's chrysobull. All was again right in the East.

In 1129 the crusader doge Domenico Michiel fell ill. Knowing that his time was short, he resigned the dogeship and took monastic vows. The newly tonsured hero was borne to the monastery of San Giorgio Maggiore, where he spent the last months of his life. His tomb, modest and inconspicuous, was placed in a small passageway leading from the church to the monastery. Yet the Venetians did not forget him. More than a decade later an inscription was added to the bare tomb:

> Here lies the terror of the Greeks and the glory of the Venetians, Domenico Michiel whom Manuel fears; a doge honorable and strong, whom all the world cherished; prudent in counsel and consummate in intellect. His manly deeds are declared by the capture of Tyre, the destruction of Syria, and the anguish of Hungary; he made the Venetians to live in peace and tranquility, for while he flourished his country was safe from all harm. You who come to look on this beautiful sepulcher, bow low before God because of him.

When the Venetians sought a successor to one of their greatest leaders, it was natural to look to Michiel's family. Yet the days of ducal dynasties had ended with the death of Otto Orseolo in 1032. Venice was a different place. Population in the city had been expanding rapidly. The success of Venetian merchants brought healthy infusions of new wealth into the lagoon, prompting increasing numbers of new families to demand political authority to match their economic clout. It was in the interest of these wealthy clans to expand the avenues of power, and that meant keeping any one family from gaining too tight a grip on the dogeship.

Their desire to honor Michiel and determination to avoid tyranny were satisfied in their final choice. Pietro Polani (1129–48) was a member of the Michiel family, but only by virtue of his marriage to the doge's daughter. He came from a new family, one that had made its fortunes in the markets of Constantinople. Early in his reign, Doge Polani favored the members of other new families, like the Dandolos, Zianis, and Mastropieros, by appointing them as judges in his court. In a city without nobles, ducal judges were as close as one could come to nobility. By Polani's reign, they were the peers of the doge. Yet, just as with the dogeship itself, power flowed from the office, not from the officeholder. Judgeships were not hereditary, nor were they very often held for more than a year or two. Depending on the occasion, one could find at this time anywhere from two to five judges in court. The doge could not conduct business without them. By the mid-twelfth century the road to the ducal throne invariably passed through the judiciary.

Among the most notable political events of Polani's reign was the institution of the Venetian "commune." Reflecting prevailing fashions in other Italian towns, the Venetians began to refer to their government in this way. On the mainland a commune denoted a newly won element of self-rule—something that Venetians had enjoyed for centuries. Nonetheless, the change in nomenclature did recognize some political and social changes at work in Venice. Power was shifting incrementally away from the doge and into the hands of an expanded ducal court, which began to include not only the judges but also a new body known as the *consilium sapientium*, or Council of the Wise. It was made up of well-connected men from important families who, in one form or another, represented the people of Venice during the day-to-day activities of the doge's court. These political reforms were slow, but in them one can see the rise of Venice's evolving representative councils.

Change also came to the Church in Venice. An ecclesiastical reform movement had swept Europe in the eleventh century, yet had little effect on Venice. The simple fact was that the Church in Venice did not need as much reform. On the Continent many of the clergy had become lax or corrupt. Priests took wives and bishops purchased their offices— an offense known as simony. The office of bishop was worth paying for on the mainland because it brought with it rich lands, wealth, and power. In Venice, where land was scarce, the bishops and the patriarch of Grado lived primarily off voluntary tithes—which meant that they were perpetually short of cash. Venetians were usually generous toward pious works, but much of their largesse found its way into monasteries or other charitable institutions. Parish tithing was a legal obligation and, therefore, conformed to only minimally at best. On the mainland, reformers worked hard to remove lay control over the appointment of ecclesiastical offices. While this was a common practice in Venice as well, it had not led to any clerical abuses. Ecclesiastical offices were simply not attractive enough in Venice to warrant corruption, and as a result, they tended to draw only the genuinely pious.

The peace between church and state in Venice was shaken, however, during the dogeship of Pietro Polani. He had nominated his boyhood friend, Enrico Dandolo, as patriarch of Grado. Accepted by the bishops of the lagoon, Dandolo was duly ordained in 1134. However, Dandolo, much like his contemporary, Archbishop Thomas à Becket of Canterbury, was changed by his high ecclesiastical office. In June 1135 the young patriarch attended the Council of Pisa, where he likely met St. Bernard of Clairvaux, one of the most famous men of his time. Bernard, a Cistercian monk, was the standard-bearer of reform in twelfth-century Europe, preaching a message of purification of every element of Christian society. It appears that Dandolo learned from Bernard the importance of ecclesiastical liberty and the duty of a shepherd of souls to instruct even the most powerful.

The city of Venice had its own bishop—the bishop of Castello—who at that time was Giovanni Polani, a kinsman of the doge. The patriarch of Grado was the metropolitan, or archbishop, with authority over all bishops in the Venetian lagoon, which stretched at that time from Chioggia to Grado. Although the patriarch's home church was on the distant little island of Grado, by the twelfth century the population center of the area had shifted dramatically to the city of Venice. For that reason, patriarchs of Grado tended to spend much of their time in the city, residing in the parish church of San Silvestro, very near the Rialto markets and directly on the Grand Canal. Officially, they were "visitors," since canon law did not allow one prelate (high-ranking member of the clergy) to reside within the jurisdiction of another. The extended stays of these patriarchal "visitors" naturally strained their relations with the bishops of Castello.

Patriarch Dandolo's zeal to promote ecclesiastical reform in Venice quickly put him at odds with Bishop Polani. One of the papacy's favored reform initiatives was to organize parish clergy into associations, called canons regular, under the monastic rule of St. Augustine. In this way, local priests lived more humbly, with more piety, and with much less worldliness. Dandolo joined forces with the Badoer clan, who were strong supporters of church reform in Venice, to oversee the conversion of the clergy of the parish church of San Salvatore, in the heart of the city, to the canons regular. When parishioners complained about this meddling in their neighborhood church, Bishop Polani ordered the priests who wished to become canons regular to abandon their plan. They refused. Bishop Polani then placed the church under interdict, meaning that the sacraments could not be performed there. Patriarch Dandolo responded by taking the parish under his own protection. The dispute between the two bishops ultimately ended up in Rome, where the pope sided with Dandolo. Against the will of Venice's bishop, the priests of San Salvatore thus became canons regular. It was a wound that would not quickly heal.

The smoldering rancor between the patriarch and the bishop soon grew into a flame that burned across Venice's political landscape. A new spark was struck sometime between 1141 and 1145, when Nella Michiel, the abbess of the convent of San Zaccaria, died. As was customary, the doge nominated a new abbess, probably one of his kinswomen. Doge Polani's nominee was forwarded to the nuns of San Zaccaria, who dutifully elected her. However, before the doge could invest the abbess-elect, the patriarch of Grado condemned the election and the investment. With classic church reform arguments, Dandolo insisted that the sisters of San Zaccaria hold a free election without lay interference; under no circumstances should the abbess receive her office from the hands of the doge. Doge Polani was outraged. It was one thing for the patriarch to squabble with the bishop over ecclesiastical jurisdiction, but quite another for him to deny the doge's right to nominate and invest the abbess of the wealthiest convent in Venice. With no obvious way to resolve the dispute, the patriarch took his case to Rome, where it would drag on for years.

In his zeal to promote reform, Patriarch Dandolo had managed to anger the two most important men in Venice. But matters were about to get worse. During the summer of 1147 a fleet of Normans sailed across the Adriatic and captured the Byzantine island of Corfu. From there they proceeded to plunder the Greek coast with little opposition. Once again the Normans were poised to invade the Byzantine Empire, and once again the emperor in Constantinople turned to Venice for help. There was never any question that the Venetians would oblige. Merchant families, like the Dandolos and the Polanis, had an enormous interest in a stable and peaceful Byzantine Empire. A Norman conquest of Greece or Constantinople would be economically and strategically cataclysmic for Venice. The son of John II, Emperor Manuel I Comnenus (1143–80), hastily sent off a chrysobull in October 1147 confirming all of Venice's commercial privileges. Doge Pietro Polani then announced to the Venetians that they would once again wage war against the Normans, calling upon them to prepare a fleet to sail in the spring.

Although the Dandolo family had every reason to favor the defense of its commercial interests in Byzantium, the good of the clan no longer carried much weight with the Dandolo who was patriarch of Grado. His eyes were no longer on his earthly family, but on the welfare of the Catholic Church. When the patriarch learned of Venice's alliance with Byzantium, he called together an assembly of clergy and laity to rebuke the doge and his policy. Faithful Christians, Dandolo asserted, should not come to the aid of the Byzantines, who refused to recognize the full authority of the pope. In a city that had long favored Byzantium, the patriarch's opposition party was small, but nonetheless determined. It included many of Venice's reform-minded clergy, including the canons of San Salvatore, as well as prominent members of the Badoer clan, who had defended the patriarch's actions since at least 1145. With this controversy, Dandolo had introduced into Venice the most expansive elements of the ecclesiastical reform that were spreading throughout Europe. Already a defender of the Church against lay interference, Dandolo took the next step, asserting his right to overrule secular leaders when their decisions threatened the Church or the spiritual well-being of the faithful.

Doge Polani's patience was at an end. He would not have churchmen dictating Venetian foreign policy. He likely issued an ultimatum to the patriarch, threatening to harm his family if he did not stand down. Dandolo remained resolute. And so, in late 1147 or early 1148 the doge lashed out at his enemies in a move unprecedented in Venetian history. He ordered the permanent exile of Patriarch Dandolo, his supporters, and all members of the Dandolo and Badoer families. To make doubly certain that the patriarch's family could never return, the doge ordered the entire Dandolo compound in the parish of San Luca to be leveled to the ground.

The expelled patriarch fled to Rome, where he informed Pope Eugenius III (1145–53) of events in Venice. Eugenius promptly excommunicated Doge Polani and placed the entire city of Venice under interdict. So severe a spiritual punishment on the eve of war with the Normans no doubt weighed heavily on the minds of the Venetians. Never before had they incurred the wrath of a pope, nor had the sacraments ever been denied to them in this way. Still, Doge Polani was unmoved. He personally took command of the war fleet, which sailed on schedule to restore the island of Corfu to Byzantine rule. Although the fleet was successful, the doge himself died on the voyage. The Norman danger thus averted, a grateful Emperor Manuel dramatically expanded the Venetian Quarter in Constantinople.

The death of the still-excommunicated Polani amid a smashing victory against the Normans allowed the Venetians to claim their reward from Byzantium while simultaneously opening a door to peace with the Church and the lifting of the interdict. The first action of the new doge, Domenico Morosini (1148–55), was to rescind Polani's exile orders against the patriarch and his faction. Indeed, he decreed that the Dandolo compound should be rebuilt at state expense. Morosini then took an oath that he would forever preserve the liberty of the Church in Venice, allowing no lay power to have influence over ecclesiastical government or elections. What took more than a century in Europe was concluded in an instant in Venice. Every Venetian doge after Morosini took an oath of office that included a clause in which the liberty of the Church was guaranteed. As a result of these rapid reforms, the separation between church and state in Venice was greater than anywhere else in the world. Venetians remained intensely pious people. That is one of the fruits of living on the perilous sea. But the Church no longer had any direct role in the Venetian government, nor did the government interfere with the Church.

As for Patriarch Dandolo, he returned to Venice triumphantly. The convent of San Zaccaria was reformed into a Cluniac house, becoming part of one of Europe's oldest reform orders. The new abbess was no relation to the doge—indeed, she was a German sent from the convent's motherhouse on the Continent. Dandolo's authority outside the lagoon grew as well. Because of Venice's increasing control over the Dalmatian coast, Pope Anastasius IV (1153–54) elevated the city of Zara (modern Zadar) to a metropolitan see. The bishop of Zara (who was also the city's ruler), therefore, became an archbishop. A few months later Pope Hadrian IV (1154–59) placed the archbishop of Zara under the jurisdiction of the patriarch of Grado. This was a remarkable move. By elevating one metropolitan over another, Hadrian had at last made Grado a true patriarchate: the only one of its kind in western Europe besides Rome. The pope did this, as Innocent III later wrote, "so that your Church would clearly possess the patriarchal dignity not only in name but also in full right." Needless to say, the archbishop of Zara did not appreciate being the only metropolitan answerable to another metropolitan. The resentment engendered would fester for a very long time.

The reforms of the Venetian Church in the twelfth century continued to be mirrored in the accelerating reforms of the Venetian state. As with most such changes, the key impetus came from an unexpected direction. Relations between Venice and the emperor in Constantinople later soured after the Venetians refused to help Manuel Comnenus with a plan to invade southern Italy. In retaliation, the emperor began cultivating friendships with Venice's commercial rivals, namely, the Pisans and the Genoese. He granted these other Italians their own quarters in Constantinople very near the Venetian Quarter. Rancor between the expatriates ran high. One day a group of Venetian residents of Constantinople raided the Genoese Quarter, spreading death and ruin until the imperial guard finally quelled the violence. This blatant act of disobedience convinced Emperor Manuel that the Byzantine Empire no longer needed Venice. It was a bold decision—one scarcely conceivable just a century earlier. But since then other Italian maritime states had grown in strength. Genoese warships were just as numerous in the Aegean as Venetian. They could see to the defense of Byzantine waters just as effectively as the Venetians, and without their arrogance—or so it seemed.

Manuel's plan of attack against the Venetians was ambitious, to say the least. In early 1171 he sent secret messages to Byzantine officials across the empire ordering them to arrest, imprison, and confiscate the property of every single Venetian they could find. Amazingly, the secret was kept. Some months before, fearing just this kind of imperial retribution for the Venetian attacks in Constantinople, Doge Vitale II Michiel (1155–72) had sent high-level ambassadors to the emperor's court to smooth things over. Manuel had assured his Venetian visitors that all was well. With a sigh of relief they returned to Venice to report the happy news.

And then, on the morning of March 12, the hammer fell. In Constantinople and every other Byzantine port, Venetian men, women, and children were rounded up and thrown into prisons. More than ten thousand were arrested in Constantinople alone. When the prisons were full they stuffed them into monasteries. Their houses, shops, and vessels—all that they owned—were taken from them. A handful of Venetians escaped. Romano Mairano, for example, was doing business in Constantinople when he was seized and thrown into prison. Faced with overcrowding, the Byzantine officials agreed to release him and a few other wealthy Venetians who could post extremely large bails. Mairano then bribed the commander of a large vessel to transport him and the other released Venetians out of Constantinople. In the dead of night, the refugees crept aboard the ship, which cast off and sailed slowly out of the imperial city's secure harbor, the Golden Horn. But when the sun rose they found the seas alive with vessels carrying Byzantine officials seeking Venetians to arrest. One imperial vessel closed in on Mairano's craft, ordering it to halt for inspection. Instead, the refugees put up full sails. The Byzantines tried to destroy the ship with Greek fire—an incendiary liquid propelled out of tubes—but failed. Mairano and his friends finally made it to Acre, where they told their countrymen about the tragedy. But Mairano's wealth and luck made him unusual. Well over twenty thousand Venetians remained in indefinite captivity.

When news arrived in Venice of this devastating blow, it was met with shock, outrage, and a fair amount of embarrassment on the part of the ambassadors who had been so thoroughly duped by Manuel. Doge Michiel summoned his high councillors, the *sapienti*, to advise him on the crisis. Chief among these councillors were representatives from the new families, Orio Mastropiero, Sebastiano Ziani (the richest man in Venice), and Vitale Dandolo (the brother of the patriarch). The councillors advised caution. The reports they had received seemed fantastic, almost unbelievable. They urged the doge to dispatch envoys to Constantinople to ascertain the facts on the ground. If the reports were true, the envoys should assess the damage, inquire as to Manuel's reasons for inflicting it, and demand release of the hostages and the restoration of their property.

The doge agreed to follow this cautious, careful approach, but events soon veered out of his control. A convoy of twenty Venetian vessels that had escaped the clutches of the emperor sailed noisily into the lagoon. With great passion the sailors told their harrowing stories to all who would listen. People poured out of their houses, inflamed with passion and eager for revenge. They gathered together, probably outside the Ducal Palace, and formed the *arengo*, the theoretical basis of all authority in Venice. As a group the people of Venice demanded a retaliatory strike against the Byzantine Empire. They ordered the doge to personally lead a war fleet of a hundred galleys and twenty transports to exact revenge against Manuel and win the release of the hostages. Doge Michiel obeyed. He had little choice. Four months later the fleet was prepared. Against his better judgment, and against the wishes of the sapienti, the doge led Venice to war against its parent state.

The imposing armada sailed along the coast of Dalmatia, quickly reinforcing Venetian control there. It then swung around into the Aegean Sea and landed on the prosperous Greek island of Negroponte (Euboea), laying siege to the capital, Chalkis. The Venetian strategy was simple: inflict as much pain as possible on the emperor until he released the captives. Realizing that the city would likely fall, the Byzantine governor in Chalkis requested a meeting with the doge and his councillors. In that meeting, the Venetian leaders made clear that they preferred a diplomatic solution to the quarrel if one could be found. In return for the withdrawal of Venetian forces, the governor agreed to send an envoy to Constantinople to urge the emperor to release the hostages.

With high hopes for peace, the doge ordered the fleet to withdraw from Negroponte to the island of Chios, where the Venetians spent the winter waiting for word from Constantinople. But Manuel Comnenus refused to receive the envoy. He would listen to no words of peace while Venetians waged war in his empire. Manuel did, however, send his own envoy, who held out hope for a negotiated settlement. On Chios the doge and his men listened to the optimistic words of the imperial messenger, who urged them to send another embassy to Constantinople. Of course, Manuel's real game is clear enough. By dangling the possibility of peace before the doge, the emperor hoped to forestall further attacks on his territories while he prepared his own forces to meet the Venetians. The ruse worked. The doge sent a group of Venetian envoys to Constantinople.

Shortly after the embassy departed, a devastating plague descended on the Venetian camp. More than a thousand men died in the first days of the outbreak. Many blamed Byzantine agents, whom they believed had poisoned the wells. There was also a good deal of grumbling against the doge, who had hardly dealt out swift vengeance against the Byzantines. In the only attack on a Greek city thus far, Michiel had withdrawn in order to pursue his original diplomatic strategy. Since then the Venetians had done little but wait—and die—on Chios. In March the fleet moved to the island of Panagia, but the plague followed. At the end of the month the Venetian delegation to Constantinople returned and gave its report. It was no better than the first. Once again it had been denied an imperial audience. However, Manuel did send another Byzantine envoy to the doge with a promise that if a third legation was sent, he would receive it.

Doge Michiel's situation was dire. His armada was crippled and more of his men were dying every day. He had already received intelligence of a Byzantine plan to attack the Venetians on Chios or at sea, so he found it difficult to believe that peace was really on the emperor's mind. But his options were limited. If he could shake off the plague, the Venetian fleet was still large enough to make trouble in the Aegean. Perhaps that threat, along with another embassy, would be enough to persuade Manuel to release the Venetian prisoners. It was, in any case, his only hope. He sent two high men, Enrico Dandolo, the son of Vitale Dandolo and nephew of the patriarch (and himself a future doge), and Filippo Greco to the emperor's court. The doge then moved the fleet first to the island of Lesbos and then to Skyros—desperately island-hopping in an attempt to lose the plague. Nothing worked. As the numbers of Venetian dead mounted, it became depressingly clear that the fleet was no longer a threat to the emperor. Indeed, it was itself in grave danger. The surviving Venetians ordered their doge to take them home, and so he did.

Manuel had won. He had punished the Venetians for their insolence and then sent their retaliatory fleet home in disgrace. He could not resist a bit of crowing. According to John Kinnamos, a member of Manuel's court, the emperor sent a letter to Doge Michiel that succinctly sums up what had become the Byzantine perception of the Venetians—a perception that struck at the core of Venetian history and identity.

> Your nation has for a long time behaved with great stupidity. Once you were vagabonds sunk in abject poverty. Then you slinked into the Roman Empire. You have treated it with the utmost disdain and have done your best to deliver it to its worst enemies, as you yourselves are well aware. Now, legitimately condemned and justly expelled from the empire, you have in your insolence declared war on it—you who were once a people not even worthy to be named, you who owe what prestige you have to the Romans; and for having supposed that you could match their strength you have made yourselves a general laughing-stock. For no one, not even the greatest powers on earth, makes war on the Romans with impunity.

What was left of the retaliatory fleet limped into the Venetian lagoon in late May 1172. Rather than revenge, Michiel brought home defeat, humiliation, and plague. Once again the Venetian people took matters into their own hands. A general meeting was held in the Ducal Palace on May 27. The doge and his councillors were there to discuss the tragedy with the assembled citizens. Things went badly from the start. Amid tears for fallen loved ones were angry cries of accusation. The people of Venice had given the doge the means and a mandate to retaliate against the emperor, yet he had done nothing of the kind. Instead, he had used the fleet merely as a tool of diplomacy. Many of the survivors angrily denounced the doge, saying, "We were poorly led, and if we had not been betrayed by the doge dragging out matters with legates, then all of these troubles would not have overtaken us!" Among the crowd stones and knives began to appear. While Michiel attempted to reason with the people, his councillors slipped out of the room one by one. Finding himself alone, Michiel made a break for the sanctuary of nearby San Zaccaria, but was overtaken and stabbed to death before getting that far.

As the body of the doge was prepared for burial, once again the popular act of regicide became bitterly unpopular in hindsight. A good man and a "lover of peace," Michiel had been put into an impossible situation by the people themselves. Marco Casolo, the doge's assassin, became the scapegoat for the people's rage, but his execution did not wash away their guilt. After an emotional funeral at San Zaccaria, the people assembled at nearby San Marco to choose Michiel's successor. Medieval Venetian chroniclers give sparse details about what happened next, but in the end the people elected not a new doge, but instead an eleven-man commission charged with electing a new doge. This was an extraordinary change, unprecedented in Venetian history. What convinced the people of Venice that they should give away their cherished right to choose their own doge?

Based on subsequent events, it seems clear that the revolution of 1172—for revolution it was—drew its breath from the sapienti, those wealthy men from powerful and largely new families that had been carving out a position for themselves between the doge and the people. Filled with grief for their loved ones and the death of their doge, the Venetian people listened attentively to these conservative, wise men. If their cautious advice to the doge had been heeded, after all, hundreds of Venetians would still be alive and they would be that much closer to securing the release of the hostages. It was the rashness of the people and the arengo that had put them on their present course. The selection of a new doge was crucially important. Would it not be better to leave it to those same wise men? Unfortunately, we cannot know precisely what arguments were made at this assembly, but we do know that when it was over, the people had given away their authority to select their doge. It was a moment of profound importance, a milestone in the creation of a new Venetian government. The last direct tie between doge and people had been severed.

The eleven men chosen for the commission were the friends and advisers of the slain doge—all of them sapienti. Not surprisingly, they elected one of their own, the seventy-year-old Sebastiano Ziani (1172–78). When Ziani's election was publicly announced (with the diplomatic insertion "if it pleases you"), the people of Venice approved the choice enthusiastically, shouting, "Long live the doge, and may we be able to obtain peace through him!"

It is impossible to adequately understand medieval or Renaissance Venice without taking into account the lessons learned by the Venetians in their failed mission of vengeance of 1172. They learned that the fury of the mob was a poor substitute for the reasoned consideration of experienced statesmen. Those statesmen, the friends and councillors of Vitale II Michiel, became the new leaders of a reformed republic. The next three doges were marked by their association with Michiel and were probably elected for that very reason. They were men who knew first-hand the importance of a doge's councillors and who feared rash actions, whether by the people or the doge. A fundamental shift was occurring in the history of Venetian government as well as in the development of the later "myth of Venice." Venice, the republic where powerful doges ruled powerful people, was becoming something different—a government in which a distinct body of elites, known for their wisdom and service to the state, began to draw into themselves the powers of both people and doge. It was not, and never would be, an oligarchy. Rather, the Venetian republic was being outfitted with new bodies and procedures, which ensured that it would act prudently, cautiously, and predictably. Not surprisingly, these are precisely the attributes that businessmen most value in a government.

Venice had been harmed gravely—but by no means mortally—by the Byzantine Empire. Banned from trading in Greek ports, the Venetians made up the business in the markets of the crusader states, especially the city of Tyre. Ziani and his successors pursued a measured, cautious approach to their ongoing state of war with Byzantium, continuing to seek the release of the long-held hostages. It would take more than a decade to achieve. In the meantime, the people of Venice had crafted a government of both church and state that was far more stable and more efficient than any other in western Europe. With a free Church, the Venetians avoided the strife that beset the German empire, where kings and emperors held tightly to their customary control over ecclesiastical appointments. With a new, more stable government watched over by those businessmen who had the most to lose by instability, the factionalism and vendettas that plagued other Italian cities withered and died in Venice.

CHAPTER 5

BETWEEN EMPIRES:
The Peace of Venice, 1172–1200

The first Venetians fled to the lagoon to escape Europe. On July 24, 1177, Europe came to the lagoon.

It started early in the morning. First, Pope Alexander III (1159–81) awoke at San Silvestro church, had an ample breakfast, and was rowed to San Marco, where he heard a High Mass. Then Doge Sebastiano Ziani and his court took a richly decorated ceremonial galley to the Lido, where they picked up the Holy Roman emperor Frederick I Barbarossa (1155–90). They then returned to the newly paved Piazzetta San Marco, just west of the Ducal Palace, where the German emperor disembarked upon a scene of pomp and grandeur that few states in Europe could match. The entire Piazzetta was festooned with long banners of the lion of St. Mark, waving in the warm sea breeze. Thousands of dignitaries and onlookers from across Europe filled the Piazzetta and adjoining Piazza, either in positions of honor or craning their necks in the crowd to catch a glimpse of the most famous men in the Western world. The emperor, his retinue, and accompanying nobles proceeded through the Piazzetta, between the two monolithic columns bearing the heavenly patrons of Venice, and halted at the church of San Marco, where the supreme pontiff of Rome was waiting on a throne surrounded by a mob of ecclesiastical lords. Such a scene was rare even in Rome. But it was happening in Venice. The lords of Christendom had come to make peace.

The events that brought the pope and the emperor to Venice's front door form the basis of a story that, with occasional embellishments, Venetians told proudly for centuries. Indeed, it is still recounted in paintings that cover the north wall of the chamber of the Great Council in the Ducal Palace. The story begins in 1158, when the Holy Roman emperor Frederick I Barbarossa issued his edicts of Roncaglia, which claimed that he was the rightful ruler of northern and central Italy, including some of the pope's territories, but, of course, excluding Venice. These claims dated back to Charlemagne, Frederick's predecessor centuries past. In truth, though, Holy Roman emperors generally had their hands full just trying to rule Germany. Northern Italian (or Lombard) towns willingly recognized the German emperor's theoretical overlordship, but vigorously refused to offer anything tangible. Frederick Barbarossa was determined to change that. He planned to extend his dominion over all of Italy and demanded the support and loyalty of the Lombard towns for a planned invasion of southern Italy to eject the Normans, who had ruled there since the days of Robert Guiscard. Although medieval popes were not overly fond of Normans, they always opposed any initiative that might give one man control over Italy, since it would seriously threaten the independence of the Papal States. Pope Hadrian IV, therefore, strongly opposed Barbarossa's plan and urged the fiercely independent Italian city-states to do the same.

Faced with the prospect of militarily subjecting Lombardy, Barbarossa was not sorry when the troublesome Hadrian died on September 1, 1159. At once the emperor sent a group of agents and a great deal of money to Rome to persuade the cardinals to elect a churchman favorable to him. They succeeded, at least partially. A slim majority of the cardinals elected Barbarossa's candidate, Victor IV. Unfortunately for them, another group of cardinals had earlier elected a respected canon lawyer and defender of Church rights, Alexander III. Barbarossa chased Alexander and his prelates out of Rome, but the kingdom of France and most of the rest of Europe accepted Alexander as the true pope. Because Barbarossa did not, a state of war ensued in Italy that would drag on for more than a decade. On the one side stood the German emperor and his string of antipopes; on the other, Pope Alexander III and the newly created Lombard League, a consortium of cities that refused to bow to Frederick. The stakes were high: the cherished independence of the Italian cities as well as that of the papacy. When Frederick finally invaded Lombardy, he headed straight for the ringleader of the rebellion—wealthy Milan. On March 1, 1162, after a two-year siege, Frederick captured and destroyed the city, sending a plume of refugees pouring out from the region.

Venice took her share of those refugees. Although they were not members of the Lombard League, the Venetians' natural sympathy was with the Italians who were fighting to keep the Germans on their side of the Alps. Pope Alexander sent the vicar apostolic, Cardinal-Legate Hildebrand Crasso, to Venice during the 1160s to oversee refugee services, communicate with nearby rebel towns, and negotiate with the Byzantine emperor for aid. Frederick Barbarossa recognized the threat that Venice posed, for it was a gaping doorway for Lombard support. In 1162 he encouraged the cities of Verona, Padua, and Ferrara—all currently under his control—to launch a naval attack on Capo d'Argine, some fifteen miles northeast of Venice at the edge of the lagoon, but a Venetian squadron easily repulsed Frederick's men. In response, Venice supported rebellions the next year in Verona, Vicenza, and Padua and began funneling money to support their defense. Venice continued to support rebellions against Barbarossa in 1165 and 1167, but never sent men to fight.

Then came 1171, the year that the Byzantines seized and imprisoned thousands of Venetians in the eastern empire. Although much of Venice's attention was focused on its hostage crisis, it could not ignore the war in Italy. The vicissitudes of the struggle were great, but by mid-1176 it was clear even to Frederick that he simply could not defeat an alliance of the pope, the Lombard towns, and the Normans of southern Italy. It was time to cut his losses and shore up his power in Germany, where his vassals had paid heavily for these foreign wars. What was needed was a peace conference to iron out the details. But where to hold such a meeting was a thorny question, for trust levels on all sides were exceedingly low. With no agreement on the location, Alexander III nevertheless left the Norman kingdom, where he was residing, in early 1177, and sailed up the Adriatic to Venice.

On March 24 the pope's vessel landed on the Lido, where the sons of Doge Ziani and a party of leading Venetians received him with honor. After spending the night at the monastery of San Nicolò, Alexander boarded a lavish state galley and was rowed to the Piazza San Marco, jammed with thousands of people eager to see the first pope ever to visit Venice.

The San Marco area had changed dramatically in the years just preceding these events. In 1172 the area outside the church of San Marco was still a sandy, grass-covered field. A river called the Rio Batario ran through it, roughly where the Caffè Florian stands today. Across that river stood a small orchard, owned by the nuns of San Zaccaria, and a parish church dedicated to the fourth-century bishop of Modena, St. Geminian. Altogether it was a pleasant place, quite in keeping with the rustic character of Venice. However, it did not at all fit with the imposing edifice of San Marco, not yet a century old, nor really even with the fortified Ducal Palace—both among the few stone structures in the city. In one of his first actions upon taking office after his predecessor's untimely demise, Doge Sebastiano Ziani ordered a complete transformation of the San Marco area. It is he who formed the distinctive L-shaped Piazza and Piazzetta of San Marco that we see today.

Ziani began by purchasing the orchard and then chopping it down. San Geminiano was likewise demolished and rebuilt at the western edge of the new piazza. (The church, later destroyed by Napoleon, is still commemorated by a plaque at this location.) The Rio Batario was completely filled in. Then the entire area was paved with stone—an extraordinary undertaking for medieval Europe. Where the Piazzetta San Marco meets the waterfront—the area known as the Molo—plans called for the raising of giant stone columns brought back from Greece by the ill-fated Doge Michiel. The former doge had actually returned with three columns in all, yet when the Venetians tried to raise one of them, it slipped out of their control and fell into the water, sinking deep into the mud of the Bacino, where it presumably still lies. Determined to put up the other two, Ziani spread word that he would handsomely pay anyone who could manage the feat. After some months, an engineer presented himself who claimed that he could do the job. All that he asked in return was the right to set up a gambling table between the columns for the rest of his life. The favor was granted, the columns were raised (by some method unrecorded in the chronicles), and the gambling commenced. Unfortunately, the engineer lived rather longer than many expected. It is said that to discourage his clients the state later decreed that all hangings should occur between the two columns, leaving the dead bodies swinging gently over the determined gamers.

On the western column Ziani placed a statue of a winged lion, the symbol of St. Mark, probably the same bronze statue that rests there today. It is an ancient work, perhaps from China or Persia, the original likely depicting a basilisk to which the Venetians simply added wings.

The other column may have received a statue of St. Theodore, the original patron of the city, although the current statue was produced in the fourteenth century.

There is no doubt that all this construction was expensive. Why, then, did the doge and his court think it a worthwhile expenditure at a time when Venice remained at war with the Byzantine Empire and many thousands of their countrymen were still held hostage abroad? Perhaps it was an outward expression of Venice's independence from the parent that had betrayed her. Or perhaps it was to provide a fitting place for the momentous meeting of emperor and pope in 1177. Whatever the case, the Piazza San Marco—the largest open gathering space in the city—would become the center of Venetian society, politics, and culture, magnetically drawing to it all visitors and, in times of crisis, all residents. In that respect, it has changed very little in the last eight centuries.

The arrival of Pope Alexander in 1177 certainly made for a fitting inaugural, and Venice's stature as a global power was put on display. As his galley approached the Piazzetta, the pope was met by Doge Ziani, Patriarch Dandolo, and the patriarch of Aquileia, Ulrich II of Treffen, all in their own ceremonial galleys. Moving to the doge's galley, the pope was seated between Ziani and Dandolo and then taken to the Piazzetta. The crowds parted as the pope, doge, patriarchs, and leading citizens proceeded to the church of San Marco, where a Mass was sung and the pope blessed the people in the church and the crowds in the Piazza outside. He then boarded the doge's galley, which took him down the Grand Canal to the patriarch's palace near the Rialto market. Alexander would remain the houseguest of Patriarch Dandolo for the next two weeks.

After a full schedule of ceremonies and the showering of Venice with many privileges, Alexander III left the city on April 9, bound for the nearby Italian city of Ferrara. There he met with representatives of the Lombard towns and the German emperor in an attempt to settle on a place for a peace conference. The Lombards, who had begun to question the depth of the pope's commitment to them, insisted on Bologna, where they felt sure they could control matters. Not surprisingly, Frederick's agents objected to this choice, suggesting Ravenna, Pavia, or Venice. Frederick himself favored Venice, because it was neutral, trustworthy, and "subject to God alone"—precisely why the Lombards opposed it. Nevertheless, after much arm-twisting, Alexander finally persuaded the Lombards to relent. To assuage their fears, the pope asked Frederick to personally remain outside Venetian territory, sending only his legates and advisers, until all sides had agreed upon a final peace. Frederick assented. Envoys were then dispatched to Doge Ziani requesting oaths of safe passage to Venice, which he promptly granted.

Frederick Barbarossa went to Ravenna, where he received regular reports from his ambassadors in Venice, while Pope Alexander celebrated Easter in Ferrara and then returned to Venice with his cardinals on May 10. Once again he was escorted grandly to San Marco and then to Patriarch Dandolo's palace at Rialto, which became the headquarters for all negotiations. Twice a day, every day, the patriarch welcomed to his palace the various agents for another round of talks. The building was filled to capacity with lodgers, including the pope, his cardinals, and other clerical envoys from across Italy. The Rialto area, always buzzing with activity, was now crawling not only with merchants but also with diplomats. In fact, all parts of Venice had their share of visitors as the city swelled with the thousands of dignitaries and churchmen hoping to affect the peace or gain favors from the emperor or the pope.

Negotiations dragged on for many weeks, yet by the beginning of July it was clear that an agreement was close at hand. In order to minimize the delays during the final negotiations, Frederick requested that he be allowed to relocate from Ravenna to Chioggia, on the southern edge of the lagoon. Sometime around July 6, Alexander granted this request, provided that Frederick renew his promise not to enter Venice without papal permission. Shortly after Frederick's arrival at Chioggia a party of cardinals and German agents were sent to gain the emperor's approval on a final draft of the peace. If he agreed, it would end the schism and grant truce to the Lombards and Normans. At the patriarchal palace, all waited in hopeful expectation.

In a city of some eighty thousand people, most of whom were filled with anxious anticipation, it is not surprising that rumors began to circulate in Venice. One of them, though, almost scuttled the peace. At the doge's court there had been considerable worry that either the negotiations or the final ceremony might be moved to another city. These worries intensified after Frederick moved to Chioggia, which was a rustic fishing town beset by "flies, gnats, and heat." No one expected the emperor to remain there for very long. The doge had vessels ready at a moment's notice to bring Frederick to the comforts of the Ducal Palace, yet he could do nothing until Alexander III gave the order. One evening, as they waited for word on the treaty draft, the doge and members of his court received an erroneous report that Frederick had approved the peace and was ready to leave Chioggia immediately. Fearing that he would go to the mainland rather than remain in Chioggia, the doge sent messengers to the patriarchal palace to determine the truth of the report. Roused out of bed, Pope Alexander told the envoys that he had no information from his cardinals and assured them that he would give permission for Frederick's transport into Venice the moment he learned that the emperor had agreed to the terms of the peace. With that settled, everyone went back to bed.

But the drama of the nocturnal visit to the pope sparked a flurry of rumors in the Rialto markets that spread quickly across the city. It was said that the doge and other leading Venetians were engaged in secret talks with Frederick to bring him into the city so that he could capture the pope and take control of the peace conference. So prevalent were the rumors that the Lombard delegates packed their bags and fled to

Treviso. The Norman delegation urged Alexander to escape lest he fall into the clutches of Frederick. However, the pope's information was rather better than that of the Venetian street. He told the Normans they should wait for definite word from Chioggia before doing anything. Frustrated, the Norman ambassadors stormed into the Ducal Palace, where they demanded and received an audience with the doge. Ziani tried to explain that the whole thing was simply a misunderstanding. He insisted that the Venetians were interested only in providing comfort for the emperor and ensuring that the peace would be celebrated in Venice. Unconvinced, the Normans returned to their vessels and sailed through the Grand Canal, blowing trumpets and announcing to anyone who would listen that they were leaving Venice because of the faithlessness of the doge. They also made a point of threatening Venetian expatriates and assets in Norman ports. As news spread, thousands of Venetians converged on the Ducal Palace, where they, too, demanded an explanation. Exasperated and frightened, Doge Ziani reaffirmed that Frederick would not be brought to Venice without Alexander's assent. He then sent envoys to the pope to beg forgiveness for the whole episode and decreed that no one in Venice was to speak of bringing Frederick into the city until Alexander ordered it.

Finally, on July 21 and 22, all the parties swore to the terms of the newly crafted peace treaty. The pope then asked Doge Ziani to bring the wayward son to him. The next day six rich galleys loaded with various important personages went to Chioggia to collect Frederick and transport him to the monastery of San Nicolò on the Lido. Meanwhile, the citizens were busy preparing the Piazza San Marco for the big event. Ships' masts were set up all along the length of the Piazzetta, each bearing the banner of St. Mark. In front of the church a dais was constructed for the pope's throne and the dozens of prelates that would surround him.

The following day, July 24, was a Sunday. Alexander III woke early and went to San Marco, where he heard Mass. He then dispatched four cardinals to the Lido to receive Frederick's renunciation of the schism and his promise of obedience to the pope. Then Doge Ziani, Patriarch Dandolo, and numerous other Venetian notables boarded the doge's galley and went to the Lido, where they greeted Frederick and brought him to San Marco. At 10:00 a.m., those on the galley disembarked and walked in procession down the center of the richly adorned Piazzetta to the church, where the pope was seated on his throne surrounded by cardinals, archbishops, and bishops. Patriarch Dandolo, who was in the procession, took his place at the pope's right hand. The emperor approached Alexander, took off his purple cloak, knelt, and kissed the pope's feet. Crying tears of joy, Alexander stood, lifted Frederick up, and gave him the kiss of peace. Bells rang out across the city and the people lifted their voices in the *Te Deum*. The "Peace of Venice" had at last been concluded.

Alexander III's visits to Venice in 1177 remained a treasured gem in the Venetian people's trove of history. Indeed, more civic rituals in Venice were tied to these events than any other. Within a century a wide collection of stories had attached themselves to the Peace of Venice, many of which were developed to explain the *trionfi*, a group of prerogatives and rituals that surrounded the dogeship. It was said that during his first visit the pope had secretly entered Venice dressed as a beggar, because he was safe nowhere else. He was found sleeping in the doorway of a church (although exactly which church remained a bone of contention for centuries), and with filial devotion, Doge Ziani and the Venetian people had given him shelter and bestowed upon him every honor. In gratitude, Alexander gave Venetian doges the right to have a white candle precede them during feast-day processions to symbolize their honor and purity of faith. When Ziani later sent letters to Frederick in Pavia urging him to make peace, Alexander (it was said) declared that the doge should not use wax seals, like all other rulers, but lead seals as the pope and emperor did. When Frederick received the lead-sealed letters, he was outraged and ordered Ziani to place the pope in irons and hand him over at once. Ziani refused, so Frederick sent a massive fleet commanded by his son, Otto, to destroy Venice and capture the pope. But the much smaller Venetian squadrons not only defeated the German vessels, but heroically captured Otto. Before the battle Alexander gave Ziani and his successors a sword, which represented the justice of the war and promised remission of sins for all those who touched it.

But the most famous of the trionfi to be associated with the Peace of Venice was the golden ring, which the pope bestowed upon the doge to be used during the Feast of the Ascension. It was said that after Ziani's naval victory against Otto, Alexander presented the doge with the ring, saying:

> Take this, O Ziani, which you and your successors will use each year to marry the sea, so that posterity knows that the lordship of the sea is yours, held by you as an ancient possession and by right of conquest, and that the sea was placed under your dominion, as a wife is to a husband.

Thus was born one of the most unique and enduring of all Venetian civic rituals. Each year on the Festa della Sensa (Ascension) the doge, patriarch, and throngs of nobles and citizens sailed out to the eastern end of the Lido, where the lagoon met the sea, and performed a ceremony in which the Republic of Venice married the Adriatic. After prayers and the pouring of holy water into the sea, the doge would cast a golden ring into it, proclaiming, "We espouse thee, O Sea, as a sign of true and perpetual dominion."

These colorful legends maintained that the Peace of Venice was settled not through complex negotiations, but simply by releasing Frederick's son Otto, who promised to persuade his father to come to terms with the pope. And so it was on Ascension Day 1177 that Frederick knelt before Alexander and kissed his feet outside the church of San Marco. In memory of that day, the pope granted a plenary indulgence to all who visited San Marco on the Feast of the Ascension. Then, it was told, Ziani, Frederick, and Alexander sailed to Ancona, where the citizens greeted them with two ceremonial umbrellas for the pope and the emperor. Alexander, however, insisted that a third umbrella be brought for the doge, and decreed that his successors should henceforth enjoy the same honor. When they approached Rome, the pope was greeted with eight banners and many silver trumpets, which he then also gave to the doge as his right. Thus the doge's trionfi were complete—the white candle, lead seals, sword, golden ring, umbrella, banners, and silver trumpets. These were ceremonial trappings associated only with the loftiest powers, yet the Venetian doge had acquired them all by serving God and his Church.

Little truth can be found in these legends. Alexander never disguised himself as a beggar and the doges' use of lead seals can be dated well before 1177. The white candle was initially a symbol of penance, used each year when the doge visited San Geminiano in recompense for destroying the earlier church without ecclesiastical permission. Like the seal, the sword, umbrella, banners, and trumpets were adopted at various times in the twelfth century in imitation of Byzantine ceremonies. As for the Sensa ritual of marrying the sea, at least part of it was already practiced during the eleventh century, when the doge attended an annual blessing of the Adriatic. It may be that Pope Alexander took part in the ceremony in 1177, or perhaps provided a golden ring. But the ritual itself was much older.

That is not to say that Venice received nothing from the grateful pope. With the energetic goodwill that a long-delayed reconciliation often brings, Alexander and Frederick decided to stay in the city for a while, rewarding the republic and other friends with privileges and largesse. Patriarch Dandolo and Alexander III were strong supporters of reform orders, particularly the canons regular. In April, during the pope's first visit to Venice, he had dedicated a new church of the canons regular, Santa Maria della Carità. Now, with the peace settled, Dandolo was in a position to ask for more favors. It appears that he directed the pope's attention to the church of San Salvatore. Three decades earlier, it had been the conversion of the clergy there to the canons regular that precipitated the bitter struggle between the patriarch and the bishop of Castello—the struggle that ultimately led to the exile of the patriarch and his family. Accompanied by Patriarch Dandolo and Frederick Barbarossa, Alexander now dedicated the newly rebuilt church. He blessed the high altar, bestowed a number of indulgences on various shrines, and celebrated the first Mass there. It was a glorious ceremony, one that the canons of San Salvatore would recount proudly for centuries. For Patriarch Dandolo it was a satisfying moment indeed.

Although Dandolo could look with pleasure on the pope's favor toward San Salvatore, he did not fare so well in other matters. In the wake of the Peace of Venice a new political landscape was conspiring against his jurisdictional interests outside the lagoon. Nowhere was this clearer than in the patriarch's long rivalry with nearby Aquileia. As long as Aquileia had supported the imperial antipope, Grado had fared well with Alexander. Yet that changed with the accession in Aquileia of Patriarch Ulrich II of Treffen (1161–82). Ulrich began his patriarchate on a belligerent note, violently attacking the cathedral of Grado, prompting Doge Vitale II Michiel to lead a counterattack that not only repulsed the invaders but captured Ulrich himself and the twelve canons of his cathedral. As a condition of their release, Ulrich promised that henceforth, every Fat Tuesday, he and his successors would send to the people of Venice a bull and twelve pigs, to represent the patriarch of Aquileia and his canons. Thus began another of the most enduring civic ceremonies in Venetian history. Each year for centuries these animals were solemnly brought to the Piazza San Marco, where, under the watchful eye of the doge and his council, they were tried, convicted, and condemned to death. The revelers would then chase the animals around the Piazza, before decapitating, roasting, and eating them. The event was so popular that in the fifteenth century, when the patriarchate of Aquileia was merged with that of Grado, the Venetian government continued to provide the annual bull and twelve pigs at public expense.

When the antipope Victor IV died in 1164, Ulrich switched sides, bringing his church into communion with Alexander III. This put him in a unique position. He had come to the throne of Aquileia through his friendship with Frederick Barbarossa. Yet the growth of Venetian influence on the mainland meant that Aquileia and its dioceses were increasingly within Venice's sphere of influence. With considerable political skill, Ulrich was able to retain his friendship with the emperor while recognizing Alexander as pope, all the while enjoying the support of Venice. He used this position to act as an honest broker during the years of the struggle and, in 1169, was made a papal legate. Now that the pope and emperor were at peace, both men wished to reward Ulrich for his services. Frederick extended the secular jurisdiction of the patriarchate of Aquileia. Alexander confirmed the patriarch of Aquileia's right to wear the pallium, a wool band reserved for metropolitan bishops, and his ecclesiastical jurisdiction over sixteen dioceses, including those in Istria claimed by the patriarch of Grado.

There remained numerous other bones of contention between Grado and Aquileia, but the pope, emperor, and doge were united in their desire to have them at last sorted out. In March 1179 Patriarch Dandolo and his bishops traveled to Rome to attend the Third Lateran Council. There, with the representatives of Patriarch Ulrich, the details of a settlement were finalized. On July 24, 1180, in the presence of Alexander III and nine cardinals, Patriarch Dandolo formally ended the ancient disputes between Grado and Aquileia.

Soon the grand and glorious party in Venice was over and the people of the city began the business of getting back to normal—or as normal as things could be while thousands of Venetians were still hostages overseas. In the early months of 1178 the aged Doge Ziani fell gravely ill. This naturally led to questions about the method of selecting his successor. The sapienti of the court clearly wanted to keep the power to choose the new doge, which they had exercised in 1172. Yet had that authority been bestowed on them indefinitely, or only as a stopgap during a time of emergency? Like the members of his court, Ziani wanted to keep the election away from the people. These men had a natural desire to concentrate power into their own hands, but they also genuinely feared the recklessness of the arengo, which had led to the destruction of the fleet in Greece and the subsequent murder of the doge. Since 1172, the doge's council had grown substantially in size, beginning to resemble what it would later become, the Great Council. In any governing body, size breeds factionalism. To avoid that problem, it was decided to select four men who would in turn choose forty from the doge's council to serve as electors of the new doge. After swearing to act in the best interest of Venice, the forty would then make their decision by a simple majority vote.

After the selection of the Four, Doge Ziani retired to the monastery of San Giorgio Maggiore, where he died in early April 1178. Three days later the Four appeared in the packed church of San Marco to read off their list of forty electors for the people's approval. Surely someone among the assembled must have noticed that the people were no longer being asked to choose their new doge, as they had throughout Venetian history, or even to approve a doge chosen by someone else, as they had done just six years earlier. Instead their approval was being sought merely for the electors of a doge. If anyone objected, however, it is not recorded. Those selected for the Forty were the most powerful and respected men in the city. Many of them were marked by their association with the murdered Vitale II Michiel, who still cast a long shadow over Venetian politics. When the Forty voted, they turned again to Michiel's inner circle, electing Orio Mastropiero (1178–92). Like Ziani, Mastropiero was a member of a relatively new family that had grown wealthy in commercial ventures and that had only recently entered the highest levels of political power in Venice. Like his colleagues, he was a conservative man who valued prudence and moderation in all things, but nowhere more so than in Venice's relationship with Byzantium. The highest order of business for Venice remained the release of the hostages, thousands of whom still languished in jail cells in Constantinople.

And yet, as uncomfortable as those cells no doubt were, they protected the imprisoned Venetians from the carnage that was soon to take place in the streets of the Byzantine capital. Emperor Manuel I Comnenus died on September 24, 1180, still at war with Venice. He left behind a twelve-year-old son, Alexius II. In the usual Byzantine fashion, a series of rebellions ensued, tainted with the virulent hatred for European Catholics (known as Latins because of the language of their liturgy) that now ruled the streets of Constantinople. In 1182 a Byzantine provincial governor, Andronicus Comnenus, took over the regency of the young emperor. To repay his supporters in Constantinople and to begin with a clean slate in the Italian quarters of the city, Andronicus signaled to the Greek citizens that they might give full vent to their hatred for their Latin neighbors—essentially sanctioning murder. The massacre of Catholics that ensued in Constantinople was brutally efficient. Greek mobs poured into the Latin quarters along the Golden Horn, murdering, raping, and torturing their victims. The easiest targets were women, children, and the aged, who were cut down mercilessly. Catholic priests and monks were also massacred. The papal legate to Constantinople was decapitated and his head tied to the tail of a dog that was chased through the bloodstained streets.

Venice's alienation from Constantinople suddenly seemed good fortune. In 1182 the only Venetians living in the city were safely in jail. In retaliation for the massacre of their citizens, the Pisan and Genoese governments declared war against Byzantium. With the Normans also preparing to renew their attacks, Andronicus had little choice but to turn to Venice for support, having alienated everyone else. At once he released all Venetian hostages and promised to make installment payments on Venetian damage claims. He also restored the Venetian Quarter to its owners. Venetian merchants flocked once more to the lucrative city on the Bosporus that they knew so well, and the released hostages began returning home in January 1183. The first restitution payments did not arrive for almost three years, but the Venetians were willing to wait. What mattered most was that the hostages were home and good relations had finally been restored with the Byzantine Empire.

When the aged doge Mastropiero abdicated the throne in May 1192, the doge's council again called the people of the lagoon to assemble at San Marco to approve the forty electors, in what they cleverly called the "customary way" of choosing a doge (although the custom had only been exercised once). The committee again selected an elderly member of one of the "new" families. There was nothing about Enrico Dandolo (1192–1205), the nephew of the patriarch of the same name, to indicate that he would be an especially effective doge. Although he could boast a distinguished career of service to the state, the eighty-five-year-old Dandolo suffered from cortical blindness—the result of a severe blow to his head almost twenty years earlier. The electors must surely have believed that Dandolo's dogeship would be short and uneventful.

They were wrong. Enrico Dandolo would become one of the most famous men in Venetian history, and his dogeship would fundamentally transform Venice from a merchant republic into a maritime empire.

Yet that was still all in the future. The old man who was led to the altar of San Marco to receive the ducal regalia seemed a small, almost helpless creature. In truth, he was a man with extraordinary energy and a keen mind who would live to be almost a hundred. The people looked on as their new doge reached the altar and took his oath of office. It is not clear how far back the doge's oath goes, but Enrico Dandolo's is the earliest to survive. It is a relatively long document, with seventeen separate sections. In good republican fashion, most of the promises concern things that the doge could *not* do. He was forbidden to alienate state funds or property, divulge state secrets, permit prohibited exports, conduct foreign diplomacy, appoint notaries, or administer communal business without the approval of the doge's council, a growing body of important Venetians who represented various portions of the city. Over the subsequent centuries the doge's oath grew ever longer, augmented with additional prohibitions. In its own way, it became much like the American Constitution, enumerating and limiting the powers of government. Dandolo's oath not only defined the extent of his authority, but also his greatest responsibility, to "consider, attend to, and work for the honor and profit of the people of Venice in good faith and without fraud."

And this he did. It is clear from the outset of his reign that Enrico Dandolo was a man of action. He ordered the first-ever codification of Venetian criminal and civil law. He dramatically reformed Venetian coinage, issuing the first token coin (the quartarolo) and the first silver coin in Europe since the fall of the Roman Empire (the grosso). The grosso, which would become an international coin of exchange, bore on its face the image of the doge receiving the banner of the winged lion from St. Mark himself. It was a bold statement of the power and reach of the Venetian government.

. . .

And yet, many challenges remained. A particular source of aggravation was the city of Zara, on the Dalmatian coast. It had chafed under Venetian political and ecclesiastical control for years, especially since the city's see had been subjugated to the patriarch of Grado. Rebellion after rebellion had been put down until 1180, when the Zarans finally won their freedom. For the next two decades Zara remained a lone holdout on the otherwise Venetian-controlled Dalmatian coast. Venetian merchants feared the pirates hidden along the Zaran coast, and the state coveted the supplies of oak in the forests near the rebel city. In 1187 Doge Orio Mastropiero had borrowed money from the republic's leading citizens to prosecute a war against Zara, but the Zarans allied themselves with King Bela III of Hungary, who constructed a strong fortress to ward off the Venetians. The war was short-lived. Almost immediately after the Venetians began their siege, Pope Gregory VIII ordered a cessation of all hostilities in Europe in preparation for the Third Crusade. Venice complied, signing a two-year truce with the Zarans. In 1190, shortly after the truce expired, Doge Mastropiero dispatched another fleet against Zara, with disastrous results. The Venetians not only failed to capture the city, but in the process lost control of the nearby islands of Pago, Ossero, and Arbe. Among Doge Enrico Dandolo's first actions was the launching of yet another strike force in 1193, recapturing the islands but failing to quell Zara's defiance.

Relations with Byzantium were also strained. Although Andronicus I had restored the Venetian Quarter and released the hostages, the doge continued to press for the restoration of Venice's trading privileges in the empire's other ports. Dandolo devoted six years to painstaking negotiations with Constantinople, culminating in a new chrysobull, issued in 1198. The new emperor, Alexius III Angelus (1195–1203), made a point of favoring the recently reconciled Pisans, whom he hoped to enlist for the naval defense of the Byzantine Empire. This naturally caused friction with the Venetians, yet aside from some skirmishes in the Adriatic, matters remained at peace. The imperial chrysobull affirmed that Venetians should be free from taxes and tolls in a long list of Byzantine ports and further stipulated that Venetian expatriates should have criminal and civil cases heard by Venetian judges in all matters except murder or riot. It was an impressive document, meticulously negotiated and crafted. Unfortunately, Alexius III disregarded most of it. Byzantine officials continued to demand import and export duties from Venetian merchants, despite gold-sealed charters and lofty promises from Constantinople.

By the turn of the thirteenth century, then, Venice had grown into a prosperous, energetic, and optimistic republic in a world of feudal monarchies. Within a few years, though, it would become something more. Unexpectedly, and quite against the will of the Venetians, their republic would acquire an empire.

CHAPTER 6

BIRTH OF A MARITIME EMPIRE:
VENICE AND THE FOURTH CRUSADE

A storm was brewing across Europe in 1201 that would soon wash up on the shores of Venice. It did not look like a storm. It looked like a small wooden boat holding six Frenchmen. But it was a storm, nonetheless. And it would rage over Venice, shaking it, stripping it, and when it had finally passed, transforming it into something altogether new.

The boat that sliced its way through a mist-wrapped February morning carried important men, who themselves represented even more important men. They brought with them news from France of a vast movement of the spirit of God. Almost three years earlier the young and energetic pope Innocent III (1198–1216) had announced a great Crusade to restore Jerusalem to Christian rule. The powerful Muslim ruler, Saladin, had crushed the Christian armies in the Holy Land more than a decade earlier, conquering Jerusalem. He had even captured the relic of the True Cross, believed by Christians to be the wood on which Christ himself was crucified. Europe's first response was the Third Crusade (1189–92), led by powerful monarchs with deep pockets and large armies. Under the command of King Richard the Lionheart of England, the Third Crusade managed to save the crusader kingdom, but not Jerusalem itself.

The Muslim conquest of Jerusalem and the capture of the True Cross were not minor events for medieval Europeans. They were clear evidence of God's displeasure with Christian society and a call—indeed a demand—for action. From the lowly serf in his fields to the exalted king on his throne, the feeling was the same: Something was wrong with the soul of Europe.

Like the rest of the Catholic world, the people of Venice were troubled by these events. Yet unlike most Europeans, Venetians had first-hand experience with them. Thousands of them lived and worked in cities of the crusader kingdom (which encompassed much of what is today Syria, Lebanon, and Israel), and as a state, Venice had already thrice crusaded. Although eight decades had passed since their last Crusade, Venetians remained staunchly proud of those campaigns. They continued to idealize their crusading doges, who had won victories for Christendom and the Republic of St. Mark.

The blind doge of Venice, Enrico Dandolo, knew all about that last Crusade, he had been there when it was called. In his early teens in 1120, Dandolo had likely stood with his father, Vitale, in the church of San Marco listening to Doge Domenico Michiel rally the Venetians to take the cross of Christ. He may well have been the only Venetian alive in 1201 who could remember the Crusade of 1122. Even by modern standards, Dandolo was a very old man; when the boat carrying six Frenchmen arrived on his doorstep he was almost ninety-four. Despite his age and his blindness, Dandolo remained strong, active, and quick-minded.

The doge could not see the six Frenchmen, but he had a good idea why they had come. In France the new Crusade, which the pope had been promoting for more than two years, was finally taking shape. At a tournament in Ecry three powerful French barons, Count Thibaut of

Champagne, Count Baldwin of Flanders, and Count Louis of Blois, had taken the vow of the Crusade, receiving on their garments the cloth cross that marked them as warriors of God. The passion and chivalric drama of the moment led thousands of other knights to do the same. The fires of pious enthusiasm were fanned further by Fulk of Neuilly, a flamboyant preacher who persuaded even the paupers to take the oath of the Crusade, although none of them could afford the journey. Rumors in Venice whispered of a magnificent army, numbering hundreds of thousands of warriors, that was forming across Europe. The Holy Spirit seemed again to be on the move through the Christian people.

Although all six of these visiting Frenchmen were of high station and chivalric warriors of exceptional caliber, none of them was a leader of the forming Crusade. But they were just as good. The three leading Crusade barons—Thibaut, Baldwin, and Louis—had hand selected these six to travel to Italy to make preparations for the Crusade. And to these trusted envoys they had given blank checks—literally. The six men carried large parchments with the seals of the barons firmly attached packed securely in their bags. Each parchment was clean, ready to be filled in by whatever agreement the envoys thought best for the future of the Crusade. They had come to Venice looking for something that Venetians had in abundance: boats.

This was the Fourth Crusade (as historians now call it). In early 1200, while warriors across Europe continued to take the crusader's vow, the leading nobles had convened a strategy session at the beautiful abbey of Soissons in northern France, hoping to solve the problem of transporting so large an army thousands of miles to the Holy Land. Earlier Crusades had made the obvious choice of simply walking. But it was, after all, a long walk and there were many kingdoms along the route that were less than welcoming to crusaders marching across their territories.

A little over a decade earlier the Third Crusade had tried a different method, sailing directly from Europe to the Holy Land. This had the benefit of being more direct and less troublesome than the traditional land route across Hungary, the Byzantine Empire, and the Turkish lands of Anatolia. But the Third Crusade was led by kings with treasure chests—especially Richard the Lionheart, who brought the vast revenues of the Saladin Tithe imposed on the people of England. The kings of England and France had the means to assemble a large fleet to carry thousands of soldiers, herds of animals, and tons of provisions across the sea.

The leaders of the Fourth Crusade, who included no kings, lacked those options. Like Richard, whom they revered, they wanted their Crusade to sail to the East, but they had neither a fleet nor the money to pay for one. They resolved not to let these problems stand in their way. At Soissons they decided that the entire Crusade would rendezvous in summer 1202 at a European port, where money would then be collected from each crusader for his individual passage and supplies. The decision of which port was left to the six envoys, who were given their blank parchments and many blessings as they headed south, across the Alps.

Why did the six choose Venice? One of them, Geoffrey de Villehardouin, later described it as a simple decision. They believed that Venice was best able to satisfy their need for a very large fleet. But there must have been more to it than that. Venice's main competitors, Genoa and Pisa, were at war with each other, so they were clearly unable to help a Crusade. The envoys may also have known that Pope Innocent had planned for Venice to take part in this Crusade from the beginning.

Three years earlier, the pope had sent a papal legate, Cardinal Soffredo, to Venice to request help for the Holy Land. Innocent may have hoped that the Venetians would respond as they had done in 1121, when Doge Michiel took the papal banner and led his people on Crusade. If so, he was disappointed. Doge Dandolo was not opposed to a Crusade. Indeed, he probably favored the idea. But Venice was a maritime power, so its previous Crusades had been against coastal cities. The target of this new Crusade was Jerusalem, miles away from the sea. Venetians could join the effort, but a land-based army was essential to see it through. Innocent knew this, too, which is why he sent another legate to France to put a stop to that kingdom's war with England. By imposing a truce, the pope hoped to raise troops for his new Crusade in France and ships in Venice.

Dandolo was skeptical about the pope's ability to end the war, but hopeful nonetheless. He ordered his two best envoys, Andrea Donà and Benedetto Grillioni, to accompany the cardinal back to Rome, where they assured the pontiff of Venice's continued devotion to the Holy Land and determination to restore Jerusalem and the True Cross to Christendom. However, they pointed out, unlike the rest of Europe, the Venetians shouldered the burden of crusading every day. Innocent's predecessor, Pope Gregory VIII, had decreed that no Christian merchant was to have dealings with Muslims, which led Venice to postpone indefinitely its plans to establish a commercial presence in Egypt. The Genoese and Pisans, although Christians, ignored the Church's restriction and continued to do a brisk business in Muslim Africa. But most Venetians steered their ships to Christian territories like Greece, the crusader states, and Constantinople. The decree cost the Venetians money, which could be used, Donà and Grillioni argued, to outfit ships and prepare fleets for a Crusade. They reminded Innocent that, unlike the rest of Europe, Venetians did not engage in agriculture. Their livelihood was overseas commerce. How would other Europeans react if Innocent forbade them to grow certain crops for the good of all Christendom?

The pope was not pleased by this line of reasoning, but he wanted Venetian help and probably saw some justice in their complaint. He responded by granting a dispensation to trade nonstrategic goods with Muslims in Muslim ports. He made clear, though, that he expected that this measure would support Venice's ability to come to the aid of

Jerusalem. Dandolo was pleased by the decision, but took no immediate action regarding the Crusade. If a Crusade army were to materialize, he would deal with the question then. In 1198 that seemed unlikely.

What a difference two years had made. The pope's legate had managed to forge a peace in Europe, and despite the unfortunate death of Richard the Lionheart, the Crusade was at last forming. Dandolo knew why these six Frenchmen had come to Venice. In a way, he had been expecting them all along.

The doge ordered comfortable lodgings near San Marco for the envoys, and after they had an opportunity to rest and refresh themselves, he paid them a visit. In his memoirs, Villehardouin relates how impressed he was with the old, blind doge, who seemed so intelligent and wise. But Villehardouin had come to make a deal—not friends. He handed to Dandolo's assistant letters of credence from the northern barons stating that the six envoys had full power to make commitments and contracts in their names and were to be treated as if they were the barons themselves.

Dandolo coyly asked the French travelers just what they wanted from the Venetians. The envoys responded with a question of their own: Did the doge have the authority to conclude an agreement on behalf of the Venetian state and people? No, Dandolo responded. Doges had not had that sort of power for some time. Indeed, they were forbidden by law even to negotiate with foreigners without the approval of the councils. The envoys asked Dandolo to convene the councils the next day.

Yet that was no simple request. By this time the Venetian ducal court had become a busy place with a long list of cases before it, many of them time-sensitive. If the envoys were unwilling to state their business to the doge, he informed them, it would be at least four days before he could get them before the Small Council and the ducal court. With that, Dandolo bade them good day.

After four days the French envoys were ushered into the ducal chamber in the old fortified Ducal Palace, which Villehardouin described as "very rich and beautiful." There in the chamber they found the seated Dandolo surrounded by the six members of his Small Council. The envoys were cordially welcomed and then, once again, asked to state their business. This time they did not hesitate:

> Lord, we have come to you on behalf of the great barons of France, who have taken the sign of the cross to avenge the shame done to Jesus Christ and to conquer Jerusalem, if God permits. And because they know that no one has as great a power as you and your people, they beg you for the love of God to have pity on the land beyond the sea and on the shame done to Jesus Christ, and to consider how they can obtain vessels and a fleet.

While heartfelt, the opening statement did not tell the Venetians anything that they did not already know. Dandolo asked them to be more specific. Just what was it that they were asking for in the way of sea vessels?

A good question—and one that the French envoys do not appear to have fully considered. Of course, much of the answer was simply outside their area of expertise. These were warriors, specialists at mustering troops, laying siege to fortifications, and prosecuting field battles. They knew all about the care and feeding of an army, but very little about boats and sea travel, let alone maritime warfare. It was probably at this point that the envoys told the doge and his council the size of the projected Crusade: 20,000 foot soldiers, 9,000 squires, and 4,500 knights and their horses, all of which would require transport out of the Adriatic and across the Mediterranean. They asked the Venetian leaders what they thought would be necessary to carry so great a force and whether such a thing would be within their financial means.

Medieval Venetians were used to making contracts for sea voyages.

At that very moment in the Rialto markets, notaries were busy drawing up just such agreements. But what these envoys were asking for was in a class by itself. To transport that many men and horses, not to mention the tons of provisions necessary, would require the largest fleet constructed in Europe since the days of the Roman Empire. It was a project of staggering size. Dandolo and his council were clearly taken aback. They had expected a Crusade, yes, but not one this big.

The doge told the envoys that they were asking a very great thing. This was no back-of-the-parchment calculation; it would require much consideration. Could the Venetians produce so large a fleet? And if they could, how much of it would need to be drafted from Venetian merchants and how much constructed? What kinds of provisions would be necessary and where could the Venetians, whose agricultural production consisted largely of gardening, obtain them? And even if all of this were possible, how much would it cost? These were serious questions and it was crucial that Dandolo and his councillors get them right. If they overextended the commune's resources or failed to ask for sufficient payment, the results could be catastrophic. On the other hand, if properly managed, the merchants of Venice could make a tidy sum while still discharging their duty to fight for the liberation of Jerusalem.

The doge told the envoys that he and his council would need time to gather the information necessary to work up a viable plan—if it could be done at all. He told them that he hoped to have something for them in eight days, although he warned that it could take longer. A bit disappointed by the delay, the Frenchmen left the Ducal Palace for what was undoubtedly a pleasant week of Venetian sightseeing. Eight days later they were again summoned to the ducal court, where Dandolo and his council awaited them.

Only at this second meeting did the envoys inform the doge and his men that the destination of the Crusade was to be Egypt, rather than the Holy Land. The Crusade leaders had chosen this strategy, first proposed by King Richard during the Third Crusade, as the best means of shattering Muslim power in the region and thereby assuring the long-term safety of Jerusalem. But it remained unpopular among rank-and-file crusaders, who took the cross to fight for the land of Christ, not the pyramids. The leaders of the Fourth Crusade planned to get around this problem by simply not telling the rank and file where they were going. The destination would remain a secret until the ships landed on the Nile delta, leaving the common crusaders no choice but to accept their new theater of war.

Changing the destination, though, would certainly have upset some of the Venetian leaders' calculations. So it is not surprising that they had much to discuss. In the end, however, the Venetians presented their proposal. Dandolo made clear to the envoys that this was not a firm offer of service. Even if the knights found it acceptable it would still require the approval of the Great Council and the arengo. The French understood and Dandolo laid out the terms.

Venice would provide transportation for one year and a large amount of provisions for the army. The cost would be four silver marks for each knight, four silver marks for each horse, and two silver marks for everyone else. The envoys persuaded the Venetians to reduce the passage cost for the horses (or perhaps the knights) to two marks. In addition, the Venetians agreed to join the Crusade themselves, supplying fifty fully armed war galleys at no charge provided that all spoils were split between the French and the Venetians.

Although the price of the fleet was negotiated on a per capita basis, it was important to the Venetians that the final contract deliver payment in lump sums. They were producing a fleet of a set size, which would need to be paid for one way or the other. They did not want to be in the business of collecting passage from each and every crusader. Instead, the French envoys agreed on behalf of their lords to pay a set amount of money, which they would themselves collect from the crusading army.

This may seem a minor point, but it was not. Indeed, it lay at the heart of the problems that would later arise and ultimately lead this project to have such transformative effects on Venice.

After talking it over, the French envoys accepted the proposal the next day. Dandolo promised to move it through the Venetian government as quickly as possible, and three days later he convened the Great Council, which consisted then of forty representatives of the people. With "wit and wisdom" he persuaded the members to accept the plan. According to Villehardouin, Dandolo then called together progressively larger groups of citizens—first a hundred, then two hundred, then a thousand—getting their approval before moving on. Villehardouin may simply be expounding on something that he had heard, but it is also possible that Dandolo was returning to the old way of doges calling together ad hoc bodies in order to approve various initiatives. Politically, it made good sense, since each approval made it less likely that the next, larger committee would turn down the proposal.

After more than two weeks in Venice, the mission of the French envoys was no longer a secret to anyone. The whole city knew that there was a plan for Venice to crusade again. Now the people needed to approve it. Thousands poured into the Piazza San Marco and as many as were able crammed into the ornate church. There they heard a Mass of the Holy Spirit, traditionally sung before any great undertaking. After Mass the doge introduced the envoys and then asked them to address the crowd—presumably through an interpreter.

The great cavern of the church was silent and still as the knights awkwardly made their way to the front. Villehardouin later remembered how curiously the Venetians stared at them, for northern lords dressed in knightly finery rarely visited this merchant port. The marshal of Champagne began with a bit of flattery, telling the congregation that the most powerful lords in France had sent them to Venice because they knew that no city had greater power on the sea. He then described the

Crusade taking shape across Europe, the thousands of warriors who were even now taking the vow of the cross and leaving behind loved ones for the sake of the faith. With heartfelt emotion, Villehardouin begged the Venetian people to join their French brothers, to have mercy on the holy city, and to avenge the shame done to Jesus Christ by the desecration of the holy places.

With his words still echoing from the golden domes, Villehardouin stepped down from the ambo and stood before the people. Silently he motioned to his five colleagues, who joined him at the front. Moved by the plight of Jerusalem, the abuse of the True Cross, and the wounds of Christ crucified again in the persecution of his people, all six of the envoys wept bitterly. Then they did something even more unexpected: They knelt before the people of Venice. Through tears of anguish Villehardouin at last spoke. He swore that they would remain there, forever on their knees, begging for the help of Venice until it was granted.

They did not have long to wait. A flood of tearful emotion had already swept through the church. No sooner had Villehardouin implored their aid than the people raised their hands by the thousands chanting, "We grant it! We grant it!" The French envoys stood up joyfully, and the vast crowd sang and cried and reveled in the moment. With this assent of the people, the Republic of Venice had again taken up the crusader's cross.

The next day the joyful French envoys were ushered into the doge's court, where the Great and Small Councils were gathered. Notaries had been busy drawing up multiple copies of the contract. This was the business side of the Crusade, where the logistical details were set down on parchment so that the grand spiritual enterprise could take place. But it was not without religious feeling that the Venetian leaders made their commitments. Holy relics were brought to the chamber, and each of the Venetian councillors swore on the precious body parts to uphold the terms of the contract. Then the blind doge was led to the relics. Tearfully, he knelt down and promised to fulfill every part of the agreement. It was a promise that he would meticulously keep.

Preparing for the Fourth Crusade was the biggest project thus far in Venice's history. The Venetians had promised to produce a fleet of some 450 major transport vessels, 50 fully manned war galleys, and many tons of provisions—all within just eighteen months. Most of the transport vessels that would carry the crusaders, provisions, and military gear were large, sail-powered roundships—the same sort that were routinely used by Venetian merchants. Dandolo and his council suspended all overseas trade, ordering Venetians to bring their merchant ships home for the June 1202 Crusade departure. This, in itself, represented an enormous expense. Turning off the flow of overseas trade cost Venice and its people dearly.

Much of the fleet also had to be constructed at state expense. Certainly the horse transports had to be built from scratch. These vessels represented a significant improvement in medieval military technology. They were equipped with a ramp that allowed the horses to be walked onto the ship, rather than hoisted, which often harmed the animals. On board, the horses were placed in their own stalls and secured with harnesses, which protected them from falling when the deck pitched.

And then there were the war galleys. These long, sleek vessels were manned by trained Venetian marines who could move the vessels nimbly with their hundred oars, ramming and boarding at will. The galleys were crucial for the defense of the fleet en route and the destruction of Egyptian naval forces when they arrived. In later centuries these vessels would have been produced in the famous Arsenale. But in 1201 they had to be built in dozens, perhaps hundreds, of shipyards dotting the city. Venetian agents were sent across the rivers and roads of the Po Valley to make advance contracts on wheat and other foodstuffs for the Crusade. The acquisition and transportation of this food—not just for 33,500 men but 4,500 horses as well—was a daunting task.

So, too, was the problem of manpower. In 1200 Venice's population stood around a hundred thousand, making it the second-largest city in Europe (after Rome). Manning the proposed fleet would require more than thirty thousand sailors and marines. The entire city probably held just enough able-bodied adult males to do it, but that would have left Venice without men, and likewise protection. Instead, the Venetians planned to send half of their men, and held a lottery to decide which half. Wax balls—half of which had a scrap of parchment in them—were placed in large containers. Priests from every parish were charged with summoning the adult males, blessing the wax balls, and then administering the lottery. Those who drew the parchments joined the Crusade. As for the other fifteen thousand men, the Venetians would need to recruit them from dependencies on the mainland and Dalmatian coast.

Before leaving Venice, Villehardouin and his colleagues borrowed two thousand silver marks as a down payment on the building of the fleet. That was the last the Venetians saw of French money for some time. The crusaders had agreed to pay for the fleet in regular installments, yet none of those payments ever materialized. Indeed, nothing at all arrived from the Crusade—except crusaders, who started showing up in June. This put the Venetians in a difficult position. If the money had been paid as promised, it would have been used to offset the costs of the fleet. As it stood, by June 1202 Venice had been forced to absorb all those costs. A great many Venetians were owed a great deal of money and risked financial ruin if they did not receive it. The stakes for them—and their doge—could not have been higher.

Although Venice had plenty of accommodations for pilgrims and travelers, it had nowhere near enough rooms for 33,500 men, let alone 4,500 horses. Instead, the crusaders were dropped off on the barren Lido, within sight of the main city and the massive fleet that now stood ready to transport them to the East. With heady anticipation, new groups of crusaders arrived on the island daily. They pitched their tents, prepared their weapons, and looked forward to proving their worth in defense of Christendom. The mood among the Venetians was just as jubilant. The arrival of the greater lords, such as Baldwin of Flanders, Hugh of St. Pol, and Boniface of Montferrat, was especially celebrated, for they brought with them powerful armies, beautiful banners, and impressive war chests.

Yet on June 29 that mood began to sour. According to the contract, on this day the money was to be paid and the fleet to set sail. Neither happened. Out on the Lido, among the fine tents, prancing horses, and campfires, only eleven thousand crusaders had arrived—and some of those were poor people with no means of support. Since individual passage was to be collected from the crusaders, this meant that the leaders could only lay their hands on one-third of the fleet's price. Like any debtor, the crusaders asked for patience: just a few weeks more, to give stragglers time to arrive.

As merchants, Venetians lived by the letter of their contracts. Murmurs and grumbling began to be heard in the market stalls of Rialto and the fishing docks across the city. They complained, of course, about the French, who should have treated their allies better by paying what they owed on time. But undoubtedly they also complained about their leaders—Doge Dandolo and his council—who had championed this suddenly questionable venture.

Matters did not improve with the passing weeks. More crusaders arrived, but only a thousand or two—nowhere near the twenty thousand for whom they still waited. Some hopes were raised when Cardinal Peter Capuano, the papal legate to the Crusade, arrived on July 22. But he brought no money. He absolved the poor and the sick of their Crusade vows, sending them back home. Beyond that, all he could do was wait for more arrivals, like everyone else.

Where were the missing crusaders? Everywhere except Venice. Although the Crusade leaders had agreed that Venice was the rendezvous point, this in no way bound individual fighters. A medieval Crusade was not like a modern army in which one joins and then takes one's place in a chain of command. A Crusade was made up of thousands of different people, each of whom had taken a personal vow to God. How a crusader fulfilled that vow was up to him. He was under no obligation to take passage at Venice simply because the counts of Flanders, Champagne, and Blois had put seals to parchment. If it was more convenient or economical, a crusader could buy passage at Marseille, or Bari, or Brindisi, or any other port with vessels heading east.

And that is just what the missing twenty thousand did. The debacle unfolding in Venice became a self-fulfilling prophecy. As more crusaders learned of the problems in Venice, they avoided the city, thus worsening the situation. By the end of July 1202 things had grown so bad that no crusader just starting off on his journey wanted to become mired in it. And on the Lido, only about 12,000 of the projected 33,500 crusaders were ready to sail.

In late July or early August the extension expired and payment was due. Dandolo asked the Crusade barons to render 85,000 silver marks so that the Crusade could get under way. Immediately passage was collected from each crusader. When that was not enough, the barons ordered every crusader to pay all that he had to make up the difference. The leading nobles handed over their rich plate and most of their war chests as an example to the rank and file. But not every crusader agreed with their leaders. From their perspective, they had paid all that was required and should not be forced to pay more simply because their leaders had misjudged the size of the army. Let them pay for their own mistakes. In the final tally the crusaders were able to gather up 51,000 marks. They still owed 34,000 more and had no way of raising it.

The Fourth Crusade was the ultimate test for the new governmental reforms instituted in the republic during the 1170s. A century earlier the people of Venice, fired by feelings of anger, betrayal, and disgust, may well have demanded that the crusaders be ejected from the city and all monies paid kept as penalty for breaking their contract with Venice. Yet thanks to the reforms, the doge and his council were now positioned as a buffer between popular outrage and prudent action. In a meeting with his council, Dandolo flatly rejected the idea of removing the crusaders from the lagoon. He pointed out that Venice's reputation throughout Christendom would suffer. He also doubted that the rest of Europe would agree that they were justified in keeping the 51,000 marks paid. Then there was the practical problem of the ejection itself. Venice had survived and flourished for centuries because no army could overcome its watery fortifications. Now a large, well-armed, and angry army was camped right on the Lido. Just how would the sailors of Venice remove the knights of France if they refused to go?

Dandolo suggested a different solution. The Venetian state could loan the crusaders the 34,000 marks still owed provided they promise to pay it back from their share of the Crusade's booty. Alexandria and Damietta were rich cities that might easily provide the spoils necessary to pay off the Crusade's debts. Since it had grown too late to sail to Egypt that year, Dandolo further proposed that as a stipulation of the loan the crusaders agree to winter at Zara. Zaran pirates had been a danger to Venetian shipping for some time, so the idea of restoring control over the city was meant to convince those members of the council who balked at risking 34,000 silver marks on a Crusade with a poor credit history. Though wary, the council approved the plan.

A few days later the doge went out to the meeting tent of the barons on the Lido. The atmosphere was tense. Like the Great Council, the Crusade leaders were not enthusiastic about Dandolo's plan. They were willing to mortgage their remaining debt against the collateral of future booty, but why should they also have to help Venice in its squabble with Zara, a fight that had nothing to do with the Crusade? Zara was a Catholic city. Dandolo, the skilled negotiator, knew that without Zara the

Great Council would not accept the compromise. He needed the crusaders to meet him halfway. He reminded them that the problem was of their own making. The Venetians had been ready to transport them to Egypt on June 29. He gave them a lesson on Mediterranean weather, explaining that winter storms made a crossing next to impossible after September. The crusaders needed a place to stay. Unlike the sandy Lido, Zara was a rich city with every sort of amenity. It was, furthermore, a rebel—something loathsome to the feudal knights. Thus, by helping their allies to perform a righteous task, the crusaders could solve two pressing problems: the moribund Crusade and the need for a place to winter. Faced with this hard calculus, the barons agreed to Dandolo's proposal.

It was not easy, but the doge had managed to forge a delicate compromise that saved the Crusade. However, the doge had omitted one critical detail during his negotiations with the Great Council and the crusader barons. Zara, the linchpin of the whole agreement, was under papal protection. The city was a possession of King Emeric of Hungary, who had taken the crusader's cross several years earlier. Emeric had no interest in crusading; he had taken the vow only to secure his throne. But when the king heard that a large army would be accompanying the Venetians in the vicinity of Zara, he lost no time reminding Pope Innocent of his rights as a crusader. By canon law, all properties of those signed with the cross were under the protection of Rome. The pope had already sent word to Dandolo that he was forbidden to use the Crusade to settle his dispute with Zara.

The doge recognized the severity of this problem, but he believed it was manageable. He argued—at least to himself—that Emeric was a false crusader who used the cross to unjustly hold what was not rightfully his. Since Emeric had no plans to join the Fourth Crusade, Dandolo reasoned that his lands were no longer under papal protection. It was a likely story, even if completely false. Nevertheless, the projected conquest of Zara was the only thing holding the Crusade together. It *had* to be acceptable to the pope.

Only one other person in Venice knew that the pope had forbidden the conquest of Zara: the papal legate, Cardinal Peter Capuano. This compromise plan put him in a difficult bind. If he condemned it, making public the pope's protection of Zara, then Peter would be responsible for the dissolution of the Crusade. Innocent would not like that. On the other hand, if he allowed it he would contravene the pope's commandments and canon law. Innocent would not like that either. So the cardinal devised a third way. He would say nothing while the fleet was readied for departure and the crusaders were loaded aboard. He would say nothing as the Crusade made its way down the Adriatic Sea. But when the Crusade fleet cast anchor before Zara, then he would speak up, and with his full authority as the representative of the pope. With the army already in the boats, no longer holed up on an island and at the mercy of Venice for provisions, things would look very different indeed. The Crusade would be saved and the Venetians would be deprived of an unjust victory.

It was an awkward plan. Leading churchmen on the Crusade naturally went to the papal legate when they heard that the army would be attacking a Catholic city. Did the pope really approve of this? No, Peter replied, he did not. He advised his fellow clergy to remain silent about the matter until the fleet had sailed, when they should do all in their power to stop the attack on Zara.

It did not take long for Dandolo to hear of the cardinal's plan. In a testy exchange, the doge told Peter that if he was going to forbid the conquest of Zara he should do so immediately, while they were still in Venice. Peter politely declined. The two men understood each other perfectly. Both had the same secret, and both planned to use it for their own very different ends. But Dandolo would not suffer this puffed-up legate to double-cross the Republic of St. Mark. He informed the cardinal that he would not be allowed to board fleet vessels unless he renounced his authority as papal legate. He was welcome to join the Crusade as one of its preachers. Outraged, Peter Capuano refused to do any such thing. Slinging threats and warnings, he stormed out of the room, packed his belongings, and left for Rome. The pope would hear of Venice's perversion of the Crusade.

With that problem seemingly resolved, Dandolo and the Venetians concentrated on the departure of the Crusade armada. Much remained to be done, and after months of delays, the lagoon was a hive of activity. Mariners rowed or sailed boats back and forth to the major vessels, loading aboard siege engines, weapons, horses, and what was left of the Crusade's provisions. On September 8, the Feast of the Nativity of the Virgin, Venetian crusaders and their French allies were invited to a special Mass in the church of San Marco. Before the bells and incense commenced, however, there was a surprise. The ancient Enrico Dandolo, in full ceremonial garb, mounted the stone steps of the pulpit. Addressing his countrymen, he said:

> Sirs, you are joined with the most valiant men in the world in the greatest enterprise that anyone has ever undertaken. I am old and weak and in need of rest, and my health is failing. But I see that no one knows how to govern and direct you as I do, who am your lord. If you agree that I should take the sign of the cross to protect and lead you, and that my son should remain and guard the country, I will go to live or die with you and the Crusaders.

With heartfelt emotion, the doge was re-creating a scene that every Venetian knew well. In 1121 it was Doge Domenico Michiel who had stood at that same podium, exhorting the Venetians to fight the war of Christ, and donning the cross as their leader. And once again the great church rang with the cries of Venetians approving their doge's request.

As cheers mixed with song, Dandolo slowly descended from the pulpit and knelt before the high altar. There the priest received the doge's vow and sewed the crusader's cross, not on his shoulder as was customary, but on his cloth crown (an early version of the *corno*) for all to see.

The ceremony-filled departure of the Crusade occurred during the first week of October 1202. The last to take ship was Enrico Dandolo, who boarded the doge's vermilion galley, adorned in his colorful robes of state. Four silver trumpets used on solemn occasions blared before him and drums rattled to attract attention to the show. The various colored banners were raised and the sides of the ships and the castles were girded with the shields of the Crusade barons, each painted brilliantly to distinguish its owner. The clergy mounted the castles or poops of the ships to chant the *Veni creator spiritus*. As Dandolo's galley began to move forward, followed by the rest of the fleet, a hundred trumpets of silver and brass signaled their departure and countless drums and tabors beat excitedly. Soon they passed the familiar Lido on the right and moved out of the lagoon and into the Adriatic. Enrico Dandolo could not see the beauty of Venice as he departed, but he could hear the Venetians cheering as they took one last look at their leader.

Venice must have seemed a quiet, empty place after the Crusade departed with half of its men and most of its vessels. While the remaining Venetians cleaned up and tried to restore some normality, they worried about the fate of their crusaders, not to mention the 34,000 silver marks owed to them. At least they could rest easier about the safety of the Adriatic when Zara was returned to Venetian control.

But things did not go quite as planned at Zara. When Cardinal Peter left Venice in a huff, he made certain to tell his friends and supporters among the crusaders about his treatment and his conviction that the Venetians were hijacking the Crusade. The most powerful of his partisans was Count Simon of Montfort, a young, pious, and exceptionally scrupulous warrior who commanded a sizable army of his own. Simon sent his friend, Abbot Guy of the monastery of Vaux-de-Cernay, with the cardinal on his trip back to Rome. There the cardinal and the abbot told the pope everything. Innocent was beside himself with rage. He immediately penned a terse letter threatening excommunication for any crusader who lifted a sword against the Zarans. The letter was entrusted to the abbot, who traveled at top speed to get it to the Crusade before it was too late.

The Crusade army encamped outside the walls of Zara on November 11. The sheer size of the force made a deep impression on the people in the city. There was no doubt that Zara would fall. The Zarans, therefore, sent a delegation to Doge Dandolo seeking terms of surrender. They received a harsh response. Dandolo would spare their lives only provided they evacuate the city at once. With little choice, the delegation agreed. Pleased, the doge told the Zarans to wait in his tent while he went to confer with his French allies.

Dandolo left the Zarans alone only a short time, but it was enough to prove decisive. Abbot Guy and his letter had arrived. With a few well-armed friends, Simon of Montfort quickly brought the monk with him to the doge's tent. There he told the Zaran delegation the welcome news that the pope had come to their rescue. There would be no attack. With profuse thanks, the Zarans returned home to tell their people that all was well.

It is not difficult to imagine the next scene in this comic tragedy. Dandolo, now accompanied by the leading Crusade barons, returned to his tent to accept the surrender of Zara. All that he found there were Count Simon, Abbot Guy, and a few other knights wearing disturbingly smug smiles. Where were the Zarans? Gone. But why? Because we told them that the Crusade would not attack a Christian city under papal protection. Confusion, shouts, anger. And then the abbot burst into the midst of the fray. Holding the pope's letter aloft, he shouted, "I forbid you, on behalf of the Pope of Rome, to attack this city, for those within are Christians and you are Crusaders!"

This was precisely what the doge of Venice had sought to avoid. He may have kept Cardinal Peter from making this proclamation, but he had failed to keep the pope from doing so by means of a scribbled letter and a curiously quick abbot. Pressed by circumstances, Dandolo had played fast and loose with the Holy See and thereby injured the traditionally warm relations between Rome and Venice. The wound would not heal easily, or soon.

Faced with the collapse of the compromise, Dandolo had no choice but to appeal to the chivalric honor of the French barons. The doge wheeled on Baldwin of Flanders, Hugh of St. Pol, Geoffrey de Villehardouin, and the other Crusade leaders, saying, "Lords, I had this city at my mercy, and your people have deprived me of it. You have promised to assist me to conquer it, and I summon you to do so." The French leaders were torn between piety and honor. What tipped the balance was the character of Simon of Montfort, who was not well liked by his French colleagues. He seemed always to have a complaint, and they believed that he either wanted to command the Crusade or see it collapse. They would allow neither, and so they agreed to attack the city of Zara. Disgusted, Simon and his men camped apart from the Crusade, refusing to have anything to do with this sinful business. After five days of assault on Zara's walls, adorned by its citizens with banners of the cross, the city fell on November 24. And the crusaders, both French and Venetian, moved in.

The siege of Zara added the specter of excommunication to the miseries of this increasingly troubled Crusade. Simon and his friends made sure that every soldier knew about the state of his soul. Perhaps he did hope to wrest control over the Crusade from the other barons, who seemed to be leading the men straight into hell. As the story spread among the French, it was invariably the Venetians who played the villain. It was they who had kept the crusaders in Venice until it was too late to sail to the Holy Land. It was they who had overcharged the knights, draining every penny from them and still demanding more. And it was they who had demanded that the Crusade attack a Catholic city, even after the pope had strictly forbidden it. In Venice the soldiers could not act on their frustrations. But in Zara they could. French crusaders began organizing themselves into bands and attacking the Venetians. The barons mounted their horses and rode swiftly through Zara's streets, quelling the fighting in one area only to have it erupt elsewhere. By morning, when the killing finally stopped, about a hundred lay dead and many more were wounded.

In an attempt to restore calm, the bishops on the Crusade issued a general absolution, lifting the excommunication that weighed so heavily on the soldiers' minds. Anyone with an elementary knowledge of canon law knew that such absolutions were invalid—only the pope could lift his own excommunication. Fortunately, few of the crusaders had an elementary knowledge of canon law, so peace prevailed for the remainder of the winter.

The conquest of Zara was good for Venice because it eliminated an enemy from its backyard, but it was not what spawned a maritime empire. The next act in that drama took place sometime around Christmas. Once again, it arrived on a boat. Into Zara's harbor sailed a smallish vessel bearing envoys from Philip of Swabia—a powerful lord who claimed to be the king of Germany, but who was still waging a war against another lord with much the same claim. The German envoys brought with them a tale of treachery and intrigue.

It was a good story, one that had begun almost a decade earlier in Constantinople. One day in April 1195 Emperor Isaac II Angelus went hunting with his brother, Alexius. What the emperor did not know was that he was the prey. As soon as Isaac was away from his bodyguard,

Alexius and his accomplices seized the emperor and gouged out his eyes. In Byzantium this was considered a humane way of conducting a coup since blind men were not allowed to rule. Isaac was placed in comfortable confinement in Constantinople and his rebellious brother was crowned Alexius III. None of this was unusual in Constantinople, although the treachery outraged the feudal knights when they heard of it.

Poor Isaac had a son, the envoys continued. His name, like that of his uncle, was Alexius. In 1200, when he was about fifteen years old, young Alexius had managed a daring escape from Constantinople aboard a Pisan vessel bound for the West. Disguised as a common sailor, he landed at Ancona and then made his way to Germany and the court of Philip of Swabia, where Philip's wife, Irene, was the young man's sister. Irene begged her husband to help Alexius, yet Philip was too busy with his own wars. Instead, he sent these envoys to the Crusade to enlist their aid for the young man.

With their story complete, the Germans urged the Crusade barons to take up the poor prince's cause. He was, they claimed, a victim of unrivaled treachery. The people of Constantinople groaned under the weight of the tyrant Alexius III and longed to accept the young man as their rightful ruler. Indeed, the envoys insisted that the Byzantines would overthrow the evil uncle as soon as the young Alexius arrived. It was only right that crusaders should defend the defenseless and liberate the oppressed. And it was merely a small side trip on their way to the East. Furthermore, if the crusaders should agree to do this for the prince, he would richly reward them. As the rightful emperor, he would provide supplies for them on their journey to Constantinople. Then, when he had punished his evil uncle and assumed the throne, he would pay the crusaders two hundred thousand silver marks—more than enough to pay their debt to the Venetians and still make it worth their while. And that was not all. He also promised to raise a Byzantine army of ten thousand soldiers and join the Crusade himself for one year. For the rest of his life he would maintain a garrison of five hundred knights in the Holy Land. And there was even something in the deal for the pope: The new emperor would make the Orthodox Church obedient to Rome, thus ending the schism between the Latin and Greek churches that had been in effect for more than a century.

It was quite a proposal and it seemed to come at the perfect time. Not only was the Crusade penniless, but in May 1203 it would run out of provisions. Taking up Alexius's cause seemed a way to fill empty stomachs and pockets, and thus preserve the enterprise. The doge of Venice certainly wanted the Crusade to succeed, but he recognized the dangers for his city and people. Venetians did the bulk of their overseas trade in the Byzantine Empire. The Venetian Quarter of Constantinople was a vibrant and profitable city within a city. Why would they wish to upset all of that? Doge Dandolo knew all about Alexius III's blinding of his brother, yet that was just the way business was done in Byzantium. Overall Venice's relationship with the current emperor was good. Dandolo himself had negotiated a trade agreement with Alexius III in 1198—an agreement that would be worth nothing if Venice sailed into Byzantine waters with an armada and a rival. Of course, they might succeed in overthrowing the emperor, but it was a tremendous gamble for Venice. Sailing to Egypt carried no such risks and offered plenty of opportunity for rich plunder.

But the decision was not in the doge's hands. Although he did not know it, a number of the Crusade leaders had already committed themselves and the Crusade to the young man's cause. The titular leader of the Crusade, Boniface of Montferrat, was a vassal of Philip of Swabia. He had actually met the Byzantine prince two years earlier when the Crusade was still forming and had promised then to find a way to use the army to help him. Boniface had gone to Rome to persuade Innocent III to allow the Crusade to take up the cause, but the pope categorically refused. Doge Dandolo also did not know that the leading Crusade barons, in particular Boniface, Baldwin of Flanders, Hugh of St. Pol, and Louis of Blois, had already negotiated a deal with Philip of Swabia months earlier, when they were all still waiting in Venice. In it, they had agreed to help Alexius in Constantinople if he would help them in the East. The doge was, therefore, under heavy pressure to accept the prince's proposal. In the end, he did.

The new plan was then revealed to the rank-and-file crusaders. The Venetians, most of whom knew the way to Constantinople well, had no objections to the change. Indeed, they may even have believed (wrongly, of course) that the pope had ordered the diversion. As for the French, they opposed it. But their leaders signed the contract anyway, and so the Crusade was bound for Constantinople.

In the meantime, Zara persisted in causing problems. In the spring of 1203 a coalition of Zaran and Hungarian fighters began guerrilla raids against the crusaders camped in the city. For the moment they were only a nuisance, but after the Crusade departed, the fighters would have a good chance of recapturing their city. Dandolo could not have Zaran pirates cruising the Adriatic at will while most of the republic's navy was gone. On April 7 the entire Crusade evacuated Zara and camped nearby. The Venetians then spent the next several weeks demolishing the city. When they had finished, only fields of rubble and churches remained to testify that a city had once been there.

As the two hundred or so vessels of the Crusade fleet unfurled their sails and made their way to Constantinople, the pope and his legate watched with frustration and anger. Innocent had no doubt that Dandolo and the Venetians had hijacked the Crusade, using it to settle scores first with Zara and now with Constantinople. Although the French crusaders had sent envoys to the pope to beg forgiveness for their sins, the Venetians had sent no one to beg for anything. Dandolo knew that the pope would insist that Venice return Zara to the king of Hungary, so he decided to wait until after its destruction to seek forgiveness. By then, however, it was too late. When the papal legate absolved the French crusaders, he also issued a formal bull of excommunication against the Venetians. Doge Dandolo told the Crusade barons that if the excommunication was made public, the Venetians would abandon the Crusade. Boniface of Montferrat obligingly suppressed the bull and that, for the moment, was the end of it. All the Venetian crusaders were excommunicates, yet only Dandolo knew of it. He would spend much of the remainder of the Crusade seeking absolution for himself and his countrymen.

On June 23, 1203, the Venetian fleet bearing the Crusade and the young Alexius came within sight of Constantinople. For the doge and the Venetians it was a familiar sight. Not so for the French, very few of whom had ever been to the imperial capital—indeed few knew that so large a city existed anywhere in the world. They had never beheld so many and such magnificent palaces, and the many domes of Orthodox churches were also a strange and marvelous sight. Constantinople was simply outside the ken of the northerners. The ten largest cities in western Europe would have fit comfortably within its walls. As the crusaders sailed north through the Bosporus directly past the city, crowds of Greeks perched on the seawalls to get a look at the massive armada. Because of the high hills in the city, many others could see the ships from rooftops or even on grassy knolls in the old acropolis (modern Seraglio Point). In a city saturated with spectacle, where the unusual was commonplace, the large and colorful crusader fleet remained a sight to behold.

The crusaders camped on the Asian side of the Bosporus, where they waited for the people to overthrow their tyrant. Nothing happened. After waiting several weeks, on July 3 all fifty of the Venetian war galleys rowed out across the Bosporus, taking up a position very close to the capital's seawalls. Doge Dandolo, Boniface of Montferrat, and the young Alexius were aboard one of the galleys, probably the sumptuous vessel of the doge. As expected, the galleys drew a large crowd of on-lookers. The crusaders displayed the prince while shouting, "Behold your natural lord!" They cried out the crimes of Alexius III and stressed that they had not come to harm the people, but rather to defend and assist them. They urged the Greeks to take action against the usurper. Instead, the inhabitants took action against the crusaders, showering them with rocks, stones, and insults. Two days later, the Fourth Crusade prepared to attack Constantinople.

Militarily speaking, the Crusade was too small to conquer something as large as Constantinople, but it was large enough to cause damage. The main Venetian assault came on July 17, when the fleet, including transport vessels equipped with castles and flying bridges, moved against the seawalls of the inner harbor. As the transports came within range the Byzantine artillery mounted on the towers began to shower down stones, although miraculously none damaged the vessels. Crossbowmen and archers from both sides fired away, filling the air with bolts and arrows. The ferocity of the defenders' missile fire kept the captains of the transports from pressing too closely to the shore. A few vessels were able to graze the walls with their bridges, but quickly retreated to avoid the deadly shower of stones. After additional failures, the Venetian assault stalled.

Then Enrico Dandolo did an amazing thing. Standing on the prow of his galley, fully armored, and with the banner of St. Mark waving in the wind before him, the blind old doge had been listening intently to the sounds of battle and the description of events from his men. When the advance of the transport vessels halted, he ordered his own galley to advance and run aground beneath the walls. Not surprisingly, his men questioned the wisdom of this tactic. Dandolo erupted in fury, promising to do bodily harm to them if they did not put his vessel onshore. And so the rowers put their backs into it and the vermilion galley moved swiftly forward. All along the line Venetian sailors watched in surprise as the doge's vessel came out from behind the transports and sped toward shore. Amid the torrents of missiles they could see the winged lion of St. Mark and behind it the figure of their doge, still standing bravely on the prow. As soon as the galley made a landing, several men grabbed the standard and planted it on the shore. This amazing display of courage gave heart to the Venetians. At once the roundships moved forward and the marines rushed to the flying bridges. Some managed to gain a foothold on the walls, while others came ashore and scrambled up ladders. The Byzantine defenders fled, allowing the Venetians to move quickly across the fortifications, ultimately capturing twenty-five towers.

The image of the old doge, face in the wind, crashing against the shore of Constantinople is deservedly one of the most enduring in the history of Venice or, for that matter, the Middle Ages. Perhaps that is why it is sometimes exaggerated. From the canvas of Tintoretto in the Chamber of the Great Council to the pages of Edward Gibbon's *Decline and Fall of the Roman Empire*, Dandolo has been depicted as the first warrior onshore, leading his countrymen into battle against the Greeks. In modern histories one often reads about the old doge waving the banner of St. Mark, shouting to his forces, and jumping ashore with the army. In truth, though, Dandolo never physically moved during the entire episode. He did not grasp or wave the banner, nor did he shout orders to the other ships (which would have been impossible in any case). He did not even get out of his galley. Dandolo carried his armor and maintained his footing on a moving vessel, something quite normal for Venetians. Anyone who has watched elderly women crossing the Grand Canal on *traghetti* (gondola ferries) weighed down by their shopping bags can attest to this. But Dandolo did inspire his men with his courage, and that is what altered the course of the battle.

Taking a small section of the walls is not the same as taking a city, but the Venetians also managed to set fire to a wealthy nearby district.

That was enough for the Byzantines, who cared little whether Isaac II's brother or son ruled them. Sensing danger, Alexius III grabbed a thousand pounds of gold and as many precious stones and pearls as he could carry and fled Constantinople. The next morning Dandolo and the Crusade leaders were awoken by messengers from Isaac II, who had been restored to his throne (despite his blindness). In an instant the crusaders were transformed from villains into heroes. The doors of the city were opened to them and the young man who had promised them all so much was crowned Alexius IV.

One hundred thousand silver marks was immediately delivered to the crusaders, a welcome bounty indeed. As the treaty stated, the money was divided between the Venetians and the French. The latter used theirs to pay off their debt to the former, which finally closed the books on their troubled contract. Still, although the French remained poor, they knew that more money was on the way. Half of the promised fee was still to be paid.

But Alexius IV was out of money. He looked everywhere for more—confiscating the property of his enemies, plundering church treasuries, even opening the tombs of emperors to relieve them of their finery. But a hundred thousand silver marks is a great deal of money, and Alexius simply could not lay hands on it. He needed more time. He offered to extend the lease on the Venetian fleet for an additional year at his own expense if the army would spend the winter in Constantinople. By March 1204, he assured them, he would be able to pay his remaining debt and join the Crusade on its journey to Egypt.

It did not turn out that way. The new emperor's increasingly draconian attempts to raise funds to pay the Venetians and French made him and them deeply unpopular among the citizens of Constantinople. Things became so bad that bands of Greeks started setting fires in the Venetian Quarter of the city as well as in other European quarters along Constantinople's harbor area. On August 19 a group of armed Pisans and Venetians retaliated, setting fires to Byzantine homes in the city center. A fierce wind blew up, spreading the fire across Constantinople's midsection. It soon became one of the most destructive urban fires in history. More than a hundred thousand Byzantine citizens lost their homes in the blaze. Byzantine hatred for western Europeans, which smoldered even in the best of times, now became a white-hot flame. All the European residents of Constantinople—including thousands of Venetians—fled their homes and moved in with the crusaders on the north side of the harbor. The battle lines were drawn.

The open hatred for the Latins made it no longer politically possible for Alexius IV to pay the crusaders anything. He tried to stall them, but in the end made it clear that they should be content with what they had received. This was a clear breach of his vow and contract—something that the feudal French and the commercial Venetians abhorred in equal measure. They threatened to "pay themselves" by confiscating goods and wealth from the suburbs of Constantinople if the emperor did not pay them what they were owed. He refused.

Thus the winter of 1203–4 was spent with the Venetians and the French joining together on various raids. The emperor remained safe behind his walls, doing nothing. He feared bringing out his numerically superior armies for the simple reason that they were cowardly, crooked, and poorly trained. As usual in the viper's nest of Byzantine politics, the government responded to the difficult situation with a palace coup. Alexius Mourtzouphlus, an imperial minister, first imprisoned and then strangled young Alexius IV. Blind old Isaac II conveniently died at about the same time. The traitor was then crowned Alexius V. With their imperial claimant dead, the Fourth Crusade declared war on Constantinople and its treacherous inhabitants.

There is a reason that the Fourth Crusade became for Venetians one of the proudest moments in their history. It was a monumental effort in which the largest, wealthiest, and best-fortified city in the Western world fell to an army of determined Venetians and their boats. The French helped, too, of course, but the attack, which came in April 1204, was solely a naval affair. Large merchant ships were lashed together two by two so that they could bring giant flying bridges to bear on Constantinople's northern seawalls. The hard-fought battle lasted several days, but in the end the Venetians and their allies successfully breached the walls and took the vast city behind them. The victory was, however, not simply due to the ingenuity of the Venetian sailors but to the extraordinarily poor quality of Constantinople's defenders. When faced with the slightest danger, the Byzantine soldiers fled like cattle.

For the next three days the westerners gorged themselves on the riches of Constantinople. Nicetas Choniates, a Byzantine senator who witnessed the sack of his beloved city, gave a graphic account of the violence with which the crusaders and other Europeans stripped clean the palaces, churches, and public places. Innumerable art treasures of antiquity were destroyed, melted down for coin, or broken apart for their precious gems. Of course, the Venetians took part in the looting as well. But, unlike the French and other Europeans, they had an appreciation for what they seized. Enrico Dandolo saved hundreds of items from destruction by having them crated up and sent back to Venice. There does not seem to have been any guiding principle behind what he chose to take—except, perhaps, that they were all rare and beautiful.

A visitor today to San Marco will see much of what Dandolo sent home. Indeed, it is impossible not to see it. The church of San Marco had sparse ornamentation in 1200. Today it is encrusted with marble slabs, arches, columns, and sculptures placed in an almost haphazard fashion wherever they might fit. Most of these came from Constantinople. Take, for example, the dark tetrarchs, mounted on a corner of the church very near the Ducal Palace. Each of these two porphyry sculptures depicts an Augustus and a Caesar (the emperor and the vice-emperor of the Roman Empire) embracing each other in a gesture of solidarity. Originally mounted on columns, they towered over a forum in Constantinople known as the Philadelphion, or place of brotherly love. There they represented the imperial structure of the late Roman Empire. In Venice, they represented nothing, but they were attractive and so they were cut to order and mounted on the bare corner. Today they share the area with tourists, who often rest there a moment before moving on to the next attraction. Few notice that the foot of one of the tetrarchs is white. It is a substitute, produced by the Venetians because the real one was lost during transit. The missing foot was discovered in excavations in Istanbul in the twentieth century and is now on display there in the Archaeological Museum.

By far the most famous objects that Dandolo saved were the four bronze horses of San Marco. Few statues have as rich a history as these fascinating steeds. These remarkable statues are life-size depictions of a team that once pulled a quadriga (two-wheeled chariot) and a bronze charioteer. The horses are a Roman copy of a Greek masterwork, and were probably cast around the time of Christ or a century or two after. In the fourth or fifth century they were moved to Constantinople, where they pulled their triumphant charioteer for centuries above the starting gates of the lavish Hippodrome. What happened to the driver is unknown, but the four horses were unbridled, boxed up, and sent to Venice. We can imagine the surprise with which the Venetians unpacked this strange gift. Why send bronze horses to a city without real ones? For a few years the Venetians argued over where to place them, but finally decided on the facade of San Marco. Why put them in Venice's most prominent location? There is no connection between St. Mark and horses, no connection between the Piazza and horses. Despite modern attempts to divine some meaning in the horses' placement, we are left with the same answer. Like every other item from Constantinople that was used to ornament the church of San Marco—both inside and out— the horses were placed on the facade because they looked good there.

For the pragmatic, no-nonsense merchants of Venice that was reason enough.

The fall of Constantinople may have been a boon to the church of San Marco, but it was a real danger to the people of Venice. The lion's share of Venice's overseas business went through Byzantine ports—especially Constantinople. The fall of the city and its empire meant uncertainty, disorder, and danger—all of which were bad for business. The doge understood this perfectly. His main objective was to restore stability to the region as soon as possible.

The first order of business was to select a new emperor. Six Venetians and six non-Venetians were chosen to make that decision. There were two main contenders for the position: Boniface of Montferrat, the titular leader of the Crusade, and Baldwin of Flanders, a powerful count with strong support among the French barons. With the six non-Venetian electors split between these two leaders it would have been a simple thing for the Venetians to hand the imperial throne to their doge. Yet Dandolo did not want the job. He was ninety-seven years old and eager to return home. More importantly, he feared that if a Venetian was elected emperor, the French would abandon Constantinople, leaving it defenseless. The Venetian electors were, however, in a position to break the tie between the other two imperial hopefuls. They chose Baldwin. It was largely a vote against Boniface, who was a friend of Genoa and whose family was closely entwined with the previous Byzantine dynasty. Baldwin brought none of that baggage and he was more likely to keep the French knights in the East. Since the Venetians did not receive the throne, the crusaders ceded the patriarchate of Constantinople to them.

On May 16, in a rich ceremony in Hagia Sophia, Catholic clergy presided over the coronation of Baldwin I, emperor of Constantinople. The event was splendid. The leading barons and Venetian nobles rode in procession to the palace to collect the emperor-elect and then proceeded to Hagia Sophia. There Baldwin was bedecked in the marvelously rich garments of a Roman emperor. Precious stones were so copious on his attire that it is a wonder he could carry them all. Even his shoes were studded with jewels. His mantle bore the imperial eagles in rubies, so brilliant that it seemed to one observer that it was on fire. Baldwin proceeded through the church to the high altar, accompanied by Louis of Blois, bearing the imperial standard; Hugh of St. Pol, carrying the imperial sword; and Boniface of Montferrat, holding the imperial crown that had just eluded him. Baldwin knelt before the altar and the crown was taken up by the crusader bishops and blessed. Then all of them, each holding the crown by one hand, placed it on Baldwin's head and proclaimed him emperor. Around the new Augustus's neck they hung a ruby the size of an apple that had formerly belonged to Manuel I Comnenus.

At once a committee was assembled to divide up the Byzantine Empire among the victors. There were a few areas that were off-limits to the committee. Crete was one. A strategic and commercially important island, Crete had previously been given to Boniface by Alexius IV as a bonus for putting him on the throne. Now that Byzantium lay in ruins, Boniface was more interested in claiming Thessalonica, the second city of the empire. He offered to sell his rights over Crete to the Genoese. But Dandolo was quicker. He purchased Crete from Boniface for one thousand silver marks.

And that was not all Venice had coming. According to an agreement among the crusaders before the conquest, the city and empire were to be divided, with one-quarter going to the emperor and the other three-quarters split between the Venetians and the French. In other words, Venice stood to receive three-eighths of the Byzantine Empire. The partition committee awarded Venice a large section of Constantinople near the harbor, the Sea of Marmara shoreline from Heraclea to the end of Gallipoli, and the city of Adrianople. Venice was also given rights to the islands of Salamis, Aegina, Andros, and both ends of Negroponte as well as the Gulf of Corinth and the Morea (Peloponnese). Finally, Venetians received all the lands of western Greece along the Adriatic Sea. Like the purchase of Crete, these awards consisted only of the right to conquer the regions. Nevertheless, Dandolo immediately assumed a new title, which Venetian doges would proudly don for decades: "lord of three-eighths of the Roman Empire." It was to be a short-lived empire, one that modern historians call the Latin Empire of Constantinople, limping along for more than five decades until it finally collapsed in 1261.

Shortly after Baldwin's coronation the aged Enrico Dandolo died. He was buried with great pomp in the gallery of Hagia Sophia—a church that dwarfed Venice's magnificent San Marco. Doge Dandolo was the only person ever to be buried there in Christianity's largest church.

Thus was Venice transformed into a maritime empire—although not all at once, and certainly not without some trepidation. As business-men, the Venetians had a natural aversion to empires. They were expen-sive, troublesome ventures that kept one from focusing on the bottom line. Venice had long ago extended its control over cities along the Adri-atic Sea, yet for Venetians that was their sea, their home. While Venetian quarters could be found in cities throughout the eastern Mediterranean and Venetian convoys sailed in exotic waters, Venice had never ex-tended political or military power outside the confines of the Adriatic.

At first the government in Venice refused to accept the lands that Dandolo had won for them. Instead, the new doge, Pietro Ziani (1205–29), issued a general license for Venetians to conquer what they wished in those territories at their own expense. Once conquered, the lands would remain part of the Latin-ruled empire with no legal attachment to the Republic of Venice. Yet this strategy of pretending that nothing had changed did not work for long. The Genoese, still fuming that Dandolo had purchased Crete out from under them, launched an invasion of the island in 1206. They also unleashed pirates, such as the infamous Leone

Vetrano, who captured Corfu and set up operations against Venetian shipping along the Greek coast.

And so Venice declared war on Genoa. The first two fleets were commanded by Ranieri Dandolo, the only son of Enrico, who had served as vice-doge during his father's absence. He successfully ejected the pirates, capturing Corfu, Coron (Koroni), and Modon and invading Crete. During the warfare he was struck by an arrow and died in a Genoese prison a few days later. The war over Crete would drag on for another five years. Finally, in 1211, the Venetians defeated Genoa and established sole control over Crete. This island would remain a cornerstone of the Venetian empire for more than four centuries.

The Fourth Crusade had transformed Venice. What was conceived as a grand war in defense of the faith had become a doorway to empire. While it was happening, though, it seemed like nothing more than a source of trouble. Not only did the crusaders leave Venice holding the bill, but the Crusade itself veered wildly off course, finally destroying Venice's greatest trading partner. With stability in the Aegean shattered, the Venetians were forced to man their war galleys, expand into the chaotic ruins, and build a new overseas empire.

CHAPTER 7

MARCO POLO'S VENICE:
PROSPERITY, POWER, AND PIETY
IN THE THIRTEENTH CENTURY

At one time it was fashionable among historians to blame the outcome of the Fourth Crusade on Venice and Doge Dandolo, reasoning that since the Venetians profited from the conquest of Constantinople, they must have planned it. In the nineteenth and twentieth centuries this explanation was seasoned with a dash of Marxism that cast religion as a tool of bourgeois oppression. Thus, it was argued, the greedy Venetian capitalists used fake piety to persuade the naive crusaders to divert to Constantinople and win an empire for them. Crusade historians have long since abandoned this fiction for the simple reason that it makes no sense. The Fourth Crusade shattered the stable markets on which Venice depended and forced Venetian citizens to spend their lives and their treasure building an empire of their own to replace one that had been, for the most part, quite acceptable to them. Nonetheless, one still runs across in novels and guidebooks (the traditional last stand for poor history) those crafty Venetians cleverly twisting the Fourth Crusade to their own ends.

The entire period of the Latin Empire of Constantinople involved careful risk management for the Venetians. True, the doge had become "lord of three-eighths of the Roman Empire," but just what did that actually mean? The Venetians never attempted to claim all the lands that had been given to them in the Treaty of Partition, remaining content to acquire islands and ports of strategic importance in the Aegean in order to safeguard their merchants. Three-eighths of Constantinople also belonged to them, yet it was not the great city it had once been. On the eve of the crusader conquest as many as four hundred thousand people lived within the walls of the capital and probably more than a million in the metropolitan area. By the 1230s the population of Constantinople had declined to around forty thousand. Much of the city lay in ruins, decimated by the fires of 1203–4 and abandoned by its citizens. Nevertheless, Constantinople remained a thriving port and the Venetians were at least able to exclude their enemies—which meant the Genoese— from doing business there. Venice was supposed to have control over the patriarchate of Constantinople, but that, too, never happened. Pope Innocent III refused to ratify the election of the Venetian monk, Thomas Morosini, to the patriarchate, although he later appointed him to the office to keep peace in Constantinople. Subsequent patriarchs were Venetian, too, but Innocent and his successors worked tirelessly to maintain the freedom of the Catholic Church in the Byzantine East—and that meant fighting any attempt to make the patriarch of Constantinople as Venetian as the patriarch of Grado.

The Venetian community in Constantinople grew substantially after the conquest. After all, it owned a large portion of the city and had no serious commercial rivals. This led to the expansion of a Venetian government in Constantinople headed by an official known as a *podestà*, who had his own court of advisers much like the doge in Venice. Friction sometimes occurred between the home and provincial governments, but there was sufficient movement of people and goods between Venice and Constantinople that the two were never estranged. In the sixteenth century the historian Daniele Barbaro claimed that the provincial government in Constantinople had become so powerful that the home government seriously considered moving the capital from Venice to Constantinople. Historians used to give this story some credence, but in truth it never happened. Not only was this momentous debate left unremarked by earlier Venetian historians, the plan itself makes little sense. Moving the capital to a troublesome colony is not a victory for the mother country but its complete demise. No colonial power in history has ever contemplated, let alone enacted, such a plan. Another complication is the fact that Constantinople was already the seat of an empire. Even if the Venetians could have removed the French rulers (not an easy prospect), it would have meant war with just about everyone. The French would naturally take it badly, but so, too, would the pope. A Crusade against Venice would then not be out of the question. In return for all this strife Venice would have acquired a dilapidated capital surrounded by enemies while leaving behind the impregnable and prosperous city of the lagoon. No one, especially not a patriotic Venetian, would seriously consider so foolish a proposal.

This is not to say that Venice gained nothing from the conquest of Constantinople. Venetian military power grew dramatically in this period—all of it in response to the suddenly dangerous world in which the Venetians found themselves. The thirteenth century saw the creation of the state Arsenale, a vast workshop for the production of war vessels that would remain active for centuries—indeed, it remains a military installation to this day. Venetian expansion into the Aegean and eastern Mediterranean Seas also came at a fortuitous time. The recent victories of Genghis Khan in China and westward had allowed stable trade routes to develop along the Silk Road stretching from the Pacific Ocean to the markets of the Black Sea, Constantinople, and Syria. At the same time, the growth of towns, revival of trade, and return of capital in western Europe meant that there was now a ready market f

Eastern luxury goods, which the Venetians were in an ideal position to exploit.

Although Venice did well in the thirteenth century, the Latin Empire of Constantinople did not. Almost from its beginning, the new state foundered. Rival Greek states at Nicaea, Epiros, and Trebizond, along with the troublesome Bulgarians, jostled for dominance in the region. Tattered Constantinople was habitually short of money and reduced to begging the West for military and economic aid. Emperor Baldwin II (1228–61) spent his teenage years traveling from one European court to the next, receiving fine meals and high promises, but very little help. He was in Paris when he learned that his barons in Constantinople had pawned the precious relic of the Crown of Thorns, venerated in the imperial city for nearly a thousand years. It appears that a consortium of Venetian merchants in Constantinople had loaned the barons a large sum of money and were given the crown as collateral. If the funds were not repaid on time, the relic would be retained and sent back to Venice. Needless to say, the Venetian merchants hoped that the money would never be repaid.

In Paris, Baldwin II begged his kinsman, the young king of France, Louis IX (later St. Louis), to redeem the Crown of Thorns. Louis agreed, provided that the emperor make a gift of the crown to the French monarchy in gratitude for its support and hope for future aid. Baldwin agreed. With that settled, Louis sent two Dominican friars to Constantinople to pay the debt and claim the relic. When they arrived, however, they heard that the Venetian merchants had already packed it aboard ship and were making final preparations to sail for Venice. It was an odd scene indeed—a creditor trying desperately to avoid payment for a loan he hoped would go into default. Eventually the Dominicans caught up with the Venetians and delivered a bill of guarantee for the loan from Louis IX. Strictly speaking, that was not payment, so the Venetian merchants had some room to negotiate. They finally agreed that they would all sail together to Venice, where the Crown of Thorns would remain until the king of France could pay the outstanding debt. This they did, although weather and Greeks unsuccessfully conspired to keep the relic from leaving Constantinople. For several months after its arrival in Venice in early 1239, the Crown of Thorns was placed proudly on display in the church of San Marco. But all too quickly it was again packed up and transported across the Alps to Paris, where Louis received it with great joy. To house the relic, he constructed the spectacular Sainte-Chapelle. Amazingly, the Crown of Thorns weathered the storms of revolution and remains in Notre Dame today.

No amount of Venetian money could save the Latin Empire. The Greek ruler in Nicaea, John Vatatzes, managed to eliminate his rivals and surround enfeebled Constantinople. It seemed only a matter of time before the city would fall to him. Nevertheless, Vatatzes continued to encourage every effort to overcome the differences between Greek Orthodox and Catholic clergy in a vain attempt to reunify the Church and thereby receive Constantinople freely from the pope himself. The theological sticking points were fairly trivial—the use of leavened or unleavened bread in the Eucharist, the procession of the Holy Spirit from the Father or from the Father and the Son, and the primacy of Rome over all other sees. What could not be overcome, however, was the ever-growing animosity that Greeks felt for western Europeans. They had always judged westerners to be rude barbarians, the descendants of those who had destroyed the Roman Empire in the West. As a result, they often chalked up theological disputes to the poor state of education in the backward West.

Yet by the thirteenth century that line of reasoning no longer carried much weight. Europe had, in fact, surpassed the Byzantine East in wealth, power, and learning. The universities in France, England, and Italy produced world-class scholars who could defend Catholic theology and refused to be dismissed with the shake of a Greek head. The proceedings of dialogues between Orthodox prelates and Catholic friars in Nicaea still survive, and it is clear from those records that the Greeks had their hands full keeping up with the new apologists. Any member of an ancient culture, supplanted by a new and occasionally ungainly one, naturally resents the upstarts. In Byzantium this resentment had been growing for centuries. The crusader conquest of Constantinople in 1204 helped to feed it, but it by no means created it.

The Venetians stayed out of such theological discussions. They were busy enough simply policing the shipping lanes between Venice, Constantinople, Crete, and Syria. It was a difficult task, but the thirteenth-century Venetian chronicler, Martino Da Canale, assures us that they were extremely successful. An extraordinary amount of cargo made its way across the eastern Mediterranean and into Venetian markets, further expanding the wealth and population of the rapidly growing city. Venice's primary rival at this time was Genoa, whose merchants did business in many of the same areas (although the Genoese remained unwelcome in Constantinople). On occasion Venetians and Genoese would swallow their dislike and band together against a common enemy, as they did with Emperor Frederick II, who waged war across Italy against the popes and the Lombards. But usually, the two powers entertained some level of aggression. It was not always easy to gauge their relations. Although Venice had an increasingly complex government to oversee their expanding empire, the Genoese did business in a much more casual manner, as families struggled against one another for dominance. Against their enemies Venetians sent war fleets; Genoese sent pirates.

In 1255 a major war broke out between Venice and Genoa. It began in Acre, the sprawling port city of the ever-diminishing crusader kingdom in Syria. Indeed, by 1255 there was little left of the old kingdom beyond Acre. But the growing danger from the Mamluk empire in Egypt did not draw the Christian groups together, so consumed were they by factionalism. The Venetians and Genoese each had their own quarters in Acre. A few years earlier a Venetian had murdered a Genoese resident, and anger over that incident grew so heated that a Genoese mob took up arms and attacked the Venetian Quarter, killing many. Venice retaliated by sending a fleet under the command of Lorenzo Tiepolo, the son of a previous doge, who broke the chain of the Acre harbor, burned the Genoese ships docked there, and occupied St. Sabas, a Genoese church or abbey on the border of the two quarters. Thus began the War of St. Sabas, a battle between two Western powers that would play out in the Eastern theater of Syria. After several major engagements at Acre and Tyre, the Genoese were at last defeated, giving Venice a bittersweet victory in a kingdom that was already approaching death.

Much the same could be said of Venice's position at that time in Constantinople. Upset by their defeat at Acre, the Genoese allied themselves with Michael Palaeologus, the regent of the Nicene emperor who would soon take the crown for himself. Like Vatatzes before him, Palaeologus was determined to win back Constantinople and Genoa was determined to help—provided that it harmed Venice in the process. Indeed, even a papal excommunication and interdict of Genoa did not shake the Genoese commitment to supporting the Greeks. In 1261 a portion of Constantinople's fortifications was left unguarded and Michael Palaeologus's nearby forces simply entered and secured the city. The Venetians in Constantinople were prepared to fight, but when Michael offered to allow them to leave with their vessels and goods intact, they accepted. And so the Latin Empire, born of the Fourth Crusade in 1204, was in an instant extinct. In truth, it had rarely been more than the city of Constantinople. After seizing the Byzantine throne for himself, Emperor Michael VIII Palaeologus rewarded the Genoese by allowing them to establish themselves in Constantinople at Galata as well as in port cities in the Black Sea. This last concession was a particularly harmful blow to Venice, for these ports were at the end of the Silk Road. The money that could be made in the Black Sea was extraordinary, and the Genoese had usurped Venice's position there.

The loss of Constantinople did nothing, however, to diminish Venice's holdings in the Aegean and the Adriatic, as well as the all-important island of Crete. Michael VIII may have hoped that the Genoese, who were now serving as Byzantium's navy, could be used to neutralize Venetian power in the region. Yet Michael's success did not transfer to Genoa. In battle after battle in the Aegean, the Venetians kept the upper hand against their rivals. Changing tactics, the emperor began to make overtures to the Venetians. He returned to their merchants some portions of Constantinople, although he still excluded Venice from the Black Sea. Finally, in 1268, the Venetians were fully reinstated in the Byzantine Empire. Once again they returned to their quarter in Constantinople, where they had done business for centuries. Genoa, of course, was less than pleased.

Although Venetians could be found in almost every market or town of any size in the East, few of them ever traveled as far away as Marco Polo—arguably the most famous Venetian who ever lived. The Polos were a well-established family in Venice who had made their fortune in overseas trade and had settled in various portions of the city. They were not adventurers, but they were good businessmen always seeking new markets. Marco's father, Nicolò, and his uncle, Maffeo, had been doing business in Constantinople in 1260—just one year before it fell to Michael Palaeologus. There they had purchased a collection of jewels and sailed north into the Black Sea with plans to sell the precious stones to some Mongol princes, who had the money and taste for such lavishness. They traveled to the court of Barka Khan on the Volga River, where they made a good return on their investment and so decided to remain for the rest of the year. Just then, however, a war between Barka and the khan of Persia broke out, making the roads back to the Black Sea unsafe. When word reached the Polos that Constantinople had fallen and Venetians were no longer welcome there, they decided to venture eastward, crossing the desert to Bukhara (today in Uzbekistan), where they remained for three years, learning the languages and customs of the Mongols while continuing to make a good living buying, selling, and offering occasional advice about the West. While there, they became friendly with some ambassadors from the khan of Persia who were on their way to the court of the new ruler of the Mongol Empire, the Great Khan, Kublai. Several Catholic missionaries had been sent to the Mongols during the preceding decades. The ambassadors assured the Polos that Kublai was fascinated by the Catholic religion and western European culture in general, and that he would lavish the Venetians with gifts and honors if they would visit him. That was enough for the Polos. They enthusiastically joined the caravan and headed east.

When the Polo brothers arrived at the court of the Great Khan (which was probably at Karakorum in Mongolia), Kublai treated them like royalty and peppered them with every sort of question about the Western world, just as the Persians said he would. He was eager to know about the Roman emperors, by which he meant the German and Byzantine rulers. The new forms of learning that could be found in European universities also fascinated him. Indeed, he wrote a letter to Pope Clement IV (1265–68) asking him to send a hundred scholars who could teach the Mongols about the *trivium* and *quadrivium* (advanced courses of study) and who could convince them of the truth of the Catholic faith. Kublai Khan was so interested in Christianity that he asked the Polo brothers to personally deliver his letter to the pope and, on the way, to acquire some of the oil used to light the lamp of the Holy Sepulcher in Jerusalem.

Duly tasked, the brothers made the long journey back to Venice, finally arriving in 1269. They discovered, however, that Clement was dead and the cardinals deadlocked on his replacement. Indeed, there would be no new pope until the election of Gregory X two years later. Gregory, who had previously been a papal legate in Egypt and Acre, was keenly interested in the Great Khan's letter. Although the westward expansion of the vast Mongol Empire worried Europeans, many also saw in it a ray of hope. The Christian West had run upon hard times, and was in desperate need of allies wherever they could be found. Muslim power had soared under Sultan Baybars of Egypt, who waged relentless jihad against Christians with his fearsome slave armies, known as Mamluks. The battered remnants of the Christian states of the eastern Mediterranean were no match for him. In 1263 Baybars led a devastating raid into Galilee and destroyed the cathedral of Nazareth there. Two years later he conquered Christian Caesarea and Arsuf. In 1266 he took the Templar fortress of Safad, massacring the inhabitants after promising to spare their lives, and he did much the same to the city of Jaffa the following year. The greatest blow to Christendom, though, came with Baybars's brutal conquest of Antioch in 1268. The sultan ordered the doors of the city closed and the inhabitants, including thousands of women and children, massacred. The atrocity shocked even Muslim chroniclers. Upset to learn that the ruler of Antioch, Count Bohemond VI, was absent for the event, Baybars even sent him a letter describing the carnage that he missed:

You would have seen your knights prostrate beneath the horses' hooves, your houses stormed by pillagers and ransacked by looters, your wealth weighed by the quintal, your women sold four at a time and bought for a dinar of your own money! You would have seen the crosses in your churches smashed, the pages of the false Gospels scattered, the Patriarchs' tombs overturned. You would have seen your Muslim enemy trampling on the place where you celebrate the Mass, cutting the throats of monks, priests and deacons upon the altars, bringing sudden death to the Patriarchs and slavery to the royal princes. You would have seen fire running through your palaces, your dead burned in this world before going down to the fires of the next, your palace lying unrecognizable, the Church of St. Paul and the Cathedral of

St. Peter pulled down and destroyed; then you would have said: "Would that I were dust, and that no letter had ever brought me such news!"

With the relentless expansion of Islamic armies into Christian territories, it is not surprising that many in the West wondered when, or if, God would act to save them. More than a century earlier a story had begun circulating in Europe of a "Prester John." It was said that this mysterious figure was a powerful and wise monarch who ruled over a vast and extraordinarily wealthy Oriental empire. Some claimed that he was the successor of one of the Magi who had adored Christ in Bethlehem. The story gained wide currency and was considered at least plausible by both peasants and potentates alike. Faced with the possibility of the extinction of the Christian West, Prester John seemed to offer a way out. If the Christians of Europe could inform him of their plight, surely he would come to their rescue by crushing their Muslim oppressors.

The Great Khan certainly seemed like Prester John. He had a vast empire that had already conquered Muslim Persia as well as the capital of the Muslim caliphate in Baghdad. Many of the Mongol leaders were, in fact, Eastern Christians known as Nestorians. Previous popes and even King Louis IX of France had written to earlier Great Khans seeking aid and information, but with less than encouraging results. In truth, the Mongols did not factor religion into their military campaigns, but simply conquered whoever was in their path. It just so happened that Muslims were in their path. Kublai Khan's interest in Christianity, however, seemed like a breakthrough. Pope Gregory X penned a reply letter, which he gave to the Polo brothers to return to Kublai. Rather than send the requested hundred scholars (which would have been expensive and difficult in any case), the pope sent two Dominicans. The Polos were also joined by Nicolò's son, the adventurous and occasionally theatrical seventeen-year-old Marco.

The group faced a long and difficult journey eastward, beset by war, storms, and severe cold. The Dominicans made it only as far as Armenia before local violence convinced them to return home. The three Polos pressed onward all the way to Beijing, now the capital of the Mongol Empire, where they found the Great Khan who was overjoyed to see them. He devoured the pope's letter and revered the holy oil from Jerusalem. But he was most impressed by young Marco Polo, with whom he became quite close. In later years he would even send Marco to represent him in distant lands. Kublai Khan particularly liked Marco's very Venetian approach to his ambassadorships. In Venice, ambassadors were essentially spies; it was their job not only to relate information to a foreign court but also to send back to the Venetian government dispatches reporting everything of importance, be it customs, rumors, or even local foods. Marco did the same for the Great Khan. For example, when reporting on the Hindus of central India, he wrote:

The people go to battle with lances and shields, but without clothing, and are a despicable unwarlike race. They do not kill cattle nor any kind of animals for food, but when they wish to eat the meat of sheep or other animals or birds they hire Muslims, who are not bound by the same laws and customs, to slaughter them. Both men and women wash their whole bodies in water twice every day, that is, in the morning and the evening. Until this ablution has taken place they neither eat nor drink; and the person who should neglect this observance would be regarded as a heretic. . . . When they drink they do not put the vessel to the mouth, but hold it above the head and pour the liquid into the mouth, not letting the vessel on any account touch their lips. When they give a drink to a stranger they do not hand the vessel to him, but, if he does not have his own vessel, they pour the wine or other liquid into his hands from which he drinks it as from a cup.

These detailed reports formed the basis of Marco Polo's famous *Travels*, a book that devotes much more attention to foreign lands than to the royal court at Beijing.

Marco Polo remained under the employ of Kublai Khan for almost two decades. His travels brought him across the length and breadth of the massive Mongol Empire and as far beyond as Sumatra and perhaps even Japan. After so long away from home, the Polos finally petitioned the khan to give them leave to return. But Kublai refused, not wanting to lose so useful a friend as Marco. He was finally persuaded, however, to allow the experienced Venetian travelers to escort an important princess to her new husband, the khan of Persia. Kublai sent them away with many ships, much gold, lavish presents, and letters for the leaders of Europe. The journey westward was not easy, and it took several years for the travelers to make their way to Persia and then to reach Trebizond, Constantinople, and finally Venice. When they arrived the three travelers, dressed in rough Mongol garb and now more than twenty-five years older, were almost unrecognizable, even to their family. Word soon spread across Venice of the dramatic return of the Polos and, of course, everyone wanted to hear their stories. Marco never tired of telling them. They were tales of wonder so filled with multitudes of people, goods, and riches that many Venetians began to suspect Marco of rather blatant exaggeration. Indeed, he was soon known on the streets of Venice as Il Milione, which is perhaps best translated as "Mr. Millions."

Although they might be suspected of hyperbole, no one could doubt that the Polos had returned with extraordinary wealth. They built a new family palazzo in the parish of San Giovanni Crisostomo, which still remains today at the Corte del Milion. Later Venetian writers told compelling stories about the return of Marco Polo, which, given the travelers' love of the dramatic, may or may not be true. In one, told by Giambattista Ramusio in the sixteenth century, the three travelers gave a lavish banquet in their palazzo to celebrate their return. During each course, servants brought new robes of the richest satins and velvets for the Polos to wear. Finally, when the feast was concluded, Marco Polo left the chamber and returned in the dirty Mongol robe that he had worn during his journey to Venice. This naturally caused a stir among the guests—and not a little indignation. Then, on cue, Nicolò and Maffeo rose, approached Marco with daggers, and cut out the lining of the tattered garment. Onto the floor spilled hundreds of diamonds, emeralds, and rubies—the magnificent tokens of the Great Khan's affection.

It was not the Polo fortune, though, that was enriching Venice in the thirteenth century. Every day in the Rialto markets sums of money that dwarfed the cascading gems of Marco Polo's robe changed hands between Venetian and foreign merchants. Venice's location near roads and rivers snaking into Europe and its maritime dominance of the Adriatic continued to make it a natural place to do business. Every sort of commodity could be found in Venice, which served as a major clearinghouse for East-West commerce. The burgeoning wealth of the Venetians could be seen clearly enough in the physical changes to the city. It was during the thirteenth century that the basic framework of the Venice that we see today was set. The canals were dredged, the land stabilized, the areas defined. No longer a collection of islands, Venice had become a single great and utterly unique city. It was probably during the reign of Doge Vitale II Michiel, whose murder ushered in Venice's governmental reforms, that the city was divided into six *sestieri* (districts) for administrative purposes. Those six—San Marco, Castello, Canareggio, Santa Croce, San Polo, and Dorsoduro—are still used today, not only for local administration but also for the delivery of mail. (Addresses in Venice are notoriously difficult to decipher because they consist of only a number and a sestiere.)

The Piazza San Marco had already begun to take on its current form in the twelfth century. In the thirteenth century the Grand Canal did as well. Before 1200 the focus of life for most Venetians was the open campo outside each island compound's church. However, as the city filled up, becoming one rather than many, the divisions between those compounds were blurred. The great open space of the Piazza San Marco became the city's campo—a place for the citizens of a unified state to gather. In the same way, the Grand Canal became its central boulevard, filled with traffic of all kinds. Where the palaces of rich Venetians had previously faced their local campi, they now turned toward the Grand Canal. The wealthiest Venetians jostled for position along the waterway, each attempting to outdo the other in grandeur. The oldest surviving such palazzo is the Ca' Farsetti, built by Ranieri Dandolo, the son of Doge Enrico Dandolo. This impressive Gothic structure near the Rialto Bridge is today used as Venice's city hall. The old conquering doge, who came of age during the mid-twelfth century, had lived in a modest wooden family home facing the campo of San Luca on the site of what is today the Palazzo Corner-Valmaran. His son, though, built a grand stone structure that provided not only visibility for the Dandolo family but also room for various brothers, spouses, and children to live undisturbed, and warehouse space for conducting the family business. This style of palazzo would become characteristic of Venice—a family home that was at once attractive and functional. However, unlike family palaces in other Italian cities, the Venetian structures remained unfortified—a feature that speaks volumes about the lack of factionalism and lawlessness in the Republic of Venice.

Although the Christian world was shrinking during the Middle Ages, the people of Europe remained intensely pious. Indeed, the victories of Islam only underscored for Christians the displeasure of God and the urgent need to repent and return to him. Lay piety movements swept across Europe, especially in the growing towns and cities of the thirteenth century. Nowhere was this more evident than Venice, which continued to expand in wealth and size. Venetians donated much of their growing wealth to ecclesiastical institutions, which in turn meant larger parish churches and the promotion of additional monasteries. In the thirteenth century this also meant the rapid acceptance of the mendicant orders. The first of these new orders was founded by St. Francis of Assisi, the son of a wealthy Italian cloth merchant. Francis and his companions gave up all their possessions to preach and minister to the poor in the expanding urban centers of Europe. They embraced humility, closely following the simple instructions that Jesus Christ had given to his apostles in Matthew 10:8: "Freely have you received; freely give." In 1210 Pope Innocent III had approved the new Order of the Friars Minor (Little Brothers), also known as the Franciscans. It grew at an astonishing rate. The friars were revered for their selflessness and holiness. As wealth grew in the commercial cities of northern Italy, many were the merchants who considered how rich men tended to fare in the parables and sermons of Christ. The Franciscans, who owned nothing, offered these wealthy men a way to spiritual fulfillment, either by joining the order or financially supporting its charitable work. St. Francis attained a level of popularity in medieval Europe similar to that of modern music and movie stars (although the quiet humility of Francis has no modern parallel in the entertainment industry). He visited Venice in 1219 on his way to join the Fifth Crusade and again in 1220 on his return from Egypt. According to tradition, Francis founded a new convent on a Venetian island, which was subsequently named for him and his voyage: San Francesco del Deserto.

The Franciscans were not the only friars in the streets of Venice. While Francis was forming his order, another preacher, St. Dominic, was working in southern France to combat the Cathar heresy, a dualist belief that rejected the Catholic Church. Innocent III approved the Dominican order in 1216 and it spread almost as quickly as the Franciscans. Like the Franciscans, the Dominicans lived and worked in the streets, owning nothing. But Dominic had founded an order of preachers equipped to defend the Catholic faith and to care for the souls of the faithful. Dominicans, therefore, valued education more than Franciscans did—at least at first. Both orders, however, typified a spirit of renewal and reform that permeated late medieval Europe.

In the early years of the Franciscan order one could support the friars with food, shelter, and other kindnesses, but little else. They had no churches—indeed, St. Francis had personally pulled apart a structure that the people of Assisi had attempted to build for him. But Francis died in 1226 and shortly thereafter Franciscan rules on property usage were modified. The Venetians, who included a good share of wealthy men concerned for the health of their souls, moved quickly to establish the friars in their own city. Among them was Doge Giacomo Tiepolo (1229–49), a man from one of Venice's old families who had served as the first governor of Crete and *podestà* of the Venetian colony in Constantinople before his election as doge. Tiepolo donated empty lands in the city to the Franciscans and Dominicans for the construction of churches. To the Dominicans went a marshy area north of the parish of Santa Maria Formosa on which the friars had already built a small oratory. Tiepolo's land grant of June 1234, which survives, has an urgency that medieval men and women often felt for the spiritual well-being of their community. "Their [the Dominicans'] presence in the city of Venice," Tiepolo wrote, "is seen by us and the entire population as a pressing necessity."

The Dominicans began at once building a stone church, which they dedicated to Saints John and Paul. The John and Paul in question, however, were not the famous apostles of the New Testament, but two fourth-century martyrs who were the patrons of the Dominican church in Rome. SS. Giovanni e Paolo (or, as it became known in Venetian, Zanipolo) was completed quickly, thanks to steady contributions from numerous devout Venetians. Indeed, so many donations continued to flow in even after the church was completed that the Dominicans decided to demolish it in 1333 and begin work on the present massive Italian Gothic structure. As preachers and theologians, the Dominicans had become the guardians of orthodox belief, the protectors of Christian truth. They were holy men and it is not surprising, then, that people wanted to be as close to them as possible. In Venice, this can be seen in the desire of doges to be buried in the Dominicans' great church. At least twenty-five Venetian doges still rest in its confines. The old practice of donning a Benedictine habit on one's deathbed and choosing burial among the monks of a monastery was replaced with a tomb among the friars wearing the coarse habit of the street preachers. The Dominicans' benefactor, Doge Giacomo Tiepolo, was buried at SS. Giovanni e Paolo in a stone sarcophagus placed in a courtyard before the church. In 1431 his tomb—which also holds his son, Doge Lorenzo Tiepolo (1268–75)—was lifted off the ground and mounted on the facade of the new Gothic church. There it remains today, to the left of the main door, largely ignored by everyone save the Venetian children who use it as a soccer goal.

Two years after Doge Giacomo Tiepolo's grant to the Dominicans, an abandoned abbey near the parish of San Tomà was likewise donated to the Franciscans. In 1250 they began construction there on a church dedicated to the Assumption of the Blessed Virgin. Santa Maria Gloriosa dei Frari (or just the Frari, as Venetians soon called it) benefited from the same levels of financial support that helped the Dominicans across town. The first Franciscan church was completed in 1338 and almost immediately a new one was begun. Like SS. Giovanni e Paolo, the new Frari was a magnificent Gothic church, rivaling the Dominican structure in every way. And, indeed, rivalry between the two orders was at least one factor in their respective efforts. Many were the prominent Venetians who wished to be buried in this soaring temple, although it was not as popular with the doges as Zanipolo. The Frari remains today an amazing structure, decorated with Renaissance masterworks, yet still maintaining its medieval ambience.

Doge Giacomo Tiepolo was also long remembered for his Statuto of 1242. This extensive codification of Venetian civil law was built on the work of Doge Enrico Dandolo (or perhaps his son as vice-doge) to produce an organized collection of laws and procedures for administering justice with regard to property claims. Because population was exploding within the confines of a shifting geography, thirteenth-century Venice had no shortage of property disputes. The wealthier and more populous the city became, the more cases came before the city's judges. In earlier centuries these were argued before the doge, accompanied later by his court, yet the rise of the wealthy middle class in Venice and the ballooning caseload forced substantial changes in the system. Plaintiffs would bring their disputes to at least two judges and be represented by at least one advocate (usually someone well acquainted with the law, or at least with the judges). Preliminary hearings and testimonies could occur at various places in the city, but the final judgment for all cases still required the presence of the doge, who had almost nothing to do with the decisions themselves. Only when the judges were deadlocked could he decide a case. Tiepolo's Statuto was of extraordinary importance, forming the basis of Venetian civil law for several centuries.

Venetian government also grew and evolved to meet the needs of the teeming metropolis. The conservative Venetians cherished their traditions, yet allied with their solid business sense was a constant search for improvement and refinement. The growing number of Venetian citizens and the skyrocketing levels of wealth continued apace. As had been true for centuries, new families who wanted political power to match their economic clout were able to percolate to the top of Venetian society. Throughout the early thirteenth century the number of councillors in the doge's court continued to grow. Indeed, the group became so large that it began meeting separately from the doge and his Small Council. This larger group ultimately became the Great Council, the engine of the Venetian republic. Like its ad hoc predecessors, the Great

Council was made up of important men from wealthy families, and as their numbers grew, they became the representatives of the people of Venice. They were not strictly representative, of course, since they were not directly elected by the citizens. Rather, membership in the Great Council was by internal election and the position was renewable indefinitely. However, the members, who numbered perhaps four hundred or more by the mid-thirteenth century, lived in parishes across the city and were closely associated with the laborers and guildsmen in their neighborhoods. Since all political power in Venice flowed from the people, the Great Council became the new face of that power.

As with any such body, there was a tendency toward factionalism and party loyalty. The Venetians, though, fought this tendency with every fiber of their will. Perhaps the well-traveled Venetians saw enough of the carnage and ruin that factional warfare had produced in other Italian cities and the Byzantine Empire to acquire a healthy fear of it at home. Or perhaps their aversion to factionalism was simply a determination by each wealthy family that if it alone could not rule Venice, no one else would. Whatever the case, the organization of the Venetian government would always be one of multitudes of checks and balances, each designed to keep any one man or group of men from acquiring extraordinary power.

This dynamic is most visible in the labyrinthine procedures that the Venetians developed to elect their doges. Gone were the days when the people would pour into an open area and begin shouting names. The election committee established in 1178 continued, although it was expanded to forty-one members to avoid the possibility of deadlock. But what if a faction was able to stack the forty-one to claim the dogeship for itself? The new Venetian system made that impossible. It was designed to filter out partisanship while enlisting the wisdom of men and the will of God to make the best choice for the people of Venice.

The election began with the assembling of the Great Council. After the procedures were read aloud, an urn was filled with wax balls, one for each member. Within thirty of those balls was a slip of parchment reading simply "Elector." The Venetians prayed before and during the assembly that God would make his will known through the drawing of lots. In random order each of the members of the Great Council walked to the urn. A boy, who had been plucked from the streets at random, withdrew a ball for each of the councillors. If it contained parchment, the member's name would be announced and he would go into an adjoining room. At the same time, any other members from the new elector's family departed from the Great Council Chamber, since only one person from each clan was allowed to serve on any electoral committee. This process naturally took some time, but at the end the thirty electors were sworn in to do their duty.

Yet it was not these thirty who would elect the doge. Indeed, this was not the end of the process, but its very beginning. Another urn was promptly produced and the thirty drew wax balls again to reduce them by lot to nine. Then those nine prayed for wisdom and elected a committee of forty men, who were summoned to the chamber to take over the process. Wax balls were again produced and those forty were reduced to twelve. The twelve survivors then cast ballots for a new committee of twenty-five electors. When the twenty-five were sworn in, they marched to the urn and drew more balls until only nine remained. Those nine then elected a new committee of forty-five men. The forty-five drew wax balls and were reduced to eleven. After so many elections and lotteries it was the solemn charge of these eleven men to elect, not the doge, but the final electoral committee of forty-one!

The meeting of the final forty-one was filled with ceremony and prayer. The electors were locked away in the palace so that they could not be influenced by anyone outside. First, forty-one parchments—each with a number from one to forty-one—were randomly distributed to the electors. Then, beginning with the elector that held number one, each would stand and nominate a Venetian to be the next doge. There was a fair bit of repetition in these nominations, since there is no record of there ever having been more than seven or eight men nominated. After the nominations the first nominator would usually say something regarding his reasons for choosing this particular man. Then the nominee himself would be summoned (if he was not already an elector) and he would make a short speech. He would then be locked away in a small room while the electors brought up every rumor or reason they could muster why the nominee should not be doge. The nominee then returned to the chamber and the objections were read to him, without attribution to any members. This was his opportunity to refute the criticisms and charges. Afterward, he was again removed and the same opportunity was given to members who wished to cite reasons why the nominee was suitable. Finally, the forty-one members proceeded in order toward the head of the room, where there was a white box (for the nominee) and a red box (against the nominee). The electors anonymously placed a red ball inscribed with a cross into the box of their choice. After the ballot, the white box was opened, and if it had twenty-five balls inside, the nominee was elected. If not, the entire process was repeated for the second nominee, and then the third, and so on.

This process of choosing the highest office in Venice was obviously not meant to be streamlined. Quite the opposite—it was meant to be so cumbersome that only God could influence it. The new doge was still presented to the people of the city for their approval, but there was no means for them to reject him short of riot. The usual response, though, was one of joy—and not only because the newly crowned doge threw gold coins to the people. The peaceful and secure election was an affirmation of the stability of Venice—and stability is not only pleasant, but extremely good for business.

CHAPTER 8

THE DISCOVERY OF THE WEST:
WAR, WEALTH, AND REFORM IN THE
EARLY FOURTEENTH CENTURY

In 1289 Doge Giovanni Dandolo, a kinsman of the conqueror of Constantinople, died and was buried with modest ceremonies in the courtyard of SS. Giovanni e Paolo. At once the complex wheels of the Venetian election system began to turn. However, for reasons that are still not clear, a large mob of Venetians assembled in the Piazza San Marco and demanded that a certain Giacomo Tiepolo be crowned as the new doge. Tiepolo was certainly a reasonable choice. His family was well respected. His grandfather and namesake was the famous Doge Giacomo Tiepolo, who had so eagerly welcomed the Franciscans and Dominicans to Venice. His father, Lorenzo Tiepolo, had also served Venice as doge and now rested with his father in the richly decorated tomb before the church of the friars. Giacomo the younger had repeatedly distinguished himself by victoriously commanding Venetian war fleets at home and abroad.

The problem was not the man, but the method. The people who assembled at San Marco were invoking a means of electing doges that had not been used in more than a century. It was supposed to have been abandoned, replaced by the new, complex election process in the Great Council. Suddenly the political reforms painstakingly enacted to free the government from the caprices of the mob seemed dangerously fragile.

This reborn arengo of citizens seemed likely to prevail. The Great Council immediately suspended its own election to see what would happen next. Had the arengo wrested back the right to elect Venice's doge, it is difficult to see how the Great Council could have held on to other powers that it had also assumed in the people's name. And had that happened, the history of Venice might well have progressed very much like that of other Italian city-states, where powerful families acquired despotic control through violence, riots, and intimidation.

But that did not happen. Out of patriotism, fear, or perhaps a little of both, the beloved Giacomo Tiepolo declined the people's honor and quickly retired to his home on the terra firma. His departure instantly deflated the movement. The Great Council, therefore, continued its deliberations and in the end elected Pietro Gradenigo (1289–1311), a distinguished public servant from one of Venice's oldest families. Although the people dutifully approved the choice, there was no mistaking the grumbling in all parts of the city.

The election of 1289 exposed a clear flaw in the Venetian republican system—but it was not in the electoral process; rather, it was in the constitution of the Great Council itself. The increasing growth of Venice's population and wealth had placed a strain on the council. As more families rose to economic prominence, they naturally sought election to the Great Council for their own members. However, the council, which already numbered some five hundred seats in 1289, was jammed full of important men from important families. Some of those families were revered for their antiquity, although no longer for their wealth. The current members of the Great Council were not, in any case, willing to make room for nouveaux riches who clamored to join the most exclusive club in Venice.

And there was also the problem of foreigners. The cosmopolitan population of the merchant city had long consisted of many foreigners, some of whom married into affluent Venetian families and thereby sought access to political power. Recent events in the East had further complicated matters by forcing thousands of Venetian citizens who had lived abroad most or all of their lives to relocate to the mother country. This was especially true after 1291, when a Muslim army conquered the city of Acre, the last remnant of the crusader states in Syria and a major port city for Venice. These returning expatriates were legally Venetian, but culturally foreign. Were they really the sort that should take a place in the Great Council?

Since the Great Council's primary job was electing people to high government positions, and since membership in the Great Council was necessary to attain those positions, the body had become the gatekeeper for power and prestige in Venice. The problem was that it also elected itself, and so its members were naturally unwilling to welcome new groups that they thought beneath them, preferring instead to defend the exclusiveness of their own positions. Tensions in Venice between those who were in and those who wanted in became palpable, and had already led to several unsuccessful proposals for reform. It seems likely that the sudden appearance of the arengo in 1289 was itself a manifestation of those tensions. Those who could not gain entry into the Great Council were sufficiently frustrated that they had decided to strip the body of one of its most important functions. That their attempt ultimately failed hardly lessened their frustration with the concentration of power.

The new doge Pietro Gradenigo and his advisers worked hard to find a solution to this problem, but it seemed that there was always a constituency that opposed any particular reform. At last, they hit upon an answer—a slow, gradual reform that would preserve the integrity of the Great Council while relieving the stresses caused by its inability to represent all the interests of the burgeoning city. The size limit of the legislative body would be instantly abolished. All Venetians currently in the Great Council or who had served in it during the four previous years could become full members for life with the approval of only twelve of the Forty—a body drawn from the Great Council that oversaw elections and the evaluation of members. In practice, these reforms meant that virtually every man who had made it into the Great Council in recent years was henceforth a permanent member. Furthermore, new members could be introduced by a simple nomination of three current members, confirmation by the doge and his court, and the approval of twelve of the Forty. The bar, in other words, was not only attainable, but even rather low. In 1297 the Great Council confirmed the entire package of reforms.

The result was a dramatic expansion of the Great Council. By 1300 it had more than 1,100 members. In other words, approximately 1 percent of the Venetian population were members of the Great Council—an extremely high rate for a representative government. (By contrast, representation in the U.S. government consists of 0.0002 percent of the population.) Violent dissatisfaction with the Venetian government withered as some two hundred new families entered the Great Council and, thereby, other high-ranking positions. New families with considerable economic clout had no problem finding their place in the reformed government. For their part, old families who had fallen on hard times were also guaranteed their positions, since they had been regularly present in the council for many years.

The genius of the new system, though, was in the number of votes from the Forty needed to confirm the admission of new members. After the first rush of applications, the pool of those who desired entry naturally subsided. The Great Council was able, therefore, to incrementally increase the number of votes in the Forty needed for admission. In short, once all those who had the means and position to serve in the Great

Council had been admitted, the members were able to slowly close the door behind them. Finally, in 1323, after more than twenty-five years of expansion, the Great Council closed that door altogether, in what came to be called the Serrata, or closing. Henceforth, all new members of the Great Council had to have an ancestor who had served in a high government position. Since those positions were filled only by members of the Great Council, this had the effect of setting in stone which families made up the governmental body.

Long ago, historians used to see the Serrata as the death of the Venetian republican system and the birth of a closed oligarchy. In truth, it was neither. The reforms that led to the Serrata had dramatically increased participation in Venetian government, making it the most representative in the world. The Serrata did not create an oligarchy, since hundreds of families and well over a thousand members were included in the council. Instead, it gave certainty to those important (and even not-so-important) families that their position in government and society could not be taken from them. The *Serrata*, therefore, had the effect of dousing the most virulent forms of factionalism in the Great Council. And it was, in any case, never a complete closure. Venetians who distinguished themselves by extraordinary service to the state could still gain membership for themselves and their family—although this was appropriately rare.

The Serrata represented the final victory of the governmental model first proposed in the upheaval of 1172. The leading citizens, those who were called the "good men" or "wise men" in twelfth-century documents, had successfully placed themselves at the heart of the Venetian republic. From the people, whom they represented, they inherited the foundation of all political authority. From the doge, whom they checked, they claimed the right to execute that same power. As a result, the Great Council became the beating heart of the Venetian government.

By the fourteenth century, the basic components of Venetian

government were in place. At the lowest level was the arengo, which included all male citizens. In practice, the arengo met only to confirm the election of doges. Above the arengo was the Great Council. Since the large size of the council made it ill-suited for rapid action, it elected a higher body known as the Forty, which served as a court of appeals and prepared some legislation for debate and voting in the Great Council. Another committee of sixty men of the Great Council, which came to be known as the Senate, was given the task of commanding fleets, naming captains, and sending embassies—all of which still required the approval of the council as a whole. In the fourteenth century the Forty was the most important committee of the Great Council, although the Senate would later supplant it in that respect. The Forty elected three heads (*capi*) as presiding officers. These three were also present whenever the doge's council met. The latter consisted of six men, probably elected from each of the six sestieri, who formed the doge's inner circle. They held their position for one year and could not be reelected for several years after. All ten men—the three capi, the six councillors, and the doge—were called the Signoria, the highest committee in the government, although completely at the command of the Great Council.

After 1323 it was possible for the Venetians to make a definitive list of those families with a right to membership in the Great Council—and, of course, they did, calling it the Book of Gold. Venice, therefore, had legally defined the boundaries of a hereditary governing class. The members of this class were referred to as "patricians" or "nobles," yet these terms can be misleading. Everywhere else in Europe, "nobility" referred to feudal landholders who exercised extraordinary powers and privileges over the people and institutions of their domain. Counts, barons, and dukes on the mainland commanded local military forces, raised taxes, and administered justice among their subjects. The Venetian nobility simply had seats in the Great Council. They were by no means above the law. No one in Venice was. Nonetheless, the position was one of great prestige. Non-noble fathers in Venice dreamed of marrying their daughters into noble families, for their grandchildren would thus be noble. Even clothing and jewelry in Venice were regulated based on class. No matter how much wealth one had, to dress really lavishly one needed to be a noble.

Because Venice's livelihood was based on the marketplace, it stands to reason that over time some of the families in the Book of Gold would do well, while others would not. In general, the patricians tried to take care of each other. Members of distinguished families that fell on hard times were often voted government jobs that offered comfortable stipends. Outside of the nobility, new fortunes were, of course, made by new families in the years after the Serrata. Over time this could have led to the same sort of imbalance that preceded Doge Gradenigo's reforms. To avoid this, the Venetians instituted a new class, known as the *cittadini* (citizens). Rather like the equestrian order in ancient Rome, the cittadini consisted of families who, by service or wealth, had lifted themselves higher than the *popolo* (common people), but who could not become noble because of the Serrata. New members of the cittadini had to be Venetian citizens resident in the city for the past twenty-five years and nominated by current members. The names of the thousands of cittadini families were inscribed in their own register known, appropriately enough, as the Book of Silver. The creation of the cittadini class provided a useful safety valve for political and factional tension. Unlike the nobility, the cittadini class was never closed, so all could aspire to it. Furthermore, as the government of the Venetian empire grew larger and more complex, new administrative positions were created that were reserved exclusively for the cittadini. They became crucial to the operation of the Venetian government and highly visible in Venetian society. And, of course, those few cittadini who reached the highest levels of wealth and service to the state could always hope for promotion to the nobility itself.

These reforms, which were carried out slowly and with great caution, saved Venice from the warfare and tyranny that beset all the other Italian city-states during the Middle Ages and Renaissance. They were not perfect (as we shall see), but they did provide a broad avenue for political expression by all Venetians, regardless of social class. Just as importantly, they offered the possibility of upward mobility—something almost unimaginable for most Europeans of that age.

Many of these benefits, however, would be enjoyed by Gradenigo's successors, not the reforming doge himself. Given the controversy that surrounded his own election, there would always be those waiting for him to misstep, and thereby prove their wisdom. Gradenigo had the misfortune to reign during tumultuous times. All of Europe mourned the loss of Acre to Muslim forces. The crusader kingdom of Jerusalem, founded by the First Crusade in 1099, had for almost two centuries safeguarded the holy sites. It can be difficult for us today to understand the depth of concern for the Holy Land that gripped Western Christians in the Middle Ages. Jerusalem was itself a relic, sanctified by the life, death, and resurrection of Jesus Christ. Crusade after Crusade had failed to restore the holy city to permanent Christian control, and Muslim power continued to grow, not just in the Middle East but across the world. Only in Spain were Christian forces able to win victories against Muslim empires. Acre was the last Christian city in the Middle East, and its conquest and destruction filled European hearts with bewilderment, anger, and fear.

For Venice, the fall of Acre was devastating, not just spiritually and emotionally, but economically as well. With their loss of dominance in Constantinople, the Venetians had come to rely heavily on Acre as a source for Eastern luxury goods. Their victory over Genoa in the War of St. Sabas had given Venetians the upper hand in this well-fortified coastal city. Now all of that was lost. Venetian merchant vessels began heading north up the Bosporus strait past Constantinople to the ports of the Black Sea in search of the same goods, but the Genoese had the advantage in those waters and recognized the opportunity to strangle the economic lifeline of their rival. After a truce expired in 1291, Genoese squadrons began openly attacking Venetian convoys in the eastern Mediterranean and raiding Venetian Crete. Even worse, they erected a naval blockade of the Bosporus, refusing Venetian vessels entry into the Black Sea. Then, in 1295, the Genoese attacked the Venetian Quarter in Constantinople, massacring many of the residents there. The Byzantine emperor Andronicus II Palaeologus (1282–1328) favored the Genoese and obligingly arrested most of the remaining Venetians. Venice declared war on both powers.

Within a matter of weeks a fleet of forty war galleys left the lagoon under the command of Roger Morosini, known as Malabranca (Evil Claw). He sailed to Constantinople, where he attacked the Genoese Quarter at Galata. He then targeted all Genoese and Greek shipping moving up and down the Bosporus. Having gained control of Constantinople's inner harbor (the Golden Horn), Malabranca prepared to attack the emperor's Blachernae Palace in the far northwest corner of Constantinople. Fearing he would lose his city, his crown, or both, Andronicus agreed to make peace with Venice, releasing all prisoners and returning all goods and monies that he had confiscated.

Another Venetian fleet, under the command of Giovanni Soranzo, managed to break the Genoese blockade of the northern Bosporus, sailing into the Black Sea and seizing the port city of Caffa (modern Feodosiya) on the Crimea. The Genoese, however, were not so easily defeated. They continued to hold their position in the Aegean and even began launching major offensives against Venice in the Adriatic Sea. In 1298 a large-scale battle took place off the Dalmatian coast near the city of Curzola (modern Korčula). There the Genoese decisively defeated the Venetians, sinking sixty-five of their ninety-five vessels, killing some nine thousand Venetians, and capturing another five thousand. Among those captured was Marco Polo. Posterity was well served by his subsequent imprisonment, for it was then that he dictated his *Travels*, which remains a priceless treasure trove of information. In 1299 the long war with Genoa finally ended, yet the subsequent peace remained uneasy.

As Venice and Genoa warred over ports and shipping lanes, Muslim powers in the Middle East continued to grow in strength. In 1302 the founder of the Ottoman Empire, Sultan Osman I, defeated a Byzantine army near Nicomedia (modern Izmit, Turkey) and proceeded to conquer much of Asia Minor. Desperate for aid, Emperor Andronicus II hired any and all mercenaries from the West, including the Grand Catalan Company, a mercenary army drawn largely from Spain that eventually became more dangerous to the Byzantines than the Turks. To pay these bills in a rapidly diminishing empire, Andronicus had for some time been debasing the Byzantine currency with which Venetians continued to conduct a great deal of overseas business. The response in Venice was the minting of the republic's first gold coin, the Venetian ducat, which would remain a rock-solid currency for Europeans for centuries.

The decline of the Byzantine Empire in the east was mirrored by a rise of prosperity in western Europe. The German empire and Italy remained fractured and turbulent, but the kingdoms of England and France were unifying under increasingly powerful monarchs. Culture and learning were blossoming in Europe, while the Christian East, once so mighty, was consigned to Muslim occupation or life among the ruins of antiquity. The Venetians, who had always lived between these two worlds, were naturally drawn to the literature, song, and pageantry of French chivalry spreading across the courts of Europe. They could also hardly fail to notice that the riches of the East, while still vast, were now largely in Muslim hands. Within the Christian world, the balance had shifted decidedly westward. This led some forward-thinking Venetians to reevaluate their age-old aversion to projecting power on the mainland. Perhaps it was time, they suggested, for Venice to acquire an empire in the West as a safeguard against the uncertainties of the East.

This strategy was tested in 1308 when war broke out between three brothers claiming control over the city of Ferrara on the Po River. One of the claimants, Fresco, sought and received Venetian military support. For the Venetians, this seemed a golden opportunity to gain substantial control over the commercially important Po. However, with the entry of their garrison into Castel Tedaldo, which commanded the city's bridge over the river, the Venetians had inserted themselves into a factional war that stretched far beyond Ferrara. In medieval Italy, political factions usually aligned themselves with one of two parties: the Guelfs and the Ghibellines. These groups dated back to the eleventh century and the disputes between the popes and the German emperors in Italy. Since those same disputes regularly resurfaced and were often mixed liberally with Italian city-state independence, German wealth, and the freedom of the Church, the parties themselves endured. Broadly speaking, the Guelfs were pro-papal, while the Ghibellines were pro-imperial (that is, German). Yet by the fourteenth century factional struggles in the various Italian cities rarely touched on those matters, so the Guelfs and the Ghibellines were usually just the accepted names for opposing parties. They could be found in every northern Italian city—except, of course, Venice.

With their arrival at Castel Tedaldo in 1308, the Venetians had allied themselves with the Ghibellines, or at least a group of them, in Ferrara. Pope Clement V (1305–14) opposed Fresco's claims, supporting instead his Guelf brothers. The Venetians pointed out that Fresco had the better claim, yet the papal legate simply countered—correctly—that Ferrara was a papal fief and therefore, as its overlord, it was Clement, not the Venetians, who had the right to decide the dispute between the brothers. Papal troops were accordingly sent to Ferrara. Although skirmishes broke out, all agreed that the matter should be resolved peacefully.

Papal legates traveled to Venice, where they offered to let the Venetians govern Ferrara as papal vassals provided they paid an annual rent of twenty thousand ducats to the Holy See. The Great Council refused. When the legates returned to Ferrara, they issued a formal bull of excommunication against Doge Gradenigo and placed Venice itself under interdict.

In the turbulent world of late medieval Europe it was not unusual to find one's self or one's state at odds with Rome. As a result, the papal arsenal of excommunication and interdict was sufficiently familiar in most places not to cause too much of a stir. This was not the case in Venice. The Venetians remained an intensely pious people with a strong devotion to the Catholic religion and their spiritual father, the pope. The Peace of Venice, in which the Venetians in 1177 had helped Pope Alexander III achieve victory over Emperor Frederick I, remained a defining moment in their own history and civic identity. The excommunication of the doge, therefore, was nothing to be dismissed. The interdict, which embargoed all sacraments in Venice, was even more serious. This was only the third time that such spiritual weapons had been used against Venice—and the Venetians did not like it.

The Great Council met at once to consider the emergency. Giacomo Querini spoke for many when he insisted that Venice withdraw from Ferrara. This whole mainland venture was not only un-Venetian, he argued, but physically and spiritually dangerous. The first duty of all states was obedience to God and his vicar on earth, the pope. In any case, the wounds of the war with Genoa were still fresh. This was no time to take on another, potentially even larger, war. Doge Gradenigo spoke for the other side of the question. Venetians, he said, needed to safeguard their future in a dangerous world. An opportunity like this to acquire firm control over shipping on the Po would not likely present itself again. The papal legates in Ferrara could easily be overruled by the pope, who was currently in Avignon. If Venice could establish itself in Ferrara, Clement would accept Venetian control of the city. After all, the Venetians had been obedient sons of the Church for centuries. The majority of the Great Council agreed with the doge, but tensions in the chamber and in the streets of Venice remained high.

A few months later word reached Venice that Gradenigo had been wrong about Clement—the pope was not at all happy about the Venetian bid to claim Ferrara. To forestall the worst, the Signoria sent an embassy to Avignon to plead their case. But events moved too quickly. On March 27, 1309, Clement issued a devastating bull against the people of Venice. It excommunicated not only the doge but the Signoria and all citizens of the Republic of St. Mark. It declared all Venetian property anywhere in the world forfeit, forbade Christians to supply food or merchandise to any Venetian, and stripped the Venetians of all legal rights. In addition, it ordered all clergy to leave Venice and its territories. The pope's attack was total and devastating. Venetians had enormous wealth invested in foreign ventures and banks as well as merchandise stored in foreign warehouses, all of which could now be confiscated. Throughout their history, a large portion of the Venetian population had lived outside Venice. Those who were in the Byzantine Empire, Crete, or other Venetian ports in the East were safe from the pope's decree. But the wealth, property, and lives of Venetians doing business in the West now faced serious danger.

And that danger had only just begun. When the doge and his councillors still refused to withdraw from Ferrara, Pope Clement declared a Crusade. Across northern Italy, soldiers began to take up the cross to wage holy war against Venice, the state that had itself crusaded more than any other in Christendom. The new crusaders joined out of piety and a desire for salvation, but also because the defeat of Venice at Ferrara would force the maritime power off the Italian mainland. As it turned out, however, the war did not last long. Disease struck the Venetian garrison at Ferrara and it was quickly defeated by the crusader and papal forces. Most of the garrison was then put to the sword, although some were blinded and released. The Venetian commander, Marco Querini, managed to escape unharmed. He returned to Venice, claiming that he was insufficiently supported by the doge and his councillors.

The Venetians had lost Ferrara, lost their garrison, and feared they were losing their souls. And this, they believed, was all because of the headstrong desire of Doge Gradenigo to expand Venetian power onto the terra firma. Those who had taken part in the arengo of 1289 that had called for the election of Giacomo Tiepolo now crowed that their candidate would never have led Venice into such ruin. Others, like Giacomo Querini, who had argued for a peaceful withdrawal from Ferrara lamented the folly of the doge's plan. Both groups pointed out that if their advice had been taken, all would now be well.

Emotions ran so high that violence erupted not only in the streets and alleyways of the city, but also in the Great Council itself. Revolution, it seemed, was in the air. Seizing the moment, a group of disaffected nobles, including Marco Querini and a number of Tiepolo family members, organized a meeting at the Querini palazzo near Rialto, where they planned an elaborate coup d'état: They would sweep away the doge and the Signoria and place in their stead the son of Giacomo Tiepolo, a swashbuckling leader known as Bajamonte. As governor of the Venetian colony in Modon, Greece, Bajamonte Tiepolo had misused state funds and oppressed his subjects in order to live like a Byzantine potentate. When he was later prosecuted for his crimes, he fled the city to sulk on the mainland. He now strongly supported the plan to free Venice from the tyranny of Gradenigo and replace it with a tyranny of his own. There was nothing special about Bajamonte Tiepolo; indeed, there were dozens just like him all across late medieval Italy—well-connected strongmen seeking to build a kingdom on the ashes of failed communes. Now, Bajamonte believed, it was his turn to do the same in Venice.

The coup was set for June 15, 1309. The armed conspirators and their supporters would assemble at the Querini palazzo before sunrise.

From there they would march over the Rialto Bridge (a wooden structure) in two columns. One group, led by Marco Querini, would head down the Calle de' Fabbri. The other, led by Bajamonte Tiepolo, would make its way through the Merceria, a busy street that then, as now, was filled with rich shops. Another conspirator, Badoero Badoer, agreed to gather men in Padua and make a simultaneous attack by sea. The three groups would then converge on the Piazza San Marco at daybreak and capture the Ducal Palace.

The plan went badly from the start. A conspirator with second thoughts about overturning the Republic of Venice informed Doge Gradenigo about the coup. Gradenigo instantly summoned the Arsenale workers, who served as a makeshift bodyguard for the doge when necessary. Members of the Forty and the Signoria armed themselves and their servants and were therefore ready for the attack with superior numbers. The weather also did not cooperate with the conspirators. Storms and winds kept Badoer's vessels from leaving the mainland, and when they finally did set sail, they were quickly captured by loyalists from Chioggia. Marco Querini and his men stormed into the Piazza only to find it filled with well-armed defenders. They were quickly dispatched, with Marco himself killed in the melee. The boisterous Bajamonte Tiepolo continued to lead his men to the Piazza, unaware of what awaited him. At the head of his group a man carried a standard that read simply "Freedom." When the standard-bearer passed into the Piazza (probably through the arch that is today below the clock tower), a woman dropped a stone mortar on his head, killing him instantly. (A carved relief dating to 1861 still depicts the heroic woman. Walking under the clock tower from the Piazza, look up and to the left to see it.) That was enough for Tiepolo. He ordered the retreat and fled back across the Rialto Bridge, which his men destroyed to prevent loyalist forces from following. Holed up in his palazzo, he surrendered only when Doge Gradenigo agreed to allow him to live in exile. As for the other leaders, Querini lay dead on the Piazza and Badoer would soon join him. After his confession under torture, Badoer was beheaded between the two columns of the Molo.

The attempted coup shook Venice's men of government, who feared another attempt, given the high emotions that still reigned in the city. Before the coup, the Great Council had ordered the city guards, known as the Signori di Notte, to make certain that no one in the city was armed. Now they reversed that decision. The Great Council was to be surrounded by armed guards at all times, and all members were themselves allowed to bear arms. Each of the sestieri was charged with providing well-trained armed guards to keep peace in its district and to come to San Marco at a moment's notice in case of emergency. To oversee these security matters, the Great Council elected an ad hoc committee known as the Ten. As with many organs of state designed to deal with emergencies, the Venetians soon found the Ten indispensable, and so it became a permanent body. Its primary functions were intelligence gathering and diplomatic missions (often much the same thing) as well as the investigation and prosecution of treason. In times of emergency, though, it could serve as a substitute Great Council, thus allowing the Signoria to act quickly to deal with matters. In later years the Ten became so powerful that members were elected for only one year and could never be reelected. The three capi of the Ten served for a month at a time and, to avoid any opportunity for bribery, were forbidden to leave the Ducal Palace during their tenure of office.

As time went on, the Ten became expert at detecting enemies of the state. Spies worked the inns and taverns, listening above all for foreign agents, but also for internal plots against the government. Perhaps the most visible face of the Ten was the famous *bocche dei leoni* (lions' mouths) scattered around the city. Modern visitors to the Ducal Palace are invariably shown the *bocca* next to the entrance of the Sala della

Bussola, yet that is only the most famous one. The purpose of the lion's mouth was to provide a means for Venetian citizens to report illegal activities to the proper authorities. These written reports, signed or anonymous, were fed to the vigilant lions and later examined by the Ten and the Signoria. In later centuries, foreigners often condemned the *bocche* as evidence of the dark, secretive, and oppressive nature of the government of Venice. Mark Twain, for example, who visited the Ducal Palace in 1867, reported in his book *Innocents Abroad* that "these were the terrible Lions' Mouths! ... These were the throats, down which went the anonymous accusation, thrust in secretly at dead of night by an enemy, that doomed many an innocent man." Much the same description still dominates most modern guidebooks.

In truth, the Ten had an extraordinarily complex system of evaluating all reports received through the *bocche*, especially those that were unsigned. The procedure, which took up many pages of precise instructions, was designed to reject almost all anonymous reports, investigating only those for which there was strong reason to believe they might be accurate. And this was only an investigation. Arrest and conviction required real evidence given in a court of law. The truth is that the *bocche dei leoni* worked so well that other government agencies began using them. One can, for example, still see various *bocche* around Venice that were used to report a variety of criminal activities. On the wall of the church of Santa Maria della Visitazione on the Zattere is one with an inscription "Denunciations [for activities] against the general health of the sestiere of Dorsoduro"—an important matter during times of plague. The church of San Martino, near the Arsenale, has a similar *bocca* for reporting heresy and impiety.

The new security measures worked so well that there was no repeat of the problems that beset the last doge's election. When Pietro Gradenigo died in 1311, the constitutional process ran smoothly, electing the aged and saintly Marino Zorzi (1311–12). Perhaps the electors hoped that the pious man could make peace with the pope, but he lived only ten months after his coronation. His successor, Giovanni Soranzo (1312–28), was the hero of Caffa during the last war with Genoa. Although he was in his seventies, he had a bit more life in him than Zorzi. His first task, of course, was to settle matters with Clement V. After promising to pay the enormous sum of ninety thousand florins, the Venetians at last received their absolution and the lifting of the interdict. The sum was so great that the Great Council had to impose a forced loan on the citizens to raise it. They considered it well worth the cost. Peace with the pope allowed the Venetians to again enter into binding agreements with their fellow Christians in Europe, and soon the damage of the ecclesiastical censure began to heal. Venice once again prospered. Of particular importance was the increase in the number of Germans who came to Venice to trade or work. So many came, in fact, that they were given their own *fondaco*, a building for lodging, storage, and conducting business. The Fondaco dei Tedeschi was built on the San Marco side of the Rialto Bridge. The original building was a wooden structure, yet in the sixteenth century it was replaced with the current stone building. Today it serves as the main post office of Venice.

Although their first venture on the mainland had proved disastrous, the Venetians found themselves increasingly drawn into matters in the West. The simple fact was that events in Italy had grown too important to ignore. The Renaissance was beginning in Florence and spreading across northern Italy. Italian cities were becoming wealthier and more powerful. In the fourteenth century most of them were controlled by the signori, tyrants who waged war against their neighbors and spent freely on mercenary companies led by condottieri—generals for hire. The Venetian republic safeguarded its citizens from tyrants at home, but it could not ignore their wars on the mainland.

The most troublesome of these signori for the Venetians were the

Della Scala brothers. Some years earlier the Della Scala family had taken control of the thriving city of Verona, some sixty miles west of Venice. Through violence, threats, and invasions the brothers had managed to claim an impressive chunk of northern Italy—their rule extended over Vicenza, Feltre, Belluno, Brescia, Parma, and Lucca. By 1329 the Della Scalas had expanded almost up to the Venetian lagoon itself with their conquest of Padua and Treviso. This represented a severe threat to the Venetians, for the Della Scalas now controlled access to the Po as well as other mainland markets. Mastino della Scala imposed stiff tolls on all Venetian goods moving on the Po or other rivers, as well as export duties on foodstuffs headed for Venice. With well over a hundred thousand mouths to feed, Venice was heavily reliant on the flow of produce from the mainland. The new taxes not only increased food prices for the average citizen, but greatly harmed Venice's religious houses, which relied on estates on the terra firma for their income and maintenance. Mastino also threatened Venice's salt industry by creating his own saltworks not far from Chioggia and defending it with a powerful fortress.

Doge Francesco Dandolo (1328–39) was an accomplished diplomat who favored negotiation over warfare. Indeed, it had been he who had successfully negotiated peace with Pope Clement V in 1313 after the mainland debacle. He hoped to do the same with Mastino della Scala. Dandolo strongly opposed entangling Venice in the problems of the mainland. Venetians were sailors, not soldiers. They were businessmen, not farmers. Waging war against the Della Scalas would mean hiring mercenaries, with all the attendant problems. But this position put the doge in the minority, both in the Great Council and among the populace. The Venetians wanted to fight this nearby threat. Word went out that Venice was hiring mercenaries, and a collection of English, French, German, and Italian bands arrived in Ravenna and were transported to the Lido. The Della Scalas had plenty of enemies willing to help shatter their grip on power. The Florentines, who had lost Lucca to the Della Scalas, sent money for the war. The Carrara family, which had lost its position in Padua, was also willing to do whatever it took to defeat the Della Scalas. And so on July 14, 1336, Venice declared war. By December, Venetian forces were nearing Padua and Treviso. Success brought more allies. The ruling families of other major Italian city-states—the Viscontis of Milan, the Estes of Ferrara, and the Gonzagas of Mantua—formed a league with Venice to crush the Della Scalas. By August 1337 the war had ended. The threat to Venice was neutralized.

Now they had to decide what to do with the spoils. In the peace treaty the Della Scalas ceded Padua, Treviso, and all their surrounding territories to Venice. The Venetians immediately gave Padua to the Carraras, who had faithfully helped win the war. Other lands were also parceled out to allies. But Treviso and its territories fell directly into Venice's hands. For the first time, the Venetians had direct control of a state in the West, causing some to worry that this in itself meant the loss of something distinctively Venetian. They governed Treviso with a collection of administrative techniques that they had learned in their eastern provinces and quarters. By a suitably complex and indirect vote, the city would elect a *podestà*, who would govern along with a large council (similar to the Great Council) and a small council (similar to the Six). In general, the government had wide latitude in matters of local administration and justice. A Venetian rector, who was appointed by and answerable to the Ten in Venice, remained in Treviso to advise and, if need be, overrule the provincial government. The system worked well, blending just the right amount of local control with colonial oversight. With some modification, this model would be reused when Venice later expanded further on the mainland.

The annexation of Treviso was Venice's first direct venture into the turbulent world of northern Italy. More would follow. Despite their long-standing reluctance to project power on the terra firma, the Venetians had come to believe that to preserve their position and extraordinary prosperity it was essential to do so. The maritime empire was becoming a traditional empire. The refugees of the lagoon were at last returning to their ancestral homes, yet no longer as victims, but as masters.

CHAPTER 9

PLAGUE AND TREASON IN
THE FOURTEENTH CENTURY

When one thinks of Venice today, the mind invariably con-
jures the striking facade it presents across the Bacino San
Marco, the wide body of water that stretches from the
Ducal Palace to San Giorgio Maggiore. The two columns of the Molo,
each bearing the city's spiritual protectors, reach skyward framing the
long entryway of the Piazzetta and beyond to the majestic church of San
Marco. Half of this scene, however, is the extraordinary Ducal Palace,
perched almost on the water's edge and stretching from the Piazzetta to
the Rio del Palazzo, over which the famous Bridge of Sighs extends. Few
buildings in the world are so often painted, photographed, or described
as Venice's Palazzo Ducale. The greatest artists and writers of the ages
have strained to express its unique beauty and its timeless serenity.

All the more surprising, then, is the fact that no one actually designed this architectural triumph. It was, instead, the result of centuries
of projects, restorations, and general improvements. It is not even one
building, but many collected under one roof. Like the government that it
housed, the palace grew slowly and in an ad hoc manner. It is the

product of a conservative people who held tightly to their traditions, history, and institutions but were still willing to modify or extend them when circumstances warranted. Nothing is more Venetian than this magnificent structure.

Its origins lay in the flames of revolution. In 976 the previous wooden palace was burned to the ground, along with the doge and his family. St. Pietro I Orseolo funded the rebuilding of the palace after his election as doge. Like its predecessor, the new building was a smallish, fortified structure along the river and close to the church. It was made of stone, and as Venetian power and wealth grew over the years, builders used increasingly valuable materials for its beautification and enlargement. The palace expanded along with the Venetian state. By the twelfth century it was no longer simply a residence for the doge, but home to most of the main organs of government. To use an American example, it was the White House, Capitol, and Supreme Court together under one roof. As time went on, newly created bureaucracies often found a home in the Ducal Palace.

As one might expect, this had the effect of giving the palace a disjointed look, not at all as it appears today. Doge Sebastiano Ziani expanded the building a bit farther toward the Piazzetta and the waterfront before the Peace of Venice in 1177, giving it a more attractive facade. Political reforms, however, put a major strain on the building, since it needed to accommodate an increasingly large number of people participating in Venetian government. When the Serrata more than doubled the size of the Great Council, Doge Pietro Gradenigo ordered the enlargement of a hall to hold them all. Yet by the time that construction was finished, the Venetians had won Treviso and the Council, which was approaching 1,300 members, had already outgrown the new room.

In 1340 the Great Council voted to extend the Ducal Palace toward the water of the Bacino, leaving only a *fondamenta*, or small section of earth along the waterfront. The primary purpose of the expansion was to build an entirely new chamber for the Great Council, which would stretch all along the water's edge. The new room was placed on an upper story with an arched atrium below to allow easy foot traffic along the shore, perhaps as a concession to those who resented the government taking over prime land on the waterfront. Whatever the case, it produced the palace's distinctive appearance. Although in style it is fourteenth-century Venetian Gothic, the palace's archways and windows give an extraordinary impression of lightness. It almost seems upside down, with the heavier portions appearing to rest at the top and the open areas on the ground. The construction of the building would be delayed many times, only finally finished in 1423. As far as we know, the latest expansion was not the work of any single architect, but of many designers, builders, and politicians, each moving it toward completion.

When ground was broken on the expansion, spirits in Venice were soaring high. The bustling, crowded city continued to reap rich commercial profits abroad and had lately begun to exert its authority in Italy. The future seemed bright. Of course, plenty of dangers remained. The Turks continued to press westward, threatening the teetering Byzantine Empire and commercial shipping from Europe. The Genoese were a constant worry. But no one guessed the direction of the gravest danger, for it seemed like the smallest of all things.

Every ship in the Middle Ages had rats. Every city had them, too. They had been the constant companion of civilization since humans first began building settlements and storing away their food. The rodent problem led directly to the domestication of cats some ten thousand years earlier, but the problem, of course, persisted. The dirtier and more populous the city, the more the rats happily infested it. By luck of geography, Venice was much cleaner than most European cities in the Middle Ages. People in landlocked areas typically dumped chamber pots and other sewage and refuse into the streets, but in Venice the streets were canals that the tides flushed clean twice a day. That was one rea-son why Venice could house more than a hundred thousand people without any method of sewage removal. But the tightly packed city con-tained plenty of food and many places to hide, and that meant a vibrant population of rats.

Before the modern age, when a ship took harbor, people, goods, and rats moved freely on and off the vessel. The rats—usually foot-long black rats—sought the food stored in the cargo holds. When the food was depleted and the ship sailed into a new port, the rats would often dis-embark, searching for other hospitable locales. The old saying "rats de-serting a sinking ship" has nothing to do with rodents leaping into the water to avoid drowning in a doomed vessel. It refers, instead, to a nauti-cal superstition that if rats left a vessel in port it was a clear omen that the ship would sink. The rats, the most experienced travelers in the ani-mal kingdom, knew a risky transport when they saw one. In an age in which sea travel was always dangerous, it did not pay to ignore omens.

Rats in Venice were nothing new, but what they brought with them in the fourteenth century was: the seed of pandemic. The black rats that scurried off Venetian merchant ships in 1348 carried fleas, which were themselves infected with *Yersinia pestis*—the bubonic plague. This bac-terium originated in China, where it had spread quickly among rat fleas before moving westward with merchants. Like Marco Polo, the plague made its way along the Silk Road to the ports of the Crimea in the Black Sea. By tradition, the plague made its first western appearance at Caffa, which the Venetians had ruled until 1307 and which was currently under Genoese control. The Mongol general Janiberg is said to have cat-apulted the plague-ridden corpses of his men into the city in an attempt to infect his enemy. It seems unlikely, however, that the disease was so well confined. Caravans from the East stopped at many Black Sea ports to sell their wares. Catapults were not necessary—just willing buyers. The Venetians and Genoese did plenty of business in those ports, and it is not surprising, then, that both cities were hit by the deadly disease first and at almost exactly the same time.

The black rats that decamped from the vessels and darted down the narrow streets of Venice were already sick. As they died, the infected fleas jumped from their dead hosts onto the skins of new, live ones—in other words, people. Although rat fleas naturally prefer rats, in a pinch they will feed on humans. Since it was not at all uncommon for people in the Middle Ages to have fleas, one or two more were hardly noticed. (Only modern hygiene has banished the human fleas that faithfully accompanied us for thousands of years.) The rat flea then regurgitated the *Yersinia pestis* bacterium into its human host, where it spread quickly to the lymph nodes and from there throughout the body.

The first symptoms of bubonic plague resembled influenza—fever, chills, headache, muscle aches—but soon included the signature "bubo," a painful swelling of lymph glands in the groin, armpits, or neck. Believing that the bubo itself was causing the disease, medieval doctors often lanced it, which, if the patient was fortunate, did no harm. It could, however, release the bacterium into the air, where it would find its way directly into the lungs. The disease could also infect the lungs anyway if it spread widely enough in the body.

Bubonic plague is a ruthless killer. Without modern antibiotics, more than half of those who contract it die within a week. If it infects the lungs, however, the plague is even deadlier. The pneumonic version causes the sufferer to cough up bloody sputum, which aspirates into the air where it can be inhaled by others. Pneumonic plague kills almost 100 percent of its victims within twenty-four hours. One can be healthy at breakfast and dead by dinner.

As a port city with an abundance of boats, rats, and people, Venice was the perfect host city for the Black Death (as it was soon called). Within a year of its arrival the plague had killed approximately half of the Venetian population—more than fifty thousand people. At least fifty patrician families were completely wiped out. The survivors were understandably filled with fear and bewilderment. With no concept of germs, medieval people were at an utter loss to explain what was happening to them. In Venice, many believed that the plague was caused by an earthquake that had damaged the city in January 1348. It was clear that the disease was contagious, but the why, how, or even what of the disease was beyond understanding. Not surprisingly, many reasoned that the plague was a punishment from God, and so they did all that they could to effect a spiritual cure. Piety movements, which were already widespread across western Europe, were supercharged by the Black Death. New confraternal organizations of prayer and charity sprang up in Venice and across Italy. Precious relics were brought out and paraded through the streets in an attempt to purify them. Patron saints and the Virgin Mary were invoked to save their people.

And eventually all those things worked. After a few years of carnage, the plague invariably faltered, unable to make headway among those who had developed antibodies against it. But new victims lived just down the road. Just as it had followed the merchants from China to Italy, the Black Death moved along the trade routes in Europe from Venice, Genoa, and Marseille to every point northward, even as far away as Iceland. Everywhere the death toll was horrendous. Millions perished—probably 50 percent of the total population of Europe died in the first decade of the disease. And this blow came only a few years after some of Europe's worst famines, brought on by a sustained period of global cooling. It seemed that God truly was smiting his people.

The survivors continued to look for explanations. Many Europeans initially suspected that Jews were poisoning the wells, though this quickly subsided when local Jews were expelled or killed with no effect on the plague's spread. Their focus then turned to the sins of Christendom—particularly the Catholic Church. For decades the popes had been based in Avignon, which, while extraordinarily pleasant, was not Rome, the Holy See of Peter. The Avignon popes were good at raising funds, so the Church's wealth had grown. This was the age of the rich satin vestments and distinctive hats of the cardinals, who were truly "princes of the Church" in wealth and power. Clerical abuses such as absenteeism and pluralism were rampant, leading many Christians to wonder what the rich prelates, priests, and monks had to do with the simple message of Christ. The Black Death was widely seen as God's retribution for the sins and excesses of his Church, leading to new calls for reform from every quarter.

Venetians were not as quick to blame the Church or to seek celestial reasons for the Black Death. Perhaps it was the fact that, unlike most Europeans, Venetians traveled to distant lands, where they saw that the plague had devastated the Mongols and the Muslims just as thoroughly as it had the European Christians. Instead, Venetian responses to the plague were much more pragmatic. They prayed, of course, but from a medieval perspective that was the height of pragmatism. They also worked hard to lessen the effects of the plague. After they discovered that the dead could themselves transmit the disease, death ships were ordered to patrol the city's canals daily, calling out for *corpi morti* (dead bodies). They drafted into service large roundships and barges for the removal of corpses, which were taken to various uninhabited islands in the lagoon and dumped into mass graves.

When the Black Death subsided in 1350, the surviving Venetians faced a problem of manpower—a crucial consideration for a maritime state that depended on the sailors and oarsmen of the war galleys. The government opened wide the doors to Venetian citizenship, offering financial incentives such as streamlined guild memberships for craftsmen in order to entice immigrants. As new people moved into Venice and children were born, the possibility of a return of the plague remained a constant danger. Trading vessels sailed into the city from all parts of the world—any one of them could be carrying the disease.

Venetians did their best to find ways to combat the problem. One of the more common sights during later Carnevale festivals in Venice was the hooded reveler wearing a bizarre mask sporting a long, curved nose. This mask was originally devised to protect doctors from the plague by placing medicinal herbs thought to combat the disease into the mask's nose cavity. In later centuries foreigners saw the doctors' attire and assumed it was part of the costumes that filled the city in the months before Lent. Although the herbs were of no use, the mask itself could at least shield its wearer from airborne bacteria. A simple cloth over the nose and mouth would have been just as effective, of course, but hardly as picturesque.

When plague took the life of Doge Giovanni Mocenigo (1478–85), the government enacted even more proactive measures. A new hospital was built at state expense on Lazzaretto Vecchio, a small island just off the Lido that had previously been owned by the monks of San Giorgio Maggiore. The Great Council passed a new law requiring those exhibiting symptoms of plague to be held at Lazzaretto Vecchio for a period of forty days, on the assumption that if they were still alive at the end of the waiting period they either did not have the plague or had survived it. In practice, though, very few ever returned from the heartbreaking misery of the plague island. If a patient did not have the disease before arriving at Lazzaretto Vecchio, it was certain that he or she would contract it before leaving. The dead were stacked like cordwood in mass graves all over the island. An excavation in 2004 uncovered more than 1,500 skeletons—and those are only a tiny sample of the bodies that still lie beneath the green grasses of that quiet island. The gruesome process birthed the word "quarantine"—from *quarantia*, the forty days that the sick were required to spend at Lazzaretto Vecchio.

So well did the quarantine seem to work that the Venetian government later expanded on the concept. On another, larger island the state built extensive dormitories, warehouses, and wharves. Henceforth, all vessels entering the lagoon were required to stop at this island, called Lazzaretto Nuovo. The vessels were docked, the cargo stored, and the crew and passengers assigned quarters. Like its older cousin, Lazzaretto Nuovo was a quarantine island, but for the healthy as well as the sick. The administrators separated the residents into those who were obviously sick, those who were obviously well, and those whose condition was not obvious. It was a massive undertaking. The buildings, which still remain, could house four thousand people, two hundred horses, and vast amounts of cargo. Modern visitors to Lazzaretto Nuovo can still see the copious graffiti of the frustrated, the bored, and the frightened. When forty days had expired, the survivors and their belongings were released and allowed to enter Venice.

The doge of Venice during the first outbreak of the Black Death was one of Venice's most extraordinary leaders. Andrea Dandolo (1343–54) had demonstrated amazing intelligence and wisdom from an early age. He became a Procurator of San Marco, a position of great legal and financial importance, when only twenty-five, and was one of the first members of the Venetian patriciate to take up studies at the still relatively new University of Padua. Not only did he complete his work, but he probably earned a doctorate in law as well. In 1343 he was elected doge at the age of only thirty-seven—the first young man to hold the office in centuries. Dandolo numbered among the ranks of a new breed in fourteenth-century Italy, the beneficiaries of growing capitalist economies that placed a high value on individualism. Well educated in languages and classical literature, these men increasingly directed their attention to matters of this world. They were the first of the Italian humanists, from whom the Renaissance would flow. Dandolo's close friend Petrarch described the young doge as "a just man, incorruptible, full of ardor and love for his country, erudite, eloquent, wise, affable, and human." Although a doge, Dandolo remained a scholar. He worked tirelessly on a new history of Venice, based on his humanist desire for accuracy in science and observation. His book, the *Chronica per extensum descripta*, drew from a variety of earlier chronicles and archival materials that have since perished. It is an extraordinary work that scrupulously avoids the hyperbole, puffery, and patriotic fabrications that so often infected Venetian chronicles in the fourteenth and fifteenth centuries. It remains one of the most important sources for historians of medieval Venice.

Dandolo's artistic interests profoundly improved the church of San Marco. Few doges have taken so keen an interest in the beautification of the "ducal chapel." Indeed, he firmly asserted that "the church was and is ours" and that it was solely up to the doge "however many burials within the church" there could be. This mattered, because he fully intended to be buried there himself. He added a new Chapel of San Isidoro to hold the relics of that Byzantine warrior saint. He oversaw the reworking of the Pala d'Oro, a magnificent golden altarpiece crafted by Byzantine masters at the opening of the twelfth century. He also expanded and beautified the baptistery, and there he was laid to rest when he died, still a young man, in 1354. He was the last doge ever to be buried in San Marco. What was the ducal chapel had become the people's church. Subsequent doges were content to be buried elsewhere.

Dandolo's reign was beset by challenges. The Venetians had once again crusaded against the Turks, wresting the city of Smyrna (modern Izmir) from them. A revolt in always troublesome Zara in 1345 led to a difficult siege and an attack from Hungary. Much of the Venetian government's attention was also consumed by another long war with Genoa, waged in the Aegean and on the Italian mainland. Both powers scored victories and costly defeats, although the Genoese had the upper hand. The real winners were the Turks, who took advantage of the strife between the merchant republics to expand their power in the region.

Foreign mercenaries also did well, as the Venetian government spent freely to defeat the Genoese. Petrarch wrote several letters and even traveled to Venice urging peace, but his friend would not hear of it.

The war with Genoa did not last much beyond the death of the doge. Weeks later the Venetians suffered a devastating loss at Porto Longo, near Modon. Genoese galleys under the command of Paganino Doria skillfully entered the port and destroyed the unprepared Venetian fleet there. Thousands of Venetians, including their commander, Nicolò Pisani, were captured and many more were killed. The Genoese now gazed with pleasure on a severely weakened Venice, but they could not deliver the deathblow. Back home the Viscontis, the ruling family in Milan, had acquired control over Genoa, and they had no interest in expensive wars with Venice over foreign ports and shipping lanes. They brought the war to a close in 1355 with Venice shaken by its close call.

The young Andrea Dandolo was succeeded as doge by an old man, Marino Falier (1354–55). In his more than seventy years of life, Falier had served Venice across a broad range of activities. He was a member of the Ten when Bajamonte Tiepolo was tried for treason. He later served on numerous diplomatic missions to Italian powers and crowned heads of Europe. In 1353 he was even knighted in Vienna by Emperor Charles IV—a distinction of great importance in an age when chivalry was glorified across Europe and had its admirers even in Venice. Falier had commanded Venetian vessels in the Black Sea and acquitted himself well in the wars against Genoa. In short, he was a perfect choice to serve as the new leader of Venice.

And that is what makes what happened next so difficult to understand. Many of the documents that would shed light on Falier's activities have not survived, so the story must be pieced together from chronicles, proceedings, and hearsay. Even Venetians at the time did not quite understand why things went so badly, as evidenced by the collections of stories they told to explain it. It was rumored that after his election Falier returned to Venice in a boat that landed in a fog at the Molo. Not sure of his exact location, the doge-elect walked between the two columns, a place where criminals were executed and that wise Venetians avoided. This omen, it was said, doomed his reign. Other writers claimed that the elderly doge had recently married a beautiful young woman, which led to a good deal of snickering and bawdy humor among the young patricians of the Great Council. One story has it that graffiti was found in the palace claiming (in graphic language) that the young wife was rather energetically unfaithful to her new husband. The offending scribblers stood trial, but received little more than wrist slaps. This leniency (according to various writers) greatly irritated the doge, who soon came to believe that the Venetian nobility was spoiled, arrogant, and no longer good for Venice.

Historians today tend to dismiss the cuckold explanation for Falier's actions, emphasizing instead his experiences as a diplomat, which made clear to him how differently politics unfolded outside the lagoon. Venice's republican government was not just rare, it was unique. The world was ruled by powerful autocrats who acted decisively, while Venice was governed by an increasingly complex constitutional system and its ever-growing bureaucracies. No other city-state in Italy still maintained a republic. They were all ruled by signori, powerful men and their families who acquired despotic control while paying lip service to republican ideals. Venice's recent losses to Genoa may have convinced Falier that to survive his country must conform to the times and embrace a dictatorship.

All of this, of course, is pure speculation. What is known for sure is that discontent simmered in Venice over the debacle of Porto Longo and that many of the *popolo* blamed their noble leaders. Morale worsened when, as an emergency measure, the government mobilized four war galleys commanded by experienced captains who were *not* members of the patriciate. Unlike the fleet at Porto Longo, these commoner vessels went on to successfully attack Genoese shipping. Common sailors and marines, as well as the skilled dockworkers in the Arsenale, took more than a little pride in these successes, and there was plenty of grumbling at the failures of the spoiled patricians.

The spark that set off the extraordinary events of 1355 occurred on the ground floor of the Ducal Palace in the naval office, which faced out toward the Bacino. Giovanni Dandolo, a nobleman and the paymaster of the naval secretary, assigned a particular man to a particular galley. There was nothing unusual about this. However, the commoner galley officer, Bertuccio Isarello, refused to accept this man, which led to a heated argument with Dandolo. Finally, Dandolo struck Isarello, who departed in a rage.

The paymaster had struck the wrong commoner. Isarello's popularity ran high among the sailors and dockworkers. He raced along the waterline (what is today the crowded Molo and the Riva degli Schiavoni) telling all who would listen of Dandolo's arrogance and suggesting that the nobleman be brought to account for his action. A large and rough group of men quickly assembled and began marching up and down the Piazzetta waiting for the hapless Dandolo to emerge. As for Dandolo, he peered nervously out the window, wondering how he would get home without being mauled. Finally, he appealed to Doge Falier, who summoned Isarello into the palace and ordered him to disband his gang and to quit threatening his betters. Isarello grudgingly obeyed.

Later that night, though, Falier summoned Isarello back to the palace for a closed-door meeting. The two were joined by Filippo Calendario, a stonemason and builder who was overseeing the current expansion work on the Ducal Palace. Like Isarello, Calendario had no love for the arrogance of the Venetian nobility. The two men were reasonably wealthy, so they naturally resented the patricians who looked down upon them. Whether the doge was animated by a similar resentment caused by comments about his wife or rather by a belief that

Apparitio Sancti Marci. The people and doge of Venice look on in wonder as a column in San Marco miraculously opens to reveal the lost relics of the saint. This thirteenth-century mosaic is one of the earliest surviving depictions of the Venetian people. BASILICA DI SAN MARCO, VENICE.

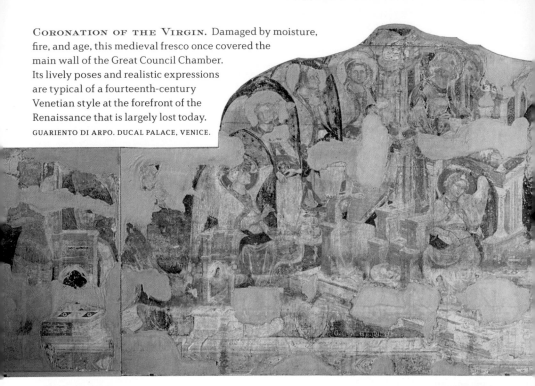

CORONATION OF THE VIRGIN. Damaged by moisture, fire, and age, this medieval fresco once covered the main wall of the Great Council Chamber. Its lively poses and realistic expressions are typical of a fourteenth-century Venetian style at the forefront of the Renaissance that is largely lost today.

GUARIENTO DI ARPO. DUCAL PALACE, VENICE.

THE PROCESSION OF THE TRUE CROSS IN PIAZZA SAN MARCO. The narrative painting style of Venice often showcased the city and its people. Executed around 1496, this magnificent painting depicts the white-robed members of the Scuola Grande di San Giovanni Evangelista as they parade through the Piazza San Marco with the relic of the True Cross.

GENTILE BELLINI. ACCADEMIA GALLERY, VENICE.

ASSUMPTION OF THE VIRGIN. Titian produced this painting in 1518 for the main altar of the Franciscan church of Santa Maria Gloriosa, where it remains today. The startling vibrancy of the religious figures—the apostles below, Mary and the angels in the middle, and God above—soon became a feature of Venetian art. TITIAN. SANTA MARIA GLORIOSA DEI FRARI, VENICE.

HEALING OF THE MADMAN. Although it depicts the miraculous healing of a madman by the relic of the True Cross in the upper left, the entirety of this narrative painting offers a snapshot of the Rialto area around 1494. The old wooden Rialto Bridge (complete with drawbridge) stands over the gondola-filled Grand Canal in the background.   VITTORE CARPACCIO. ACCADEMIA GALLERY, VENICE.

THE LION OF ST. MARK. Vittore Carpaccio's depiction of the symbol of the Venetian Republic quickly became one of the most famous ever rendered. The winged lion, which traditionally represented St. Mark, is shown with his paw resting on a book. The words (*Pax tibi Marce evangelista meus*) are not from the Gospel of Mark, but from a divine prophecy that Venetians believed foretold that the body of St. Mark would forever rest in Venice. In the classic Venetian narrative style, Carpaccio sets the busy Bacino San Marco as the backdrop of his allegorical painting.   VITTORE CARPACCIO. DUCAL PALACE, VENICE.

BATTLE OF LEPANTO. *(above)* The painting depicts two scenes, both important to the success over the Turks at Lepanto in 1571. The glorious naval battle rages below while the saintly patrons of the crusaders plead to the Virgin Mary for victory. From left to right they are St. Peter (patron of the Papal States), St. James (patron of the Hapsburg empire), St. Giustina (on whose feast day the battle took place), a shrouded figure representing Faith, and St. Mark (patron of Venice). To the right an angel fires flaming arrows down upon the Turks.
PAOLO VERONESE. ACCADEMIA GALLERY, VENICE.

NEPTUNE OFFERING TO VENICE THE RICHES OF THE SEA. *(left)* Venice, the Queen of the Seas, reclines, resting her left arm on the lion of St. Mark. With her right arm she commands Neptune, who pours out before her the riches of the sea. This allegory perfectly represents a Venetian maritime domination that was only a memory by the time Tiepolo painted it around 1745.
GIOVANNI BATTISTA TIEPOLO. DUCAL PALACE, VENICE.

THE SKY OF SIGHS. In 2009 the clothing maker Sisley incorporated the famous Bridge of Sighs into a giant advertisement that covered both sides of the Rio di Palazzo and much of the Ducal Palace. Controversial billboards helped offset the costs of reconstruction work taking place behind them.
PHOTO BY ROBYN LAKEMAN.

Venice needed a single ruler (or by both), he suggested that the three of them join forces in a plot to overthrow the republic.

They crafted a methodical plan, although not a very wise one. Calendario and Isarello would assemble twenty trusted men and charge each of them with raising another forty. All eight hundred men—primarily laborers and sailors—would then secretly assemble in the Ducal Palace on the evening of April 15, 1355. The doge would summon the Great Council and the conspirators would then storm the room, killing all the hated nobles. They would then acclaim Doge Falier as "Lord and Master" of Venice. One gets the feeling that the satisfying murder of the haughty nobles was the real purpose of this plan, since the rest of it was not well thought out. Killing the Great Council, after all, was not the same as murdering the nobility. A great many noblemen were on assignments or doing business overseas—and, of course, there were always the women and children, who were forbidden to attend the council. Yet the plan's greatest problem was that it required eight hundred mouths to keep absolutely silent about it—something unknown in human events.

As the leaders fanned out across the city recruiting conspirators, word quickly spread of something afoot. The doge claimed that it was only a minor problem and even arrested some of those who gathered in the Piazza San Marco to air grievances against the nobles. But the *bocche dei leoni* of the Council of Ten filled up with reports of treason, either as conspirators had second thoughts or nobles were warned by commoner friends to stay home on April 15. The specific nature of the evidence does not survive, but the Ten were quickly convinced that the doge himself might be involved in the plot. On the night of April 14, invoking emergency powers, the Ten called the doge's councillors, the criminal judges, the Signori di Notte, and the leaders of the six sestieri. This group ordered the arrest of Calendario and Isarello, who when questioned quickly implicated the doge. The leaders then told all nobles in the city to arm themselves and ordered the sestieri to send guards to San Marco.

The parishes posted guards, too, while others patrolled for any signs of insurrection. The great coup had collapsed before it had ever really begun.

As a matter of history, when a state's leader is accused of treason, the usual result is chaos and upheaval. One thinks of the execution of Charles I in England or Louis XIV in France, but one could just as easily point to the factional violence in most Italian states in the fourteenth century. Venice's complex constitutional system, however, did not even tremble at the strain. Everything worked in a cool, rational, and calm manner. And because the state remained firmly stable, even with the betrayal of its executive, the people, too, remained calm. There was no street violence, no riots, no lynchings—only the Venetian republic and the justice it dispensed. The Council of Ten formed a tribunal consisting of nine of them (excluding one, because he was a Falier), twenty of the most respected nobles in the city, the six ducal councillors, and one state attorney. This body then heard the cases of Calendario and Isarello and the other ringleaders, finding them all guilty. They were immediately hanged from the upper story of the Ducal Palace facing the Piazzetta. Because of their popularity, Calendario and Isarello had bits placed into their mouths to keep them from inciting the crowds below.

The trial of the doge was a simple, albeit anguishing, affair. The aged Marino Falier immediately confessed to everything, asserting that he deserved to die for his crimes. The tears and sorrow that he demonstrated makes his part in this saga all that much harder to comprehend. He had nothing to gain by overthrowing a government that had lifted him to its highest position. He had no children, so founding a dynasty was clearly not his plan. It may be, as some historians have argued, that he believed that Venice would be better served by autocracy. But if so, it is odd that he offered no defense based on this reasoned position. Instead, his reaction before the court was one of pitiful repentance for a foolish crime. It is just what one might expect from a man who had been so enraged by arrogant mockery against himself and his wife that he rashly set forces in motion that he could not control.

On April 17, 1355, guards stripped Marino Falier of his regalia and led him into the courtyard of the Ducal Palace. He climbed the great staircase, probably the same as the current Scala dei Giganti (Stairway of the Giants), to stand where all doges stood when they took their oath of office. The executioner, with his glistening longsword, stood directly behind him. This was not a public execution, but a somber private affair in which the government dealt with a distasteful, yet necessary matter. With one swing the executioner severed Falier's head. Both body and head tumbled to the base of the stairs. The chief of the Ten then carried the bloody sword to the balcony of the palace and showed it to the crowds below. "Behold," he shouted, "justice has been done to a traitor."

One might expect that the execution of the doge would lead to some measure of instability in Venice. Indeed, members of the government thought so, too, allowing all patricians to arm themselves for some time afterward. But life soon returned to normal and the matter was quickly put behind them. Marino Falier was buried in his family tomb, in the Chapel of the Madonna of Peace in the Scuola Grande di San Marco, near so many other doges in the church of SS. Giovanni e Paolo. (When the tomb was opened in the nineteenth century the severed head was found to have been placed between the traitor's knees.) Petrarch traveled to Venice the following month and heard of the startling events, but even he could not understand why the doge had taken part in such a plan. As a man who enjoyed the favor of Italian despots, Petrarch was not quick to condemn Falier. Indeed, he showed great empathy for him, suggesting that the Venetians should have extended more mercy toward the old man. Nonetheless, Petrarch understood the essential lesson of Falier's punishment. "Those who are for a time doges," he wrote, "I would warn to study the image this sets before their eyes, that they may see as in a mirror that they are leaders not lords, nay not even leaders, but honored servants of the State." With but a little blood, Venice had defiantly remained a republic.

Ten years later the heart of that republic, the Great Council, at last convened in its new grand chamber. This massive space, which today seems like an ornate ballroom, was filled with the desks and benches of hundreds of council members. Plague had reduced the patrician population so severely that it would take more than a century to fill the room completely. Beautiful frescoes (now lost), depicting some of the most important events in Venetian history, decorated the walls of the chamber. The north wall bore scenes of the Peace of Venice, while the south wall likely displayed the victories of the Fourth Crusade. At the head of the room, the great artist Guariento di Arpo produced a monumental fresco, *Coronation of the Virgin*. (Portions of it have been recovered and can be seen in the nearby Sala dell'Armamento.) Along the top of the walls were placed individual portraits of every doge, with plenty of room for more. In 1366, only a few months after moving into the chamber, the council decreed that the portrait of Marino Falier should be covered over. It seems likely that this was accomplished by simply hanging a dark curtain over the portrait. So important was the memory of this treason to the Venetians, though, that when fire destroyed the doges' portraits in 1577, the restorers painted an image not of Doge Falier, but of the curtain that had previously covered his portrait. On it can be found the words *"Hic est locus Marini Faledri decapitate pro criminibus"* (Here is the place of Marino Falier, decapitated for his crimes). It remains one of the most remarked-upon features of the Great Council Chamber.

Although Venice remained extremely prosperous, the decades after the execution of Marino Falier produced significant setbacks for the republic. King Louis of Hungary allied with lesser powers to force Venice out of Dalmatia, a land that it had ruled since the eleventh century. The once-lengthy title of the doges was reduced to "By the Grace of God,

Doge of the Venetians et cetera." Still, Venetian fleets continued to maintain unquestioned mastery of the Adriatic Sea, so the trade convoys were unaffected. Business, in fact, remained quite good in the 1360s and 1370s. Although the Genoese had seized the city of Famagusta on Cyprus, the Venetians simply shifted their trade markets to the southern part of the island. More importantly, armed with a papal dispensation to trade with Muslims in nonstrategic goods, the Venetians established themselves in Syria and Egypt. To avoid problems in the Mongol Empire, much of the spice trade from India began making its way through the Indian Ocean and the Red Sea, making the markets of Alexandria a source of rich profit for Venetians.

As they had done for generations, the Venetians and the Genoese continued to compete for advantage in the Aegean, Constantinople, and the Black Sea. There was, nonetheless, a feeling of unfinished business between the two powers. The Genoese resented the peace that had been forced on them in 1355, sure that they could have won their struggle with Venice once and for all. As the Genoese government convulsed between factions and interests, the Venetians were able to avoid war, but only for a time.

CHAPTER 10

FROM VICTORY TO VICTORY:
THE WAR OF CHIOGGIA AND THE
BIRTH OF THE MAINLAND EMPIRE

In October 1372, in the city of Famagusta, on the island of Cyprus, the king of Jerusalem gave a banquet. Of course, no king had actually ruled in Jerusalem for almost two centuries and this particular king, Peter II, was no exception. But as the newly crowned monarch of Cyprus, the sixteen-year-old ruler was entitled to the crown of Jerusalem and he certainly had no reason not to take it. The celebratory banquet, though, did not go at all well. Even as the lavishly dressed attendees took their places in the sumptuous banqueting hall, a palpable tension filled the air. Earlier in the day the young king had made a public procession through the streets of Famagusta to celebrate his new crown. As the crowds pressed in, a group of Venetian residents rushed in to take the right rein of the monarch's horse—a position of honor normally reserved for princes or prelates. Seeing this, the Genoese, who also had a large community in the city, rushed forward as well, grabbing the left rein and loudly insisting that it was they who deserved the right. Shouts and insults flew as each side tugged and pushed the other, with the terrified horse and the bewildered teenager caught in the scuffle. Finally,

King Peter's uncle, the prince of Antioch (another city long ago lost to Christendom), pressed into the fray with some of his men and forced the Venetians and the Genoese to return to their places among the crowd. He then took up the horse's rein and himself led the king to his palace.

At the evening banquet the Venetians and the Genoese were seated at tables far across the room from each other, and at first, all went well. Guests offered many speeches and toasts to the health of the new king. Indeed, there were so many toasts with so much Cypriot wine (known for its potency) that what little restraint remained among the angry Italians after the morning's fracas quickly evaporated. Shouts and insults between the Venetians and the Genoese began again, followed by threats, shoves, and finally outright fighting. The Genoese had come prepared. From their cloaks they produced daggers and even a few swords. The Venetians had not arrived without a few hidden weapons of their own, but they had much the worst of the fight. Enraged at the disturbance, the king called for the palace guards, who rushed in noisily, sized up the situation, and attacked the Genoese. Some of the Genoese were killed in the banquet hall; guards carried others to nearby balconies and threw them down to the street, five stories below. When news of the brawl spread beyond the palace, the people of Famagusta, also blaming the Genoese, stormed their quarter and burned their warehouses. By morning, the smoke of the bloody conflict still hung heavy in the air.

Hostility between the Venetians and the Genoese was intense, so intense that they could scarcely be put together in the same room, let alone the same city, without violence. It was a contempt bred of familiarity. Venetians and Genoese understood each other perfectly. Both sought fortunes in the East and found the other forever in the way. They were enough alike to grasp each other's stratagems and different enough to despise them. Many on both sides welcomed open conflict. War, it seemed, was the natural state of affairs between Venice and Genoa.

What no Venetian imagined, though, was that the next war, waged within only a few years of the knife fight in Famagusta, would threaten the survival of Venice itself.

Its seeds were sown not just in the banquet brawl, but in the overall political morass of the East. Although the once-great Byzantine Empire was but the faintest shadow of its former glory, the Venetians and the Genoese continued to jockey for position in Constantinople and its access to the ports of the Black Sea, still a source of goods from eastern and central Asia. The big news in the eastern Mediterranean was the dramatic expansion of the Ottoman Turks, a Muslim power that had settled in Anatolia more than two centuries earlier. Nicaea (modern Iznik) in northwest Asia Minor, not far from the capital, fell to their armies in 1331 and nearby Nicomedia did the same in 1337. The work of the Crusades finally undone, most of Asia Minor quickly came under Turkish rule. Only the waters of the Aegean and the straits of the Hellespont (Dardanelles) and Bosporus (and the Christian fleets that sailed them) kept the Turks from crossing into Europe itself.

As surprising as it may seem, it was the Byzantine Greeks themselves who ferried the Turks across those waters. In 1351 another in a long line of civil wars between those contending for the ruined throne of Constantinople raged across the shrinking Byzantine Empire. Fearful that he would lose his crown, Emperor John VI Cantacuzenus enlisted the powerful Turks to fight on his side. He rowed an army of ten thousand Turks across the straits and stationed them near Gallipoli, where they quickly put an end to the civil war. Although the strategem saved Cantacuzenus's power, the empire—and indeed all of Europe—was imperiled. The Ottoman forces soon began raiding the fields of Thrace while the emperor tried to bribe them into returning home to the Asian side of the waters. Then, in 1354, an earthquake brought down the fortifications of the city of Gallipoli and the Turks quickly captured and fortified it for themselves. The gateway to Europe was thus opened.

A growing and very reasonable fear of the Turks gripped Europeans in the fourteenth, fifteenth, and sixteenth centuries. Under the sultans, the Turks expanded their power at an alarming rate, making no secret of their desire to conquer the Western infidels. For nearly eight centuries, the Christian world had been shrinking, the victim of the extraordinary power of the medieval Muslim states. The Crusades, which had been launched to restore the Holy Land to Christian control, were retooled in the fourteenth century to defend Europe itself from Turkish invasion. The danger was grave indeed.

Pope Innocent VI (1352–62) called for new Crusades to push back the Turkish advance, and no state responded with greater enthusiasm than Venice. Although Emperor John V Palaeologus, who took the throne in Constantinople in 1354, promised to become Catholic himself and re-unify the Catholic and Orthodox churches in return for crusader help, he could offer nothing in terms of military support. Byzantium relied completely on Genoa for its naval defense—and the Genoese liked it that way. Indeed, when Byzantines had tried to build their own navy, the Genoese living in Galata (a suburb of Constantinople) burned it in the harbor.

The rivalry between Venice and Genoa in the fourteenth century, therefore, played out against the backdrop of Byzantine decline and Turkish ascendancy. The Venetians naturally favored international cru-sading efforts, since they promised to remove the Turkish threat and dis-rupted Genoa's power in the Aegean and the Bosporus. For precisely those reasons, the Genoese looked on Crusades with suspicion. Emperor John V at first clung to the Genoese for aid, even giving them the island of Chios in payment for their services to the empire. The Venetians, for their part, offered to cancel the Byzantine government's enormous debt—a debt that included the pawning of the imperial crown jewels—if the emperor would cede to Venice the island of Tenedos (modern Boz-caada) as a base for a Crusade against the Turks. A small, triangular island of no more than fifteen square miles, Tenedos was chiefly remembered as the spot where the ancient Greeks had hidden after placing the great wooden horse before the gates of Troy. Although it had little instrinsic value, the island's strategic location could significantly reinforce Venice's access to Constantinople and the Black Sea, since it commands the Dardanelles, the southern straits by which vessels must enter the Sea of Marmara and pass north to the capital. The Genoese naturally opposed the trade and so, unwilling to upset his defenders, the emperor rejected the Venetian offer.

Venice continued to contribute men and vessels to the Crusades and other operations against the Turks throughout the 1360s, but with only marginal successes. The Ottoman foothold in Europe was not an easy thing to reverse. Although a Crusade led by Count Amadeo of Savoy managed to recapture Gallipoli, Turkish forces had by then conquered all of Thrace, west of Constantinople. In 1369 the Turks seized Adrianople (modern Edirne) in the heart of Thrace and transformed it into a new western capital for the Ottoman Empire. Constantinople now lay completely surrounded—a bit of Byzantine flotsam in the vast sea of the Turkish empire. Serbian and Bulgarian leaders, who had for centuries threatened the Byzantines, were forced to become vassals of Sultan Murad I (1362–89). Even Emperor John V, the successor of the Roman Caesars, paid tribute and did homage to the Ottoman sultan.

Desperate for Western aid against the Turks, John V personally traveled to Rome. There he proclaimed himself a Catholic in return for the promise of even more and greater Crusades. On his return journey he stopped in Venice, an extraordinary visit for a number of reasons. The large and wealthy city of the lagoon remained proud of its heritage as a city of refugees who had fled the chaos of the West to maintain their allegiance to the emperor in Constantinople. Now, for the first time in its history, the emperor of Byzantium had come to Venice. But the glory of the Roman Empire had faded irretrievably in the past nine centuries, making for an awkward encounter. John did not find the Venetians particularly obedient, nor did the Venetians find the pauper emperor much to their liking. For one thing, John continued to owe Venetian bankers and the Venetian state a great deal of money. Since the loan contracts were severely overdue, and since John rejected every proposal for settling his accounts, the Venetians at last detained him as an insolvent debtor. While legally sound, the house arrest of the Byzantine emperor proved just as unpopular among Venetians as it was among Europeans and Byzantines. Seeking a way out, the Venetian government offered John their best deal yet. In return for the much-desired little island of Tenedos, the Venetians would cancel all the empire's outstanding debts, return the Byzantine crown jewels, and even provide John with a princely sum on which to travel. They would also, of course, let him leave. After some delay, John finally accepted the proposal. However, when it came time to pay up, John's son Andronicus refused to hand over Tenedos. Instead, John's other son, Manuel, raised the money himself to pay off the Venetians and thereby free his father. Despite the Venetian government's desire to get its hands on Tenedos, it had little choice but to obey the rule of law. When, in 1371, the emperor's debts were paid in full, he was promptly released.

But the matter of Tenedos persisted. After his return home, John V found himself not only short of funds but forced to defend himself against another coup, this one led by his son Andronicus. After suppressing the rebellion, John could not bring himself to execute his son or even to blind him—the usual punishments for failed coups. Instead, he split the difference, partially blinding and imprisoning him in the hope that this would end the matter. A few years later, in 1376, Venetian ambassadors in Constantinople finally persuaded the troubled emperor to sell Tenedos to Venice for thirty thousand ducats and the return of the crown jewels. Word was sent to the people of the island that Venice was to be their new protector, although their churches would remain under the jurisdiction of Constantinople, and the Venetian lion and Byzantine eagle would fly side by side on every wall and tower. The Genoese, who were unaccustomed to having emperors disobey their orders, moved quickly to depose John. A large band of armed Genoese broke into the imperial prison and released Andronicus, bringing him back to Galata, where he found the representatives of Sultan Murad waiting to help him in his bid for the throne. With Genoese and Turkish troops, Andronicus broke through a city gate, seized power, and threw his father and younger brother, Manuel, into the same dark prison he himself had only just escaped. When it came time to parcel out rewards, Andronicus IV (1376–79) handed Gallipoli back to the Turks, and Tenedos, which the Venetians had just purchased, to the Genoese.

For most Venetians, losing Tenedos to the Genoese was simply unacceptable. Combined with their base at Galata, it would give the Genoese the power to harass or even halt altogether Venetian commercial traffic to Constantinople and the Black Sea. The small Greek population of Tenedos found Genoese rule equally unacceptable. They were proudly loyal to John V, refusing to have anything to do with the rebel Andronicus. When the Genoese arrived to claim their prize, the Byzantine governor of Tenedos refused to surrender and beat off a Genoese attempt to take it by force. Shortly thereafter the Venetians arrived to a grand welcome with joyous songs and a parade of crosses. This the Genoese could not allow. They commanded their Byzantine emperor Andronicus to seize Venetian citizens and goods in Constantinople and even to arrest the Venetian baillie (an official who oversaw the Venetian community in Constantinople) and his councillors. The senators in Venice responded by sending additional war galleys, led by Carlo Zeno, to reinforce Tenedos and raid Byzantine properties near the capital. Finally, in November 1377, a combined fleet of Genoese and Byzantine forces attacked Tenedos. After a difficult and deadly engagement, Zeno and his men repulsed the assault, forcing the invaders to withdraw. Venetian and Genoese blood had been spilled in battle. The time for diplomacy between the powers had again come to an end. Back in Venice, the Great Council declared war on Genoa.

The War of Chioggia, as it came to be known, was the fourth, largest, and last of the wars between Venice and Genoa. Before it was over, the battle would spill across the Mediterranean and even into the Venetian lagoon itself. It is perhaps not surprising that a struggle of such magnitude would give rise to larger-than-life heroes who led it. The first was Carlo Zeno himself. As with all national heroes, Zeno's early life is wrapped in tall tales, some of which may be true. His father, Pietro, had been killed in 1343 during Venice's Crusade against the Turks at Smyrna. His family later marked him for a career in the Church, so he was sent first to the papal court in Avignon and then to the University of Padua for his studies. The bookish life, however, did not appeal to Zeno. Then, as now, there were plenty of taverns and diversions near the university, and Zeno made frequent use of all of them. Impoverished by gambling losses, he sold his books and joined a mercenary army—a promising, if often brief, career in late medieval Italy. Five years later he returned to Venice and, with no job prospects, again took up a clerical position, this time in a church in Patras, a thriving Greek port city in the northern Peloponnese with a large Venetian population. But church life still did not suit Zeno, so, despite his religious office, he organized and led several attacks against Turks in the region. Later, after challenging a knight to a duel, Zeno was dismissed from the church. He married and relocated to Constantinople, where he conducted business for several years. It is not clear what role he played in the Venetian purchase of Tenedos, but there is no doubt that he was on the island when the Genoese came to claim it.

More traditional than Zeno, but no less accomplished, was Vettor Pisani, a well-seasoned naval commander. Charismatic, sometimes rash, but with a down-to-earth demeanor unlike that of many of his fellow patricians, Pisani had a strong following among the common Venetian people. He had distinguished himself at the Battle of Porto Longo in 1355, during the last war with the Genoese, where he had served under his uncle, Nicolò Pisani, who died in the defeat for Venice. When the War of Chioggia began, Zeno was ordered to Negroponte, to look after Venetian interests in the East, while Vettor Pisani received the banner of St. Mark from the hands of the doge, who named him Captain of the Sea, the highest military office in Venice.

The Venetians hoped to overwhelm the Genoese with an offensive surge. Pisani was sent with a squadron of galleys to enter western waters near Genoa and attack at will. Zeno, who commanded a similarly well-armed naval force, received a more flexible mandate. He was to prey on Genoese shipping and interests in the East wherever he found them vulnerable, while still maintaining watch over Venetian vessels and colonies there. Both Venice and Genoa scrambled for allies in the war. Not surprisingly, they both found willing support among their enemy's closest neighbors, who naturally hoped to use the war to thwart the local powerhouse. The Genoese allied with the king of Hungary, who controlled Dalmatia and hoped to extend his power into the Adriatic. The Carrara family, who still ruled nearby Padua, joined the Genoese in an attempt to eject Venice from the mainland entirely. On the other side of Italy, Venice allied with Bernabò Visconti, the ruler of Milan, who was eager to reexert control over Genoa.

In April 1378 Vettor Pisani's fleet sailed out of the Adriatic, rounded the peninsula, and in May engaged a Genoese squadron not far from the Tiber River, capturing or destroying at least half of it. Along with some booty, he also took aboard a number of Genoese nobles, who were transported back to Venice to be held in comfortable confinement for the duration of the war. Pisani then sailed to the Aegean, where he added more galleys to his fleet before returning to the Adriatic, Venice's own sea. He put into port at Pola (modern Pula) and sent a message to the Senate requesting permission to return home for refitting and supply. But the

Senate denied his request, insisting that he remain at Pola, where his fleet could better protect the spring convoys making their way through the Adriatic. This put Pisani in a difficult, although not unmanageable, position. At the time there was no reason to expect trouble so deep in Venetian territory. Early in the summer of 1379, though, a sizable Genoese fleet of more than twenty galleys appeared off Pola. Although Pisani opposed a direct engagement with them, his fellow officers insisted that anything less would be cowardice. Bowing to their opinion despite his reservations, Pisani led the attack, which managed to isolate the Genoese commander's vessel and kill him. Relief swept through the Venetian ranks; it seemed they had won the day. However, just then six additional Genoese galleys rowed out from behind a hill and moved swiftly to ram the Venetian vessels. Caught by surprise, the Venetian fleet fell into disarray and was soon forced to surrender. Hundreds were killed or taken prisoner, but Pisani's vessel and a few others managed to escape. They sailed into Venice with the frightening news that the Genoese had gained control of the upper Adriatic.

Upon his arrival, Vettor Pisani was immediately arrested on the charge of poor leadership and abandoning a battle while it still raged. He was quickly tried and found guilty on all counts. The court stripped him of his rank, forbade him to hold public office for five years, and sentenced him to six months in prison.

While Pisani languished in jail, Venice's enemies continued to press forward. Hungarian forces closed off the rivers and roads to the north, while the Carraras in Padua did the same to the west. With Genoa in control of the Adriatic, the three powers had managed to isolate Venice, cutting it off from access to food and trade. Before long Genoese vessels could be seen sailing just off the Lido and the entrance to the lagoon near the monastery of San Nicolò. The cold fear of conquest, a stranger to the Venetian lagoon for centuries, now gripped the hearts of its citizens. The call went out for mercenaries, who came quickly enough once payments were assured. The land forces on the Lido were commanded by the condottiere Giacomo Cavelli, whose mercenaries had served Venice well in previous wars. An emergency committee of seven officials began sitting round the clock in the Ducal Palace, ready to respond to the expected invasion of the lagoon. When that happened, the bells at San Nicolò were to ring out the alarm, followed by the bells in the great Campanile of San Marco, and finally by all the bells in more than a hundred churches across the city. Each parish was charged with assembling armed men and bringing them to the Piazza San Marco at a moment's notice.

The attack finally came in August 1379. A combined force of Paduans and Genoese sailed into the lagoon and, after a bloody battle, conquered Chioggia. No foreign power had come this close to Venice since the Magyar invasion in 899. Yet this time the threat was more dangerous. The Magyars, as well as the Carolingians and Huns before them, had brought land forces that captured the periphery of the lagoon, but had no obvious way to advance into its watery core. Now that core was the city of Venice—one of Europe's largest and wealthiest urban centers. And the attackers were not simply land armies, but included Genoa, a great maritime power. The frightened Venetian government at once called for negotiations, hoping to talk their way out of the noose that was closing around them. The invading allies responded that they would hear no words of peace until they had bridled the proud horses of San Marco.

Things looked dark indeed for Venice. Much of the navy was off with Carlo Zeno, and no one knew where he was or when he might return. In so great an emergency, the government imposed a forced loan on wealthy Venetians to raise funds for mercenaries to man the forts of the lagoon. The resulting property assessment, called the *estimo* of 1379, is a boon for getting a closer look inside the city at this time, for it reveals the names and parishes of thousands of Venetians as well as estimates of their landed wealth. Those named in the *estimo* were required to buy government bonds in accordance with their means. Venice was also short on fighting men, so rather than casting lots (as was the common practice) the government conscripted *all* able-bodied men to defend the city. In the Arsenale, new war galleys bristling with oars were produced in record time, yet the oarsmen and marines that would serve aboard them were in reality shoemakers, cooks, and accountants. These new sailors needed to be trained to fight and to row—and soon.

The government appointed a new Captain of the Sea to replace Pisani, a puffed-up patrician named Taddeo Giustinian. His appointment did not warm the hearts of the popolo, who, as at Porto Longo, were blaming the present disaster on the arrogant nobility. Vettor Pisani was a noble, yet he had a unique rapport with the commoners. In the streets of Venice people grumbled over the shameful way that the government had treated him. The defeat at Pola, they insisted, was not his fault but that of the government leaders. It was they who had refused Pisani's request to return home for resupply, probably because they were jealous of his successes and eager to see him fail. Many common Venetians resolved only to serve if commanded by Pisani. Unmoved, the new galley commanders set up desks for enlistment on the Molo, but true to the people's word, only a trickle of men came forward. Meanwhile, several hundred men from Torcello arrived saying that they stood ready to fight under Pisani's command. When Doge Andrea Contarini (1367–82) informed them that Taddeo Giustinian was now the captain general, they cursed and went home.

As the invaders began to press forward toward the Lido, Doge Contarini finally prevailed upon the Senate to release Vettor Pisani. The senators did so reluctantly, perhaps fearing that the beloved admiral would use his popularity to overthrow the government. But Pisani was no Julius Caesar. He quietly left his cell and went immediately to Mass, where he received Holy Communion. He then appeared before the doge, to whom he promised every loyalty. When he later entered the Piazza San Marco, he was, of course, mobbed by thousands of ecstatic Venetians shouting, *"Viva Vettor!"* But he sharply corrected them, saying, "That's enough of that, boys! Say 'Viva the good Evangelist San Marco!'" A few days later Pisani took his seat at one of the galley registration desks on the Molo. He was surrounded by hundreds of men who pushed and shoved to enlist under his command. At last giving in, the government restored Pisani to his former position as Captain of the Sea.

With the internal strife resolved, the Venetian people and government worked diligently to ward off the common threat. Nearly forty galleys were produced and stationed at key locations around the lagoon. Every day galleys rowed between Giudecca and the Lido, training the craftsmen and day laborers to propel a war vessel. At last, in December 1379, the Venetians were ready to counterattack the enemy clustered in and around Chioggia. The plan was a variation of the one used against Pepin more than five centuries earlier. The Venetian lagoon appears to be a sea, but in reality it is a shallow pool with an average depth of about three feet. Vessels navigate the lagoon only by following the rivers and channels that lie hidden below the deceptive waves. Although Chioggia is surrounded by water, vessels can reach it only by means of a few waterways. The Venetians planned to cut off those waterways. Venetian war galleys would defend a group of heavy barges and cogs (large sailing vessels) filled with stones, which would be brought to the channels near Chioggia and sunk. Galleys, some carrying the new technology of stone-ball cannons, would then batter Chioggia's defenses, attempting to take back the island. The operation was launched on December 22, led by the elderly doge and accompanied by Vettor Pisani. It met with great success. Against the odds, the Venetians managed to turn the tables on their enemies. They surrounded Chioggia, although the Genoese on the island remained defiant.

The war had begun at Tenedos and continued in clashes and

skirmishes across the Mediterranean, but its most desperate battle was fought at Chioggia. The Genoese worked hard to clear the channels and repel the Venetians, still hoping that their blockade of the lagoon would bring the city to its knees. But the Venetians received a much-needed dose of good news on January 1, 1380, when the long-absent Carlo Zeno sailed into the lagoon with fourteen well-armed and expertly manned galleys. His mission to disrupt Genoese shipping had been an unqualified success. With their forces tied up in the Adriatic, the Genoese had been unable to defend themselves against Zeno's attacks. His patrols between Genoa and Sicily had netted numerous Genoese vessels and tons of precious cargo. Zeno had then sailed to Tenedos, which he fortified, and then successfully preyed on Genoese shipping in the Aegean and eastern Mediterranean. At Rhodes he had even captured the *Richignona*, the largest Genoese cog of its day bearing a cargo valued at half a million ducats. When he put in at Crete, which remained a Venetian colony, Zeno received orders to return to Venice at once. After refitting his ships, he did just that, culminating in his magnificent arrival in the lagoon on January 1.

With Carlo Zeno and Vettor Pisani working together, Venetian spirits soared. Zeno, the old swashbuckling mercenary, was especially useful for dealing with the frequent scuffles between the various Italian and English mercenary companies working for Venice. Indeed, when Genoese supplies in Chioggia were finally depleted, they attempted to bribe Venice's mercenary leaders to switch sides—something not at all uncommon in those days—but Zeno thwarted the plan. With all options exhausted, in June 1380 the Genoese on Chioggia finally surrendered the island. The worst was over for Venice. Over the next year Venetian fleets kept busy taking back the Adriatic Sea. Vettor Pisani died during those battles, and Carlo Zeno succeeded him as captain general. In 1381 the long and difficult War of Chioggia finally came to a close with the painstakingly negotiated Treaty of Turin. Venice lost little, but neither did she gain. The island of Tenedos—the cause of the war and still a bit-ter bone of contention between the two powers—went to the treaty's honest broker, Count Amadeo of Savoy, who, it was hoped, would use it as a base of operations against the Turks.

For Venice, the spoils of the War of Chioggia were measured not in booty, but in survival. Although Venice was the capital of a large and prosperous maritime empire, it had nonetheless come within a hair-beadth of conquest. It survived because the republican government, for all its complexities and inefficiencies, remained rock solid even during enormous adversity. Although they had disagreed with their govern-ment in the matter of Vettor Pisani, the Venetian people expressed that disagreement peacefully. Once again, the Venetians' love for their repub-lic won out over their attraction to any one man. As Pisani himself had said, it was not to him, but to San Marco, the symbol of Venice, that the people owed their allegiance. That belief not only carried them through the war, but ensured that they were poised to capitalize on the peace.

Within a month of signing the Treaty of Turin, the Venetian government awarded thirty commoner families permanent membership in the no-bility. In part, this was a recognition of the extraordinary contributions that they had made toward the war effort. However, in so great a strug-gle as the War of Chioggia, virtually all Venetian citizens had made ex-traordinary efforts. What set these thirty families apart was their wealth. It cannot be stressed enough that the patrician nobility in Ven-ice was not a static, landed gentry like that in most other places in the world. It was instead a large group of families with a right to serve as representatives of the "people of Venice" in the Great Council and to hold high offices in the government. Because Venice was a capitalist so-ciety based on international commerce and entrepreneurialism, it was natural that over time some family fortunes would rise while others would decline. Throughout their long history the Venetians had repeatedly made adjustments to membership in circles of power based on those fluctuations—whether it was the new families of the eleventh century who became the "good men" of the doge's court or the families that gained admittance to the Great Council during the fourteenth-century Serrata. To make no adjustments would have produced dangerous imbalances whereby old yet financially weak families ruled over new economically powerful ones, a state of affairs no republic could endure. The War of Chioggia, therefore, provided an opportunity for the government to again co-opt those Venetians who were in the best position to help or, if excluded, to harm the Republic of St. Mark.

Of course, new arrivals into any elite group are often looked down upon, and the Venetians were no exception. Old families (many of whom had been new families only a few centuries earlier) referred to themselves as the *longhi*. These included stalwarts such as the Dandolos, Michiels, Zianis, Mastropieros, Morosinis, and Gradenigos. Researching and producing genealogies became popular in fifteenth-century Venice as noble families sought to link their distant ancestors with the first tribunes or other early settlers in the lagoon. In the sixteenth century Marco Barbaro produced his massive compendium of Venetian family genealogies, which laid out the real and sometimes imagined histories of Venice's noble clans. Although the longhi did have impressive pedigrees, much of the early history that they now claimed was simply wishful thinking. The newer patrician families were known as the *curti*. It is sometimes said that relations between the longhi and the curti were poor, but there is little evidence of it; in fact, the two groups frequently intermarried and voted for each other in state elections. While the longhi may have enjoyed a certain prestige, it was often mitigated by their relative poverty and increasing dependence on government stipends to make ends meet. Given the natural rise and decline of family businesses based on commerce rather than agricultural estates, it is not surprising that the curti grew in power during the next few centuries—indeed, virtually all the subsequent doges were members of the curti.

The War of Chioggia badly bruised Venice's economy, but did not undermine its fundamental soundness. Disruptions in trade coupled with punishing forced-loan levies on the citizens had taken their toll. Yet Venice's rulers were businessmen. They understood finance and worked hard to pay off debts and restore government bonds as a safe investment. Genoa did not fare as well. Torn by civil wars and factional violence, the city passed from one ruler to the next. Genoese merchants also began to spend more of their time in the western Mediterranean, searching for profitable markets there. It was not an unreasonable decision. The Turkish advance into the Balkans continued apace throughout the late fourteenth century. The Ottoman Empire was becoming the superpower of its age, and the sultan could raise large and well-trained armies of foot soldiers and cavalry. He also had the Janissaries, an elite unit made up completely of slaves taken from their Christian parents during infancy and raised in military barracks to be warriors par excellence. Europe had no comparable military force. Even the Crusade of Nicopolis in 1396—perhaps the largest Crusade yet launched—was utterly destroyed by Ottoman forces. It seemed nothing could stand in the way of the Turks.

The Venetians did not even try. They were sailors and their field of battle was the sea. Fortunately for them, the Ottoman Turks had little interest in naval matters, leaving control of the Aegean largely to Venice. Venetian patrols continued to make their way through the Adriatic and Greek islands, and Venetians still held colonial bases at Negroponte, Crete, Modon, and (most recently) Corfu. Indeed, the relentless advance of the Ottoman Empire actually opened up opportunities for Venice, as various Greek or French lords decided that it was better to sell their Balkan port cities rather than lose them to the Turks. In this way Venice greatly expanded its overseas colonies, acquiring Durazzo, Scutari, Lepanto, Patras, Argos, Nauplia, and even Athens as well as several additional Greek islands. Provided that the sultan's rights were respected and sufficient payments made, the Venetians were allowed to keep all their new acquisitions.

Venice moved quickly to gather up these crumbling fragments of the Byzantine Empire, in part to keep them away from Genoa but also as insurance against the day when the ancient empire would be no more. By 1400 the Byzantine emperor Manuel II Palaeologus (1391–1425) ruled little more than Constantinople, and even that was besieged by the armies of Sultan Bayezid I (1389–1402). Desperate for aid, Manuel left the capital on a two-year fund-raising tour of Europe. The Renaissance in the West had created a strong appetite for Greek and Roman antiquity, so there was a good deal of interest in the emperor and his colorful entourage. Everywhere he went, Manuel was received with unbounded enthusiasm. Crowds poured out to cheer the brave, yet humble, emperor who had become a symbol of defiance against the Turks. After touring Italy, Manuel arrived in Paris, where King Charles IV lavishly entertained him. The following year he was the guest of King Henry IV in England, where he was similarly celebrated. Manuel's trip had a powerful impact on European fashions and Western perspectives of the East. But the large sums of money and vast armies that his hosts promised never did materialize.

With little help against an implacable foe, it seemed that the last chapter of the long history of the Byzantine Empire had at last been written. But remarkably Constantinople was saved by powerful forces that it neither controlled nor truly understood. A Turkish/Mongol leader named Timur (or, as he became known in Europe, Tamerlane) led a huge Mongol army into Anatolia and demanded the immediate surrender of all Turkish lands there. Sultan Bayezid abandoned his siege of Constantinople and amassed his forces near Ankara to fend off the eastern invasion. What followed was one of the largest engagements of the Middle Ages. Timur and his Mongol armies not only crushed the Ottoman forces but captured Bayezid as well. According to some reports, Timur kept the sultan on display, chained in a cage like an animal. The loss of the sultan and much of the army led to a mad scramble for power in Turkish lands, which eventually resulted in a brutal civil war between Bayezid's three sons. Ottoman power, which had caused all of Europe to tremble, suddenly evaporated. Timur swept through Asia Minor and then, as quickly as he came, returned to the East, where he later died. The ruins of the Ottoman Empire lay strewn everywhere. Anatolia was awash in petty emirs and Ottoman princelings competing for the throne. In Thrace, Bayezid's oldest son, Suleiman, managed to gain some measure of control in Adrianople, but he was weakened by the continued civil war. Fearing a new Crusade from the West to save Constantinople, in 1403 Suleiman returned a number of lost territories to the Byzantine Empire, including Thracian ports, the Peloponnese, various Aegean islands, and even the city of Thessalonica. He furthermore abolished the annual tribute and the vassalage of the emperor. It was an amazing reversal.

For Venice all the news was good. The demise of the Ottoman Empire in the east mirrored a similar decline of Genoa in the west. Beset by internal strife, Genoa gave itself (for a time) over to the kings of France, who would govern it until 1409. This did not eliminate the danger for Venice, for there were always companies of Genoese freebooters patrolling eastern waters seeking their own profit. But Genoa no longer controlled its own foreign policy, so the possibility of another full-scale war was greatly diminished. Nevertheless, Venetian foreign policy remained complex as kingdoms and empires continued to shift dramatically in the fifteenth century. As a result, the governmental body charged with overseeing foreign affairs, the Senate, came to dominate the Venetian government. The Great Council remained the repository of all political authority in Venice, yet the need for rapid decisions based on an extensive network of diplomats meant that in practice the Senate began to play the largest role in steering the ship of state. It was the Senate that swiftly deflected the attempts of Francesco Carrara, ruler of Padua, to cut off land trade routes between Venice and Germany. When diplomacy failed, the Senate allied with Gian Galeazzo Visconti, the ruler of Milan, in a war to eliminate the troublesome Carraras once and for all. By the time that war ended, Venice had managed to restore complete control over Treviso. A few years later, after Visconti's death, Venice further expanded its mainland holdings to include Padua, Vicenza, and Verona. In 1400 the Venetian Senate even began dividing its registers of deliberations between *terra* and *mar*, land and sea. The Venetians were acquiring a mainland empire to rival their maritime one.

Across the waves, Venetian trade stretched to the eastern Mediterranean and the Black Sea, energizing the economy at home. Indeed, by 1410 Venice had rebounded from the War of Chioggia so strongly that the Dalmatian port cities asked to be returned to Venetian rule, finding it preferable to being fought over by the thrones of Hungary and Naples. The galleys and merchant vessels of Venice sailed out of the Adriatic and across the waves in search of profit—and they found a great deal of it. Spices were the most famous cargo, because they were rare, expensive, and much desired in western Europe. But there were a great many more. The rapid depopulation of Europe due to plague had produced a severe labor shortage within a well-established and still vibrant economy. The cost of labor (and thereby the individual incomes of most Europeans) rose, which in turn provided an economic incentive for producing labor-saving devices. The Venetians themselves had begun using some new ship designs such as cogs, which had single masts and could be managed with smaller crews. There was, of course, no way to skimp on military manpower on state galleys, but since all the Mediterranean powers were equally harmed by the plague, this only meant that fewer vessels took part in naval engagements. The great battle off Pola in 1379 consisted of scarcely forty vessels. Compare that with pre-plague fleets, like that of the Fourth Crusade, which numbered well over three hundred major vessels. Venetian galleys in the fifteenth century continued to escort merchant convoys through the waters of the Adriatic and Aegean. Goods unloaded in Venice were then sold to merchants who bore them northward, across the Alps. Along the way, the state taxed every transaction and the Venetian economy flourished.

Safe trade routes overland had traditionally not been a concern of Venetians, who very deliberately focused their attention on the lagoon and the sea. Since northern Italy was fragmented into competing communes and petty regional powers, there was little fear that all routes could ever be closed. But by the late fourteenth century the rise of the signori had produced powerful and expansionistic states in Italy that could conceivably cut off Venice's access to the trade routes, produce, and raw materials of the mainland. Indeed, that had been the goal of Genoa and Padua during the War of Chioggia. The Venetian government responded by first neutralizing the threat posed by the Carrara family, and then establishing colonial rule over lands stretching from the lagoon all the way to Lake Garda, near Verona. Once Venice was established as a mainland power, however, it was difficult for its people not to be drawn further into Italy's politics and wars. Although the cities that Venice acquired were largely left to govern themselves, they nonetheless required Venetian officials, which provided lucrative jobs for nobles needing work. In short, a careful expansion of Venice's empire onto the terra firma seemed not only prudent but natural.

And there was no shortage of opportunity to do so. In 1418 the king of Hungary allied with the patriarch of Aquileia, who ruled Friuli, to the north of Venice. Their aim was to launch strategic assaults on Venetian strongholds to deprive Venice of both Istria and Dalmatia. The plan was beset, however, by delays and obstacles, so it never fully materialized.

The Venetians nonetheless responded by attacking and defeating the patriarch's forces, which received no support from Hungary because of renewed Turkish threats on its borders. In 1420 the capital city of Udine fell and the patriarch was forced to cede all of Friuli to Venice. The mainland holdings of the Republic of St. Mark instantly doubled.

By 1423 Venice's expansion into Italy had brought its people to a new crossroads. The powerful Visconti family in Milan had rallied under the rule of Filippo Maria after the death of Gian Galeazzo. Milan held Lombardy in its grip and was extending its authority southward. The question for the people of Venice—a question that would have been unimaginable to their ancestors—was what to do about it. There were at this time five major Italian powers: Naples, which ruled southern Italy and Sicily; the papacy, which ruled Rome and central Italy; Florence, which ruled Tuscany; Milan; and Venice. When the Viscontis began their new conquests, Florence reached out to Venice for support. It was an attractive request. Like Venice, Florence was a republic—at least at times. It was also the birthplace of the Italian Renaissance. Steeped in the florid literature of civic humanism, Venetian patricians were naturally amenable to Florentine pleas to join a war against the tyranny of the Visconti despots.

But Venetians had never before contemplated a land war of such magnitude. The Viscontis of Milan were not to be trifled with. They currently ruled Genoa, something that made them in every way more dangerous to Venice. Furthermore, a war with Milan—as with all Italian wars in this age—would have to be fought by mercenaries under the command of condottieri, powerful generals who sold their services to the highest bidder. And that would be expensive. In his *Lives of the Doges*, Marino Sanudo tells us that the eighty-year-old Doge Tommaso Mocenigo (1414–23) spoke out strongly against Venice's entry into this war. With death approaching, the doge made an impassioned appeal to his countrymen not to mire Venice in campaigns of conquest on the terra firma. He did not call to mind their shared history of isolation from the problems of Italy, nor the dangers of building empires that one cannot sustain. Instead, in good Venetian fashion, he explained precisely why a war against Milan made no business sense. Peace had brought prosperity to the people of Venice. The state debt had been greatly reduced, and each year goods worth more than ten million gold ducats flowed through the ports and markets of the city. As an economic powerhouse, Venice already consumed the fruits of Lombardy, which were traded freely in its markets. Why, the doge asked, would Venetians willingly bring fire and sword to Lombardy and in the process impoverish themselves with military expenditures? He condemned Francesco Foscari, the leading proponent of the war, as a lying scoundrel interested only in expanding his own power, even if it meant the economic ruin of Venice. Venetians had before them a choice: Follow the old ways of honor and profit in the islands, ports, and quarters of the eastern Mediterranean, or turn toward Europe, its states, and its wars.

Weeks later Mocenigo died, and the Venetians elected Francesco Foscari (1423–57) as their new doge.

Foscari began preparing for battle almost immediately. In 1425 the republics of Florence and Venice formally declared war against Filippo Maria Visconti, the lord of Milan, with the stated aim of preserving the freedom of Italy. It is fitting, then, that during the next three decades all of Italy was at some point involved in this war. Venice's forces struck deep into Lombardy, capturing Brescia in 1426 and acquiring Bergamo by treaty two years later. The twists and turns of this long and complex war need not detain us here; suffice it to say that it was a typically Italian affair, full of treachery, violence, and shifting allegiances. The main actors in the struggle were, of course, the condottieri. These expert mercenary generals commanded enormous wages, which were bid ever higher by the warring states competing for their services. Condottieri were contracted military leaders, working under a *condotta*, or contract, that bound them to a specific state for a specific period of time and for a specific sum. Although Venice sent officials to accompany its condottieri in the field, their primary purpose was simply to express broad war objectives and to keep watch on their investment. The details of the campaigns, though, were left to the individual condottieri. By their nature, these warlords did not choose sides. While they were under contract to one state, they were obligated to wage war efficiently and effectively for it. When that contract expired, however, the condottiere was a free agent and could just as easily switch sides, waging war against his former employer.

Overall the Venetians found the system to their liking. Indeed, without condottieri and their mercenary armies Venice could not have waged land wars at all. Since successful generals who capture large swaths of territory can often become tyrants, Venetians were also amenable to a system that kept military leaders at arm's length and allowed them to be easily dismissed. Not everything went smoothly, though. Francesco Bussone da Carmagnola had won Brescia and Bergamo for Venice, but as he advanced toward Milan to press his advantage, he suddenly and unexpectedly halted. No amount of bonuses or promises from the Venetian government could persuade him to take up the offensive again. Agents of the Council of Ten subsequently learned that Carmagnola was secretly negotiating with Filippo Maria Visconti, for whom he had worked earlier. This sort of treachery could not be excused, but punishing a man with a mighty army is not a simple thing. The Ten, nonetheless, devised a plan. The condottiere was invited to Venice in 1432 to discuss strategy. When he arrived, he was welcomed joyously in the Piazza San Marco with high honors and much celebration for his victories. When the party concluded, he was promptly arrested, tried, and beheaded between the two columns on the Molo.

In 1447 Venetian prospects seemed to brighten when Filippo Maria Visconti died without a male heir. The people of Milan overthrew the

Visconti family (again) and proclaimed a new republic. Yet even this did not end the war. With help from the new ruler of Florence, Cosimo de' Medici, the condottiere Francesco Sforza became Duke of Milan and was able to push hard against Venice's continued march westward. By 1453 there seemed no way to stop the war and no end to the number of mercenaries willing to fight it.

But then everything changed. Unbelievable news began spreading across Europe, shaking everyone who heard it. The last Christian state in the East had been destroyed by the roaring advance of Islam. The ancient empire that had once seemed eternal, that had civilized western Europe and given birth to Venice itself was no more.

Byzantium had fallen.

CHAPTER 11

DEATH OF A PARENT:
THE FALL OF CONSTANTINOPLE AND
THE RISE OF THE OTTOMAN TURKS

The first Venetians were Roman citizens, refugees of the empire's collapse in the West, and loyal subjects of its emperors, who still reigned in Constantinople. The Byzantine Empire was in every way the parent of Venice, and as the centuries passed, the child grew to independence, maturity, and strength. There were, of course, quarrels, but Byzantium and Venice were simply too closely related to forever go their separate ways. By 1400 the Byzantine Empire, then over a thousand years old, had grown withered, weak, and sick. The Republic of Venice, approaching the pinnacle of its own power and glory, was forced to grapple with the painful realities of the decline and death of its parent.

Once, long ago, Roman emperors had executed grand plans of expansion and progress. Emperor Manuel II Palaeologus prayed only that the empire would not fall during his lifetime. His prayer was answered, although only just. In Manuel's day the length and breadth of the largest empire in Western history had been whittled down to the city of Constantinople. The capital and the empire had become synonymous. Various groups held the districts and islands outside the walls of the emperor's city. The Genoese had their independent walled colony at Galata, just across the harbor from Constantinople, as well as several other islands, including Lesbos and Chios. Various Greek despots and princelings ruled over their own small patches of territory. The greatest power in the region, though, was the Ottoman Empire, which had fully recovered from the blow it had received in 1402 at the hands of Timur. Sultan Murad II (1421–44), reigning in the Ottoman capital of Adrianople, was determined to wipe away the last remnants of the Christian Byzantine Empire. In 1422 he began sieges of both Constantinople and Thessalonica. The latter, long known as the second city of the Byzantine Empire, had been restored to the Byzantines by Suleiman in 1403, but Murad meant to have it back.

Venice's foreign policy in the East during the early fifteenth century can best be understood as a strategy of defiant struggle against the collapse of the old order. Although Constantinople had little left to offer Venice, save a port along the way to the Black Sea, the Venetians nonetheless treated the emperors there with every deference and respect, despite their unpleasant encounter with the debtor John V a few decades earlier. Every five years they dutifully sought an imperial chrysobull—an elaborate gold-sealed document bestowing privileges on the Venetians and permission to do business throughout the Byzantine Empire. Although the emperors still owed Venice a great deal of money (a fact noted in the chrysobulls themselves), the Venetians could not bring themselves to treat the successors of the Roman emperors as petty despots, outward appearances notwithstanding.

To conduct profitable business in the East, the Venetians needed safe and secure shipping lanes and ports. Since 1204 they had adopted a policy of acquiring Greek islands and colonies along the trade routes to Constantinople and Syria. This policy was stepped up as the Turks dismembered the Byzantine Empire. The Venetian Senate had no illusion that it could challenge Turkish power as it spread across Greece, Bulgaria, Serbia, and Albania. But it was determined to retain Venetian maritime access to the markets of the East. Venice controlled most of the Dalmatian coast, the island of Corfu, the cities of Modon and Coron, Negroponte, many Greek port towns such as Nauplia, numerous Aegean islands, and, of course, Crete. They naturally took pride in any victory over the Turks, who continued to march relentlessly toward western Europe. Venetians reveled in the Crusade history of their republic—no state in Europe had so frequently crusaded. But they could not fight every battle. Wars continued to rage throughout Europe, and no one, except the popes, the Venetians, and the states on the ever-advancing Ottoman border, seemed to notice the danger posed by the Turks.

Murad's siege of Constantinople in 1422 set more than a hundred thousand Turkish troops against a Byzantine defense force of less than ten thousand. But Constantinople's defenders had the mammoth triple land walls of the ancient city, which had repelled every invader since their construction in the fifth century. The Ottoman siege lasted four months before Murad finally called it off. The city's survival seemed a miracle. Indeed, the Byzantine Greeks attributed it to the intercession of the Virgin Mary, who had always been the special protectress of Constantinople. Some claimed to have seen an angel on horseback riding along the walls of the city, deflecting every attack.

Unfortunately, Thessalonica had no such angelic defender, and the people of the city feared what would happen to them when their city again fell to the Turks. The Byzantine governor there—the title was Despot—was the son of Emperor Manuel II, a young man named Andronicus, who was crippled by leprosy or perhaps elephantiasis. Rather than lose his city, he sent an intriguing offer to the Senate in Venice. If the Venetians would commit to the protection and provisioning of Thessalonica, they could have the city as their own. The senators did not take long to accept the offer, but it was an emotional, not a practical, choice.

To have the second city of the Byzantine Empire, the coveted jewel of Macedonia, offered to Venice seemed impossible to turn down. Even the senators emphasized that they accepted Thessalonica "for the honor of the Christian faith and not out of ambition for dominion." It also helped that the new doge, Francesco Foscari, favored a bold expansion of the Venetian empire. He had championed Venice's entry into the war against Milan—a war that was still raging across northern Italy—and favored a strong Venetian response to Turkish aggression in Greece. Naturally, he also supported the acquisition of Thessalonica. Its successful defense would certainly bring honor to Venice, although whether it would do the same for its profit was an open question.

Once a thriving commercial center, Thessalonica had been reduced by the Turkish siege into a starving, ramshackle husk sheltering some twenty-five thousand residents who had been unable to flee. On September 14, 1423, the Feast of the Exaltation of the Cross, the city of Thessalonica formally became a part of the Venetian empire. The Greek citizens lined the streets leading to the harbor to cheer and welcome the Venetians, who brought with them troops, weapons, and most important, food. The banner of St. Mark was solemnly hung from the city's walls and planted in the central square. But matters in Greece were worse than previously thought. Back in Venice, even while the roads and canals echoed with celebrations, word arrived that the Turks had stepped up their efforts to capture Thessalonica. More ships, more men, more money, and much more food were needed to sustain it. The Senate sent everything requested. It also sent an ambassador, Nicolò Giorgio, to the court of Sultan Murad to negotiate peace. Giorgio explained that the Venetians had taken the city in order to keep it out of the hands of other, less honorable Christians—a clear reference to the troublesome Genoese. The sultan was unamused. He arrested Giorgio and demanded the immediate surrender of Thessalonica. The senators in Venice were outraged. They dispatched more war vessels to Thessalonica "so that the said Turk and the whole world should be made aware that the arrest of the ambassador was and remained a serious and scandalous offense, that Venice prized the city of Thessalonica and had no intention of relinquishing it."

The struggle over Thessalonica dragged on for years, costing the Venetians dearly in both treasure and blood. And yet, for all their efforts, the Venetians could not reconcile the sultan to their ownership of Thessalonica or even attain a level of cooperation from the city's own citizens. Ingratitude mixed liberally with loud complaint was the near constant refrain from the Greeks of Thessalonica. They avoided helping with the defense of their city, but regularly berated the Venetian governors for not providing sufficient food and amenities to meet their needs. The old Greek prejudice against Venetians always ran strongest when Greeks were at their weakest, so it is not surprising that it was given full vent in the streets of Thessalonica. Although the Venetians had guaranteed their property, civil rights, and the independence of their Church, the Greek citizens still complained that it was irksome to have so many Venetians moving freely about the city. In June 1425 they sent an official delegation to Doge Foscari complaining about the Venetian duke of Thessalonica, Bernabò Loredan, and his captain, Giacomo Dandolo. They insisted that the doge order his men to keep their distance from the Greeks. They also demanded more food and more money, which they believed the Venetians should spend on repairing Thessalonica's walls and other buildings. The doge tried to comply, offering higher prices for independent merchants to deliver food to Thessalonica, but it was not enough to please the Greeks.

In 1426 Sultan Murad ordered his army of some thirty thousand troops to storm the walls of Thessalonica. Along those walls the Venetians had stationed seven hundred crossbowmen, who rained a blizzard of deadly bolts down on the attackers. They were assisted by five galleys in the harbor, which may have brought small cannons as well. The battle raged throughout the morning, until at last the Turkish commanders sounded the retreat. More than two thousand Turks lay dead on the fields outside the city. Yet the Greeks within remained unimpressed. Indeed, they had only begun to plumb the well of their ingratitude. Leading Greeks began to advocate surrender to the Turks. Some of them remembered the old days of Turkish rule, between 1387 and 1402, and claimed that it was in every way preferable to Venetian government. Although they admitted that the Turks could be cruel overlords, the Venetians were impertinent sailors who could not bring dinner on time. To quell the unrest, the Venetian authorities arrested and exiled some of the most vocal advocates of surrender. The sickly former Despot, Andronicus, was sent back to Constantinople, where he became a monk in the monastery of Christ Pantocrator.

But resentment in Thessalonica continued to grow. A second delegation of Greeks arrived in Venice in 1429, bringing with them a detailed list of thirty-one grievances against the Venetians. Most of these dealt with the amount of food that Venice was providing and the means of its distribution in the city. But they also demanded that Greek residents be allowed to leave the city if they no longer wished to live there. The Senate apologized for the food difficulties and promised to rectify them, but refused to allow Thessalonica's citizens to abandon their city. The Turks were not invincible; indeed the Venetians had repelled them only a few years earlier. The Senate continued to insist that Thessalonica could be saved.

Unfortunately, only the Venetians still believed this. The captain of Thessalonica, Giacomo Dandolo, went to Adrianople to try again to negotiate peace with the sultan. Like Giorgio before him, Dandolo was put in chains and thrown into a Turkish prison, where he died a few weeks later. Venice had no choice but to declare war. The Genoese, always eager to assist any foe of Venice, quickly allied themselves with the Turkish sultan.

The final attack on Thessalonica came in March 1430. The sultan himself led a massive army of more than a hundred thousand men out of Adrianople and against the battered city. He did not mean to return without the matter settled once and for all. With him he brought enormous siege engines pulled by camels, whole battalions of archers, and as many rock-throwing cannons as he could find. Greeks who had earlier fled the city assured Murad that the population had no desire to defend itself against his benevolent rule. The arrival of his forces, they said, would be a signal for the citizens to kill their Venetian masters and open wide the gates to the Turks. No doubt these Greeks correctly gauged their countrymen's desires, but not their will to challenge the well-armed Venetians, who were under orders to defend the city at all costs. Once again the Venetians were forced to take on the job with little help from the Greeks. Indeed, they had to post guards to watch over the Greeks, some of whom were caught digging tunnels to escape and to allow the Turks to enter.

On March 29 the assault began. The Turkish archers fired so continuously that one defender claimed that it was impossible to raise a hand above the fortifications without having it pierced by an arrow. The "man-made thunder" of the cannons echoed across the battlefield, keeping the defenders from repeating their crossbow attacks, which had worked so well in 1426. The Turkish soldiers pressed forward, raising scaling ladders onto the battered walls. The Venetians fought hard, but the sheer number of Turks was simply overwhelming. Finally, a lone Turk, armed only with a dagger clenched in his teeth, climbed a ladder and found a single wounded Venetian defending a tower. He killed him, hacked off his head, and threw it down to his companions, urging them to join him on the wall. The attackers scrambled up and over the walls and began a bloody sack of Thessalonica that would not long be forgotten. Churches were despoiled, women raped, and every Christian who could be found was enslaved or put to the sword. The Venetians fought with grit and resolve. More than two hundred of them perished, including the son of the Duke of Thessalonica. When it became clear, though, that all was lost, the Venetians fled to the harbor, where they boarded their vessels and sailed home. They would travel many miles before escaping the terrified screams of Thessalonica and the smoke of its immolation.

The loss of Thessalonica was a bitter defeat for Venetians at a time when their other war in Italy was going reasonably well. After seven long years, the loss of hundreds of Venetian lives, and spending more than 700,000 gold ducats, they had nothing to show for their efforts at Thessalonica save the hatred of those they had tried to save. It was time to make peace. In September 1430 they concluded a treaty with Murad in which they agreed to relinquish their claim to Thessalonica and pay a sizable sum of money. In return the sultan promised to respect Venice's Greek holdings and to keep Turkish warships out of the Aegean Sea. The trade routes, at least, were safe.

The extraordinary violence unleashed at Thessalonica convinced Emperor John VIII Palaeologus (1425–48) that Constantinople could survive only if another major Crusade was launched to force the Turks out of Europe. The West had been sending Crusades to defend Byzantium for centuries—indeed, the First Crusade had been called in 1095 for precisely that reason. But since then the Orthodox Greeks had acquired a reputation in the Catholic West as enemies of the Christian faith, a people who would rather make deals with Muslim conquerors than defend the lands of Christendom. Their behavior at Thessalonica did nothing to challenge that judgment. The Greeks' refusal to accept the authority of the pope over the Church only added to their image in Western eyes as prideful, arrogant, and rebellious—not the sort that one is inspired to save from ruin. John therefore believed that if Byzantium was to be saved, it was necessary to end the schism between the Greek Orthodox and Roman Catholic churches. For centuries, Greeks had maintained their disagreements with Rome because no ecumenical council had ruled on the matters in dispute. They did not accept the authority of the pope to pronounce judgment on them. The key, then, was to call a council that would be truly ecumenical, one that no Greek could gainsay.

As it happened, the decade of the 1430s was a particularly good time to call such a council. A church reform movement in Europe, known as conciliarism, had grown out of the universities and was spreading across the West. Conciliarists argued that councils of bishops and other prelates should be called regularly to advise and instruct the pope; some conciliarists even argued that councils should replace papal authority altogether. In 1431 the Council of Basel convened and was soon taken over by conciliarists, who hoped to see papal power severely curtailed. Ironically, a weakened pope was the last thing that Emperor John VIII wanted to see. For his plan to work, he needed a pope in the old medieval mold, one that could rouse the soldicry of Europe to take up arms against the Turks and save their Christian brothers and sisters in the East. Pope Eugenius IV (1431–47), himself a Venetian of the wealthy Correr family, understood this well enough. He opened negotiations with John regarding the prospect of a new council, a fully ecumenical council that would bring the Christians of the world together to heal the schism and, not incidentally, shut down the conciliarists at Basel into the bargain.

Venice assisted with these negotiations, ferrying Byzantine ambassadors back and forth to Italy and offering encouragement. Church schism was not a major issue for the Venetians, who had long ago come to terms with the fact that although they were themselves obedient Catholics, their Eastern trading partners were not. But Venice did support any initiative that would bring Europeans together to fight the Ottoman Turks. Thessalonica had taught Venice that it did not pay to go it alone. The Turks were simply too powerful, and when the war ended, the harm fell solely on Venice. Crusading remained a powerful aspect of Venetian identity, but Venetians were no longer willing to charge off to fight the infidel while the rest of Europe watched.

At last the plans were set. In 1437 Eugenius IV transferred the Council at Basel to Ferrara and called the prelates and leaders of Christendom to attend. In effect, this closed down the Council of Basel, which had been a thorn in the side of the papacy for six years. The few moderates left at Basel headed for Ferrara, leaving behind only the most radical conciliarists. These declared Eugenius's bull of transfer invalid and even sent envoys to Constantinople to invite John to come to Basel instead, promising him full support. The emperor rejected this dubious offer. He was going to meet the pope, the only man who could call a Crusade. More than six hundred Greek prelates, including Patriarch Joseph II of Constantinople, and Emperor John boarded papal galleys and made their way west. The council at Ferrara would indeed be ecumenical.

Although the galleys flew the papal flag, they were nonetheless Venetian and so quickly joined the regular Venetian merchant convoys heading back home. The aged Greek clergy and sumptuous imperial court could not travel quickly, so they wintered at Venetian Modon before heading up the Adriatic and arriving in Venice on February 8, 1438. The Venetians were ready for them. This visit was something special. Not only had the emperor himself come to the lagoon, but he had brought with him his court, his clergy, and indeed almost all the high officials still left in the once-great empire. The government of ancient Rome had landed in Venice. They had come to heal Christendom, to restore the rent garment of Christ as the first step toward turning aside the centuries-long ascendancy of the Muslim world. Modern observers, with our perfect hindsight, might scoff at the pageantry and proud words of the moment, passing them off as a futile attempt to save a doomed relic of the medieval world. But it did not look that way in 1438. There was real optimism, real hope, and a real belief that God would soon deliver his people. For the Venetians, this was compounded by a filial devotion to their parent state, which even in its darkest hour sought out God's will.

On February 9 Doge Francesco Foscari boarded the magnificent ducal galley, itself a floating palace, known as the *bucintoro*. Banners bearing the imperial eagle of Byzantium streamed along the sides of the vessel, while from the prow waved the winged lion of St. Mark. The richly dressed oarsmen wore caps with both state symbols figuring prominently. The bucintoro was not the only vessel in the Bacino. The entire sea was filled with boats ranging from large merchant vessels to small gondolas. Brass horns and strings played music, while the bells of the city rang in celebration. The doge crossed from his vessel to that of the emperor, who waited on an ornate throne, with his brother, Demetrios, seated to his right. Foscari removed his ducal *corno* and bowed low before the emperor. Then, at his invitation, the doge of Venice took the lower throne to the left of the emperor. Cheers arose from the ships and shores of Venice, celebrating the arrival of the Byzantine emperor and his government in so grand a fashion that one might imagine that they still ruled an empire. The rich vessels then rowed to the Molo, where more ceremonies and celebrations took place. Then the mass of boats moved slowly down the Grand Canal, as spectators hailed the Byzantine dignitaries with flags and handkerchiefs from the windows and doors of the magnificent palazzi. When the boats reached the Rialto markets, the merchants and bankers joined in the celebration. So that the emperor's ship could pass, they even raised the wooden Rialto Bridge—something rarely done given the disruption to the businesses planted on it. Finally, the watery parade docked at the ornate Byzantine-style palace built by Giacomo Palmier in the thirteenth century and purchased by the Venetian government in 1381 (the modern Fondaco dei Turchi). There the emperor and his court would lodge during their stay in Venice.

The Byzantine dignitaries were overwhelmed—not only by the welcome, but also by the sheer wealth of Venice. They quickly made themselves comfortable. Although the Venetian government had voted a thousand ducats for their upkeep, the Byzantines quickly burned through that. Indeed, before they were finally ready to say good-bye, they had accumulated more than three thousand ducats in bills. During his two-and-a-half-week stay Emperor John received numerous envoys from Europe's leaders. He even heard from the conciliarists at Basel, who again urged him to come to their council rather than that of the pope. As before, he politely declined. Finally, on February 27, the mob of Byzantine political and religious leaders boarded their vessels and left Venice, bound for Ferrara.

For more than a year the Greek Orthodox and Roman Catholic prelates, theologians, and philosophers hammered out their differences at the church council. It was a grand affair. An international collection of well over a thousand leaders of the Christian faith converged upon Ferrara from as far away as Egypt and Ethiopia. For the first time in centuries all five of the ancient patriarchates of Christianity were assembled. Fearing a plague in the area, the council left Ferrara in late 1438 and reconvened in Florence. The grandeur of the event was not lost on the cradle of the Renaissance. Indeed, the artist Benozzo Gozzoli even depicted the richly adorned Emperor John VIII as one of the Magi in his famous fresco in the Medici Chapel. Across the Alps in Basel, the once-fashionable council withered as its attendees excused themselves one by one to take part in the events of Ferrara and Florence. With only a single cardinal and eleven bishops remaining, the Council of Basel deposed Pope Eugenius IV and elected Duke Amadeo of Savoy as Pope Felix V. Scarcely anyone noticed. Felix was never recognized as pope outside Switzerland and his own Savoy. Many of those he appointed as cardinals declined the honor. Amadeo held on to his papal title for ten years before finally submitting to the pope in Rome, thus ending the last papal schism in the history of the Catholic Church.

At last the work of the theologians, prelates, and politicians in Florence was complete. Amid great celebration Pope Eugenius and Emperor John formally signed the document of union on July 5, 1439. The long separation between the Greek and Latin sides of Christianity had finally come to an end—at least on paper. The emperor and his clergy were sincere enough, but they misjudged the power of certain factions in the Byzantine East, some of whom would accept no union with the West, no matter the conditions. Yet those problems still lay in the future. For the moment, Christians rejoiced that East and West were reunited and looked forward to a new Crusade to drive the Turks from Europe.

The sultan had not been idle while the West debated its theological differences. To the contrary, he mobilized a large army to threaten Constantinople in John's absence, hoping to capture it before any Crusade could materialize. The Byzantine delegates made their way back to the threatened city in various groups. Emperor John was among the last to return. He remained in Florence for a month and then traveled to Venice, where he was warmly welcomed and so decided to stay a bit longer. Since East and West were reunited, Doge Foscari suggested that they pray together in the church of San Marco at a Mass to be sung by Greek clergy according to the Orthodox rite. Although the Venetians meant to celebrate the union and honor the Greeks, it was a difficult pill for some of them to swallow. Until recently, Greek clergy were accustomed to ritually purifying altars that had been used by Catholics.

John left Venice in October 1439, arriving back in Constantinople in February 1440. He brought news of Christian unity and much-needed aid from Europe. Yet, some of his subjects—particularly the monks—responded to the news with anger and resentment. It is a mistake (although a common one) to assume that all or even most of the Greeks rejected the Council of Florence/Ferrara and the union agreed upon by their emperor and patriarch. In fact, most Greeks accepted it willingly and with much hope. It was only after the fall of Constantinople that the fictional cry "Better the Turkish turban than the Roman miter!" was uttered or put to paper. But a vocal minority of Greeks did oppose the union with the Catholic Church and they fought every effort of the Byzantine government and Orthodox ecclesiastical authorities to implement the decrees of the ecumenical council.

Back in Rome, Pope Eugenius kept his word. He immediately called a Crusade to rescue the Byzantines, and a tithe was proclaimed across western Europe to fund the effort. Because of the Hundred Years' War, the kingdoms of England and France found it difficult to participate, although Duke Philip of Burgundy joined with many French knights. The bulk of the Crusade's forces came from Poland, Wallachia, and Hungary—those kingdoms most at risk from Turkish invasion. Led by John Hunyadi of Transylvania and King Ladislas of Hungary, the Crusade of Varna (as it came to be called) set forth into southeastern Europe in 1444 with more than twenty thousand men.

Venice, too, joined the Crusade, with a fleet of eight war galleys commanded by the Captain General of the Sea, Alvise Loredan. They met up with four galleys belonging to Philip and ten from Pope Eugenius and headed eastward with the plan to sail to the Black Sea and up the Danube River to assist the foot soldiers marching east. The ten papal vessels, however, were in reality Venetian galleys manned by Venetian crusaders, although commanded by Cardinal Francesco Condulmer and flying the papal standard. In other words, the pope had contracted his entire fleet from Venice. Unfortunately for the Venetians, the pope does not appear to have believed in paying for it. The Senate complained bitterly that Venice had spent enormous amounts of money on the Crusade, yet the pope continued to delay spending anything at all, even for his own vessels. Unable to wait any longer, the Venetian crusaders sailed out of the lagoon flying two flags, hoping that the pope would make good on his promises.

The Crusade of Varna began well. The army of eastern European crusaders marched into Turkish territory and captured the cities of Nish and Sofia. Sultan Murad, who was busy with matters in Asia Minor, offered a ten-year truce with all Christian powers in return for the removal of the Crusade from his domain. King Ladislas, eager to neutralize the Turkish threat to his own kingdom even for a decade, quickly accepted the offer in July 1444. Meanwhile, the Venetian Crusade vessels had arrived at Gallipoli, where they received news of the truce. They were ordered by the Senate to hold their position there at the Hellespont. This they did. However, two hundred miles to the northeast the land-based Crusade army was torn by widespread dissatisfaction with the truce. Many soldiers complained that they were trading away their hard-won victories only for a short-term promise of peace. Finally, the cardinal-legate on the Crusade absolved King Ladislas of his oath of truce that he had sworn to the sultan. In September the crusaders crossed the Danube and continued their march against the Ottomans. When Murad heard of this in Asia Minor, he was enraged. He ordered his forces in Europe to be assembled, and he personally traveled to the suburbs of Constantinople, where he crossed the Bosporus and met up with his army. The Venetian crusaders, still holding at the Hellespont, knew nothing of the crusader army's decision to break the truce and so they did nothing to impede the sultan's trip westward. After taking command of his forces, the sultan engaged the land army of the Crusade at the city of Varna in Bulgaria. He destroyed it utterly. The cardinal-legate and the king of Hungary were killed in the bloody battle, and thousands more crusaders were captured and decapitated. Only a few Christians survived to make their way home. As for the Venetian fleet, it remained at the Hellespont, completely unaware that the Crusade was over.

Most Europeans blamed the disaster at Varna on those crusaders who had broken their truce with the sultan. But the pope also took the opportunity to blame Venice. Had the Venetians moved against the sultan as he crossed the Bosporus, the pope maintained, Murad would not have been able to return to Europe and command his forces against the Crusade. Instead, the Venetians stood idly by while the Turkish leader rushed off to crush the Christian forces. Eugenius refused to pay for the Venetian vessels and men he had contracted. The Senate responded that its crusaders in the fleet at Gallipoli had done all that they could do, given the situation. They did not know that the Crusade army had foolishly broken the truce with Murad. The Venetian crusaders had spent a difficult winter holding the Hellespont while enduring Turkish attacks. It was not right, the Senate insisted, that the pope should refuse to pay what he had promised, especially to such faithful crusaders.

Once again the Venetians were betrayed by the fickle nature of crusading in the late medieval world. Not only had the pope refused to honor his commitments, but Venice was once again at war with the Turks. The Genoese living in the Galata suburb of Constantinople had been ideally positioned to stop the crossing of Murad, but they had done nothing, remaining completely out of the Crusade effort. Venice, on the other hand, had joined the Crusade and thereby found itself at odds with both sultan and pope. Although it still had not been paid, the Venetian fleet remained off Gallipoli threatening Turkish operations until Venice finally concluded a new peace treaty with the sultan in February 1446.

Emperor John VIII died in 1448 and was succeeded by his brother, Constantine XI (1448–53), a pious and honorable man who humbly took the crown of a ruined empire. In 1451 Sultan Murad also died, leaving the powerful Ottoman Empire to his nineteen-year-old son, Mehmed II, whom history would name "the Conqueror." Mehmed believed that the Ottoman Empire represented the new, divinely ordained order. As such, it was destined to erase the last remnants of the ancient Roman Empire and take its place as the ruler of the world. As Rome's capital, Constantinople must become the seat of the sultanate.

Mehmed did not wait long to move his plans forward. He raised tens of thousands of Turkish troops and ordered them to assemble at Constantinople. In April 1452 Mehmed began constructing a great fortress, Rumeli Hisari, just north of the city where it commanded the Bosporus strait, designed specifically to stop enemy sea traffic between the Black Sea and Constantinople. With its completion and the arrival of some hundred thousand Turkish soldiers, Mehmed had effectively encircled the Byzantine capital on both land and sea. It was not the largest force that had ever besieged Constantinople, but it remained impressive. And Mehmed also brought something altogether new: large gunpowder artillery. The triple land walls raised by Theodosius II had stood impregnable for a thousand years, but their architects could never have envisioned the danger of powerful cannons firing day and night for weeks on end. Truly, the old world was passing away.

In Venice the plight of Constantinople was a source of serious concern. Constantine XI sent envoys to the lagoon in early 1452, begging for aid. He urgently needed gunpowder and breastplates and begged the Venetians to send warships to Constantinople as soon as possible. The senators sent the requested supplies at once, but the military aid was more difficult. Venice had become a major Italian power and its ongoing war with Milan continued to drain its military and economic resources. The senators assured the Byzantine envoys that Venice would help, but urged them to persuade Florence and the papacy to join the effort as well. Several months later the Senate sent a letter to Pope Nicholas V (1447–55) asking him to call a Crusade and to move with all speed to defend the Christians of the East. They also urged those cardinals who were Venetian to argue in the Roman curia for the rescue of Constantinople. Nicholas did what he could on such short notice. He sent two hundred archers from Naples as well as Cardinal Isidore, the former Greek Orthodox archbishop of Kiev, as his legate. Spirits soared in Constantinople at the arrival of the pope's men. As a symbol of their determination to remain united, on December 12, 1452, a Mass was concelebrated in Hagia Sophia using the Orthodox and Catholic liturgies. It was the first time that the union had come to the greatest church in the Byzantine world. It would remain there for as long as Hagia Sophia remained Christian.

Events at Constantinople upset Venetians not just emotionally, but economically as well. Access to the Black Sea, especially the markets of Tana (modern Tanais), was a major element in continued Venetian prosperity. And the only passage to the Black Sea ran through the Bosporus strait and past Constantinople. When Mehmed completed Rumeli Hisari, he announced that no vessels were to sail past it without first receiving permission and paying a toll. Powerful cannons mounted on the fortress underscored his demand. Several Venetian vessels managed to run the gauntlet, probably before the Turks had an opportunity to properly sight their guns. In August 1452, though, a Venetian merchant vessel carrying barley was struck by the cannons and sank. The commander, Antonio Rizzo, and some thirty crewmen were brought in chains to the sultan. Mehmed ordered Rizzo to be impaled along the roadside and the remainder of the Venetians decapitated. The truce had clearly come to an end.

Great Constantinople, which had once teemed with almost one million inhabitants, now had only fifty thousand people living among its broken ruins. Only the walls remained in good repair. Most of the residents were women and children. Less than five thousand Greek fighting men could be found to defend their capital. They were assisted by about two thousand foreigners, largely consisting of Venetians, with some Cretans, Genoese, and other Italians in the mix as well. The Venetian defenders were a stew of expatriates living in Constantinople and ships' crews who just happened to be there when the siege began. Among them was Nicolò Barbaro, a ship's surgeon who later wrote his memoirs of the event, as well as several ships' captains, including Gabriele Trevisan, Alvise Diedo, and Giacomo Coco.

In December 1452 the Venetian baillie, Girolamo Minotto, called a meeting of his councillors and other leading Venetians in the city. He put before them a simple question: Should they remain in Constantinople and fight, or board their vessels and flee? When the vote was counted, the decision was clear: The Venetians would stand with the Byzantines. Minotto decreed that no Venetian vessel should leave Constantinople until the siege was lifted. He immediately sent letters home informing the Venetian government of the danger and their resolve to meet it.

When Minotto's letters arrived in February 1453, the Venetian Senate moved swiftly. It ordered a squadron of fifteen war vessels to be prepared for departure in April. The fleet would be commanded by Captain General Giacomo Loredan, who was to make all haste to Constantinople and assist with its defense. The Senate also sent ambassadors to Rome and to other monarchs urging them to send to Constantinople whatever aid they could. Yet only Pope Nicholas V responded to Venice's call. He sent three Genoese vessels laden with arms and provisions in March and offered to fund several galleys from Venice. The preparation of the warships in Venice, though, met with infuriating delays. Finally, the Senate ordered Loredan to sail with five vessels and to pick up additional ones from Corfu, Modon, Crete, and other Venetian colonies along the way to Constantinople. Help was coming, but events were moving fast.

Back in Constantinople the emperor pleaded with the Genoese residents of Galata, the walled suburb across the harbor from the capital, to join the Christian defenders, but they refused. They insisted on Genoa's neutrality in the matter, hoping to keep their lucrative positions with whoever won the contest. The Venetians, on the other hand, fully committed their wealth and lives to Constantinople's defense. The Senate had already sent an ambassador to Sultan Mehmed II, insisting that he withdraw from the city. Recognizing that Byzantium hardly posed a threat to the Turks, the Venetians argued that their long-standing residency in Constantinople essentially made the city a colony of the Venetian empire. The implication was clear: The capture of Constantinople would not end a war, but start one against a powerful adversary. Emperor Constantine XI underscored that assertion when he allowed some one thousand Venetians to parade along Constantinople's land walls, waving their standards bearing the winged lion of St. Mark for the Turks to see. Indeed, the emperor himself remarked that Constantinople had come to belong more to Venice than to the Greeks.

None of that mattered to Mehmed. His guns continued to fire, and the defenders kept up their desperate resistance. On April 12 Mehmed ordered his fleet to break the defensive chain and take the Golden Horn, the harbor that lay between Constantinople and Galata. But the Venetians won the day, repulsing the Turkish attack and saving the chain. Mehmed was not so easily discouraged. On the night of April 22 the Turks managed to haul more than seventy smaller craft over the hills of Galata and deposit them directly into the secured harbor. The Genoese, who watched the whole operation, did nothing. In the morning, the surprised defenders rushed to their vessels. Giacomo Coco led a naval attack that was betrayed by a Genoese spy, and the Turks quickly overwhelmed him. Coco's vessel was blasted by cannon fire, killing him and his crew.

What happened to the promised aid from the West? The Genoese ships sent by the pope were stalled at Chios by winds from the north. Because Captain General Loredan's fleet had to be cobbled together along the way, its progress was seriously delayed. It limped toward Negroponte, where Loredan tried to coordinate additional rendezvous with local governors and the home government. He hoped to make Constantinople by June. On May 3 Emperor Constantine sent a lone vessel to slip past the Turkish blockade to see if help was coming. The scouts returned with the disappointing news that nothing was on the horizon. The city's defenders would just have to hold out longer.

But their time had run out. By mid-May the sultan had assembled his full forces and the walls had been battered for nearly a month. On May 28, as they watched the Turkish forces draw up in ranks, the defenders recognized that the main assault was finally coming. Minotto assembled the Venetians and ordered them to the walls. "For the love of God and for the sake of the City [Constantinople] and the honor of the Christian faith," he exhorted them, "let every man be of stout heart and ready to die at his station."

The attack came before dawn on May 29, 1453. Mehmed sent wave upon wave of warriors against the walls, starting with those of low quality and finishing with his elite Janissaries. Fierce and terrible fighting raged for hours. Finally, at a point on the northern portion of the land wall, the Genoese commander, Giovanni Giustiniani, fell wounded in battle. Concluding that all was lost, he insisted that his men retreat, bearing him to their vessels so that he could escape. Giustiniani's flight set off a panic along the walls that allowed the Janissaries to press in. The Venetian forces were surrounded and captured. Seeing that "the City" was taken, Constantine XI, the last emperor of the Roman Empire, tore off his imperial purple and plunged into the fray near the Gate of St. Romanus. It was a noble end to an ancient empire.

As was the custom, Sultan Mehmed II allowed his victorious troops to sack the city of Constantinople for three days. They found little wealth, but many people to kill, capture, rape, or enslave. The Venetian leader, Girolamo Minotto, was arrested and, along with his son and seven other Venetian patricians, executed. He had warned his countrymen that their lives were staked on the defense of Byzantium, and he bravely gave his own when the time came. Hundreds of Venetians and thousands of Greeks were rounded up by the Turks and executed or sold into slavery. A handful of well-off Venetians were able to purchase their lives and return home, bearing heartbreaking stories of bravery and defeat.

The fall of Constantinople shook western Europe in a way that is hard for us to imagine today. Although the Byzantine Empire had long been weak, the frequent and unfulfilled prophecies of its impending doom had led many to assume that it would weather this storm, too. The destruction of the last Christian empire in the East meant that western Europe now truly stood alone against the powerful Muslim world. Mehmed certainly did not mince words. After conquering Constantinople, he promised to unite the younger and elder sisters under his rule—a clear reference to Rome. No European doubted that the Turks would be coming soon.

For Venetians, the events of May 29, 1453, were not just frightening, but devastating. It was not simply that the Ottoman sultan now controlled the straits, or that he had killed hundreds of Venetian citizens, or even that he had seized hundreds of thousands of ducats' worth of Venetian property. All of these were upsetting, of course. But it was the intangible sense of lost heritage—lost history—that cut the deepest wound. During joyous and lavish ceremonies just fifteen years earlier the Venetians had celebrated and honored the Byzantine emperor with real filial devotion. Now all of that was gone. The aged and infirm parent of the Republic of Venice had at last passed away.

CHAPTER 12

SOWING AND REAPING:
MEDIEVAL VENICE AND THE
BIRTH OF MODERN FINANCE

Medieval Venetians were greedy, money-grubbing scoundrels.

At least that is what many people believed. In truth, of course, they were no more avaricious than other Europeans. What set them apart was their utter reliance on a system of free-flowing capital. Medieval Europe was a largely agrarian economy. Most Europeans worked the land, either as serfs or peasants. The wealth of Europe's kings, nobles, and clerics was based above all on cultivation. Land produced the agricultural surpluses necessary to fuel a manor-based economy and funded skilled medieval warriors. Few medieval Europeans consumed goods that were produced more than a few days' journey from their homes. Most exchanges, therefore, were in kind—a barter system with little or no money involved. Although money came increasingly into use in Europe after the eleventh century, it was found primarily in cities and towns and at fairs. In rural areas, where most of the population lived, the great, leather-bound account books of the manor or monastery still recorded payments in candles, wine, livestock, and beer.

In Venice, where land was scarce, trade was the very heart of the economy. And to trade the vast array of goods that made their way into the markets of Venice, only money would serve. The Venetians were just as earnest about making money as other Europeans were about raising a bountiful crop. As they regularly reminded their neighbors, Venetians did not plow fields, but sailed the seas for their livelihood. So, yes, money indeed held importance in the city of the lagoon. The Venetians spent it, saved it, and eventually minted it. They also found new ways to work with it and to make it work for them—innovations that still shape our world today.

It is difficult for us to imagine a world without money. But that is what Europeans faced in the centuries after the fall of the Roman Empire. Political, economic, and legal uncertainties made the old Roman coins unreliable, so they were quickly abandoned. Money, however, is a crucial tool for ensuring that both sides in a bargain get a square deal. If, for example, someone offers to trade one cow for two pigs, how is one to know if that is a fair transaction? Cows and pigs, after all, are very different beasts. If both, however, are valued according to a third commodity, things become much clearer. So, if a cow was widely recognized as being worth five hides and a pig worth three hides, then the aforesaid offer is clearly a bit light. The owner of the cow needs to offer a bit more. One hide would do it—or something else valued at one hide.

In this example, hides are the currency because they are the means by which different commodities are valued—they allow dissimilar items to be traded easily. Hides do have a utilitarian value. One can use them to produce armor, cover a book, or make a drum. But no one needs ten thousand hides, which a rich man would likely have in any hide-currency economy. In other words, the currency need not be utilitarian in any way. It must simply be something that is generally accepted as a measurement of worth—in just the same way that other weights and measures must be generally accepted or else they are useless. A currency must also be something for which the supply is limited—otherwise, it has no capacity for measurement. A useful currency should also be portable (unlike hides) and durable. Portability allows for the easy transfer of wealth, while durability allows that wealth to be saved. This is crucial, for a durable currency allows a seller to give away his or her goods in exchange for that currency with the sure knowledge that it can be exchanged again at a later date for something of equal worth. It allows a person to amass a great deal of wealth over time—far more than would be possible in a system without money.

Since currencies require widespread acceptance, states are the only entities with the means to produce, enforce, and monitor them. In the pre-modern world states minted coins out of precious metals, thereby guaranteeing a certain weight and fineness for each coin. Someone with a pound of silver would find it very difficult to purchase anything, since merchants would insist on testing the silver content (fineness) and the weight of every piece for every transaction. Instead, it was much easier to deliver that silver to the state mint, where it was used to produce coins of an accepted value. The state, of course, charged a fee for this service, but it was well worth it. Each coin was stamped with the symbols of the state, making clear what sort of coin it was and what state guaranteed its worth. Unlike in the modern world, the value of a pre-modern coin lay in its metal content, not the words or numbers stamped upon it. For that reason, coins of different states could be used in any market in which they were familiar. Indeed, before the twelfth century few European states minted coins at all. Venice did not. Before the twelfth century, Venetians used Byzantine coins (bezants, hyperpers, and others), coins from Muslim states (known as saraceni), or imperial coins from Verona.

Although Charlemagne minted few coins, he nonetheless established in western Europe the basis of a monetary system that was itself based loosely on the old Roman one. The core of the system was the silver coin known as a denarius. Two hundred forty denarii would weigh exactly one Roman pound (libra). Twelve denarii were worth one of the old Roman solidi. The system, then, was simple: 1 libra = 20 solidi = 240 denarii. When European states later produced their own currencies, they continued this system. This is, for example, the famous English system of pounds, shillings, and pence that was used until 1971. Although the system was clear and therefore always used for accounting, it rarely corresponded to the actual coins in use. Only in England did the denarius retain its original content of 1.5 grams of 0.925 fineness silver. Elsewhere, new coins were minted with increasingly less silver content and more copper. This watering-down of the coinage allowed the minting state to enrich itself, but at the cost of price inflation. As soon as merchants learned of the lower quality of the coin, they naturally demanded more of them. Older, higher silver-content coins were then hoarded and often melted down—just as a silver Kennedy half dollar or Washington quarter will today be kept rather than spent. In Continental Europe devaluations of coins had become so common that by the twelfth century most denarii (pennies) were largely copper. Pennies minted in Pavia in the 1160s had only 0.2 grams of silver and those minted in Verona only 0.1 grams! This was only enough silver to give the coin a deceptive shine when it came out of the mint—a shine that would quickly darken with handling. (A silver coin that turned copper red when rubbed was said to "blush with shame.")

As the Middle Ages progressed, Europe and the Middle East developed a trimetallic monetary system. "Black money" consisted of debased pennies, halfpennies, and other low-value everyday currencies made primarily of copper. "White money" referred to coins with high silver content that kept their shine despite handling. Finally, "yellow money" consisted of high-value gold coins, minted as pure as technically possible. Because gold was (and is) much more valuable than silver, gold coins were used only for very large transactions. Their portability, however, made them useful for Venetian merchants purchasing tons of cargo in faraway ports.

A medieval farming village might not care overly much about the silver content of the few coins that made their way through the small local markets. But for Venice, where commerce and trade were the lifeblood of the community, a sound currency was absolutely critical. Uncertain coin values meant uncertain markets—something no businessman wants. During much of the twelfth century Venetians who engaged in small domestic transactions used the Veronese penny and another small penny of their own, which weighed less than half a gram and had 25 percent silver content. For large commercial transactions they used the coins of the Byzantine Empire or the crusader kingdom of Jerusalem. However, the monetary situation in the Middle Ages shifted as quickly as the political picture. The decline of the crusader kingdom in the 1180s led to the debasement of its currency. By 1187, when Saladin conquered Jerusalem, gold coins minted in the Holy Land were only 68 percent fine. Matters were not much better in the Byzantine Empire. Venetian merchants often stipulated payments in the Byzantine hyperper, a high-value gold coin seven-eighths fine. Because the physical hyperper was relatively rare (like a thousand-dollar bill today), Venetians usually exchanged the aspron trachy, a coin originally worth one-third of a hyperper and composed of 30 percent gold, 60 percent silver, and 10 percent copper. More than any other coin, this was the one most familiar to twelfth-century Venetian merchants. But economic and political problems in Byzantium took their toll on the aspron trachy. By the middle of the twelfth century, Emperor Manuel I Comnenus had debased it sufficiently that it was valued at four rather than three to the hyperper. Subsequent emperors debased it even further so that by 1190 it took six aspron trachy to purchase one hyperper.

These fluctuations in coinage at home and abroad were, of course, destabilizing to Venetian trade. To restore stability, Doge Enrico Dandolo, the famous leader of the Fourth Crusade, ordered the production of an entirely new Venetian currency. This momentous step gave Venice much more control over its economic destiny. Dandolo discontinued production of the old Venetian silver penny and replaced it with two new coins. The first was the low-value *bianco,* or halfpenny, which weighed about half a gram and had 5 percent silver content. With a cross on one side and a bust of St. Mark on the other, the coin was valued at one-half of a Veronese penny. He also minted a new coin, the *quartarolo,* or quarter-penny. With virtually no precious metal, this was the first token coin (with no inherent value) minted in Europe since ancient Rome. Like modern coins (which still mimic the copper, silver, and gold colors of the Middle Ages) the quartarolo was meant to be used for very small daily purchases.

Although important domestically, neither of these coins solved the problem of the devalued trade currencies. In dealing with this problem, Enrico Dandolo and his council would make their mark on international currency for more than a century. They issued the *grosso,* the first high-value coin minted in western Europe in more than five centuries. The grosso weighed about 2.2 grams and had the purest silver content that medieval technology could produce: about 98.5 percent fine. The design of the coin left no question that it was meant to replace Byzantine coins as a medium of international trade. The Byzantine aspron trachy was struck with an emperor and a saint both grasping a cross or a labarum on the front and an enthroned Christ on the back. In clear imitation, Dandolo's grosso depicted himself and St. Mark grasping the banner of St. Mark on one side with Christ enthroned on the reverse. The grosso established Venice as a major player in European and Mediterranean currency markets. It was followed up in 1284 with the minting of the first Venetian gold coin, the ducat, a high-value currency modeled on the Florentine florin. It was an attempt—ultimately successful—to create a stable commercial currency under the control of the Venetian state.

At 24 karats, the Venetian gold ducat was also as pure as the technology allowed. It quickly gained wide acceptance across the Mediterranean and Europe, where it remained a well-respected currency for centuries.

The Venetians' innovations extended not just to currency but also to the development of new financial "products," many of which are still in use today. Chief of these was the invention of deposit banking. Scholars still debate whether the first bank appeared in Florence or Venice; in any case, the Venetians were certainly early adopters. Without deposit banking modern economies would be impossible. Banks are not only a means of safeguarding money, but also a method of maintaining a constant and energetic flow of capital within a complex economy. Without deposit banking money that is saved is hidden away and removed from the economy—it does nothing except preserve its original worth. Deposit banking, however, allows saved money to be loaned and invested, thereby producing more wealth. Since the heart of deposit banking is lending, one might imagine that it began with the moneylenders or pawnbrokers of the Middle Ages. It did not. It came, instead, from those whom Christ had chased out of the Temple—the money changers, whose ability to navigate the multiplicity of monies was as vital in the Middle Ages as it was in antiquity.

As the previous pages attest, the medieval currency system was complicated. There were many different coins with values not stamped upon them, but decided by the market. A merchant at a fair or in the Rialto stalls might bring many different coins with him to purchase goods. All of these needed to be evaluated for soundness and then exchanged for a common currency. Traditionally, money changers provided that service, taking a commission on the amounts exchanged, much like modern currency exchanges encountered in airports. If, however, a merchant had a large amount of money and planned to buy many different goods over the course of several days, it was cumbersome to keep exchanging funds for every transaction. Instead, at some point in the eleventh century merchants at Rialto began to deposit all their money with a money changer, who would record the amount in his ledger. When the merchant later made a purchase, he would go back to the money changer and request the amount needed. The money changer would give it to him in the proper currency and mark the debit on his ledger. The merchant would then return to the seller and pay for his goods.

What transformed this convenient practice into deposit banking was its widespread adoption in Venice. As time went on, it became standard practice for merchants to deposit their funds with money changers, and the market sellers did the same. This meant that the money changers had accounts on their books for an increasing number of people. It did not take long before transactions that had previously been done with coin were executed instead on the money changer's ledger. A buyer and seller with accounts at the same money changer would go together to his table and ask that the purchase price be deducted from the buyer's account and added to the seller's account. There was no counting out or weighing of coins necessary. The entire transaction was quick, convenient, and safe. Thus was established the *giro* system, from *girare* (to circulate or rotate).

During the eleventh and twelfth centuries that was about as far as the system went. The real potential for economic growth lay in the ability to extend credit to customers by allowing them to overdraw their ledger accounts. Since a great many Venetians, including common citizens, deposited their money, a money changer with many accounts could allow overdrafts provided that all the depositors did not demand their funds returned at the same time. But well into the thirteenth century this sort of activity was still considered to be a betrayal of trust. Some money changers in Venice did extend credit, but only for their best customers and only occasionally. In Florence, the practice was even rarer.

In time, the money changers became so important to commercial transactions that the Venetian government began to regulate them. They clustered together in the Campo San Giacomo di Rialto, the church square in Venice's busy financial district. Each money changer sat on a *bancherius* (bench) with a small table on which he kept a ledger, a pen and ink, an assay scale, an abacus, and a bag of coins. After a while these men became known by where they sat—they were the *bancherii* (benchers)—in other words, bankers. Although their benches and stalls have long since disappeared, the covered archway that protected them and their customers still surrounds the campo. And it is still known today as the Sotoportego del Banco Giro.

In the late thirteenth century Venetian money changers (now bankers) began loaning money more regularly. Before issuing a license, the state required the banker to deposit, with the state, a large sum of money as bond, which would be used to pay off depositors if the bank failed. Because the bonds were invariably less than an active bank's total liabilities, depositors in a failed bank generally received only a fraction of their money back. It appears that this discrepancy led some bankers to disappear with their deposits, letting the state keep and distribute the much-smaller bond. To deal with this problem, sometime before 1318 the government required that bonds be posted by a third party—someone other than the banker himself. This backer, usually an investor with a close association with the banker, had a clear interest in making certain that the banker obeyed the laws, remained solvent, and stayed put.

Venetian banks offered a variety of other financial services as well. Customers could deposit items of value or sealed bags of coins with a banker—the equivalent of a safe-deposit box—for which the banker charged a fee. By 1300, Venetian bankers also offered conditioned deposits that would be paid back at some point in the future with interest, like modern certificates of deposit. But it was the transfer of funds from one account to another that was used on a daily basis. In Florence, this occurred largely by one party writing a note instructing the banker to transfer funds out of his account and into that of the note's bearer—in other words, a check. In Venice, though, the easy access to the bankers' tables at Rialto meant that checks were rarely used. Instead, the two parties would present themselves before the banker and instruct him to make the changes in his account books. The oral nature of most of these transactions struck outsiders as unusual. The German knight and traveler, Arnold von Harff, who visited Venice in the 1490s, noted that "the moneychangers are seated around the square, and they hold the money that merchants consigned to them in order to avoid the counting out of cash. When one merchant pays off another, he gives that person an assignment in bank, so that very little cash passes among the merchants."

By the sixteenth century, Venetian banks were born and died with much fanfare. The opening of a new bank by a new banker was heralded with parades, food, and revelry as a means to drum up attention and deposits. Once a bank was established, it was closely watched by its depositors, including the Venetian state, which was one of the banks' largest customers. It did not take much to frighten depositors and, thereby, start a run on the bank. The clearest cue was simply the death of the banker. Even in those cases where investors promised to maintain a bank after its founder's demise, the fear of losing some or all of one's deposit invariably led to a run that killed off even the most solvent firm.

The development of deposit banking greatly increased the amount of working capital in Venice, and thereby the overall size and growth of the economy. But it did that only insofar as the deposited funds were loaned out at interest. This posed a problem during the Middle Ages since Christians were generally forbidden to charge interest, which was the sin of usury. Christ had commanded his followers to "love your enemies, and do good, and lend, expecting nothing in return" (Luke 6:35). The Catholic Church, therefore, had repeatedly condemned usury in the proclamations of popes, such as Alexander III; the canons of councils, such as Lateran III in 1179 and Lyons II in 1274; and the writings of theologians, such as St. Thomas Aquinas. Usury featured as a common complaint in medieval sermons as preachers sought to cleanse the faithful of the sin. Before the economic expansion of the twelfth century, most moneylending in Europe was done by Jews, who were obviously not subject to the laws of the Church. In most cases, this took the form of simple pawnbroking, the giving of small loans on the collateral of items of value. Some Jewish moneylenders, however, built very large businesses, lending to major monasteries, lords, and even kings. While profitable, this brought its own dangers. Powerful, debt-ridden lords can be dangerous creatures. In the case of the Jews, there was a strong temptation for a king to expel them and repudiate all obligations to them. That is, in fact, what happened in England in 1290 and in France in 1306.

Venice did not expel the Jews, but neither did it welcome them with open arms. Jews were allowed to live and work in Venetian overseas colonies as well as in the terra firma cities, but the city of Venice itself was a different matter. Before the sixteenth century Venice forbade Jews to live in the city at all, although the state made occasional exceptions. After the War of Chioggia in 1379 the government responded to the need for more credit by allowing Jewish moneylenders to come to Venice, but they were moved to Mestre on the mainland after the crisis had passed. Jews were welcome to come to Venice to do business, but they could remain in the city no more than fifteen days per year and were required to wear a yellow badge or yellow cap. A few Jews managed to get around these laws, particularly highly valued doctors and wealthy merchants.

The Jews returned to live in Venice as a result of another war. In 1509 the armies of the League of Cambrai spread across the Venetian terra firma, causing a flood of refugees to rush for the safety of the lagoon capital. Among them numbered a great many Jews. When the emergency had passed, the Venetian Senate decided to allow the Jews to remain for five years. Its reasoning was simple. The state coffers were empty and the Jews were willing to pay handsomely for the right to lend money and do other business in Venice. Furthermore, Jewish pawnbroking provided a much-needed service for Venice's poor, who could not afford to have accounts with banks. At first the Jews were free to live wherever they pleased, but this soon led to complaints from clergy as well as parents who discovered their children fraternizing with Jews of their age. Calls for expulsion sounded throughout the city, but the Senate chose a more moderate path. In 1516 the government ordered all Jews to move to a new location on the northern outskirts of Venice, which had formerly been the site of a foundry, or *ghetto*. Despite the modern connotation, the world's first ghetto was neither a slum nor a prison, but a prosperous neighborhood in which Venice's Jews thrived. The buildings—higher than any others in Venice—clustered around the central squares, while the rich synagogues became showplaces. Although moneylending and medicine were the most visible Jewish professions, most Venetian Jews held jobs not unlike those of their Christian neighbors. They were particularly known for their secondhand shops, which stocked exotic merchandise much sought after by high and low alike. But it was the small-scale moneylending that was most important to the Venetian state and ultimately the reason that the Jews were tolerated. As the Senate legislation of 1553 boldly asserted, "This Council has permitted the Jews to dwell in our dominions for the sole purpose of preventing Christians from usurious lending in violation of both the divine and civil laws."

Northern Europeans, less used to seeing Jews or moneylenders, tended to look on the residents of Venice's Ghetto with suspicion. One thinks of William Shakespeare's *The Merchant of Venice*, written around 1597. The villain of the play, Shylock, is a miserly Jewish moneylender who loans the good-hearted Antonio a large sum of money. When Antonio is unable to repay on time, Shylock demands the agreed-upon pound of flesh as payment. The famous Shylock typecasts not only Venetian Jews but Venice itself. Since the seventeenth century, historians, leaders, and writers have tended to view medieval and early modern Venetians through the beguiling lens of Shylock. Even today medieval Venetians are often described as greedy and conniving merchants seeking profit above all—always quick to demand their pound of flesh. The stereotype is inaccurate, but durable nonetheless.

Pawnbrokers were useful for quick loans, but wealthy and established investors in Renaissance Venice could find better terms at the banks. Although the Catholic Church continued to condemn usury, its definition began shifting in the thirteenth century. Even St. Thomas Aquinas agreed that it was lawful to charge a fee for financial services. Therefore, a bank lender might justify interest on a term loan by identifying it as a fee for collecting the funds, transferring them, or seeing to their repayment. Other theologians maintained that a lender had the right to charge a percentage of the amount loaned in compensation for income that the money might have produced had it been available to the lender for investment. In practice, this meant that reasonable rates of interest could be charged, although long-term rates over 10 percent were generally considered usurious, even in Venice.

Christians were also allowed to receive payment for the use of their money if that money made them partners in a particular enterprise. In other words, if funds were invested in a project and the funds were themselves at some risk, then the investor had the right to receive the fruits of that investment. This was crucial for another of Venice's financial inventions—the *colleganza* (a form of partnership).

The colleganza was an innovative solution to an enduring problem. Long-distance shipping was the foundation of Venice's economy, yet it was an activity that was both expensive and dangerous. A Venetian merchant needed a sound vessel, an experienced crew, and a large amount of money with which to purchase goods in various ports. He must also deal with the uncertainties of the voyage. Sea travel (indeed, all travel) in the Middle Ages was perilous. Storms and dense fog plague the Mediterranean, particularly during the winter months when medieval seamen would remain in port. Shipwrecks were common. Although Venetian state galleys patrolled the Adriatic and later offered convoy protection services along the major trade routes, the risk of piracy never disappeared, and grew even more pronounced during Venice's wars with other maritime powers.

A commercial voyage, therefore, constituted a major risk. Of course, it also had the potential for great reward. Goods purchased cheaply in the markets of Corinth or Sparta could be sold at extraordinary markups in the stalls of Constantinople, Acre, or Venice. Medieval Venetian merchants, therefore, looked for ways to lessen the risk so that one bad voyage would not wipe them out. In the ancient world, merchants typically took out a "sea loan"—a high-interest loan, usually more than 20 percent, which the merchant would use to fund his voyage. The interest rate was steep because repayment of a sea loan was canceled in the event of shipwreck, piracy, or other cataclysm. Although this allowed merchants to mitigate some risk, it was not a perfect solution. It required that a merchant find a lender with sufficient funds to bankroll a voyage and who was willing to assume significant risk. It also necessitated that the merchant's net profit on a voyage be at least 20 percent or he would lose money on the venture. Finally, although the sea loan alleviated the risk of lost cargo, it did not cover the loss of the vessel itself.

Because the Venetian economy relied on voyages that were both profitable and plentiful, it is not surprising that new methods of financing those voyages began to appear in medieval Venice and other Italian maritime cities. The Venetian colleganza quickly replaced the sea loan in the eleventh century. There were various versions of the agreement; however, each had certain things in common. In its simplest form, an investor, known as a *stans*, would fund a particular voyage. The merchant, who usually owned the vessel, was known as the *tractans*. He promised to use the money of the stans in whatever way seemed best to maximize profits on the voyage. The tractans had a great deal of freedom to assess which foreign ports he would visit, which goods he would purchase, and when he would return home. At the completion of the voyage—usually within one year—a general accounting would be conducted, subtracting all expenses and determining the net profit. The stans would then receive his initial investment back plus three-quarters of the profit. The tractans would take the remaining one-quarter of the profit. In this way, both the investor and the merchant had a vested interest in maximizing profits, rather than just completing a voyage. Merchants were thus no longer required to pay all expenses and turn a 20 percent profit in order to have a voyage break even. Any net profit made the voyage worthwhile.

Obviously, if a voyage produced no profit at all, no one in the colleganza received anything. Unlike with sea loans, however, if the vessel or cargo was lost, the investor did not automatically lose all of his investment. If any funds remained, the expense of the lost vessel was deducted and the remaining money (if any) was returned to the investor. Still, this high level of risk versus return made the colleganza a wager that only the wealthy were willing to take. That changed, however, in the twelfth century when merchants began adapting the colleganza to allow for *multiple* investors instead of just one. In this way, when a successful voyage returned to Venice, the three-quarters of profit paid to the stans was divided among all the investors according to the amount that they had individually invested. Multiple investors were purchasing shares in a particular voyage, much the way modern investors purchase shares in a corporation.

This single innovation enormously expanded the capital available for overseas trade while diluting the overall risk to investors, who could now diversify their investments rather than staking them on a few high-risk ventures. Venetians could simultaneously invest in a wide array of voyages. If one or two ended badly, others would make up the loss. Doge Ranieri Zeno, for example, held shares in 132 different voyages when he died in 1268. Although these colleganza shares could be sold or traded, they represented a relatively short-term venture, so no market for them developed, as it would for other financial instruments such as municipal bonds. However, the multiplicity of investors in a single voyage significantly lowered the financial bar for participation in this activity. Even Venetians of modest means could purchase a small share in a voyage. These small investments dramatically increased the capital available for underwriting overseas trade.

With all the dangers inherent in medieval commerce it would seem to be a good market for insurance. And it is true that some insurance products were developed in medieval Venice. By the fourteenth century, wealthy investors could be found to insure individual voyages against loss. These were not insurance companies, just groups willing to gamble. A merchant who insured his voyage could much more easily draw investors, since there was no possibility that the investment would not be returned. However, the steep premiums were yet another expense, so profits on insured voyages were usually much lower. In practice, though, few voyages bothered with insurance. Diversification of investments was sufficient for most investors to ensure an overall profit margin. For their part, merchants were generally content to recoup the loss of a vessel or cargo by charging it as an expense against profits.

These various complicated financial innovations required painstaking record keeping. The sole owner of an enterprise can figure out profit and loss on the back of an envelope. However, when there are numerous investors, it is imperative to be able to demonstrate that all are receiving their due. Furthermore, the Venetian government had strict laws regarding what could or could not be shipped, stored, or charged against profits. The need for maintaining clear records of complex transactions led to one of Venice's most profound financial inventions: double-entry bookkeeping.

While it may not seem exciting, the development of double-entry bookkeeping fundamentally changed business in the West. Indeed, without it, the later Industrial Revolution could not have been sustained, and modern corporations would be unthinkable. The technique was first described by Fra Luca Pacioli, a Franciscan mathematician who lived and taught in Venice between 1465 and 1475. Although he is sometimes credited with its invention, Pacioli insisted that he was merely describing a common practice among Venetian merchants. The foundational concept of this form of record keeping is that all transactions are dual in nature. There is always a credit and always a debit to be recorded, and these two must balance at all times. So, for example, rather than recording a payment received for services rendered, a Venetian merchant would record a movement from cash to revenue.

Double-entry bookkeeping may well have developed precisely to deal with the complexities of the multiple-investor colleganza. Because it records both assets and liabilities and the effect of transactions on them, double-entry bookkeeping allowed merchants to easily calculate profit and loss in otherwise complex systems. Just as importantly, it makes the detection of error or fraud much simpler, since everything must balance every day. (Pacioli himself warned that a merchant must not go to sleep before the day's accounts were fully balanced.) Thus, when a ship's captain returned to Venice, his investors and the state need not take his word for how much profit he had obtained. Every penny of every expense or income was accounted for in his ledgers, and auditors were careful to make certain that it all balanced. Even in today's infinitely more complex corporate systems, embezzlement and theft are still usually detected because the books do not balance.

Double-entry bookkeeping was itself a major reason for the adoption in Europe of something that one can find on this very page—Arabic

numerals. Originally developed in India, this system of numerical nota-
tion was adopted in Persia and then spread into Arab North Africa, from
whence it entered medieval Europe in the eleventh century. However,
Arabic numerals, like Arabic letters, were foreign and therefore not understood or adopted by most Europeans. With the low level of mathe-
matical skill required even among Venetian merchants in the twelfth
and thirteenth centuries, Roman numerals were sufficient. This changed
as business transactions became more complex. Sometime in the fourteenth century Venetian merchants began adopting Arabic numerals
for bookkeeping, although they retained Roman numerals for dates
and other everyday numbers. The reason was simple: Doing math with
Arabic numerals is much easier. Furthermore, the neat columns of
Arabic numerals fit logically into those of double-entry bookkeeping.

Where was all this business taking place? Where did Venetian merchant vessels go when they sailed out of the busy lagoon? The answer
depends a great deal on the period. Before 1200, Venetian captains
steered their ships freely to whatever ports offered the most profit. In
general, Venetian merchants left Venice with coins and cloth, hoping to
buy silk, alum, or a host of other commodities in the East. The goal was
to put into a port with low prices on one commodity and then sail to
another where it could be sold at a higher price. More goods would then
be loaded aboard in that port and the merchant would repeat the process, always seeking to maximize profit. This required not only a good
head for business but also a constant stream of news. The Venetian businessman relied on the gossip of the marketplace as well as letters from
friends, family, and partners abroad. His goal was to make as many profitable transactions as possible before returning to Venice at the end of
his colleganza period.

This freewheeling way of doing business was greatly moderated in
the thirteenth and fourteenth centuries. The collapse of the Byzantine
Empire made the waters of the Aegean and eastern Mediterranean

far more dangerous—especially during periods of war. To provide safety for Venice's merchants, the state organized regular convoys to Constantinople, Acre, Cyprus, and occasionally other destinations. War galleys initially protected these fleets of merchant vessels, but in the late thirteenth century the Venetians combined the merchant vessel and the oared galley into one design—the merchant galley. This sizable vessel, with three banks of oars and a large crew of rowers, could carry many tons of cargo and keep to a timetable, even when the winds did not cooperate. In an age before ships' cannons, a vessel's primary defense was the number of men on board. The Venetian Senate was charged with producing these vessels and organizing the seasonal convoys so as to maximize profit for Venice's merchants.

Large convoys usually left the lagoon twice a year for a given destination. They did not just duck into whatever port seemed profitable at the time. Like a locomotive train, they had a specific destination and a schedule to keep, and passengers could embark and disembark along the way. Venetian merchant vessels might join a convoy after its departure and leave before its arrival, taking advantage of the safety and drawing on news reports. The use of convoys did not end independent merchant runs, but it did reduce them significantly. In any case, the changing political situation in the East no longer made the port-hopping merchant model profitable after the mid-thirteenth century. Instead, Venice itself had become the final destination for almost all Venetian voyages leaving Eastern ports. With the decline of Constantinople and the fall of Acre, only Rialto had the trade connections necessary to make it a true clearinghouse of goods. This, of course, was all to the benefit of the Venetians, who reaped great profits and imposed plenty of taxes.

By 1400 Venetian overseas trade had settled into a system that would remain stable for decades. The Senate still organized regular convoys, which made their way to Greece and then sometimes on to Tana, Cyprus, Alexandria, and the wool markets of Flanders. The state still provided merchant galleys, but no longer at state expense. Instead, merchants bid for the right to place their goods aboard these vessels or even to control them outright. Merchants who avoided the convoys and sailed on their own generally headed to Greece for wheat or fish or to the bustling markets of the Black Sea. At Tana, at the mouth of the Don River, Venetian merchants loaded aboard Eastern luxury goods, like silks and spices, or furs, which always brought a solid profit.

Tana was also a good market for slaves—indeed, the word "slave" is itself derived from the Slavic people who were sold in Tana and brought to western Europe. Some of these slaves were sent to Cyprus for agricultural work, although many of them—particularly the young women—ended up in Venice, where they were used as domestic servants, concubines, or both. Like all medieval Europeans, Venetians were uneasy with the concept of slavery. Those who could afford slaves tended to view them as servants who would one day earn their freedom. In the wills of fourteenth-century Venetians, slaves were invariably freed. Indeed, it was customary to leave money for the dowry of female slaves who had been manumitted. Venetians understood well that owning a slave was not conducive to entering heaven, so they were careful to rid themselves of the liability at their death and even to turn it into an opportunity for pious charity. The Venetian government closed public sales of slaves in 1366, although they could still be had for another century via private contract.

Because so many of the profitable trade routes now terminated in Venice, there was no longer a need in the fourteenth century for a traveling merchant sniffing out profitable runs between various ports. This, in turn, led to the rapid decline of the colleganza. Instead, Venetian merchants began doing business without ever leaving home. Informed about prices overseas, they would purchase goods at Rialto and then pay to have them placed aboard vessels heading to a specific destination. The vessel's captain was no longer a merchant himself, but simply someone providing transportation for a fee. The ship's scribe carefully recorded the ownership of all goods loaded aboard, producing a document that would later be called a bill of lading. The merchant would then send instructions to his agent in the destination port regarding the collection, warehousing, and sale of the goods that he had sent. He would also order the agent to purchase certain goods in that city and send them back to Venice, where the merchant would receive and sell them. These commission agents usually received a flat 3 percent of everything they bought or sold. Unlike the colleganza merchant, the commission agent did not care whether a transaction made a profit, since he received no share in it. Instead, the commission agent sought to maximize his volume by acquiring a reputation for efficient, fair, and timely execution of all instructions received.

During the Middle Ages, Europeans developed a number of agricultural innovations, such as new plow designs and crop rotation methods, which added to their overall prosperity. In just the same way, the people of Venice, who neither sowed nor did they reap, developed new financial instruments to expand their own wealth. In both cases, the tools of daily life were significantly improved. For Venice, where capitalism grew and flourished, the results were astounding. Freedom and free enterprise had built a wonder nestled in a busy lagoon—the most unlikely of all places.

CHAPTER 13

THE PERILS OF SUCCESS:
THE APOGEE OF THE VENETIAN EMPIRE

F ew things foster unity like a common enemy, which is precisely what Europeans faced in 1453. With the fall of Constantinople and Sultan Mehmed II's promise that he would extend his conquests into Italy itself, the wars that raged between Western powers began to seem trivial and foolish. The Hundred Years' War between France and England came to a close that very year. Venice's long war in Italy, which seemed intractable only a few months earlier, quickly ended as Italian eyes looked fearfully to the Turkish East.

The Treaty of Lodi, signed on April 9, 1454, committed the five great powers of Italy—Venice, Florence, Milan, Naples, and the Papal States—to a firm peace in order to prepare for an expected Turkish invasion. The treaty envisioned a balance in Italy, in which the great powers kept their hands to themselves and the smaller states in check. Venice was the largest and most powerful of the five, yet also had the most to lose, for the Venetians ruled not only much of northern Italy but also a maritime empire that lay directly in the path of the sultan.

Amid the lamentations and prophecies of doom that the conquest of Constantinople elicited among Europeans there were also more than a few recriminations. Cruelly, many of those fell upon the people of Venice. Had they sent more ships, more troops, more money, and done all of it more quickly, it was said, Constantinople might have been saved. Of course, those who pointed fingers at Venice, more often than not, had failed to lift those same fingers to aid Byzantium. Only Venice and the papacy had sent military aid to Constantinople, and Venice had sent the lion's share. Hundreds of Venetians had given their lives to defend the ancient city. It was galling to hear that they had not done enough.

When the looting and carnage in Constantinople ended, Sultan Mehmed II proclaimed the city the new capital of the Ottoman Empire, and he began at once working on its reconstruction. For a thousand years Constantinople had been the head of a great Christian state. For the next nearly five hundred years it would rule the largest Muslim empire in the world. The young and ambitious Mehmed was determined to restore the dilapidated city to its former glory. Calls went out for builders and architects to begin work in the capital. Justinian's masterpiece and for centuries the heart of Greek Orthodoxy, the church of Hagia Sophia, was promptly converted into a mosque. Most of the remaining churches, however, were allowed to remain Christian. The patriarchate of Constantinople was relocated to the Church of the Holy Apostles, on which Venice's own church of San Marco had been modeled centuries earlier. The patriarch remained there only a few years before Mehmed ordered the church demolished and his own Fatih Camii (Mosque of the Conqueror) built in its place. In this way, the traditional site of the Byzantine emperors' tombs would become the final resting place of the city's conqueror.

For Constantinople to flourish, it needed people. Mehmed ordered the Ottoman government to move there, but he needed to reinvigorate the abandoned markets and fill up the empty streets and neighborhoods. He offered tax incentives to bring Turks to the city, and Greeks as well. Indeed, he extended full amnesty to all Greeks who wished to settle in Constantinople. And settle they did, by the thousands. Within a decade the Greek population of Ottoman Constantinople grew many times greater than it had been before the Turkish conquest. Thus began the long history of the Greek people under Turkish rule. Since the Catholics had been unable to save them from conquest, the Greeks repudiated the Council of Florence and its unification of the Catholic and Orthodox churches. It soon became commonplace among Greeks to say that the conquest of Constantinople was God's punishment for their apostasy at Florence.

Yet not all Greeks remained among the Turks. Those with money or influence fled to the West. Indeed, many Greek aristocrats had been shipping their wealth and belongings to Italy for years before the fall of Constantinople. Much of Hagia Sophia's plate gold had been sent to Venice. Not surprisingly, many Greeks arrived in Venice after 1453, seeking a new home. Unlike the Greeks in Constantinople, those in Venice still upheld the Council of Florence, but they nonetheless petitioned the Senate to allow them to have a regular church for their Greek liturgy. Establishing a new liturgy in Venice was complicated, largely for jurisdictional reasons, yet the senators finally assigned the Greeks the church of San Biagio, near the Arsenale. It saw much use, for the number of Greeks in Venice continued to climb. By 1478 more than four thousand called it home. In 1539 the Greeks were given land in the center of Venice to build a new church, which is today San Giorgio dei Greci. Completed in 1573, it remains the oldest of the churches in Europe built by the Greek diaspora. The Masses celebrated in San Giorgio were sung in Greek, yet remained in communion with Rome. At some point in the late sixteenth century, however, the Greeks returned to the old rites and quietly separated themselves from the papacy. No one noticed. Today San Giorgio dei Greci remains a Greek Orthodox church directly under the jurisdiction of the patriarch of Constantinople.

San Giorgio is not the only legacy of the Greek diaspora in Venice. Cardinal Bessarion, who had been the Greek Orthodox metropolitan (archbishop) of Nicaea and took part in the Council of Florence, felt a close bond with Venice. In his will he left to the people of Venice his massive collection of Greek manuscripts salvaged from Constantinople, which included works by authors such as Plato, Ptolemy, and Apuleius. These precious volumes became the foundation of a new Venetian state library, the Biblioteca Marciana. Housed in the Procuratie Nuove, just across the Piazzetta from San Marco, the Marciana remains one of the most important libraries in the world. Amid the throngs of pigeons, tour groups, and coffee shops, one can still today spy the odd scholar making his or her way quietly into the unassuming doors, behind which are preserved the treasures of the ages.

The peace that Venice concluded with Sultan Mehmed II after the conquest of Constantinople was extremely fragile. No one doubted that the Ottomans meant to press westward, which would naturally put them at odds with Venice's colonies in Greece and the Aegean Sea. Europe's kings and princes regularly paid lip service to the pressing need for Christians to stop warring against one another and unite against the common foe. Their words were sincere, but they were only words. And words would not stop the juggernaut of the Ottoman Empire.

In August 1458 the famous humanist, Aeneas Silvius Piccolomini, was elected pope, taking the name Pius II (1458–64). Few popes since Innocent III felt as strongly about their obligation to bring peace to Christendom in order to turn back the Muslim peril. For Pius II, the conquest of Constantinople ended nothing. Europeans, he believed, must cease their petty wars and join together in a mighty Crusade that would restore Byzantium to Christianity and force the Turks completely off the continent. One of Pius's first actions was to call a congress of Europe's leaders to meet at Mantua in June 1459. Yet, although he received many attractive letters borne by well-dressed messengers and filled with fine words, it was clear that Mantua would not be the show of solidarity for which Pius had hoped. The opening of the congress was delayed for months, and still only a handful of delegates attended. Undaunted, Pius proclaimed a new Crusade. It was a medieval gesture in an early modern world. Some, like the French, were still upset with the pope for unrelated decisions, and therefore refused to join any Crusade. Others, like the Germans, promised mighty armies, yet never delivered a single soldier. Still others accused Pius of cynically beating the drum of holy war so as to avoid calls for reform in the Church.

Venice showed no such misgivings. As Europe's most frequent crusading state, the republic stood ready to take up the cross of Christ and make war against the enemies of Christendom. However, it would not do so alone. The Venetian delegates at Mantua made a point of reminding the attendees that only Venice had sent aid to Constantinople. It would no longer be pulled into wars with the Turks in which many Europeans enrolled, but for which only the Venetians showed up. If clear evidence emerged that the Crusade of Pius II would become a reality, Venice would be among its strongest supporters. Otherwise, the Venetian delegates preferred not to discuss the matter.

Venice's response to Pius's plea was not unexpected. Indeed, the pope had long ago developed a rather strong opinion about Venetians that was destined to echo through the centuries, even to our own time. Pius wrote in his *Commentaries:*

> Venetians never think of God. And, except for the state, which they regard as a deity, they hold nothing sacred, nothing holy. To a Venetian, that is just which is good for the state; that is pious which increases the empire.

That this could be said about a people who routinely fought difficult and expensive wars against Muslims demonstrates the expectations that

Europeans had for the city of the lagoon. In 1460 Venice still commanded a fleet and an empire of extraordinary size. The wealth of Venice was beyond great. It was legendary. Its fleets had no equal in the Mediterranean. Therefore, in the courts of France, England, Germany, and even Italy, the Turkish peril was increasingly seen as a Venetian matter. Indeed, in states like Milan and Florence, people actually *hoped* for Turkish advances that might draw back the Venetian power that extended across northern Italy.

None of this, however, brought Pius II any closer to his Crusade. The embittered and elderly pope decided to shame Europe's leaders into joining by announcing his own intention to take the crusader's cross and promising to personally lead the expedition. The armies and fleets of Christendom, he said, were to meet him at Ancona in 1464. From there they would launch the Crusade. Promises from states such as Burgundy flowed in, although it was clear that many princes were cautiously eyeing their rivals rather than preparing for departure. In Venice, though, the pope's example filled the people with hope and a firm resolve. Cristoforo Moro (1462–71), a former crusader himself, was elected doge and the Great Council voted almost unanimously to launch a Crusade fleet with Moro at the helm. In preparation for the war, the Senate made an alliance with Hungary and informed the Ottomans that their fragile peace was now at an end.

Pius II was delighted when he heard that Venice had joined the Crusade. He sent a consecrated sword to Doge Moro in gratitude, and the two old men exchanged letters in which they looked forward to a brighter future for the beleaguered West. As with many of his writings from his days before becoming pope, Pius came to believe that he had been wrong about the Venetians and their attitude toward the faith. While Venice prepared for war, the pope traveled to the rendezvous point. However, his health was failing and by the time he reached Ancona in July 1464 he was bedridden, beset equally by disease and heartbreak. From his room in the bishop's palace he watched the wide harbor below, prepared to accommodate a mighty armada but occupied by only two papal galleys. Aside from a few mercenary bands, the town was completely untroubled by military camps. The pan-European Crusade that would break the back of Ottoman power and save Christendom had proved a fantasy, nurtured by noble lies and flourishing only in the dashed hopes of a broken old man.

And then, on August 12, the alarm went up in the city of Ancona and shouts of joy could be heard in the halls of the palace. A Venetian fleet of more than twenty major vessels led by Doge Cristoforo Moro sailed proudly into the harbor, ready to crusade. Like the pope, the Venetians were stunned to discover that they were the only ones to keep their promise to the Vicar of Christ. Moro asked to see Pius, but was told that he was too sick with fever to receive anyone. Two days later, the pope died. His cherished dream, which had been merely humored in the courts of Europe, died with him. No Crusade would challenge the plans of Mehmed the Conqueror.

Once again the Venetians had responded to the call to defend Europe, and once again they found themselves alone in taking it seriously. The pitiful situation at Ancona was precisely what the Venetians had sought to avoid—a declaration of war against the Turks to join a Crusade that did not, in reality, exist. But they were now at war, and the people of Venice were determined to win it. The fleets were dispatched to Venice's colonies with orders to push back the Turkish advance. In truth, they could only nudge it here and there while defending Venetian holdings. Occasionally things went well for Venice, as when they were able to extend their control of the Morea (Peloponnese). But such victories were usually rewarded back home by anti-Venetian alliances among Italian powers, which sought to carve up Venetian mainland territories while the republic was preoccupied with the Turks. During the first six years of the war, Venice poured lives and wealth into the struggle with little reward and less gratitude. Pope Paul II (1464–71) offered indulgences to those who would assist Venice in its holy war, yet no one gave it a moment's thought.

Despite their great efforts, the Venetians managed to hold their own against the Ottomans only because the sultan was distracted by other wars against Christian powers in the Balkans. After conquering Bosnia and executing its last king, Mehmed then crushed the last of the Albanian resistance and soon brought that territory, too, into the growing Ottoman Empire. By 1470 he was already planning his next move westward. Mehmed was a man who thought big. He had every intention of capturing Italy, which would open the way for the complete conquest of western Europe. He ordered the creation of a mighty fleet built along Western models with the aim of becoming the first Muslim power to command the Aegean Sea—and that meant removing Venice. Along with a large army and powerful cannons the Turkish fleet descended on the island of Negroponte, a prosperous Venetian colony since 1390. Mehmed II personally commanded the Ottoman forces as they battered the walls and chased away Venetian attempts to relieve the capital city, Chalkis. On July 12, 1470, the city fell. No one was spared. Men, women, and children were sold into slavery or killed in the most brutal fashion. According to later accounts, the Venetian governor of Negroponte, Paolo Erizzo, begged not to be beheaded. His wish was granted; he was instead cut in half at the waist.

The loss of Negroponte fired the Venetians to redouble their efforts against the Turks. At considerable expense the Arsenale was expanded to produce more war vessels more quickly. The war with the Turks had become stratospherically expensive. The Venetians were spending more than a million gold ducats per year on the effort, requiring the sale of additional war bonds and the levying of more taxes. It is a testament to the strength of the Venetian economy that it withstood the strain year after year. But without help, the Venetians could not continue indefinitely. They were unable to stop the Turkish conquests on land, which now stretched all the way to Friuli. At one point Venetians who crammed onto the top of the Campanile of San Marco could see the smoke of Turkish conquests in the distance. Even on the sea, the Venetians struggled to hold their own, enjoying only occasional help from the Knights Hospitaller of Rhodes, Naples, and the papacy.

An unexpected windfall came in 1475 when the famous condottiere Bartolomeo Colleoni died. For more than forty years, Colleoni had served Venice in her Italian wars, although, like all condottieri, he also served other powers. In his will, Colleoni left to the Venetian people 216,000 ducats and lands valued at more than half a million ducats to support the Crusade against the Turks. In return, Colleoni asked that a statue of himself be erected in the Piazza outside the church of San Marco. The Great Council was glad to have the money, but unable fully to grant Colleoni's last wish. Venice was a republic, not a dictatorship of the sort that littered Italy. No man, not even the doge, could have a statue of himself set up in the Piazza of the people. And so the Venetians did the next best thing. Recognizing Colleoni's reverence for the patron saint of Venice, they commissioned the great artist Andrea del Verrocchio to produce a life-size equestrian statue of Colleoni, which was then set atop a monumental pedestal and placed in the open plaza outside the Scuola Grande di San Marco (today Venice's hospital). The council's decision is often described in guidebooks and histories as a typically tricky Venetian deal, whereby the clever merchants outwitted the wealthy Colleoni. It was nothing of the sort. The placement of Colleoni's statue was not a requirement of his will, but simply a request. Placing it outside the Scuola Grande di San Marco not only associated the statue with the saint, but also put it directly adjacent to the church of SS. Giovanni e Paolo, the resting place of doges and heroes. Today the magnificent statue still surveys the busy campo with a quiet dignity it would have lost altogether among the pigeons and postcards of the Piazza San Marco.

Even with Colleoni's windfall, the Senate finally concluded that Venice could no longer sustain the war with the Turks. As early as 1475 it had begun negotiations with Mehmed, but these did not bear fruit until 1478. Eager to press on to more permanent gains, the sultan signed a treaty of truce with Venice in January 1479. He was in a position to dictate the terms. Venice was forced to accept the loss of Negroponte, Lemnos, and most of the former Venetian territories on the Greek mainland. Albania, which had previously been bequeathed to the people of Venice, was completely given over to the Turks, except for the city of Durazzo. Despite these losses, the remainder of Venice's territories remained intact, including the Cyclades and, most important of all, Crete. Venetian merchants were permitted to return to Constantinople and to have their own *podestà*, provided they paid an annual tribute of ten thousand ducats to the sultan.

By 1480 Venice was exhausted and wounded by her long war with the Turks. The enemy stood flush with victory. No sooner had Mehmed made peace with Venice than he launched a major assault against the Knights Hospitaller on their island fortress at Rhodes. The Knights were the last of the old crusading military orders still active in the eastern Mediterranean. More than 150 vessels and fifty thousand Ottoman troops descended on Rhodes, besieging fewer than four thousand Knights. The brutal siege stretched on throughout the summer of 1480, but ended when the Knights courageously beat back a general assault, forcing the Turkish forces to retreat in disarray. The upset marked a rare victory against the Ottoman Empire, and was much celebrated in Europe. Mehmed apparently hoped to eliminate certain Christian powers in the eastern Mediterranean—namely, Venice and the Hospitallers—before advancing westward into Europe. He failed in that, but succeeded in exhausting both powers sufficiently that they were no longer an immediate problem. The sultan ordered the forces that had assaulted Rhodes to sail westward.

In 1453 Mehmed had promised to conquer the old Rome on the banks of the Tiber just as he had conquered the new Rome on the shores of the Bosporus. His subsequent conquests in the Balkans and Dalmatia laid the foundation for his invasion of Italy. On July 28, 1480, the invasion began. More than 120 Turkish vessels landed near the Italian city of Otranto, the easternmost city in Italy, just across the Adriatic from Turkish-controlled Albania. In a matter of days the Turks had captured the strategic port and visited a brutality on its citizens extreme even for them. Eyewitnesses described the elderly rounded up and beheaded and the children shackled and sold as slaves. The nobles of the city were decapitated and their heads placed on lances. The Turks stripped the churches bare and turned them into stables. Bishop Stefano Pendinelli and all of the city's clergy were bound together and executed. The monasteries were ransacked, the nuns were raped on the church altars, and the precious relics of the saints were cast to the dogs. The passion and deaths of the "eight hundred martyrs" of Otranto would not be forgotten and, indeed, are still celebrated there today.

No one doubted that Otranto was to be the beachhead for the Turkish conquest of Italy, just as Gallipoli had once served for their invasion of Greece. Pope Sixtus IV sent news of the calamity to the kings and princes of Europe, calling on them to come to Italy to repel the invasion. Yet no one, least of all the pope himself, believed that such a call would be answered. In Rome the papal curia joined thousands of foreign diplomats hastily packing their bags to flee north. Although many of the Italian powers proclaimed a coalition to expel the Turks, nothing tangible came of it. Italy, including Rome itself, lay almost completely defenseless.

Because Venice had just recently negotiated a peace with Mehmed II, it was widely believed in Europe that a secret condition of that peace was Venetian support for the invasion of Italy. After all, Venice had no love for the rulers of Naples. This was compounded by the fact that the Venetians were unwilling to commit to, or even speak of, fighting the Turks after their conquest of Otranto. For the people of Venice, this criticism was infuriating. After more than fifteen years of holding off the Turks, they were now held culpable for the Turkish attack on a dozing Europe. The capture of Otranto mortified the Venetians as much as any other Christians, but they insisted that they would not again be drawn into a war with the Turks without allies. It was all well and good for the French and the English to beat their breasts over the Turkish invasion; they were, at least for the moment, out of the sultan's reach. Venice was not.

Fortunately for western Europeans, they never had to fight that war against the Conqueror. On May 3, 1481, in circumstances that still remain suspicious, the forty-nine-year-old Mehmed II died. The church bells of Venice rang out in celebration, joined by cannon fire and shouts of adulation from revelers dancing around bonfires. Similar festivities erupted across Europe as the news quickly spread. A succession struggle between Mehmed's sons diverted Ottoman attention away from the sultan's grand project, leaving the Turkish garrison at Otranto bereft of support. When the forces of Naples arrived there, the garrison quickly surrendered and returned to Albania. As quickly as it had appeared, the danger to Italy and western Europe had been averted. With a handful of promises from Europe's leaders to fight the Turks, Pope Sixtus insisted that they seize the moment and permanently safeguard Italy by launching a Crusade to take back the Balkans. "This is the time of deliverance," he wrote, "of glory, of victory, such as we shall never be able to regain if it is neglected now." But the evaporation of the immediate threat likewise dissolved what little determination the European powers had mustered to fight the Turks. There would be no grand Crusade. Many were the Venetians who now congratulated themselves on not joining Europe's latest flight of imagination.

The new Ottoman sultan, Bayezid II (1481–1512), was too busy fighting his brother and rival, Cem, to bother about European conquests. When Cem eventually came under the custody of Pope Innocent VIII (1484–92), Bayezid abandoned the idea of an Italian campaign altogether. Likewise, the sultan eased relations with Venice, reducing tariffs on Venetian goods and even canceling its annual tribute.

Despite a century of challenges, by 1490 Venice had actually reached the pinnacle of its power. The tiny archipelago of islands had truly become a far-flung empire. Even the recent losses to the Turks had been more than made up for by the acquisition of Cyprus, through the Venetian noblewoman Caterina Corner, the former queen of the island. The Venetian Senate oversaw colonial governments in the eastern Mediterranean, Greece, and central Italy. It maintained an expert diplomatic corps that was active in every court in Europe. Business in Venice remained brisk, and the wealth that poured into the city was substantial. Much of that wealth was paid to architects, stonemasons, and artists who built magnificent family palazzi towering along the broad avenue of the Grand Canal and almost every other canal and waterway in the city. Venetian pious donations transformed modest wooden churches and monasteries into stone and marble showplaces jammed with every form of religious art and filled with the chant and incense of a devout people. The stunning Venice of the Renaissance that still draws millions of visitors every year was built with the wealth accumulated in this vibrant period.

And yet, Venice itself remained a creature of the Middle Ages. Born in the ruins of the Roman Empire, it had grown and thrived in a medieval world—a world that was depicted in contemporary maps as centered on Jerusalem, with Europe, the Mediterranean, and the Middle East clustered around it. That world was now passing away. If a Venetian was asked to name the greatest threat to the republic in 1490, he would likely have pointed to the awesome might of the Turks. Yet the Turks, too, were children of the Middle Ages. The seeds of Venice's later decline lay not in any one people or one man, but rather in the coming of a new age—an age that neither the Venetians nor the Ottomans would ever successfully navigate. In France, England, and Spain monarchies were stitching together powerful kingdoms out of formerly recalcitrant fiefs. The result was the rise of powerful states with resources that dwarfed those of Italian cities—in time, even those of Venice itself.

And the world itself was growing. For decades the Portuguese, under the patronage of Prince Henry the Navigator, had been exploring the western coast of Africa. These voyages were a direct response to the rise of Muslim power in the East. In the first place, Henry sought the kingdom of Prester John, the fabled Christian emperor who Europeans hoped would one day save them from the Islamic threat. In the second place, his voyages sought to bypass the Muslim monopoly on Far Eastern goods, which made their way westward by caravan and were sold at premium prices in the markets of Constantinople, Syria, and Alexandria. The Portuguese hoped to cut out the middleman by establishing direct access to the Indies, where luxury goods like cinnamon from Ceylon, nutmeg from the Moluccas, and pepper from Malabar were available in abundance. No Venetian shed a tear to learn that Africa seemed to stretch endlessly southward, foiling every Portuguese attempt to find its end. But in 1488 the inevitable happened. Bartolomeo Dias returned to Lisbon with news that he had discovered the Cape of Good Hope. Africa could indeed be circumnavigated.

Four years later the Genoese captain Cristoforo Colombo (Christopher Columbus) persuaded the Spanish crown to fund an expedition to bypass Africa by sailing westward to the spice islands. Columbus believed that the world was much smaller than the ancient Greeks had calculated it to be. He concluded that the rich goods of the East were actually just beyond Spain's western horizon. He was wrong, but for nearly a decade after his discovery of the New World in 1492, there remained uncertainty about just what he had found. And then, in 1499, the Portuguese explorer Vasco da Gama returned to Lisbon from a voyage around Africa to Calicut (modern Kozhikode) India. He brought with him merchandise worth more than fifty times the cost of his expedition.

The sensational discoveries of the Portuguese and Spanish explorers made for good stories, but they also proved a direct threat to Venice. If Eastern goods could be purchased in India at a fraction of their cost in the markets of Egypt or Constantinople, then Venice's complex system of trade routes was in danger of becoming obsolete. As with all new ventures, many dismissed the routes to the Indies as impossibly difficult or merely a passing fancy that would not catch on. But the business-savvy leaders of Venice knew better. In 1501 a Venetian envoy to Lisbon wrote to the Senate confirming the Portuguese achievement and noting its extraordinary potential for undercutting Venetian trade. The nobleman Girolamo Priuli, who kept an extensive diary of current events, wrote:

> This is more important to the Venetian state than the war with the Turks or any other war that could occur. . . . And if this route continues—and already it appears to me easy to accomplish— the king of Portugal might just as well be called the king of money. . . . The entire city [of Venice] is thunderstruck that in these times such a new route should be discovered, never known or heard of by our ancestors.

Priuli worried that the Portuguese discovery would "rip out the heart of Venice," depriving it of its commercial income and causing it to expire "like a child deprived of milk and food."

Not all Venetians shared Priuli's pessimism. They pointed out that the distances between Portugal and India were vast and would require enormous expenditures to secure for safe trade. The Mamluk sultan in Egypt, after all, would not sit idly by while the Portuguese sidestepped his markets. He would use his powerful navy to attack Portuguese shipping in the Indian Ocean—a body of water so large that little Portugal could never hope to control it. In short, they argued, Portugal had bitten off more than it could chew. Venice's traditional trade routes were safe.

The pessimists and optimists were looking at different sides of the same problem. For decades the wharves of Lisbon had been stacked high with pepper, sold at four times less than it cost in Venice. But the continued success of Portugal's routes to India relied on its king, Manuel I (1495–1521), who poured enormous resources into their defense and upkeep. He built artillery-equipped fortresses along thousands of miles of African coast and sent war vessels to patrol the Indian Ocean. Manuel paid for this, not for modern economic reasons, but for very medieval religious ones. He was determined to use the new route to India as a Crusade strategy to break the back of Muslim power in the region and recapture Jerusalem. Although his explorers had dramatically expanded the size of the known world, Manuel still saw the holy city as its very center. When Manuel died in 1521 his successor, John III (1521–57), abandoned the Crusade idea and pulled back royal funding of the Indian routes. As a result, the cost of spices in Portugal soared as Portuguese merchants were forced to absorb more of the costs of maintaining them or the losses of failing to do so. That, in turn, allowed Venetian merchants to reestablish themselves as the reliable venue for quality spices from the Far East. Throughout the remainder of the sixteenth century, the spice trade remained extremely profitable to Venice.

But the pessimists continued to insist that Venice had staked its prosperity on a doomed business model. In an age in which European explorers crisscrossed the globe, Venetians could not expect things to remain the same. The future lay in the Atlantic. The rise of Spain, England, and France had cut Venice out of that ocean, locking it into the medieval Mediterranean world. The pessimists argued that Venice must turn its attention to building a mighty Italian state to offset its future losses on the sea. And many of them did just that. Wealthy Venetians, mimicking the styles and customs of the French, began building rich villas and opulent estates on the terra firma. Many of these still survive, attesting in their majesty to the pinnacle of Venice's achievement and, paradoxically, also the advent of her decline. For the pessimists were right—at least in the end. Portugal was unable to fully exploit the new routes to India, but the Dutch and English would. By the mid-seventeenth century the wealth of the Far East was pouring into those new markets, leaving Venice to find other ways to generate revenue.

Given the potential threats to Venetian trade posed by the Ottoman Empire and the voyages of discovery in 1500, the Senate turned toward a policy of extending Venetian dominion farther into Italy. Perhaps some senators even envisioned a united Italy under Venetian rule. That desire, whether real or imagined, nevertheless spawned many enemies. At the dawn of the sixteenth century, Italy, which was broken into numerous states and cities, was a ripe target for the unified monarchies of France, Spain, and the German empire. Venice, as the largest single Italian state, stood in their way. Her extraordinary power was also resented by Italian aristocrats, who saw no reason why they should bow to the patricians of Venice. All of this created a complex powder keg of competing interests that could go off at any moment. The job of the Senate and its diplomats was to ensure that it did not—or at least if it did that Venice was not harmed in the explosion.

The senators failed in that, although the damage was not as severe as it might have been. The spark was struck on the northern frontier of the Papal States in Romagna, and in particular the city of Faenza and the coastal towns of Cervia and Rimini. Although theoretically under papal rule, these areas had in practice become independent, thus paving the way for the Venetians to move in. Pope Alexander VI (1492–1503), who strongly opposed the Venetian incursion, died on August 18, 1503, and Venetian diplomats and operatives in Rome worked hard to ensure the election of a new pope more sympathetic to Venetian interests. They got their wish on November 1, when Cardinal Giuliano della Rovere was elected, taking the name Julius II (1503–13). Della Rovere had long been a supporter of Venice and a foe of Alexander VI (who was a member of the Borgia family). Back in Venice, the senators congratulated themselves that they could now move forward with their acquisition of the Romagna and The Marches without too much trouble.

But Julius II, whom history has dubbed "the warrior pope," had other ideas. Like all his predecessors during the previous seven centuries, the new pope insisted on the independence of the Papal States, and no amount of Venetian flattery or bribes would budge him from that position. When the Venetian ambassador to Rome suggested that Venice would simply hold and administer the lands in question for the pope, just as Venice had always served the Holy See, Julius retorted, "The Venetians wish to use us as their chaplain, but they shall never do so." In purely military terms, Venice had the strength to take what she wished. But when a pope is involved, nothing is ever in purely military terms. When Venetian forces began their march south, Julius retaliated by excommunicating Venice and quietly opening talks with Spain, France, and Germany.

None of this escaped Venice's network of diplomats and spies, which was without question the best in the world. The Senate, however, believed that the divisions between these powers were sufficient to keep the pope's plan from becoming a reality. And it did its best to widen those divisions whenever possible. When the German (Holy Roman) emperor Maximilian I invaded Italy in 1508, he was just as eager to take Milan and Genoa away from the king of France as he was Verona and Vicenza from the Republic of Venice. In the event, he did neither. With some French help, Venetian mercenary forces were able not only to stop Maximilian, but even to capture imperial territory in Friuli as well as the city of Trieste.

Venice's impressive victories only inflamed the pope's rage and worried just about everyone else. Julius II responded by calling a Crusade against the Turks and all enemies of the Church. Whether Venice belonged to the latter group was, for the moment, left to the imagination. At a subsequent meeting in Cambrai, in northern France, Emperor Maximilian I and King Louis XII of France joined numerous other smaller states, including ultimately the papacy itself, to declare a holy league— an association of powers determined to crusade. However, rather than planning how best to defend Europe against Turkish invasion, the League of Cambrai busied itself with the dismemberment of the Venetian empire. Only by destroying the greatest proponent of the Crusades, they asserted (although not in those words), could this new Crusade be successful.

Of course, none of the participants in the league had any intention of disturbing the sultan's plans, whatever those might be. They cared only for what piece of Venetian territory they could pluck from the carcass of the lion. According to the Treaty of Cambrai, after Venice was defeated Julius II would receive back all of Romagna and Maximilian would reclaim Friuli and Trieste in addition to the rest of the Veneto, including Treviso and Padua. The king of Hungary would take Dalmatia, the Duke of Savoy would have Cyprus, and the king of Spain, who already ruled the southern Italian kingdom of Naples, would take Venetian Apulia. Since France already ruled Milan and Genoa, King Louis would seize all neighboring Venetian territories in Lombardy. The tiny states of Mantua and Ferrara were also allotted a few crumbs. In short, the League of Cambrai meant to turn back the clock on the Venetian empire, returning the republic to its lagoon.

The Venetian Senate's policy of sowing discord among the greater powers now lay in ruins. Venice was alone, isolated, and the target of one of Europe's greatest Crusades. As they had done during the War of Chioggia, the people of Venice poured their energy and their wealth into the struggle in a manner scarcely conceivable in that age. An enormous army led by the condottiere Nicolò di Pitigliano and his younger cousin Bartolomeo d'Alviano met an equally enormous French army just east of Milan at Agnadello. It went poorly for the Venetians from the start. Their lines were broken and their mercenary armies scattered. Soon the Italian cities of Venice's mainland empire began falling like dominoes to the French and the Germans. No amount of bribery or cajoling could persuade the cities to stand firm with Venice, for their leaders believed that the foreigners would prevail and they were tired of Venetian pretensions to being an Italian power in any event. Even a Venetian appeal to Italian nationalism failed to elicit a response. Instead the forces of the league continued to press in. Soon, all that was left to Venice on the mainland were Mestre, Treviso, and Friuli.

The government and people of Venice were astonished at the rapid collapse of their Italian provinces. For some days after receiving the news, the people appeared to be in a stupor of fear and disbelief. The annual Sensa ritual of the marriage to the sea took place on May 17, just two days after news of the defeat at Agnadello arrived. Almost no one showed up—the Piazza San Marco was cavernously empty. No one had the heart to celebrate Venetian greatness after so smashing a defeat. And the threat was by no means over. Although none of the league members could directly threaten Venice's lagoon, they might be able to blockade it. Quickly, the Venetians began hoarding food, preparing for the worst. The Senate ordered a round-the-clock watch on all entries into the lagoon.

Surprisingly, there were some Venetians who did not believe that the losses on the mainland were necessarily a bad thing. Girolamo Priuli wrote in his diary that there were those who predicted that if the Venetians were ejected from Italy, they would once again "devote themselves to the sea and going on voyages and, besides gaining profits, would become valiant men and experts in the ways of the sea and every other undertaking, and perhaps that would be of more benefit to the Republic of Venice than the income received from the mainland." Priuli lamented that young Venetian nobles were so enamored of their lavish estates that they no longer ventured to distant lands seeking profit. Something fundamental to the Venetian character was being lost, sinking into a pool of the terra firma problems that the founders of Venice had fled. A maritime empire makes money, but the Italian territories of Venice did not. Indeed, they did little but drain Venetian funds as new fortifications were built and greedy condottieri were paid. Priuli was sympathetic to the argument, as perhaps any Venetian who looked to Venice's unique history might be. But, in practice, Priuli knew that the Venetians would never accept the humiliation of losing their Italian possessions. At least not without a fight.

Indeed, the Venetians had only begun to fight. A mass levy of men from Venice was raised, and from hundreds of rowed boats across the length of the lagoon the Venetians launched a surprise attack on German-held Padua. They were assisted by additional forces at Mestre and Treviso, led by Andrea Gritti. Their victory at Padua turned the tide of the war. Already revolts in the rural areas were handicapping the League of Cambrai. Common folk in the countryside had discovered that they much preferred Venetian government to the harsh rule of the hated French and Germans. Gritti followed up his victory with a successful advance of mercenary and native troops. As some members of the league realized that the war might not be so easy after all, they began reconsidering their membership. That gave the Venetian diplomats all the traction they needed. Spain switched sides. Julius II himself made a separate peace in return for full control over Romagna and a large pile of money. But the war, nonetheless, continued for five more years. It is a tale of shifting alliances, betrayals, treachery, and mercenary armies marching the breadth of Italy. In 1516, when the War of the League of Cambrai had at last ended, nothing at all had changed. Venice had recovered all her former Italian territories.

If the war did not alter the Venetians' situation, it did transform their outlook. They had been lucky. The Venetian empire survived, but only through the determination of her citizens and the skill of her diplomats. The struggle made clear to Venice how the sands of European power had shifted beneath her. The new powers—especially Spain, France, and England—were surpassing in wealth and military might anything that Venice could reasonably hope to attain. These were the first truly global powers, with empires that stretched far beyond the old world that Venice knew so well. Venetian foreign policy soon began to reflect those hard truths. Venetians remained proud of their crusading heritage and continued to stand as a bulwark against further Turkish invasion of Europe. Yet as the sixteenth century progressed, that service was increasingly less necessary. As Europe's great kingdoms grew to unprecedented heights, the Turks and the Venetians were slowly left behind. Still wealthy, Venetians continued to consume French culture with abandon, but they could not challenge French power. And after 1516 they no longer tried.

CHAPTER 14

MOST SPLENDID AND SERENE:
VENICE AND THE RENAISSANCE

For a thousand years people came to Venice to do business. The city was a vibrant commercial center—indeed, a birthplace of modern capitalism. Awash in riches and the seat of extraordinary power, Venice was a place of action—where decisions were made, deals were struck, and fortunes were won or lost.

Today people come to Venice for the art. It is an irony that the rich trappings of Venice's wealth—the lavish art and architecture of the city—is all that is left of its grandeur, and all that anyone really cares to see. The customhouse is shut tight, the Arsenale no longer echoes with the sound of saws and hammers, the markets at Rialto no longer buzz with the exchange of commodities, and no government at all resides in the gilded halls of the Ducal Palace. Venice is an abandoned mansion, an exquisite corpse. The life that brought it into being has long since left, yet its outward beauty endures. And, truly, it is beautiful.

Much of the Venice that we know today is the product of a flurry of artistic output during the fifteenth, sixteenth, and seventeenth centuries—at a time when the republic had already begun its slow decline. This is not to say that Venice was not beautiful before the fifteenth century, but it had a very different sort of beauty. As we have seen, Venice lived in the West, but its gaze was ever on the East. As a child of the Byzantine Empire, Venice naturally adopted the artistic style of its sophisticated parent. This can still be seen, staring out from the mosaic-covered walls of scattered churches in Ravenna that escaped the plundering of conquerors and the zeal of iconoclasts. Venetians most admired this style of art during their first millennium, and they used it to adorn their holy places.

Artists in the Middle Ages were craftsmen—much like goldsmiths, cobblers, or blacksmiths—trained to create a product. And just as blacksmiths did not sign horseshoes, the identity of medieval artists and architects has almost always remained unknown. Yet the beauty of their creations still testifies to their skill. Although the church of San Marco was modeled on the Church of the Holy Apostles in Constantinople, the identity of the person who oversaw its construction remains a mystery. Greek artists were surely employed to produce the mosaics adorning the interior of San Marco, most of which were executed in the twelfth, thirteenth, and fourteenth centuries. Like that of all Byzantine churches, San Marco's beauty is internal. The open area beneath the grand cupolas was designed to draw the worshipper's attention skyward, toward the heavens. Biblical scenes, the lives of saints, and important events in Venetian history cover the upper walls and ceilings. Lit by hundreds of candles, the interior powerfully evokes the presence of the sacred.

The exterior of San Marco was another matter. Following Byzantine practice, the church's outside wall consisted of exposed brick with very little ornamentation. Over the centuries, as San Marco and its Piazza became more important to the people of Venice, that changed. The greatest improvements occurred after 1204, when ships laden with treasures from conquered Constantinople arrived in Venice. Rich marbles and reliefs were mounted on the exterior of San Marco in almost haphazard fashion. Similarly, items such as the dark tetrarchs (mounted on a corner), the "Acre" columns (placed before a now-closed entrance on the Piazzetta), and the bronze horses (set on the front balcony) were used to decorate the church at the center of Venetian civic life.

Beyond San Marco one must look hard to find evidence of Venetian art before the fifteenth century. The best example is Torcello's church of Santa Maria Assunta, which has along its back wall a breathtaking mosaic of the Last Judgment produced in the twelfth century. At one time all the churches in Venice were decorated in this way. But then came the Italian Renaissance, and zeal for this new artistic style quickly swept away the medieval mosaics and frescoes. Few churches were spared. However, in a quiet part of Venice there is still a place where one can get a feel for the medieval parish church: San Giovanni Decollato (St. John the Baptist Beheaded) in Santa Croce, tucked away between San Giacomo dall'Orio and the Fondaco dei Turchi. At least a thousand years old, the little church is a precious gem, covered in a traditional ship's keel roof and adorned with Byzantine columns. Overshadowed by the larger San Giacomo dall'Orio, it did not see much use during the Renaissance or baroque periods, and so it was largely left alone. At some point in the early nineteenth century the church was abandoned entirely. Its inside walls were plastered and it was used for storage. In 1994, however, San Giovanni Decollato was reopened after extensive restorations, revealing a window to a Venice that had long since passed away. Chipping away the plaster exposed beautiful medieval frescoes depicting St. Helena, the Annunciation, the four Evangelists, and St. Michael defeating Satan as a dragon. It is a place of quiet reverence—something almost extinct in the modern city.

Venice's earliest palazzi were likewise built along Byzantine lines, although with uniquely Venetian modifications. One of the oldest is

Ca' Farsetti, which stands very near the Rialto Bridge. Built by Ranieri Dandolo before 1209, the palazzo exhibits the classic rounded arches opening to doors, windows, or balconies all across its facade. The Ca' Farsetti has many of the features that would become standard for Venetian palazzi. The ground level, which opened directly onto the Grand Canal, was designed for commerce. There a merchant vessel could be loaded or unloaded and goods stored. The family also kept smaller boats on the ground floor, along with oars, sails, and occasionally a bedroom for a servant or slave. At the back of the ground floor a door opened to a private courtyard with a well and stairs to the upper levels, where the family lived. Upstairs could be found a wide hallway flanked by a ballroom, dining room, and sitting room for entertaining. Family quarters frequently spread across several floors as different nuclear families claimed separate sections of a palazzo owned by a common ancestor.

Venice's palazzi are most striking for their open doors and windows, designed to facilitate communication, commerce, and the circulation of air. Elsewhere in Italy, aristocrats built fortified compounds with iron bars on the doors and windows, thick walls, and mighty towers to defend the family during the factional warfare that so often raged across their cities. Such precautions were unnecessary in Venice. Nothing speaks more eloquently of the genius of the Venetian republican system than the rows of rich and utterly defenseless palazzi that still crowd the sides of the Grand Canal, and every other canal in Venice. The owners of these ornate palaces were powerful men with all of the enemies that power brings. Yet they never conceived of the idea that those enemies, who were fellow Venetians after all, would wage war against them in their homes. Venetian politics was rough and often treacherous, but it rarely turned to violence. Allegiance to the republic, rather than to any one man or dynasty, served Venice very well.

By the fourteenth century Venetian architects began joining together two foreign influences often encountered by their well-traveled merchants. The Gothic style of pointed archways had swept through France and, by extension, the crusader states in Syria. So, too, Islamic architecture seen in Alexandria made its way into Venetian designs. The result is what is often called Venetian Gothic. It is characterized by pointed arches accentuated with various designs along an open facade. The Ducal Palace is the prime example of this style, yet it can be seen in numerous other private palaces, such as the Ca' d'Oro, with its colored stones and ornate traceries of golden colors.

The Italian Renaissance was born in Florence in the fourteenth century and quickly traveled to Venice by way of Padua. It was characterized by a rebirth (thus the term *renaissance*) of classical models of architecture, sculpture, and literature. Renaissance artists, like Renaissance humanists, searched the ancient past for a way forward. They rejected the flat medieval styles, perfecting instead new techniques that sought to breathe life into their art. Unlike medieval craftsmen, these new artists cultivated a celebrity status, not only signing their works, but overseeing busy studios of apprentices. In Florence the Renaissance was pioneered by artists such as Filippo Brunelleschi, Donatello, Masaccio, and Leon Battista Alberti.

Venice's adoption of these Renaissance styles was itself a remarkable break with the past, for the Venetians had always favored the sophisticated East when it came to artistic expression. But times were changing. The flame of Byzantium was flickering and even Venice turned its attention to the Western terra firma. Among the earliest Renaissance artists in Venice was Jacopo Bellini. The son of a Venetian tinsmith, Bellini worked under Gentile da Fabriano, who produced various now-lost works for the Great Council in 1408. Bellini accompanied his master to Florence, where he remained for some years learning the new artistic techniques pioneered there. Later, Bellini traveled to Bruges, where he was introduced to the use of oil paints on canvas—a medium that would forever change Venice.

The seat of high culture in fifteenth-century Venice was not at the governmental center, but in its outskirts at Padua. There, since 1222, a university had flourished that drew the best minds in Europe and provided an excellent education for Venice's elite. After returning to Venice, Bellini set up shop in Padua with his two sons, Gentile and Giovanni. They were likely influenced by the arrival in 1443 of Donatello, who lived in Padua for about a decade. His masterwork during those years was the equestrian statue of the condottiere Erasmo da Narni, otherwise known as Gattamelata (Honey Cat). This magnificent life-size bronze was the first such statue produced since the days of ancient Rome. It remains there still, just outside the main entrance of the Basilica of St. Anthony.

Jacopo Bellini and his sons later moved to Venice, where they found their expertise in the new Renaissance style in high demand. Under their influence, the Venetians abandoned the fresco and adopted canvas and oil paintings. This was a matter of pure practicality. Although frescoes were generally easier to produce, they did not fare well in the humid, salty air of the Venetian lagoon. To avoid the peeling and fading that plagued Venetian frescoes, patrons began ordering the new oil paintings on canvas. Often these were giant canvases specifically constructed to cover entire walls. In the Great Council Chamber on the second floor of the Ducal Palace, fourteenth-century frescoes that depicted the Peace of Venice, the Fourth Crusade, and the Coronation of the Virgin had badly faded during the last hundred years. Gentile and Giovanni Bellini produced large canvases of the same subjects, although updated in style, which were then hung over the original frescoes.

Both Bellini brothers remained in demand in Venice and beyond. Gentile commanded extraordinary sums for his exquisite portraits. Indeed, in the 1470s he became the portrait artist of the doges. The honor of having one's image executed by Gentile Bellini was so great that the Senate employed it as a diplomatic tool. Gentile was, for example, sent to

Germany, where he painted a portrait of Emperor Frederick III. He was not only well paid, but even given a knighthood by the grateful monarch. Similarly, in 1479 the Venetians sweetened the deal for peace with the Turks by agreeing to send Gentile to Constantinople to paint a portrait of the sultan. Mehmed the Conqueror, who hoped to soon rule Italy, was intrigued by the artistic innovations of the Italian Renaissance and eager to be immortalized by its techniques. Gentile's portrait of Mehmed, which today can be seen in London's National Gallery, remains a fascinating study of this enigmatic man.

Wealthy patrons for Venetian Renaissance painters could also be found in the city's various *scuole*. Despite their name, these were pious fraternal organizations with a devotion to a particular saint or relic. Although nobles and non-nobles could join, by the fifteenth century the men of Venice's scuole were usually well off and politically connected. At a scuola's meetings and banquets members had an opportunity to network and generally enjoy one another's company in a grand hall. The scuole also undertook numerous charitable works, provided some death benefits for their members, and routinely staged elaborate processions in the city. In other words, with the exception of the religious element, the scuole were not unlike fraternal organizations today.

The various scuole in Venice engaged in some competition with one another, which manifested itself in the size and lavishness of their processions and halls. They were eager to adorn their walls with the latest and most beautiful art extolling, of course, their own organizations, and here they turned to the Bellinis. Gentile was commissioned to produce several canvases depicting scenes in the history of the Scuola Grande di San Giovanni Evangelista's greatest relic, a fragment of the True Cross. Around 1496 he painted *The Procession of the True Cross in Piazza San Marco*, and then a few years later *The Recovery of the Relic of the True Cross at the Bridge of San Lorenzo*. Both of these works (now in the Accademia Gallery in Venice) were commissioned to tell the story of miracles: the first about a cure and the second about a discovery. Yet the miracles in these two paintings are lost amid a busy panorama of the people and places of Venice. *The Procession* is really a depiction of the Piazza San Marco, filled with the members of the scuola and a host of other Venetians of all ranks. *The Recovery* is much the same, set on the canal of San Lorenzo. The object of both paintings is Venice itself and the people who lived there. This narrative style—filling the canvas with people, events, and structures tangential to the subject of the work—would remain an enduring feature of Venetian Renaissance paintings. It was a marked change from Roman or Florentine methods, which populated their paintings with stylized classical architecture or ideal forms.

Giovanni Bellini had as successful a career as his brother, although he tended to focus more on religious subjects for Venice's churches and monasteries. Among his most famous are the *Transfiguration* (now in Naples) and *St. Francis in the Desert* (now in the Frick Collection in New York). After Gentile's death in 1507, Giovanni became the unquestioned master of oil painting in Venice. His studio was filled with young artists, responding to the rising demand for art among Venice's institutions and elite, and fueled by the extraordinary wealth of the city.

Giovanni Bellini's most famous pupil was Tiziano Vecelli, better known as Titian. It is impossible in so short a space to do justice to the life and artistic output of this giant of Venetian painting. During his long life, Titian produced hundreds of canvases and acquired a fame that spanned Europe. Titian, more than any other artist, cemented Venice's reputation as a leader in art. Like his predecessors, he composed works for the government, churches, and scuole. His magnificent *Presentation of the Virgin in the Temple* was produced for the Scuola Grande di Santa Maria della Carità. It remains there still, in the Accademia Gallery, which is the heir of the old scuola building. Titian's most famous work, though, is surely his *Assumption of the Virgin,* completed in 1518. For more than two years he labored over this massive canvas, to be hung over the high altar of the Franciscan church of Santa Maria Gloriosa dei Frari, where it remains today. Titian's rich use of light and color in this masterpiece draws the observer ever upward, from the terrestrial to the angelic hosts bearing the Virgin Mary and finally to God in heaven.

As Titian's fame spread, the courts of Europe called him to paint the portraits of leaders such as Pope Paul III and Empress Eleanor of Portugal. He was summoned to Augsburg, where he painted a series of portraits of the ruler of the largest empire in history, the Holy Roman emperor Charles V. His famous equestrian portrait of Charles V was the first of its kind, establishing a new genre of royal portrait style. Titian remained active until his death at around ninety, when he was one of thousands of victims of a plague that ravaged Venice in August 1576. So great was his fame that the government made an exception to its law about the disposal of the bodies of plague victims, which were usually dumped onto an island or into the sea. Instead, Titian was buried with full honors, as he had wished, in the glorious church of the Frari, made more glorious by his own works.

Although not as famous as Titian, his contemporary Vittore Carpaccio flourished by providing paintings for the usual clientele of patricians, scuole, and the government. Much of his work for the Ducal Palace was lost in fires, but his famous *Lion of St. Mark*, executed in 1518 for the Treasury Office, not only survives but has become a symbol of the city to this day. Like his teacher, Gentile Bellini, Carpaccio filled his backgrounds with the sights and people of Venice. His winged lion strikes a familiar pose, one paw on the open Gospel, yet in the background can be seen the Bacino San Marco with ships, faraway campaniles, and the Ducal Palace itself. Carpaccio's biggest customers were the scuole. He painted a number of works on the life of St. Ursula for the scuola dedicated to her. Like the works of Bellini, Carpaccio's *Healing of the Madman* has precious little miraculous in it, but much that is mundane. Set in the

Rialto area, the scene is filled with people, gondolas, and the old wooden Rialto Bridge. In the distance can be seen many houses and the forests of chimneys that defined Venice's cityscape then, as now.

Artistic culture in Venice benefited greatly from current events in Rome, although that was not immediately evident at the time. The lavish patronage of the pope had made Rome the center of the Renaissance. That changed in 1527 when Charles V invaded Italy and his unruly and largely Protestant soldiers sacked Rome. Talent quickly fled the Eternal City, much of it landing in Venice, where the demand for art coincided nicely with the money to pay for it. One transplant was the brilliant architect Jacopo Tatti, known as Sansovino. Doge Andrea Gritti commissioned him to repair, update, and beautify the main civic center of Venice around San Marco. The Piazza and Piazzetta were no more dirty, noisy, or disorderly than before, but Doge Gritti hoped to transform them into something akin to the beautifully decorated open spaces found in Rome. At great expense the government began buying out the owners of stalls in the area, some of whom had done business there for centuries. In their place, Sansovino built the Biblioteca Marciana, directly across the Piazzetta from the Ducal Palace. It was later expanded to include the state mint, or Zecca. Almost immediately after its construction, the vault over the main hall of the library collapsed and, in good Venetian fashion, Sansovino was arrested and charged with gross negligence. He was forced to rebuild the structure with a flat roof at his own expense.

The mishap did not damage Sansovino's career. Indeed, he was appointed Proto of the Procurators of San Marco, the highest architectural position in the city, and in this capacity he redesigned several parts of the Ducal Palace. His best-known additions, though, are the stairways. He replaced the old ceremonial stairway in the palace's courtyard with the new Scala dei Giganti, a sweeping marble staircase flanked on both sides by massive statues of Mercury and Neptune, representing trade and the sea. Sansovino also designed the famous Scala d'Oro (Golden Staircase) in the palace's east wing, leading to the chambers of the Senate and the Ten. His work extended to churches, updating their form to the latest styles. He designed, for example, San Francesco della Vigna, San Martino, San Giuliano, and San Geminiano. For twenty years Sansovino worked on the palace of the Corner family, known today simply as Ca' Grande. Like all of his designs, and those of his contemporaries, the styles of classical Rome, evoking the humanism of an ancient age, were used to replace the medieval Gothic wherever possible.

Among Venice's architects, however, none can rival the reputation and legacy of Andrea Palladio. The son of a miller in Padua, the young Andrea was apprenticed to a stonecutter, who apparently treated him badly. In 1524 he fled Padua, taking up residence in Vicenza. There he gained the attention of Gian Giorgio Trissino, a humanist who recognized the young man's talent for architecture. Since Andrea had no surname, Trissino called him Palladio, meaning "wise one." With Trissino's patronage, Palladio was able to travel to Rome to study and measure ruins, seeking to re-create the glory of the ancients. His reading there included Vitruvius's *De architectura*, a first-century treatise on Roman methods and the only architectural work to survive from antiquity. After Trissino's death in 1540, Palladio went to Venice, where he met the wealthy and powerful patrician Daniele Barbaro. Like many Venetian nobles in those days, Barbaro was a well-educated man of letters. He had served as ambassador to the court of Elizabeth I in England and as representative to the Council of Trent, which had set the reform agenda for the Catholic Church after the disruption of the Protestant Reformation. Barbaro was later made a cardinal and even elected patriarch of Aquileia. He encouraged Palladio's genius, bringing him to Rome in 1554. Two years later Barbaro and Palladio published a new edition of Vitruvius.

Palladio's architectural style, based firmly on classical models, found its most energetic employment in the magnificent mainland villas of wealthy Venetian nobles. He designed dozens of them, including Daniele Barbaro's own Villa Barbaro. The Palladian style, as it came to be known, would become the new face of Western architecture for centuries. It was, in short, a revival of antiquity. Within its solid, clean lines and towering columns, it celebrated a Roman and Greek past reborn in a new age of virtue and self-confidence. Palladio spelled out its elements and methods in his seminal work, *The Four Books on Architecture*, published in 1570. During the eighteenth-century Enlightenment, Palladian architecture became the embodiment of reason in building, dispelling the superstition of the medieval "Gothic" (that is, barbarian). It spread across Europe and into the colonies, even arriving in British North America. There the well-educated country gentlemen embraced Palladio as the architect of a new age. Thomas Jefferson read Palladio and used his methods when designing his own estate at Monticello. Likewise, the design of public structures in Washington, D.C., was largely based on Palladio's work. American government buildings so often resemble ancient temples precisely because of the architectural styles forged by Palladio.

It is no exaggeration to say that Andrea Palladio changed the face of Venice. As the classical style became the rage, he was in high demand to design new buildings or redesign old ones. In some cases he simply placed a new classical facade over a medieval structure, as at San Pietro di Castello, where the white steps, columns, and capitals replaced the bare bricks of the medieval building. In other cases he designed entirely new buildings, such as the Redentore church on Giudecca or the church of Santa Lucia (where the train station now stands). His most visible masterpiece, however, was the new church of San Giorgio Maggiore, facing the Bacino San Marco—an unmistakable part of the Venetian cityscape. With the creation of this church the Bacino had become majestically framed much as it is today. The last element in the group, the church of Santa Maria della Salute, was added during the next century. Like the Redentore, the Salute was built in thanksgiving for the departure of a terrible plague. Although it owed much to Palladio, the Salute, which was completed in 1687, is very much a product of the baroque period, with its elaborate decoration so favored in Venice.

In 1577 a disastrous fire broke out in the Ducal Palace and quickly destroyed most of the sections toward the sea, including the Great Council Chamber. The Venetian government asked architects to submit ideas for the palace's repair, reconstruction, or rebuilding. Given the tastes of the time, it is not surprising that most architects considered the fire to be a providential opportunity to rid themselves of a medieval eyesore. Palladio favored tearing the whole thing down and starting fresh with a new, classical structure. In another city, one ruled by a monarch with a penchant for the arts, Palladio would surely have had his way. But Venice was a republic, and the people of Venice—steeped in a conservative commercial culture that valued stability—would hear nothing of such alterations to their house. The Ducal Palace was a cherished part of their history. It belonged to them and they would not give it up.

While the architects and officials argued, the Great Council held its meetings at the Arsenale, in a warehouse used to store the fleet's oars. The members were naturally eager to see things moved along. At last the decision was made to repair the Ducal Palace, restoring the lost portions just as they had been. It was also decided to remove the prison from the palace, building a new structure across the canal for that purpose. To avoid the problem of having to cross the canal with guards and criminals, the famous Bridge of Sighs was extended between the two buildings. Although decorated ornately on its exterior, the Bridge of Sighs was meant to be a maximum-security construction.

The restoration of the Great Council Chamber posed a problem when it came to decoration, for the paintings and frescoes depicting the Peace of Venice, the Fourth Crusade, and the Coronation of the Virgin had been lost in the fire. So long had these scenes decorated the council room that it seemed unthinkable not to replace them. The large canvases that today adorn the walls of that vast room are the results of a major government project to restore what was lost to the flames. Certainly the most spectacular is *Paradise* by Jacopo Robusti, otherwise known as Tintoretto. The largest oil painting on canvas in the world, *Paradise* dominates the head of the room. Tintoretto, who was in his seventies, prayed that he would be awarded the commission, saying that he hoped to experience paradise by painting it. He painted the massive seventy-four-by-thirty-foot canvas largely in sections at the Scuola della Misericordia, which was not far from his house. The pieces were then transported to the Ducal Palace, where they were stitched together and the final work was done. Because the aged Tintoretto found it difficult to climb ladders, his son, Domenico, completed many of the final details. While Tintoretto kept the Virgin Mary as the focal point of his work, he greatly expanded its depiction of heaven and its inhabitants. Indeed, the work consists of a great sea of faces, most painted from live subjects, who people the heavenly realm. It was a constant reminder to the assembled council members of the reward for good and honorable service to God and to Venice.

As his name suggests, Tintoretto was the son of a dyer. When he was young and had demonstrated a talent for art, his father placed him as a pupil in the workshop of Titian. For some reason, Titian took a dislike to Tintoretto and within a few weeks the pupil had departed to begin his own career. Without Titian's connections (and, indeed, with the active dislike of Titian's partisans), Tintoretto had to be particularly aggressive in seeking contracts. He was a whirlwind of energy, bidding for projects wherever he found them, and there were many projects to be had. Unlike Titian, Tintoretto hardly ever left Venice, being always busy with the next job. The Scuola Grande di San Rocco numbered among his best customers.

Tintoretto's muscular style typified the Mannerism that was popular during the High Renaissance, but his use of color and light was unique to him. The speed with which he produced his paintings won him plenty of contracts with the Venetian government, particularly after the fire of 1577 when there was a rush to restore the governmental complex. These included the famous *Bacchus with Ariadne Crowned by Venice* and *The Forge of Vulcan*. Tintoretto's political work shared a style with other Venetian artists, such as Paolo Veronese—a style evident on the walls of the Ducal Palace, where there are many pictures that include multiple doges, but few portraits of a single doge. As citizens of a republic, Venetians were careful never to extol one man too much. This was a marked departure from artistic subjects elsewhere in Europe, which often depicted a king, pope, or other ruler in grand style. Instead, the focus of the paintings in the Ducal Palace was on the institutions and people of Venice. Occasionally, Venetians would adopt the ancient Roman practice of depicting their republic as an allegory. This can be seen marvelously in Palma il Giovane's *Allegory of the War of the League of Cambrai* (1582) or that masterpiece of nostalgia, *Neptune Offering to Venice the Riches of the Sea* (ca. 1745) by Giovanni Battista Tiepolo. Tintoretto's own contribution to this genre, *Venice, Queen of the Sea*, can be still seen on the ceiling of the Senate chamber.

The sixteenth century also saw the creation of Venice's most famous bridge, and the only one before the modern era to span the Grand Canal—the Rialto Bridge. Because of the frenetic activity at the Rialto markets, a bridge had been a necessity since at least the thirteenth century. Several wooden bridges had been built at Rialto over the centuries, each with a pulley system to allow sailing vessels bearing their cargoes to pass through. This was no longer a consideration in the sixteenth century, however, since the large galleons docked and unloaded their goods at warehouses near the Bacino San Marco. The Venetian govern-ment, therefore, announced a competition to design a new stone bridge—one that need only be high enough to allow local traffic and state galleys to pass under it. The greatest architects of the day, includ-ing Palladio and Michelangelo, submitted proposals. But the govern-ment declined to fund a work of art in the middle of a marketplace unless it had some commercial application. Instead it gave the contract to Antonio da Ponte, the lead architect overseeing the restoration of the Ducal Palace after the 1577 fire. His design was not only graceful but useful. With its three separate pathways, it could move traffic quickly and efficiently. Its market stalls, which faced inward toward the central path, allowed the government to rent out new space in an area in which property values were astronomical. In short, the Rialto Bridge perfectly answered the Venetians' desire for both beauty and profit, while main-taining the honorable traditions of the past.

The extraordinary demand for artistic and architectural products among Renaissance Venetians was fueled by two things they had in abundance: education and money. The money came, as it always had, through international commerce and trade. Yet by the sixteenth century much of Venice's wealth was also generated by a boom in local industry. The wars on the mainland had played havoc with Italian craftsmen, who found it difficult to conduct business amid the cannon fire and raids of mercenary armies. Venice, a city that no enemy had ever captured, seemed extremely attractive for those looking for a new place of busi-ness. After all, the extensive trade routes that terminated in Venice en-sured that any craftsman could find the materials that he needed to produce finished goods. Populous Venice also had plenty of ready, sometimes educated workers.

The largest industry to take root in sixteenth-century Venice was woolen textiles, followed closely by silk production. By 1600, in a clear sign of the times, more people worked in the silk industry in Venice than built boats. Numerous other specialty industries also developed in the lagoon, including leatherwork and jewelry. Lace made on the island of Burano soon became coveted across Europe, just as it remains among tourists today. This century also saw the rapid development of the glass industry on Murano. Venetian glass gained a wide reputation for excellence and the artistic skill of Murano's glassblowers became legendary. Aside from producing glassware and decorative items, the craftsmen also created precision hourglasses, crucial in an age of oceanic voyages.

Education levels in Venice had always been among the highest in Europe. Merchants, after all, must be able to read, write, and count. By the late fourteenth century a humanistic education, preferably at the University of Padua, was becoming a standard for Venetian patrician men. Humanism thrived on a diet of classical literature—a commodity that was extremely expensive before the fifteenth century. However, around 1450 Johannes Gutenberg created the first movable-type printing press in Europe. The printing press dramatically reduced the cost of books, which previously had to be copied by hand. Coupled with new techniques in paper production, the printing press ushered in a new age of education, communication, and thought that would ripple through the centuries. Few people in medieval Europe learned to read because there was nothing for them to read. The printing press changed that.

Movable-type print was invented in China, yet there it had nothing like the effects that it would have on Europe. The reason is simple. In China, printing presses were controlled by the imperial government and used for the needs of a complex bureaucracy. In Europe, the printing press was controlled by no one. It was, instead, an entrepreneurial opportunity. Anyone with money and some idea of which books would sell could purchase a printing press and set up shop. For Europeans, therefore, printing became a craft, not unlike making barrels, caulking ships, or painting portraits. Because it had the potential for great profits, printing expanded rapidly.

It should not be too surprising, then, that printing soon arrived and flourished in Venice. The Venetian government was, by its nature, business friendly, and certainly Venice was safe. By the sixteenth century, printers also had to contend with local governments or church tribunals, both Catholic and Protestant. While the Inquisition in Venice paid attention to what flowed from the city's presses, it tended to move slowly and often gave the publisher the benefit of the doubt. Paper and ink were readily available in Venice, along with the technical know-how to build and maintain machines. Most importantly, the high literacy rate among Venice's elite sustained a strong local market for books.

By 1500 nearly a quarter of all publications in Europe were produced in Venice. The most famous, and probably the largest, press in the city was that of Aldus Manutius. A humanist from Bassano, Manutius invested much of his fortune in the publication of Greek classics for the growing audience of humanists in Europe. He established his press in Venice not only because it had become a center for printing, but because it had a large library of Greek manuscripts from Constantinople, as well as a population of Greeks who could help with their publication. The Aldine Press soon gained a reputation for producing the best scholarly works in Europe. In 1501 Manutius adopted the now-famous symbol of a dolphin around an anchor for his press. This image became so associated with excellence in publishing that it was quickly copied by presses everywhere—and, indeed, until recently was the logo of Doubleday. The organization and capacity of the Aldine Press were truly extraordinary. It employed dozens of printers, scholars, and proofreaders.

Among the latter was the young Desiderius Erasmus, who would go on to become one of the most famous humanists of his age. As he looked back on his first job, though, Erasmus had little good to say about it. He complained of the long hours, poor working conditions, stingy bosses, and bad food ("a morsel of shellfish caught in the sewer"). Whatever

Erasmus's complaints about the Aldine Press, it seems to have taken the young scholar in stride. The busy workshop was always in need of help. According to one of Erasmus's biographers, the Aldine Press had a sign above its door that read:

> Whoever you are, Aldus earnestly begs you to state your business in the fewest possible words and be gone—unless like Hercules to weary Atlas, you would lend a helping hand. There will always be work enough for you, and all who come this way.

To increase sales, Manutius developed several innovations that fundamentally shaped Western book production. During the Middle Ages, books came in all sizes, but in general they tended to be large. Since most books were religious, it made sense to produce larger codices designed to stay put on an altar or at a table in a monastic library. Since the first printed books competed for sales with traditional manuscripts, it is not surprising that they, too, were large. The Gutenberg Bible, for example, is 12 x 17.5 inches. Most printed books were produced in quarto, which meant that a large sheet of paper was printed with four pages on each side and then folded into four parts, cut, and bound into a book. Manutius wanted to bring the size, and thereby the cost, of the book down. He therefore produced the world's first octavo book—eight pages were printed on each sheet, which was then folded one more time before cutting and binding. This produced a book not much larger than a modern paperback. To fit more print on each page, the Aldine Press adopted a new compact, slanted script, later (and still) called italic. These smaller books were not only cheaper but also portable. The octavo was a huge success—so much so that it was immediately copied by other presses across Europe.

By the end of the sixteenth century Venice had firmly established itself as a center for arts and culture. The rude community of fishermen, sailors, and merchants had grown up. In later centuries Venetians would continue to innovate in other cultural fields, particularly in music. However, on the canvas, the great period of innovation was winding down. Giants like Titian, Tintoretto, and Veronese proved difficult acts to follow. By the eighteenth century the epicenter of European culture had clearly shifted to Paris. Still, Venice remained important. Tiepolo, who perfected the ceiling painting, was in great demand outside Venice.

As European wealth grew in the eighteenth century to unprecedented levels, art collectors began to cast their gaze on Venice. The Venetian practice of using canvases rather than frescoes seemed good fortune to art lovers with deep pockets, who began buying up Renaissance masterpieces from Venetian families and churches that were down on their luck. The problem became so acute that the Council of Ten ordered a detailed inventory of all canvas paintings in Venice and strictly regulated their purchase by foreigners, a desperate attempt to hold on to a legacy that was slipping out of their fingers.

The greatest of all of Venice's artistic masterpieces, however, was Venice itself. The city of the lagoon, adorned by some of the greatest artists of all time, had become a showplace like none other. Wealthy visitors in the eighteenth century, many of whom were English tourists, paid large sums for newly executed paintings of the city. To meet the demand, an industry of Venice-scape painters arose—one that still flourishes today. The most famous of these was Giovanni Antonio Canal, known as Canaletto. An accomplished landscape artist, Canaletto turned his considerable talents to producing highly realistic scenes of Venice. English tourists snapped up his works, bringing them home to remember their trip. When war on the Continent in the 1740s disrupted English travel to Venice, Canaletto moved to England to be closer to his clientele. Although his early scenes were painted from life, his later ones obviously were not. Indeed, Canaletto produced many capriccios— fantastic scenes of an imagined Venice with monumental statues, classical temples, and nonexistent bridges. His other works, though, still preserve the image of the city in the eighteenth century—an image that is surprisingly similar to the Venice of today.

The beauty of Venice's landscape is unusual, for it is an entirely artificial one. Imposing buildings seem to float on a water canvas that both frames and reflects their splendor. It is an image frozen in time—a Renaissance city that remains unchanged, unmoved. Its magnificence is an enduring monument to a wealthy, powerful, and culturally vibrant republic at the peak of its history. And yet, unlike the monument of stone and water, that greatness would not last.

At the age of one thousand, Venice was entering old age.

CHAPTER 15

FOR GOD AND ST. MARK:
THE WARS AGAINST THE TURKS

Just as Venice reached the apogee of its power in the sixteenth century, so, too, did the Ottoman Turks. Yet Turkish power was greater than anything Venice or any other contemporary European power could muster.

Ruling from Constantinople, Sultan Selim I, "the Grim" (1512–20), had already crushed the Mamluk empire, thus capturing Syria, Palestine, Egypt, and the Muslim holy sites in Arabia. The Ottoman Empire now controlled three-quarters of the Mediterranean shoreline and all of the Black Sea. With so vast an empire the resources available to the Turks were truly staggering. Selim made no secret of his desire to use those resources to fulfill the dreams of his grandfather Mehmed II. He meant to conquer western Europe, thus extinguishing the last flame of Christendom left in the world.

Europeans engaged in a widespread and well-justified panic. Pope Leo X begged the monarchs to put aside their wars and band together into one great Crusade for the defense of Christianity. Diplomats and churchmen shuttled from court to court, eventually securing the approval of King Henry VIII of England, King Francis I of France, Emperor Maximilian I of the Holy Roman Empire, and King Charles II of Spain for a general peace and the formation of a new Crusade. In the council chambers of Europe a flurry of plans were drafted, each more optimistic than the last. The final plan envisioned a three-pronged attack on the Turks that would drive them not only out of Europe, but entirely out of the Middle East, restoring the Holy Land to Christian rule once more.

Of course, nothing of the sort ever happened. When Emperor Maximilian died in 1519, the planned Crusade became merely a talking point for the kings of France and Spain, who competed fiercely for the vacant imperial throne. When Charles II of Spain won the day (thus becoming Charles V of the Holy Roman Empire), Francis I refused to join with the hated Hapsburgs and even opened formal relations with the Ottoman sultan to oppose their common enemy. The following year, although only in his fifties, Sultan Selim died. His son and successor, Suleiman, was known to be a scholarly young man with no taste for warfare. Europeans breathed a sigh of relief. The Venetians, who had refused to join Leo X's Crusade until it consisted of more than plans and paper, did the same.

But Suleiman the Magnificent (1520–66), as he came to be called, was both scholarly and warlike. Upon assuming the throne, he wasted little time pursuing the conquest of Christian Europe. He boldly led a vast army to Belgrade, capturing it in August 1521 and opening the way to Hungary and the German empire beyond.

Before prosecuting a major war in Europe, Suleiman decided to rid himself of dangers and distractions from Christian powers in the East. Chief of these were the Knights Hospitaller, the great crusading order based on Rhodes that had for centuries launched attacks and raids on Turkish holdings in the Aegean and Asia Minor. Previous attempts by the Ottomans to extract the Hospitallers from their island stronghold had failed, but Suleiman was determined to succeed. Much to the dismay of the Venetians, the Ottoman Empire had become a real naval power under Selim the Grim. Suleiman used that new weapon, sending almost four hundred vessels to Rhodes along with an army of a hundred thousand, which he led personally. Seven thousand determined Knights held out for nearly six months before they finally accepted the inevitable. The sultan was gracious in victory. In return for the surrender of Rhodes, Suleiman allowed the Knights to march honorably out of their fortifications under colors and with the respectful attendance of the Turkish army. They were then free to board their vessels and sail unimpeded to Sicily. Ultimately, the Knights relocated to the island of Malta, where they remained until 1799.

The fall of Rhodes sent shock waves across Europe, but nowhere more violently than in Venice. The maritime portion of its empire (known as the *stato da mar*), already battered by previous wars with the Turks, was in grave danger. The days when Venetian war vessels could patrol the eastern Mediterranean without fear of challenge had suddenly come to an end. Indeed, Venice was being edged out by the enormous fleets of Suleiman and the growing presence of Spanish vessels seeking out the enemies of the Hapsburgs, such as the French or the Turks. The problem became more acute in 1532 when Suleiman appointed the North African pirate Hayrettin Barbarossa ("Red Beard") as admiral of the Ottoman navy. His policy of attacking Christian vessels first and asking questions later was obviously bad for Venetian shipping.

In 1526 Suleiman invaded Hungary with a powerful land army and numerous cannons. The king of Hungary, Louis II, quickly organized his country's defenses, but it was too little and too late. At the Battle of Mohács the Ottomans crushed the Hungarian forces, and went on to capture the capital of Buda and eventually to conquer the bulk of the kingdom. Hungary, the longtime enemy of Venice, was no more.

Venetians, like all Europeans, could only mourn its loss. The

Ottomans had penetrated deep into Catholic Europe and there seemed no good way to stop them. Indeed, far from halting their advance, the Most Christian King Francis I of France had actually allied with the Turks in a war against Charles V and his Hapsburg empire. In 1529 Suleiman led an army of more than a hundred thousand soldiers directly into Austria and besieged Vienna itself. Torrential rains forced the sultan to leave behind his largest artillery and greatly slowed his progress. Had he had good weather, Suleiman would probably have captured the city, leaving the rest of Germany to his mercy. However, the defenders tenaciously held out, and Suleiman was finally forced to retreat. A second attempt in 1532 similarly failed.

Venice's policy toward the Turks remained delicate. On the one hand, it was willing to answer the call to crusade, provided that other Europeans did the same. Too often the Venetians had found themselves at war with the Ottomans simply because they alone took a Crusade plan seriously. On the other hand, Venice's Mediterranean colonies and her merchants in the East now operated in what was quickly becoming a Turkish lake. The Senate did its best, therefore, to steer a middle course, seeking above all to maintain peace. That looked like appeasement to some Europeans—and, to be fair, it was. Charles V blamed the Venetians for refusing to join his fleet, led by the Genoese captain Andrea Doria, which captured Tunis in 1535. Yet the Venetians understood that short-lived raids would not stem the Ottoman advance. Already Suleiman had established control over North Africa, had ridden triumphantly into Baghdad, and was preparing to conquer Persia. In short, Suleiman was unifying the Muslim world under his rule. It was foolhardy to poke him with a stick—even a Hapsburg stick.

Suleiman responded to the capture of Tunis with a far-reaching plan to attack the Hapsburg empire—which included Spain, the kingdom of Naples (southern Italy and Sicily), the Holy Roman Empire (Austria and Germany), the Netherlands, and the vast New World territories of New

Spain. The sultan made an alliance with Francis to begin a coordinated assault in 1537. French forces would invade Flanders, while the Ottoman armies would press in from Hungary. Combined Turkish and French vessels would simultaneously wrest the kingdom of Naples from Charles. France, the very homeland of the Crusades, was actively supporting the Muslim invasion of Europe, proving that religion was no longer the only line that defined sides in the new great struggles.

To support all these naval operations, Suleiman sent ambassadors to Venice requesting that the republic join the French and the Turks. Doge Andrea Gritti (1523–38) politely declined. Apart from the problem of allying with the Muslim enemy of Christendom—something contrary to Venice's cherished crusading past—the Venetians had no desire to see the Ottomans (or any other power) control both shores of the Adriatic Sea. Suleiman did not take the doge's response well. After increasing taxes on Venetian merchants in Syria, he ordered Turkish vessels to further harass Venetian shipping. When a threatened Venetian warship eventually returned fire, the Ottoman Empire declared war on Venice.

Suleiman's first objective of the war was securing Corfu, which had been part of the Venetian empire since 1386. This strategic island was crucial to Venice's control of the southern Adriatic. A Turkish army of more than twenty thousand soldiers with many large cannons soon landed there; without immediate help, it seemed that Corfu would surely fall. And no help was forthcoming. Andrea Doria sailed his imperial fleet quietly by without challenging the Turks. In the end, though, Corfu was saved, but only by weather—the bane of Suleiman's ambitions in Europe. Fierce rains hampered the artillery and spread dysentery among his army. After three weeks, the Turks retreated.

Venice did not fare as well elsewhere. One by one Suleiman began plucking away Venice's Aegean colonies. Skyros, Patmos, Ios, Paros, Aegina—all fell to Barbarossa and the awesome might of the Ottoman fleets. These were brutal conquests. On Aegina, for example, the entire male population was executed and the women and children were sent to Turkish slave markets in Constantinople. Venice also lost her last two colonies on the Greek mainland, Nauplia and Monemvasia, both on the east coast of the Morea (Peloponnese). As long as this lopsided war continued, Venice's overseas colonies were in grave danger. Finally, in 1540, Venetian ambassadors managed to make peace with Suleiman by agreeing to pay a war indemnity of 300,000 ducats. It was a bitter defeat, but at least the *stato da mar* survived, although reduced, weakened, and still threatened. It consisted of Cyprus, Crete, Tenedos, and six Ionian islands.

The Venetians had no more trouble with Suleiman. They continued to do business in the Ottoman Empire and enjoyed several decades of peace and prosperity. As the power of the great European kingdoms grew in the mid-sixteenth century, the likelihood that the Turks could advance much farther west diminished. Suleiman had twice failed to capture Vienna, and his later attempt to destroy the Knights Hospitaller on the island of Malta in 1565 similarly failed. The great sultan died the following year. He was succeeded by a hedonistic son, Selim II (1566–74), known as "the Sot" because of his predilection for good wine. The new sultan quickly made a truce with the Holy Roman emperor Maximilian II.

Selim and his advisers appear to have decided to focus on softer targets for expansion, and in that capacity Venice's maritime empire naturally recommended itself. In 1570 the Sublime Porte (as the Ottoman government was known) informed the Serenissima (Most Serene Republic, as the Venetian government was known) that it must immediately hand over the island of Cyprus. This rich and important island had been a Venetian possession for more than eighty years. It was said that Selim coveted the fine Cypriot wines, yet that has the tinny ring of a bad joke rather than indicating a genuine motive. If wine is all he was after, he need only have asked and the Venetians would have gladly delivered whole oceans of it to his table with many blessings. For all his debauchery, Selim knew that a sultan must wage jihad, and it only made sense to do so where the possibilities of success were best.

In Venice the Senate defied the Ottoman ambassador, promising to defend Cyprus with the full might of the republic. The Arsenale quickly geared up for wartime production, and within a few months a massive fleet of more than a hundred vessels had been assembled, each flying the winged lion of St. Mark. The Senate also sent an alarm across Christian Europe, calling for aid against this latest attack of the Turks. Predictably, only those powers with something to lose by Ottoman expansion in the Mediterranean responded. Pope Pius V (1566–72) outfitted twelve vessels. King Philip II of Spain (1556–98), the son of Charles V and inheritor of the Hapsburg empire (minus Austria), sent a fleet of fifty vessels under the command of Giovanni Andrea Doria, the great-nephew of the famous Genoese admiral. It was an impressive fleet of nearly two hundred major vessels that assembled at Crete. However, there were incessant delays in getting under way. In part these were the fault of Doria, who did not trust the quality of the Venetian ships and men. In the end, the armada never made it to Cyprus, leaving the Venetians to their fate.

The Turkish invasion forces, which ultimately numbered some two hundred thousand soldiers, captured Nicosia, the Venetian capital of Cyprus, after a siege of several months. Governor Nicolò Dandolo was beheaded, the city sacked, and the people killed or sold into slavery. Because Famagusta was the best-fortified city, the Venetian captain general Marcantonio Bragadin decided to make his stand there. The charismatic Bragadin knew that his people could not forever withstand the might of the Turks, but he put his hopes in the fleet that was said to be assembling at Crete. Those hopes were, of course, misplaced.

The long, grueling siege of Famagusta began on September 17, 1570. Venetian artillery pounded the attackers as well as the siege towers that they built. The Turks responded by sapping the walls and periodically launching major assaults, assisted by powerful artillery bombardments.

Bragadin and his soldiers defended the city bravely, but as the months dragged on without significant relief from the West, he faced severe shortages in food, gunpowder, and men. Finally, on August 1, 1571, almost one year after the siege had begun, Bragadin asked for terms of surrender. The Turkish commander, Lala Mustafa Pasha, was delighted. The capture of Cyprus was taking much longer than had been expected, and Sultan Selim in Constantinople had registered displeasure. Mustafa granted the inhabitants of Famagusta terms not unlike those given to the Knights Hospitaller when they surrendered Rhodes. In return for peacefully handing over the city, the people would be free to depart unmolested and honorably. Venetians and any others who wished to leave the island would be escorted by the Turkish fleet to Crete. It was a good deal, sealed with the signet ring of the sultan himself.

A ceremony was planned for August 5. Bragadin, dressed in his crimson robes of state, was accompanied by his senior officers and about two hundred other guards of honor. With the Ottoman forces looking on, they proceeded out of the gates and into the pavilion of the pasha. They brought with them the key to the city and a gift of rich silks. Seated on a velvet stool, Bragadin formally relinquished control of the city and asked Mustafa to transport them to Candia (Heraklion, Crete) as he had promised. Mustafa made a few inquiries about missing Turkish prisoners and reports that food, wine, and oil in the city had been destroyed, but these were mere trifles. What really concerned him came next.

You all want to leave, and I have put at your disposal the galleys of the Gran Signore [sultan]. Who among you will stay as security with me to see that these galleys and caramusalini [vessels] come back, now that your fleet is in Candia? You must give me a hostage, and let it be one of these Venetian gentlemen.

Bragadin responded, "But, my lord, this is no part of our accord. You promised to send us all off in freedom and to give us the ships to take us." Mustafa admitted the truth of this, but insisted that the deal must be altered. If he sent his fleet to Crete and it was destroyed there, the sultan would quite literally have his head. He could not take that chance. Bragadin responded, saying that the Venetians would keep their part of the bargain and so should the pasha. He pointed out that after the surrender the Venetian commanders and soldiers were now private citizens. He had no authority to order any of them to become a hostage. The concept of such liberty seems to have been lost on Mustafa. He responded that if the Venetians would not leave an officer, then let one of the officers order a captain to act as hostage. But, Bragadin reiterated, the captains, indeed all Venetians, were free men, no longer under any obligation to obey their former commanders. Besides, a prince should uphold his word. Hostages were not part of the bargain.

At this Mustafa exploded in rage. He stood up, clapped his hands, and turned toward Bragadin, saying, "And so you have written to Candia in order that your fleet may be on the watch, because you will surrender on agreement to be escorted to Candia, so that according to some such plan we should lose this entire armada, the property of the Gran Signore. Tie them all up!" With that, the pasha's men produced rope and bound them all. Mustafa then clapped his hands a second time and the slaughter began. With only a few exceptions, all the Venetian commanders and soldiers in attendance were cut down, along with all the Christians from Famagusta who had come to watch the ceremony. Hundreds of Venetians who had gone to the harbor expecting to board vessels were placed in chains and shipped off to the slave markets. In the pavilion, with the bodies of his men strewn around him, Bragadin stretched out his neck and commended his soul to Christ. Mustafa ordered his ears and nose cut off and then threw him into a cell to rot.

During the next week Mustafa tried to quell the violence that he had initiated. After all, the sultan would not welcome the conquest of the city without a population of taxpaying inhabitants. It appears that Mustafa received word of a Christian armada made up of Venetian and Spanish vessels forming at Sicily. He likely concluded that this was sure evidence of Bragadin's treachery. This was the fleet, he believed, that would have destroyed the Turkish vessels had he been foolish enough to send them to Crete. Bragadin was roused from his cell and given to the soldiers as sport. He was forced to carry a large sack of soil on his back while trumpets heralded his progress. His tormentors demanded that he convert to Islam, but he refused, saying, "I am a Christian, and thus I will live and die. I hope my soul will be saved. My body is yours. Torture it as you will." He was then tied to a chair and hoisted up the main yard of a Turkish galley for all to see and mock. Next, he was taken down and brought to the city center, where he was tied to a pole and flayed alive. He endured the tearing of his skin from his flesh without a murmur until the executioners reached his stomach, when he cried out, "Into your hands, Lord, I commend my spirit!" and died. After his skin was completely removed, the Turks stuffed it with straw and hung it from the city gates.

Sultan Selim was well pleased when Mustafa Pasha later presented him with not only Cyprus but also the heads of the Venetian commanders and the skin of Marcantonio Bragadin. But his pleasure was fleeting. For the armada that was assembling in the West really was aimed against the Ottoman Empire. Pope Pius V had declared a Crusade, offering the usual indulgence for those who took the cross in defense of the faith. More than half of the two hundred vessels of this new Crusade fleet were Venetian. The rest were from the pope or Philip II's domains. The commander of the fleet was the young and charismatic Don John, the illegitimate son of Charles V. The crusaders were further inflamed by the news they received from Cyprus. The passion and death of Bragadin inspired them all, but especially the Venetians.

The Crusade set sail and encountered a Turkish fleet of about equal size off Lepanto in Greece on October 7, 1571. What followed was one of the most famous naval engagements in history. The Battle of Lepanto lasted approximately five hours. It was, in a real sense, Christendom's last Crusade. For nearly two years Catholics across Europe had prayed the Rosary for the success of the mission, which Pope Pius had specially commended to the intercession of the Blessed Virgin Mary. For several hours before the attack all the crusaders on the vessels prayed the Rosary, begging God to give them victory through the intercession of his mother. As the Christian galleys approached the Turkish lines, Don John ordered all flags to be lowered and the standard of the Crucifixion to be raised on every ship. They were no longer Venetians, Genoese, Neapolitans, or Spanish. They were Christians. The zeal of the crusaders, with the images of fallen Cyprus still burned into their mind, was plain. It brought them to victory that day. The crusader ships smashed the lines and captured the Turkish command vessels, including that of the pasha himself. By the end of the day the Turks had lost 113 vessels, the Christians only 12. The crusaders captured 117 Turkish vessels, freed fifteen thousand Christian galley slaves, and looted extraordinary riches from the pasha's ship. In one glorious engagement, the bulk of the Ottoman navy had been destroyed.

The Battle of Lepanto had an electrifying effect on Europe. It was the first time that a major attack against the Ottomans had actually succeeded. Europeans had long come to see the Turks as nearly invincible, but Lepanto proved otherwise. Church bells pealed across Europe, even in Protestant countries where the very concept of Crusade was abhorrent. For one brief moment Europeans were united again in a common faith and a common victory. In Venice, lamentations for the fallen heroes of Cyprus were replaced with cheers of "Victory! Victory!" Venetians were proud of Lepanto, but like Don John they credited the intercession of the Virgin for the stunning success. Pope Pius V declared October 7 henceforth to be celebrated as the Feast of Our Lady of Victory. It is still celebrated by Catholics today as the Feast of Our Lady of the Rosary. In Venice, this certainty was immortalized in the powerful painting *Battle of Lepanto* by Paolo Veronese. Above the warring fleets, which are almost an afterthought in this composition, are the heavens in which the patron saints of the states that joined the Crusade are seen imploring the Virgin to assist the valiant Christians below.

A few years later, a Venetian survivor from Cyprus was doing business in Constantinople. There he managed to steal the skin of Bragadin, which had been placed in the Ottoman shipyards. It was brought back to Venice, received as a returning hero, and buried with full honors in the church of SS. Giovanni e Paolo. The stunning monument, which depicts the Venetian martyr's death, still holds his remains today.

The Battle of Lepanto held great psychological importance for all Christians, but especially for the Venetians. In truth, though, it had little lasting effect. Selim ordered the fleet to be rebuilt, and so great were the resources of the Ottoman Empire that it was done within the year. The battle itself had been, by the standards of the time, rather old-fashioned. Cannons had played only a minor role in the engagement, since the majority of rowed galleys could not accommodate them. Instead, the real action took place with handguns or close-quarters fighting between galley crews. This type of warfare was not much different from that practiced in naval engagements during the Middle Ages. By contrast, the navies of France and England boasted massive galleons with long rows of heavy cannons belowdecks. These powerful warships did not engage the enemy directly, but fired devastating broadsides, destroying them from afar. Although the Venetian Arsenale would produce these powerful ships of the line, it did so only much later, and Venetian sailors never fully mastered them.

Venice is commonly described as entering its period of marked decline after 1600. It is worth remembering, though, that Venice's decline, like that of its enemy the Ottoman Empire, was relative, not absolute. Very little in the Republic of St. Mark was shrinking. Yes, the *stato da mar* had lost much, but an energetic rise of industry made up for those losses. Venice remained a place of commerce, culture, and learning. Its fleets were larger in the seventeenth century than they had ever been before. Its nobles were for the most part wealthy aristocrats with grand palazzi in Venice and magnificent villas on the terra firma. It boasted a solid government, a sound currency, and a content people. In short, Venice prospered.

But it did not prosper as much as the emerging powers, such as France or England, and that was the problem. These kingdoms boasted colonial empires that stretched across the globe, bringing riches and every sort of commodity to their markets. Their economies surged, which in turn allowed them to field larger armies and develop new and more effective weapons. Relative to these powerhouses, which experienced a worldwide growth unprecedented in human history, Venice was in serious decline. So, too, were the Ottomans. Although they went from victory to victory, the Turks could not keep pace with the rapid technological, scientific, and economic growth taking place in western Europe. No one could—not even the greatest empires of the New World, Asia, or Africa. For Venetians, who lived in western Europe but whose gaze was traditionally on the East, it became increasingly clear that at least in terms of pure power, they were being left behind.

In one respect, that of revolution, the Venetians were quite content to be left behind. The rise of the middle class in Europe had begun. During the seventeenth century new segments of society that were well off, well educated, and non-noble chafed against a medieval system of hereditary privilege, resulting in an increasing demand for reform that sometimes turned violent. The English had executed their king, Charles I, and abolished their monarchy in 1649. Venice, a middle-class society without a monarchy, landed nobility, or peasantry, was immune to these particular pressures. But it was not immune to calls for reform, the most effective of which were aimed at the Council of Ten. Originally charged with investigating and prosecuting treason, corruption, and espionage, the Ten had expanded its reach into other aspects of state expenditures and even foreign affairs. Since membership in the Ten was inherently transitory, the power grab can be attributed to the cittadini secretaries and staff of the body. Like congressional staff in modern America, these professionals held long-term government positions and were therefore eager to see their own power grow.

In 1582 and 1583 the Great Council curbed the power of the Ten, returning foreign affairs solely to the Senate. Because the Ten was still charged with investigating criminal activities at all levels, it established a subcommittee of three men who would deal with the Senate or the doge. These three were called the State Inquisitors. In time, their duties expanded to include crimes committed by any nobles. The Ten and the Inquisition continued to operate under strict rules of law, although by modern standards their methods might seem questionable. Because secrecy was of the utmost importance, the accused were usually not informed of the charges against them. They had no right to face their accusers and there were no appeals. The nobility naturally disliked the Ten, but there was no arguing with its efficiency. It sometimes made mistakes, as it did in 1622 when it executed Antonio Foscarini for selling state secrets. But it was quick to admit them and attempted to make amends. In an age of Enlightenment, though, foreigners found the mysterious Ten, its inquisitors, and its *bocche dei leoni* distasteful. So did some of the more progressive-minded Venetians. But attempts to reform the Ten in 1628 and 1762 failed for the simple reason that the body worked well. With a powerful patriciate, equal justice for all Venetians was possible only if accusers of important men could be guaranteed anonymity. The Ten had kept the government stable for centuries. Venetians were loath to lose it when the world around them was so unstable.

As European powers were establishing colonial empires on a global scale, the Senate contented itself with trying to hold on to what it had, while attempting, whenever possible, to restore what was lost. It fought various little wars in the seventeenth century against the Hapsburgs and various pirates. In 1645 the Turks attacked Crete, a Venetian possession for more than four centuries. The siege of the capital, Candia, would last for the next twenty-two years. The Venetian fleets scored impressive victories against the Ottomans, and even managed to reclaim some areas of Dalmatia. Because of its long duration, the defense of Crete became a celebrated cause in Europe, the subject of much talk and writing, but only a little assistance. Finally, in September 1669, the captain general of Crete, Francesco Morosini, surrendered the island. Venice was allowed to retain some small bases there and on two other islands, Tinos and Cerigo (Kithira). Along with Corfu, that was all that remained of Venice's maritime empire.

In 1683 the Ottoman Empire launched the first major offensive against western Europe since the days of Suleiman the Magnificent. The grand vizier, Kara Mustafa Pasha, led a large army to Vienna itself, which was crushed by a combined army of Austrians and Poles. The European victors insisted that the time was ripe to undo the Ottoman conquests in the West and called on Venice to join the effort. There was serious reluctance in the Senate to opening a new war with the Turks, but also a desire to win back what had been lost. Besides, as some argued, if Venice refused to take part in an anti-Turkish campaign that was already on the march, then it would be well remembered later when Venice needed help against the Muslim foe. While the Poles and Austrians liberated Hungary, the Venetians, under the command of Francesco Morosini, waged war in the Aegean and the Morea. The Venetians recaptured a number of Greek islands and even established themselves again on mainland Greece. After capturing Corinth, Morosini's forces moved on to Athens, which they bombarded. As it happens, the Turkish governor of the city was using the Parthenon, which was at that time a mosque, as a storehouse for gunpowder. When a Venetian mortar went astray and pierced the roof of the Parthenon, it ignited the powder and caused a terrific explosion. The ruins of the Parthenon that one sees today are the result. After capturing Athens, Morosini ordered some of its antiquities to be sent to Venice. These were the days of Venetian "lion collecting," when captured sculptures were often sent home as trophies. Morosini sent two large lions from Athens's Porto Leone to Venice, where they still gaze patiently out near the entrance of the Arsenale.

The war with the Turks ended in 1699 with the Treaty of Karlowitz. As a member of the effort, Venice had a place at the negotiation table. For the Turks, Karlowitz represented a humiliating defeat—the first time in their history that a sultan had accepted a permanent territorial loss. According to the treaty, Austria received Hungary and most of Transylvania, Poland took Podolia, and Venice reclaimed most of Dalmatia and the Morea (Peloponnese). Karlowitz taught the Ottomans that they could no longer challenge Europe's great powers. Venice, however, was another matter. In 1714 a large Turkish fleet descended on the Peloponnese and quickly ejected the Venetians. They pressed on to Corfu, which was once again saved, this time by Venetian resolve and the willingness of Charles VI of Austria to declare war on the Turks. Hapsburg assistance was a double-edged sword, though, for when Charles made peace in 1716 he forced Venice to do the same, despite the Venetians' strong desire to reclaim the Morea.

Thus ended the last war between Venice and the Turks. In truth, they no longer had much left to fight about. Without colonies in Greek waters or on the Greek mainland, Venice had returned to its traditional home, the Adriatic Sea. And even that it could no longer call its own. Although the Adriatic was legally recognized as Venetian waters, the great powers routinely ignored the technicality. In May 1702 the annual Marriage of Venice to the Sea ceremony on Ascension Day was canceled because a French war fleet had sailed dangerously close to Venice during the War of the Spanish Succession. The ominous irony was not lost on observers.

Venetian commercial shipping continued its own decline in the eighteenth century, yet still remained healthy. British, French, and Dutch merchants did business directly in Constantinople, where they had the clout to extract good tariff rates from the Porte. Venice lacked that clout and so her merchants in the East competed at a disadvantage. Although all commercial shipping in the Adriatic was no longer required to dock at Venice, duties were still collected as if it was. This important source of income for the government was threatened in 1719 by Charles VI's proclamation that Trieste was henceforth a free port, where goods could make their way into or out of Austria and points northward without paying duties or tariffs. Venice remained the preeminent port in the region, but it was no longer the only port in the region.

Since Venice in the eighteenth century could not seriously challenge the great European powers, and since those powers frequently challenged one another, the Senate adopted a new policy of strict neutrality. This was difficult in northern Italy, where French and Austrian monarchs so often vied for power. But Venice's diplomats managed it. Dwarfed by the might and the economies of the great powers, the Republic of Venice nevertheless prospered. At almost 150,000 people, the city of Venice was as large as it had ever been—although now tiny compared with Paris, Berlin, or London. Another nearly two million people lived in Venice's mainland territories, where agriculture flourished, boosted by the cultivation of corn (maize). Amazingly, the Republic of Venice had become a food exporter!

It had also become something more. In its unique beauty, its impressive antiquity, and its flourishing culture, Venice was no longer just a place, but a destination. It was not just a city; it had become an icon.

CHAPTER 16

MASKS, OPERA, AND LOVE:
VENICE THE TOURIST DESTINATION

Venice has always welcomed foreigners. During the Middle Ages the hostels, markets, and wharves of the teeming city echoed with a babel of tongues. From across the known world travelers came to Venice to do business or find passage to faraway destinations. That changed in the seventeenth century. As Venice slipped into political obscurity, it arose as a destination in its own right. Increasingly secular in outlook, Europeans no longer made the religious pilgrimages that had brought them to Venice on their way to Constantinople or Jerusalem. Rather than relics to venerate, the new travelers of the seventeenth and eighteenth centuries sought the unusual, the interesting, and the beautiful. Venice fit that bill. It became something altogether new—a tourist attraction.

By 1700 Venice looked much as it does today. It presented the visitor with an artificial beauty of stunning structures mirrored by water and light. The stone-paved Piazza San Marco stretched between the classical structures of the Procuratie to the Byzantine splendor of the church of San Marco to the Gothic ambience of the rich Ducal Palace. Gondolas and barges filled waterways, rowed by expert oarsmen and carrying passengers and goods from one part of the city to another. The lavish palazzi echoed with laughter as masked revelers danced and feasted the nights away. From the imposing Salute to the bustling Rialto to the towering columns of the Molo, Venice was not only a vibrant city, it was a museum. And many people came to marvel at its exhibits.

The arrival of European tourists was warmly welcomed by a city that had lost revenue from its traditional venues. The visitors, after all, were not common gawkers. Before the nineteenth century only the very wealthy could afford the expense and time that foreign travel demanded. Venice's tourists were—for the most part—well dressed, well educated, and well supplied with funds. Most came from England, France, and Austria. They brought with them servants, guides, sometimes whole retinues. It did not take long for Venetian entrepreneurs to realize the worth of these new visitors and to devise new ways to attract more of them.

The most obvious attraction in seventeenth-century Venice was Venetian art. Visitors poked their heads into the city's two hundred churches, marveling at the rich canvases and sculptures. They rented rooms in the grand palazzi and gaped at the beauty of the canals reflecting the diversity of architecture, Gothic, Palladian, and baroque. And they came to see the Venetian festivals, set against so glorious a civic space.

By 1600 the Venetians had discovered that the number of foreign visitors swelled during two festivals in particular—Carnevale and Sensa. The latter was the uniquely Venetian spectacle of marrying the sea, which dated back to the twelfth century and took place on Ascension Day. Amid much pageantry the doge and leading government officials would board the bucintoro, a richly decorated, multilevel galley used only for state ceremonies. Joined by myriad other vessels, they then rowed out to the edge of the Lido, where the Venetian lagoon met the Adriatic Sea. There the doge would cast a golden ring into the water and shout, "*Desponsamus te Mare, in signum veri perpetuique dominii*" (We espouse thee, O Sea, as a sign of true and perpetual dominion). The late spring–early summer ceremony became so popular with foreigners that the Venetians purposely enhanced both its duration and its lavish decoration in an attempt to attract more of them. A new bucintoro was put into service in 1606, festooned with images and statues of gilded sirens riding sea horses, leaping dolphins, fierce Hydras, the god Mars, and, of course, a pride of lions of St. Mark.

Even more foreign visitors came to Venice for the annual Carnevale celebrations. Meaning "good-bye to meat," Carnevale was the traditional festival that culminated on Fat Tuesday, the day before Ash Wednesday and the start of the rigors of Lent. Almost every city in Europe had some sort of pre-Lenten celebration. At some point in the fourteenth or fifteenth century, Venetians began wearing masks during their Carnevale revels—a custom already popular in other large Italian cities. The mask allowed greater freedom from social conventions and responsibilities, and generally added to the merriment. As a by-product, it also allowed foreigners to join in the festivities as natives. Why Venice's Carnevale became so popular with tourists is still not clear, but there is no denying that it did.

As with the Sensa, the Venetians and their government began to devise ways to extend the size and duration of Carnevale. This was not terribly difficult. Although the Sensa occurred on one day, the Carnevale was simply a period of time before Lent. It could reasonably be extended for days, weeks, even months. To keep the paying customers in Venice longer, new diversions were developed and offered during Carnevale.

The most famous of these was opera. Although it was once thought that opera was invented in Venice, it probably originated around 1600 in Florence or Mantua, where it was performed privately in aristocratic courts. It was the Venetians, though, who capitalized on the idea and established opera as a popular art form. Indeed, the very character of Venice quickly democratized the aristocratic pastime. During the 1630s public opera houses appeared in Venice, selling tickets that almost any-one could afford (at least for standing room). The great composer Clau-dio Monteverdi came to Venice in 1613 and later produced acclaimed operas for the Venetian public, including *Il ritorno d'Ulisse in patria* (1641) and *L'incoronazione di Poppea* (1642).

Venetian opera was in every way larger than life. Composers such as Francesco Cavalli and Antonio Cesti produced powerful works with stunning orchestral arrangements, amazing arias, and spectacu-lar scenes. Venetians loved special effects—magic spells, shipwrecks, storms, and anything else that went boom. Within just a few decades opera houses could be found across the city. The first was the Teatro Tron, not far from Rialto. It was followed by the Teatro di SS. Giovanni e Paolo, the Teatro San Moise, and the Teatro Novissimo. By 1700 there were seventeen opera houses in Venice. The opera season was attached directly to the Carnevale; as one grew, so did the other. By the mid-1600s the two seasons began in early January or, when Lent came early, even the day after Christmas. The cultured elite from across Europe rushed to Venice to take in the music and attend the numerous masked balls, each more lavish than the last.

Venice had become a pleasure not only to the eyes but also to the ears. And although opera was Venice's most popular musical form in the seventeenth century, it was by no means the only one. Venetian crafts-men constructed the best organs in the world, and crowds packed into Venice's churches to hear them played. Even the foundling hospitals be-came a source of new music. These charitable organizations housed or-phaned or abandoned children. The boys were trained in a craft and released when they turned fifteen. Girls' hospitals, however, educated their children in a variety of arts to help them find a husband, or at least employment in a noble household. Chief among those arts was music. Girls' choirs singing richly varied sacred music at the hospitals became highly accomplished and their well-attended concerts a welcome source of revenue. Girls with extraordinary musical talent were even paid to continue to sing for the choruses after they came of age.

The most famous of the Venetian composers for girls' choirs was Father Antonio Vivaldi—known as the Red Priest because of his brightly colored hair. Vivaldi was a violin virtuoso at the Ospedale della Pietà for girls. Between 1703 and 1733 he wrote dozens of concertos, cantatas, and other religious vocal arrangements for the hospital's renowned choir. He also composed operas—more than ninety by his own count—which were performed at a variety of theaters in Venice and abroad. His best-known work, though, was his series of violin concertos, *The Four Seasons*. Like other Venetian composers, Vivaldi was in high demand in the courts of Europe. At various times he composed pieces for King Louis XV of France and Emperor Charles VI of Austria.

Vivaldi seemed to have mastered every form of Venetian music. Yet like the forms themselves, his popularity eventually waned. By the 1730s opera had spread beyond Venice, and new styles were being performed in Naples, Paris, and Vienna. Venetian opera did not disappear, but it was no longer the cutting edge of musical entertainment. Vivaldi traveled to Vienna to find work, but found his services no longer required. He died there penniless in 1741.

In 1650 Venice had a near monopoly on opera. But in 1750 it could be found in every big city in Europe. Responding to the diminishing market, theaters in Venice began switching to spoken-word plays, which had flourished in Paris thanks to Molière. Here again, the Venetian emphasis was on the loud and fantastic. Theater audiences were encouraged to boo and cheer the characters. Indeed, gondoliers often received free admission simply to elevate the boisterousness of the event. Tragedies were the natural direction for indoor theater. Venetians enjoyed comedies, too, but these were thought to be the fare of the lower classes, performed on outdoor stages. Fifteenth-century Venice had seen the invention of the commedia dell'arte, a decidedly lowbrow entertainment in which a troupe of actors performed an improvisational comedy using stock characters that the audience knew well. Most such comedies revolved around a pair of lovers thwarted by an old man who eventually married with the help of a wise and witty servant. The actors wore masks that clearly defined their roles: Harlequin, a clever, humorous rake; Pantalone, a greedy, hook-nosed old miser; Columbine, the beautiful love interest; and so on. The story was, in any case, unimportant. The crowds gathered to see the acrobatic slapstick, hear the music, and laugh at the dirty jokes. And since the entire play was improvised, it was worth attending more than once. Beginning in 1738 the Venetian playwright Carlo Goldoni cleaned up the commedia dell'arte and brought it into the theaters for the amusement of the tourists and Venetian nobles. A few of the stock characters remained, but the improvisation was abandoned. Goldoni's plays drew large audiences, but they were always considered somewhat un-Venetian by locals, who saw spoken-word plays of any sort to be inherently French. Like Vivaldi, Goldoni finally left Venice, taking up a position in Paris in 1762.

The ranks of Venice's foreign visitors grew even larger in the eighteenth century, thanks to swarms of young English gentlemen on the Grand Tour—itself a remarkable cultural phenomenon. During the 1700s England experienced a dramatic increase in wealth, fueled by an expanding global empire and technological advances that would culminate in the Industrial Revolution. In short, a great many English were not just rich, but distinguished citizens of a vast empire. It became conventional wisdom, as Edward Gibbon put it, that "foreign travel completes the education of an English gentleman." According to John Locke, the reasons for this "may be reduced to these Two, first Language, secondly an Improvement in Wisdom and Prudence, by seeing men, and

conversing with People of Tempers, Customs, and Ways of living, different from one another, and especially from those of his Parish and Neigh-
bourhood." And so, after finishing their basic education, a great many
young English gentry would leave their country, traveling with a tutor
and servants, to spend several years seeing the sights on the Continent.
It became a defining feature of their class—so much so that the practice
even traveled to North America. An eighteenth-century gentleman who
could not speak with knowledge of Rome, Milan, Venice, or Paris was
simply no gentleman.

Rome was always the primary destination of the Grand Tourists.
There one could walk among the ruins of antiquity, marveling at the
artistic treasures of the Renaissance papacy. It was the Eternal City, the
capital of the last great world empire. Aside from Rome, the English
tourist had many other destination options, although Naples, Florence,
and Milan would naturally figure highly on any Italian tour. It was also
expected that one would spend some time in the countryside, learning
the customs of the quaint common folk.

Next to Rome, Venice was the most popular destination on the
Grand Tour. It was scarcely conceivable that a young Englishman would
miss it. Venice, after all, held a special place in the English consciousness, being the setting of numerous English novels and plays, including
two by Shakespeare. The English had also come to see in the island republic a kindred spirit. After the Glorious Revolution of 1688 the English
had established a constitutional government that strictly limited the
powers of their monarch. Venice's "mixed" system of government, in
which there were large and small councils presided over by an executive, seemed very similar. Just as the English had a king, House of Lords,
and House of Commons, the Venetians had a doge, Senate, and Great
Council. More importantly, the Venetians had maintained this government for more than a millennium. Clearly it worked, which was a com-
forting validation of the new English system. English observers never

failed to mention that the doge, for all his pageantry, had very little power. Like the English, Venetians pursued commerce and industry and had once ruled a scattered overseas empire. As Protestants, the English did not warm to Venice's Catholicism, but even there they found something to praise. The English had cheered the Venetians in 1606, when they withstood a long papal interdict, refusing to bow to Rome's will. The hero of the defiance, Fra Paolo Sarpi, was widely read in England. The centuries-old Venetian custom of separating ecclesiastical and secular authority now seemed both new and enlightened. In short, English visitors were usually well disposed to Venice even before they arrived.

The *milordi* (as the traveling Englishmen were called) stayed in hostels or rented accommodations in palazzi, depending on their circumstances. Like other travelers, they often timed their arrival with Venice's festivals and the theater season. An English set of travel instructions advised, "Go from Rome by way of Loretto to Venice, so as to be there the beginning of May, at which time the Ascension begins, which is a better sight than the Carneval at Venice." Thousands of tourists took this advice, filling the city in the days before the celebration. Lady Mary Wortley Montagu, who stayed briefly in Venice during the Sensa, wrote, "I cannot absolutely set the day of my departure, though I very sincerely wish for it, and have reason more than usual: this town being at present infested with English, who torment me as much as the frogs and lice did the palace of Pharaoh."

On Ascension Day the Bacino would fill with gondolas, many now carrying Grand Tourists eager for a close-up view. The English divine Richard Pococke, who saw the spectacle in 1734, sent home a long description of the doge's galley, the bucintoro, which was yet another new and more lavish model put into service only seven years earlier. It was, he believed, "the finest ship in the world. . . . The floor is wood laid in handsom figures, every thing else you see in side and out is finely carv'd and gilt all over in the most beautifull manner . . . at the helm is the

Doges gilt throne the Nobles being rangd all down." The German polymath, Johann Wolfgang von Goethe, attended the Sensa in 1786, and wrote of the bucintoro: "The ship is itself an ornament; therefore one may not say that it is overloaded with ornaments, and only a mass of gilded carvings that are otherwise useless. In reality it is a monstrance, in order to show the people that their leaders are indeed wonderful."

The Sensa, a long-treasured civic ritual for Venetians, had become a giant spectacle for tourists. And that is precisely why it became more elaborate as time went on and the power of Venice waned. The irony was not lost on many foreigners—especially the English, who knew well enough that the Republic of Venice could no longer claim dominion over her bride, the Adriatic. The English churchman John Moore, who made the tour in the 1770s, described the marriage ceremony, saying, "The sea, like a modest bride, assents by her silence, and the marriage is deemed valid and secure to all intents and purposes. Certain it is the time has been, when the Doge had entire possession of, and dominion over, his spouse; but for a considerable time past her favours have been shared by several other lovers." The English poet Thomas Gray put it more succinctly: "Next to Venice by the 11th of May, there to see the old Doge wed the Adriatic Whore."

Carnevale events were less spectacular, but drew greater crowds— nearly fifty thousand by 1700. Dressing up in costumes was, of course, part of the fun. In the seventeenth century almost any costume would serve, although there was a fondness for commedia dell'arte characters. The problem with inventiveness, though, was that revelers were expected to act the part of their costumes. Dressing as a Roman, for example, obligated one to speak Latin or else risk a thrashing from masked commoners. After 1700, guidebooks advised tourists to dress as the Venetian nobility did, with a *bauta* (cape), a *tabarro* (cloak), a white mask, and a tricornered hat. This soon became the unofficial costume of Carnevale.

Aside from masks and opera, a multitude of other activities awaited those who visited Venice for Carnevale. In the eighteenth century more than seventy casinos, called *ridotti*, would open their doors during the weeks before Lent. Most were small affairs, set up in various palazzi near San Marco. Some, however, like the Ridotto Grande, were lavish baroque salons. The only game played in the ridotti was *bassetta* (Basset), which held a mystique and association with wealth similar to baccarat today. Both games, in fact, are extremely simple with almost no place for strategy or skill. Bassetta was essentially a lottery, with a press-your-luck element that made it both addictive and extremely costly. Players placed bets on individual cards, hoping that the dealer would reveal the same card as a winner from his own deck. Winning cards (as in baccarat) could be bent in order to let a successful bet ride. Theoretically, it was possible for a single wager to pay off sixty-seven times its value, yet the odds against that were extraordinary. In fact, the game very consciously favored the dealer, who by law had to be a noble and who was often the owner of the establishment. In short, it was the perfect casino game—one that seemed winnable to the player, but in fact was a bonanza for the house.

Seventeenth- and eighteenth-century travel books almost invariably urged visitors to skip Venice's ridotti, which they claimed were both dangerous and crooked. But the tourists flocked there nonetheless. Part of the allure was the requirement that all players be masked, allowing the game and the subterfuge to extend to both friends and lovers. Indeed, many young foreign aristocrats went to the ridotti hoping to meet beautiful masked noblewomen, released from the cloistered captivity of their palazzi only during Carnevale. It was widely rumored that Venice's miserly old husbands hated the season, but "the Venetian Ladies are impatient for these Occasions, and their Husbands equally watchful to preserve the Honour of the Marriage Bed." Travel books advised their readers to resist the temptation, since the husbands often hired men to watch their wives and physically beat anyone who became too familiar.

Although sex-starved Venetian noblewomen may have been scarce, the same could not be said of Venetian prostitutes. As a port city, Venice had always boasted a vibrant sex trade. During the Middle Ages and Renaissance common prostitutes did business in the Rialto district, close to the merchants and sailors. High-class courtesans, known as *cortigiane oneste*, could also be found. These were well-educated consorts, much coveted by the nobility, both in Venice and abroad. Veronica Franco, the famous sixteenth-century Venetian courtesan, had her portrait painted by Veronese and even counted King Henry III of France among her clients. In the seventeenth and eighteenth centuries, both forms of prostitution were still active in Venice—indeed, the practitioners had greatly expanded to meet the new foreign demand. It is no exaggeration to say that Grand Tourists who headed to Venice did so as much for the sex as they did for the culture. Almost every traveler's account of Venice published during these centuries devoted significant portions to prostitution.

In 1608 the English traveler Thomas Coryat estimated that some twelve thousand prostitutes worked in Venice, and that number only increased. No longer confined to Rialto, they had spread throughout the city. According to writer Fynes Moryson, they were "free to dwell in any house they can hyre, and in any streete whatsoever, and to weare what they list." Travelers strolling through the narrow streets of Venice were presented with a wide selection of prostitutes doing business at all hours. In his 1749 tour book, Thomas Nugent noted:

> Of these [prostitutes] there are whole streets full, who receive all comers; and as the habits of other people are black and dismal, these dress in the gayest colours, with their breasts open, and

their faces all bedaubed with paint, standing by dozens at the doors and windows to invite their Customers.

English and other European tourists who could afford to visit Venice during Carnevale could also usually afford a cultured, high-quality courtesan. They need not look far. Indeed, competition among the courtesans was so fierce that they adopted a variety of techniques to snare customers. Coryat reported that if one hired a gondola for a ride, the gondolier "presently will carry you to some Curtezans house, who will best pay him for bringing her Customers, as if there were no other recreation but only with women." In a letter of March 1751, the Grand Tourist Edward Thomas wrote, "Whenever I walkd the Place of St. Mark I observed several Fellows in Cloaks come up to my Servants . . . and importune them to bring me to some of these Ladies; and in the Island of Murano a child not 8 years old came to them on the same errand." Yet another strategy was for the courtesan to feign interest in the visitor and only reveal that her interest was professional when they had arrived at her chamber. Thomas recorded one such incident:

The next day we went to see a Church and hear a musical Performance, and this young Gallant could not forbear making love to a Lady, richly dress'd and bedeck'd with Jewels tho she was on her knees and thumping her breast. She, to our great surprise, before all the People lifted up her Vail and ogle'd him presenting her hand to him to lead her to her Gondola. The bait took and he handed her into the Gondola and the moment he was in with her she becond to the Gondoleers, who were in handsom liveries, to row off with him in view of all the People, who set up a loud laugh and said she was one of the greatest and most dangerous Strumpets of the City.

Frivolity and debauchery had become major industries in Venice. They were, therefore, an important source of revenue—particularly in an age in which shipping revenues continued to decline. The Venetian government strictly regulated and heavily taxed both prostitution and gambling. By the eighteenth century the vices that were readily available in Venice were so well known that to have outlawed them would have stricken Venice from the Grand Tour. As Johann Wilhelm von Archenholz put it in 1785: "After the great decline of trade at Venice, the visits of travellers became the greatest resource of the nation; it was therefore necessary to adopt milder laws, in order not to deter them from visiting a country which can by no means do without them."

No figure better defines this period in Venetian history than the famous Giacomo Girolamo Casanova. Born in 1725, the son of an actor and an actress, Casanova moved boldly across the landscape of eighteenth-century Venice. With wit and charm he attracted noble patrons, who paid for his education and his entry into elite society. Above all, Casanova loved love. He moved from one sexual conquest to the next. A regular at the finest balls and the most raucous ridotti, Casanova proclaimed, "Cultivating whatever gave pleasure to my senses was always the chief business of my life; I never found any occupation more important." After abortive careers in the Church, the military, and the theater, he took to gambling as well as cavorting in salons and coffeehouses, discussing the newest ideas of the Enlightenment. His passion for Freemasonry brought him to the attention of the State Inquisition. He was arrested in 1754 and sentenced to five years in the Piombi (the Leads), the old prison in the Ducal Palace directly below the lead roof. After a difficult stay, Casanova staged a daring escape in which he climbed onto the roof, entered a side window, and made his way through the heart of the governmental complex during the deserted hours of the early morning. The remainder of his life was just as exciting. He traveled the length and breadth of Europe, meeting the most powerful and interesting people of his time, including Madame de Pompadour, Jean-Jacques Rousseau, and Benjamin Franklin. His numerous adventures included elaborate cons, exciting duels, diplomatic missions, and espionage. He wrote plays, essays, a novel, and, of course, his enormous memoirs, which won him eternal fame and helped define Venice in the modern world as a place of pleasure, culture, and dark designs.

Eighteenth-century Venice was a city of opulence and decadence, and those two themes most strike one in the guidebooks and memoirs of the period. It had become a city of pleasure, the Las Vegas of its day. But for all the frivolous merrymaking, Venice remained true to its ancient heritage. The republic, despite its snarl of checks and balances, remained solid and stable. Although most of the maritime empire had disappeared, Venice continued to govern a sizable chunk of mainland Italy, including important cities like Padua and Verona. And the business of Venice remained business. Much of Venetian wealth was now generated by foreigners flocking to their city of spectacles, but a great deal was also produced by local industries and international trade. The world was changing. And just as their ancestors had done for centuries, Venetians adapted to those changes to secure the honor and profit of Venice.

CHAPTER 17

A MEDIEVAL REPUBLIC
IN THE MODERN WORLD:
THE UNITED STATES, FRANCE,
AND THE FALL OF VENICE

T hanks to the Grand Tour, by the mid-eighteenth century Venice was well known to the French and English elite. In general, the English thought better of it than the French. Enlightenment thinkers in both countries praised Venice's antiquity and the stability of its republic. The Enlightenment of the seventeenth and eighteenth centuries drew breath from Europe's burgeoning middle class and was nurtured in the salons, coffeehouses, and market squares of every major city. At root was the resistance of a new class of wealthy businessmen to the old privileges of aristocracy and monarchy. They demanded a new order, one that would replace tradition with reason, birth with merit, and serfdom with liberty. They imagined a new world in which reason reigned supreme, privilege was abolished, and all men were free. In that light, Venice looked quite favorable, particularly when compared with the absolutist monarchies that still ruled in France, Spain, and Austria.

The Enlightenment ushered in the modern world. Those states that could not adapt eventually passed away. Yet for Venice, adaptation was unnecessary; it had embraced these essential concepts a thousand years before they became fashionable. For some, like the English, this was validation of the effectiveness of free government. For others, like the French *philosophes*, it was mildly irritating to discover that their avant-garde ideas were not so innovative after all. As a result, the French in this period tended to cast Venice into the morass of medieval history, stirring it together with the dark despots that they loved to hate. This opinion mattered, for Venice's survival would one day hinge on French perceptions. French authors regularly described Venice as living through a period of decadence before its final demise. Abraham-Nicolas Amelot de la Houssaie's influential *Histoire du gouvernement de Venise*, published in 1676, blamed Venice's decline on a weak-willed policy of neutrality, foolish expansion on the terra firma, cumbersome administrative procedures, and a propensity to compromise. Although Rousseau enjoyed a blissful year (1743–44) in Venice, taking in the opera, the choirs, and the other "famous amusements," he nonetheless concluded that the city "has long since fallen into decay." The Venice of Voltaire's *Candide* (1759) was thoroughly decadent. The two principal Venetian characters are Paquette, a prostitute who gives Pangloss syphilis, and Count Pococurante, who complains of utter boredom among too many women and too much art, music, and literature. Montesquieu declared simply that Venice had "no more strength, commerce, riches, law; only debauchery there has the name of liberty."

As we have seen, though, the English, who enjoyed a constitutional government and were the freest people in the world, saw much of themselves in the island Republic of Venice, and were hardly so bearish on its prospects. English writers routinely praised the Venetian government's centuries-old ability to avoid tyranny and to guarantee liberty for its citizens. Nonetheless, like the French, they denounced the Council of Ten and the State Inquisition, which they believed acted without restriction or any measure of justice. As John Moore wrote in 1781, "While you admire the strength of a constitution which has stood firm for so many ages, you are appalled at the sight of the lion's mouth gaping for accusation."

The Enlightenment ideas that had percolated in Europe's coffee-houses and salons were put to the test by the revolutions of the late eighteenth and nineteenth centuries. The first of these was the American Revolution. The Declaration of Independence, which set out its principles, was drawn directly from the philosophies of Enlightenment thinkers like John Locke and Adam Smith. It held that "all men are created equal, that they are endowed by their Creator with certain unalienable rights, that among these are Life, Liberty, and the pursuit of Happiness." It was a manifesto for what had come to be called Liberalism: a belief that all should be free to pursue their goals, no matter their birth.

The Founding Fathers of the United States meant to craft a republic that would stand the test of time, even outlasting what was in their estimation the greatest republic ever, ancient Rome. Men like Thomas Jefferson, John Adams, and Benjamin Franklin were well educated in the classics and knew as much about Venice as any English gentleman (although none of the three had made the Grand Tour as young men). One might think that the extraordinary longevity of Venice's republic would recommend it as a model for the new country. But it did not—at least not completely. Like English writers, Jefferson and Adams praised the checks and balances that guarded Venice against tyranny, but otherwise considered it to be an "aristocratical republic" (as Adams put it).

John Adams devoted an entire chapter to Venice in *A Defence of the Constitutions of Government of the United States of America*, published in 1787. The book provided a short history of Venetian government, not altogether accurate, and probably based on Amelot de la Houssaie. According to Adams, early Venetians had created a democracy, but it had been thwarted by tyrannical doges. In the twelfth century they formed a republic in which each sestiere elected members to the Great Council. Over time, however, the members of the council were able to deprive both the doge and the people of their power, culminating in the Serrata, which made membership in the council hereditary. "Commerce and wars soon turned the attention of the rest of the people from all thought about the loss of their privileges." This, in Adams's view, was where Venice had faltered.

"Great care is taken in Venice, to balance one court against another," he wrote, "and render their powers mutual checks to each other." Yet even that praiseworthy attribute of Venetian government was itself, Adams believed, a mechanism for the nobility to maintain control. A pure republic, Adams (and Jefferson) argued, was one that balanced the powers of the chief magistrate, the aristocracy, and the common people. "In Venice, the aristocratical passion for curbing the prince and the people, has been carried to its utmost length." Adams was faced, however, with the obvious fact that the chief magistrate and people in Venice had not risen up to seize power from the nobility, as they had done in Europe's absolutist states. He explained this stability by attributing it to the dark power of the Council of Ten, which Adams believed crushed all opposition to the constitution. He fully embraced the myth of the omnipotent State Inquisitors:

> This tribunal consists only of three persons, all taken from the council of ten, who have authority to decide, without appeal, on the life of every citizen, the doge himself not excepted. They employ what spies they please; if they are unanimous, they may order a prisoner to be strangled in gaol, or drowned in the canal, hanged in the night, or by day, as they please; if they are divided, the cause must go before the council of ten, but even here, if the guilt is doubtful, the rule is to execute the prisoner in the night. The three may command access to the house of every individual in the state, and have even keys to every apartment in the ducal palace, may enter his bed-chamber, break his cabinet, and search

his papers. By this tribunal, have doge, nobility, and people, been kept in awe, and restrained from violating the laws, and to this is to be ascribed the long duration of this aristocracy.

Adams was certainly correct that the Council of Ten had powers beyond what a modern liberal state would condone, but it also had powerful mechanisms to keep it in check. Strict term limits, for example, ensured that members did not arbitrarily wield a power that could soon be used against themselves. Adams was right—the Ten kept stability in Venice. But that was not because it protected the nobility, but instead because it provided an efficient method to force the ruling families to live well within the rule of law.

For more than a thousand years Venice had been the only republic in the world—one that flourished in an age of kings, emperors, and tyrants. It did so, as we have seen, because it was a state built purely on commerce. Like ancient Athens, which built a similar empire of commerce, medieval Venice teemed with entrepreneurs seeking their fortunes. They would not abide a system that denied them political authority that matched their economic clout. Throughout Western history capitalism and representative government have always walked hand in hand. When the first grows, the second must follow.

In the seventeenth century European thinkers began to rediscover republican government, but only in the eighteenth century were new states founded on those principles. The birth of an entirely new republic in North America across the Atlantic Ocean, while the world's oldest republic still lived on in the Mediterranean, is intriguing. How did Venice welcome the news of the American Revolution? What was the relationship between the United States and the Republic of Venice during the two decades that their respective histories overlapped?

Venetians were not unaware of the new birth. Their ambassador in Paris, Daniele Dolfin, sent home regular dispatches, keeping the Senate fully apprised of the American Revolutionary War. Dolfin met frequently with Benjamin Franklin, who expressed an admiration for Venice and a desire to visit. Franklin was in Paris to secure an alliance with King Louis XVI, which was finally concluded in 1778. Dolfin wrote several times to the Senate asking for instructions on how he should approach Dr. Franklin—as a foreign ambassador or just a foreigner? The difference was crucial, for it went to the heart of Venice's recognition of the United States. Like American delegates to other royal courts, Franklin naturally hoped for Venetian recognition. In Madrid the Venetian ambassador, Antonio Cappello, even entertained the American delegate, William Carmichael, in his home. The dispatches from Paris, Madrid, and Vienna continued to ask the senators for guidance on how they should answer the petitions of this "new Republic."

The Senate responded that its diplomats should not recognize the United States as a free and independent state. To do so would strain commercial relations with Great Britain and, more importantly, jeopardize Venice's status as a neutral power. At all costs, it must maintain that neutrality. Only this, the senators believed, would preserve the Republic of St. Mark in an age of great powers. Not until 1783, after the Treaty of Paris had ended the war and Great Britain itself recognized the United States, did Venice do the same.

Despite Venice's aloofness toward American independence and John Adams's own reservations about Venice, the United States nevertheless quickly sought formal ties with the Republic of Venice. In December 1784 Adams, Jefferson, and Franklin wrote a joint letter to Daniele Dolfin:

Sir,

The United States of America in Congress assembled, judging that an intercourse between the said United States and the Most

Serene Republic of Venice founded on the principles of equality, reciprocity and friendship, may be of mutual advantage to both nations, on the twelfth day of May last, issued their Commission under the seal of the said States to the Subscribers as their Ministers plenipotentiary, giving to them or the majority of them full power and authority, for the said States and in their name, to confer, treat and negotiate with the Ambassador Minister or Commissioner of the said Most Serene Republic of Venice vested with full and sufficient powers, of and concerning a Treaty of Amity and Commerce, to make and receive propositions for such Treaty and to conclude and sign the same, transmitting it to the said United States in Congress assembled for their final ratification.

We have now the honor to inform your Excellency that we have received this Commission in due form, and that we are here ready to enter on the negotiation whenever a full power from the said Most Serene Republic of Venice shall appear for that purpose.

We have further the honour to request of your Excellency that you should transmit this information to your Court, and to be with great respect

> Your Excellency's
> Most obedient and
> Most humble servants
>
> John Adams
> B. Franklin
> Th. Jefferson

This was to be the only written correspondence that would pass between the world's oldest and youngest republics. When it arrived in Venice, it was promptly ignored. Hearing no response, Dolfin, who seems to have struck up a friendly relationship with Franklin and perhaps the other Americans as well, wrote again to the Senate. He pointed out that similar treaties were being concluded in Paris between the United States and France, Holland, Prussia, and Portugal, so there was no reason for Venice to remain aloof. In earlier dispatches Dolfin had expressed optimism for the future of the United States, noting the extraordinary size of the country ("three times that of France") and its potential for expansion (he believed that a war with Spain over Florida was inevitable). At the very least, the senators should respond to the American offer.

The Senate's response disappointed Dolfin, as well as Benjamin Franklin, who was preparing to return home: Venice declined to enter into a treaty with the United States. Although Great Britain had accepted American independence, relations between the two remained tense. The Senate worried that a treaty of friendship might cast doubts on Venice's neutrality should war again break out. As for commerce, the senators had no reason to believe that any would occur between the United States and Venice. Venetians did almost no business in the Atlantic, and while American vessels traded in the Mediterranean, none had ever come to Venice. Indeed, the Senate had good reason to believe that they never would. Shipping in the western Mediterranean was plagued by Barbary pirates based in Algeria and Morocco, to whom governments paid protection money to have their flagged vessels left in peace. During the Revolution, American vessels were left alone, since they were allies of France. But since acquiring its independence, the United States could no longer hide behind the French flag. Jefferson paid Morocco to secure safe transport in June 1786, but no agreement was worked out with Algeria until 1795. For the time being, then, American-flagged vessels would find it very difficult to do business with Venice or her colonies.

Even without the pirates, trade with the United States held little appeal. Venice had goods that the United States wanted, such as glass and textiles, but not vice versa. The English ambassador to Venice, Robert Ritchie, reported that:

> the Americans are attempting to begin a kind of trade with this State [Venice]; I say a kind of trade, for they do not order goods on their own account . . . but instead of that, they give long lists of European goods, which would answer well according to the price noted, and as long lists of American goods, very few of which would answer at all if sent in return. But it will not do; the Venetian merchants are not easily cajoled into such schemes.

The final and perhaps most important reason that Venice refused to establish relations with the United States is that the senators doubted that the new republic would last. America's first attempt at establishing a written constitution—the Articles of Confederation—had failed. In October 1787 the Venetian ambassador to London, Gasparo Soderini, sent a translation of the new American Constitution to the Senate. He informed the Senate that it was very similar to the British system of government, simply "changing the name of the king to the President, of the House of Lords to the Senate, of the House of Commons to the Congress [sic]." The legal codes in the United States were also, he assured the senators, "completely like those in England." The Venetians concluded that the United States was drifting back to its mother country. Indeed, Ritchie had earlier described the new country as "independent in name only."

Venice's interest in the "new republic" of the United States was real, but the centuries-old Venetian conservatism could not conceive that it would ever succeed. Venice kept the United States at arm's length because Venetians did not make long ocean voyages, they had no interest in American goods, and they worried that the new state would soon collapse. The general feeling among Venetians was that the United States was just too new, too wild, and too unstable to survive.

As it happened, it was the Venetian republic that would not survive. And in a supreme irony it would die at the hands of a liberal republic, executed for the crime of medieval tyranny. During the momentous years between 1789 and 1794 all of Europe watched as the French people, awash in the ideas of Liberalism and buoyed by the American experience, overturned their monarchy and established a new republic. Let us not rehearse the long and bloody history of the French Revolution; suffice it to say, it did not go as smoothly as the American one. The Revolution targeted first the monarchy, then the nobility, the Catholic Church, and finally the wealthy middle class, which had itself spawned the Revolution. The result was not merely chaos and bloodshed. Out of the mayhem the French had produced a new and burning nationalism.

For Venetians, patriotism was nothing new. Indeed, Venetians were sometimes criticized for loving their state more than God. Since patriotism was virtually unknown in the Middle Ages, such criticisms are not surprising. Large kingdoms, such as France or Spain, were a collection of diverse regions each with its own language, customs, and concerns. They were bound together only by their theoretical allegiance to a king and their Catholic faith. The French Revolution changed that. The people of France—everywhere in France—had become French citizens. All now stood equal before the law, with no privilege, no nobility. They had, they believed, thrown off the shackles of Church and aristocracy and were leading the way into a new world of right and reason. Little wonder, then, that this new revolutionary France soon declared war on almost all its neighbors, which were, of course, monarchies. Counter-revolutionaries needed to be acquainted with Madame Guillotine, whether they were found in France or abroad. In a way, the French had rediscovered their medieval crusading zeal, only this time they were bringing to the world not the cross but liberal revolution.

The Revolution had fused France into one, very dangerous, state. It produced Europe's first national army, a permanent conscripted force of unprecedented size and effectiveness. France's leaders found the army useful to crush not only external enemies, but internal ones as well. After the Reign of Terror ended with the execution of Maximilien Robespierre in 1794, a new republic was formed in Paris with a bicameral legislature and a five-man executive committee known as the Directory. Because the new government proved bitterly unpopular in the Paris streets, the leaders needed a military commander who could maintain order no matter the cost. They found their man in a poor Corsican who had worked his way up the ranks of the national army: Napoleon Bonaparte. After proving himself as the commander of the Army of the Interior, Napoleon was appointed commander in chief of the Army of Italy in March 1796. His assignment was to "liberate" northern Italy from the oppression of the medieval Hapsburg emperors and then to press on toward their capital of Vienna, spreading a healthy dose of "liberty, equality, and fraternity" along the way.

Historians of Venice often cast Napoleon as a bête noire, determined to crush the Republic of St. Mark just as he would wipe away so much else in the world that remained medieval. In truth, Napoleon and the Directory were hunting bigger game. The Hapsburgs had long been the enemies of France. Now history (and the French) demanded the extermination of the Hapsburg dynasty, the defenders of absolute monarchy. To conquer Vienna would not only strike a blow against medieval despotism but also rocket Napoleon to new heights of power, perhaps even to challenge the Directory itself. Destroying poor, weak, and stridently neutral Venice was hardly worth the general's effort. This is not to say that Napoleon would not have welcomed the fall of Venice. Subsequent events prove that he had no love for it. But it was never the objective of his Italian campaign.

As a war of titans raged in Italy, Venice had the misfortune to be stuck in the middle. Napoleon went from victory to victory in Lombardy, finally capturing Milan in May 1796. His army pressed eastward, defeating Hapsburg forces with ease and establishing new liberal governments in many Italian towns. All of them were to be organized into two Italian republics, both puppets of France. The last Austrian stronghold in Italy was Mantua. Napoleon besieged the city for months, but it continued to hold out. Austrian forces made several unsuccessful attempts to break the siege, marching from the north, directly across Venetian territory. This greatly upset the French general. Why, Napoleon asked, did a neutral state like Venice allow France's enemy to wage war by crossing its lands? The Venetian Senate responded that an ancient treaty allowed the Austrians to cross in order to reach their own territories. Napoleon dismissed the excuse. He knew all about Venice and its history—or at least he knew the popular myth of Venice, propagated in Amelot de la Houssaie's history and a thousand guidebooks. Venice was no republic, he believed, but a cruel oligarchy in which the slightest dissent was punished by the Council of Ten and its State Inquisitors. Of course, he reasoned, the aristocratic Venetian rulers would support the monarchist Hapsburgs!

Napoleon used the Austrians' entry into Venetian territory as an excuse to do the same himself. When the Austrians were allowed to occupy a Venetian fortress at Peschiera on Lake Garda, Napoleon threatened to capture nearby Verona and burn it to the ground. Only by surrendering the city to the French could it be saved. Thus did Venice lose the second city of its mainland empire. Francesco Pesaro, the leader of a party of nobles that favored rearming Venice, had earlier urged the government to ally with Austria against Napoleon. Now, as Napoleon found his march to Vienna delayed by the ongoing siege of Mantua, he offered his own alliance between Venice and France. The Senate stridently rejected both proposals, continuing to believe that neutrality was Venice's only hope for survival in a dangerous modern world.

Mantua fell on February 2, 1797, and the last of the Austrian forces retreated across the Alps to Tyrol, crossing Venetian territory along the way. Napoleon gave chase, but not before having the French ambassador to Venice, Jean-Baptiste Lallement, present a series of democratic reforms to the Great Council. Implementing these, he suggested, would prove the friendship between Venice and France. They included the election of representatives, the abolition of the State Inquisition, and the release of all political prisoners (of whom Venice had none). More than a thousand members of the Great Council met on March 24 to consider and vote on Napoleon's reforms. They received five votes in favor.

French troops who remained in Italy were tasked with maintaining the peace and overseeing the creation of the new Italian republics. In fact, though, they often abused their authority, taking what they wanted from the population, be it coin, dwellings, or even women. Across northern Italy a deep hatred of the French flourished, which itself led to a new Italian nationalism. Nowhere was this truer than in Venice's former provinces, where people had grown accustomed to the rule of law and a stable government. Rebellions soon began to break out here and there, the largest in Verona, where armed bands began chanting *"Viva San Marco!"* in the streets, and targeting French soldiers whenever possible. The uprising continued to grow through Holy Week and Easter Week 1797. In the disorder, several hundred French soldiers were killed and many more imprisoned. When Napoleon heard of this, he flew into a rage. He had no doubt that the attackers had been armed and supported by Venice. While it is true that some of the partisans were Venetian militia, they were not acting on orders from the Senate. A popular uprising against the French was the last thing that the government in Venice wanted.

As the French brutally crushed the Easter uprising, Napoleon began to reconsider his drive toward Vienna. The campaign was taking longer than he had anticipated—a development for which he now blamed

Venice. For various political reasons Napoleon wanted to wrap things up quickly and return to Paris. He decided, therefore, to make peace. On April 18 he agreed to the Preliminaries of Leoben, a framework agreement that ended the war between France and Austria. In it, Emperor Francis II of Austria agreed to surrender Belgium, accept the loss of Lombardy, and acknowledge France's new frontier on the Rhine. In return, Napoleon ceded to Austria all of Venice's mainland territories, even those he did not currently possess. It was time, Napoleon believed, to return Venice to the sea.

With the apparent demise of their mainland empire the Venetians took refuge in their lagoon, which had defended them for more than a millennium. What they did not know was that it could defend them no longer. Two days after Napoleon's agreement with Austria, three French vessels patrolling in the Adriatic entered the Venetian lagoon. The fortress at San Andrea fired across their bows, which caused two of them to retreat. The third vessel, named the *Libérateur d'Italie*, was apparently unable to turn as quickly. Two small Venetian warships quickly blocked its path, and a collision occurred. What happened next is still not clear. Although the French commander, Jean-Baptiste Laugier, shouted his surrender, both sides began firing their weapons. After a clatter of shots and billows of smoke, cooler heads finally prevailed. But by then five Venetians and five Frenchmen lay dead, Laugier among them.

Napoleon already believed that the Venetians had been covertly waging war against him. Not only had they supported his enemy the Hapsburgs, but they had waged guerrilla war against his troops through their proxies. Even before news of the *Libérateur* reached him, Napoleon had thundered to Venetian deputies, "What of my men [at Verona], whom you Venetians have murdered? . . . Any government unable to restrain its own subjects is an imbecile government and has no right to survive." Napoleon fully believed the caricature of Venice as a ruthless and lawless tyranny where dark intrigues kept the people cowering in fear. Well, he would not cower. As he turned back from Austria, Napoleon again demanded that the Venetians immediately release all their political prisoners. "If not, I myself shall come and break your prisons open, for I shall tolerate none of your Inquisitions, your medieval barbarities. Every man must be free to express his opinions." The Venetian deputies were amazed that Napoleon was so poorly informed about Venice and its government. They told him that Venice (unlike France) had no political prisoners and that the State Inquisition not only operated under strict adherence to the law, but was much loved and trusted by the people. Napoleon would have none of it. For him, the myth of Venice *was* Venice. He shouted back, "I will have no more Inquisition, no more Senate! I will be an Attila to the Venetian State!"

Napoleon's famous "Attila" comment can be found in every history of the Republic of Venice. It is just too delicious to leave out. But it was not, as it is regularly interpreted, the general's pronouncement of Venice's death sentence. Even Napoleon's grasp of history was not that bad. For centuries, Attila the Hun had been credited with giving birth to Venice by waging war on the mainland. To Venetians, Attila was almost a city founder, for his attacks on Aquileia, Padua, and elsewhere had led directly to the settlement of the Venetian islands. As for Napoleon, he meant what he said. He would be an Attila by depriving Venice of its mainland possessions, sending its people scurrying back to the lagoon. He had, after all, promised those lands to the emperor in Vienna. But Napoleon did not yet envision the destruction of the Venetian state.

News of the *Libérateur* changed his mind. This, Napoleon thundered, was an act of war, and he meant to prosecute that war. He wrote to the Directory in Paris, "I am convinced that the only course to be taken now is to destroy this ferocious and sanguinary Government." Recalling the French ambassador to the Republic of Venice, he informed the Venetians that to avoid war with France they must immediately evacuate Italy and prepare to enact a series of democratic reforms.

Desperate, the Venetian government obeyed, still protesting its neutrality. There was no longer any hope of resistance. Unlike Attila, Napoleon had very large cannons, which could bombard Venice from the shore. He set them up and encamped his soldiers within sight of Venice at the end of April 1797. On May 3 Napoleon again wrote to Paris: "I see nothing that can be done but to obliterate the Venetian name from the face of the globe."

Venice was a flurry of activity during the next week. Hundreds of patricians packed their bags and fled the city. Many of them feared that the famous French guillotine would soon grace the Piazza San Marco and that they would be among its first customers. Other nobles rushed to their mainland villas, hoping to hold on to them despite the French occupation. On the streets and canals of Venice, confusion reigned. The Arsenale workers, always among the city's most bellicose defenders, insisted that Venice not surrender without a fight. In the coffeehouses of the Piazza, Jacobins (liberal sympathizers of the French Revolution) applauded Napoleon as a harbinger of modernity. Most common Venetians simply watched and waited. There was a strange unreality to it all. For Venice, these were truly uncharted waters.

On May 9 Napoleon's secretary, Joseph Villetard, delivered to the Venetian government a final ultimatum. To escape utter destruction, the Venetians must abolish their republic. The long list of demands included (again) the release of political prisoners, the creation of a provisional municipal government, the formation of a democratically elected legislature, and the planting of a Liberty Tree (the symbol of the French Revolution) in the Piazza San Marco, around which the people were to dance with joy while burning the flag of San Marco. To ensure order, the Municipality was to invite three thousand French troops into the city and turn over all major governmental buildings, including the Ducal Palace.

It is an extraordinary testament to the continued vitality and stability of the Most Serene Republic of St. Mark that even at the moment of its death it proceeded deliberately, lawfully, and in an orderly fashion. On Friday, May 12, 1797, the Great Council of Venice convened for the last time. Because of all the recent departures only about half of the members attended. Doge Lodovico Manin (1789–97) solemnly entered the chamber and took his customary place at the rostrum, Tintoretto's magnificent *Paradiso* behind him. Outside on the streets and Piazzetta below could be heard the chanting of the people: *"Viva San Marco! Viva San Marco!"* With tears streaming down his face, the doge proposed a motion: To preserve the religion, lives, and property of the people of Venice, the Great Council should abolish the constitution of the republic and surrender all of the council's authority to a provisional democratic government—one that would, of course, be a puppet of the French.

There was no debate. In truth, there was nothing left to debate. The decision had been made for them. As they had done for centuries, the members of the Great Council lined up to cast their ballots. The final vote was 512 yeas, 20 nays, and 5 abstentions. With that, history's longest-surviving republic ceased to be. After more than thirteen centuries, the Republic of Venice was sacrificed on the altar of republicanism.

A new era had dawned in Western history in which there was apparently no room for the old. And yet, even as the masters of that age built new republics on the model of ancient Rome, they scarcely noticed that it was the Venetians who were the unbroken thread to antiquity. They truly were Rome unfallen—a republic transplanted to the lagoons when the ancient world was ending. Now that thread was broken. The storks had flown. And once again a new world was born.

The Republic of Venice is one of history's greatest marvels. Its passing, like the passing of all great states and ages, cannot fail to evoke some measure of sorrow, for it reminds us that ours are transitory as well. If one should seek a fitting eulogy for the Republic of St. Mark, though, it is folly to contend with William Wordsworth's masterful poem "On the

Extinction of the Venetian Republic," penned just five years after its demise.

> Once did She hold the gorgeous East in fee;
> And was the safeguard of the West: the worth
> Of Venice did not fall below her birth,
> Venice, the eldest Child of Liberty.
> She was a maiden City, bright and free;
> No guile seduced, no force could violate;
> And, when She took unto herself a Mate,
> She must espouse the everlasting Sea.
> And what if she had seen those glories fade,
> Those titles vanish, and that strength decay;
> Yet shall some tribute of regret be paid
> When her long life hath reach'd its final day:
> Men are we, and must grieve when even the Shade
> Of that which once was great is pass'd away.

CHAPTER 18

A CRISIS OF IDENTITY:
VENICE IN THE NINETEENTH CENTURY

Within hours of the fall of the Republic of Venice, cannons were mounted on the Rialto Bridge and orders given to fire on anyone found looting or otherwise acting lawlessly. The precaution was hardly necessary. So accustomed were the Venetians to orderly government that even the death of that government could not break them of the habit. A few Venetian patriots chased down Jacobins or others suspected of pro-French sympathies, but order was quickly restored, and with a minimum of casualties. The transition from ancient republic to modern municipality took all of three days.

The crisis of Venetian identity would endure much longer. The extinction of the Venetian state had a profound and lasting effect on the Venetian people. Venice was no longer an actor on the world stage. Quite the contrary, it had become an object to be manipulated, observed, even defined by outsiders. Venice ceased to be the master of its own fate, but quickly became a curiosity or bauble in the hands of world powers. This is not to say that the Venetian people became helpless pawns; as we will see, they acted in the interest of their city when they thought it was possible. But their range of activity had been severely curtailed, their agency taken from them along with their republic. After 1797 it was no longer even clear what it meant to be a Venetian, since citizens in that state no longer existed. For this reason throughout the remainder of this book the emphasis will necessarily shift somewhat from the people living in Venice to the foreigners who interacted with it. It was the foreigners—the generals, statesmen, authors, and artists—who would craft a new modern Venetian identity, one very different from that of the medieval Republic of St. Mark.

The sixty members of the new Municipal government approved by the French, which included nobles as well as non-nobles, met in the Great Council Chamber on May 16, 1797. All were Venetian Liberals who believed that Venice's future lay with the revolutions of a new age. Few of their fellow Venetians agreed with them, but for the moment that did not matter. They viewed the new Municipality not as a break with the past, but simply as a reformed continuation of the old government. The presence of French soldiers garrisoned throughout Venice suggested otherwise.

So did the Municipality's actions. It ordered that every image of the winged lion of St. Mark was to be destroyed, including even those on the exterior of the Ducal Palace depicting Doge Andrea Gritti and Doge Francesco Foscari kneeling before the lion. (The sculptures there today are modern reproductions.) Merely to utter *"Viva San Marco"* was punishable by death. The new government outlawed the famous Venetian festivals, Carnevale and Sensa. A Liberty Tree—the symbol of the French Revolution—was placed in the center of the Piazza San Marco, where a relatively small group of French supporters danced and celebrated the "liberation" of the Venetian people. Not far away a bonfire consumed the Book of Gold, which for four centuries had recorded the names of Venetian patrician families, as well as the doge's corno and vestments. Most Venetians watched the ceremony with incredulous disdain. For more than a millennium they had been the freest people in the world. They had no need of liberation. Still, given the circumstances, it was much better to let the French have their party and say nothing. One Venetian onlooker, who quietly jeered at a woman who kissed the leaves of the Liberty Tree, was immediately arrested and jailed. Now, at least, Venice had the political prisoners that Napoleon had sought.

The absurdity of events only grew during the next few months as the zeal of the Venetian "revolutionaries" reached new heights. In June the Municipality issued a proclamation praising Bajamonte Tiepolo, the would-be tyrant who in 1309 had attempted to overthrow the republic and replace it with his own despotic rule. The members of the Municipality claimed that Bajamonte had, in reality, been a freedom fighter who had died trying to topple the closed ruling aristocracy led by the evil doge Pietro Gradenigo. Of course, in truth, Gradenigo had actually *expanded* participation in the republic. No matter. The Municipality proclaimed him the author of the hereditary nobility. Having thus manufactured both a hero and a villain, it sent a delegation to Murano, where a Liberty Tree was planted and the mortal remains of Doge Gradenigo scattered to the winds.

The Venetian supporters of the Municipality were not traitors. They truly believed that Venice would rise again as a democratic city. As nationalism spread across Europe, it kindled the dream of a united Italy in Italians across the shattered peninsula. Venice's democrats had every reason to believe that a new Venice, remade in the image of the Enlightenment and supported by the French, would rise to become the leader of a new Italy. They were, however, badly deceived. The French brought words of Liberal revolution, but in truth they remained in Venice only to safeguard it as diplomatic currency. In the Treaty of Campoformio, signed on October 18, 1797, Napoleon handed over all the former Venetian mainland territories to the Hapsburgs, just as he had promised in the Preliminaries of Leoben some months earlier. He now threw in the city of Venice for good measure. When news of the treaty reached Venice, the sense of betrayal among Venetian democrats was intense. Their champion, Napoleon, the great dispenser of liberty, had abandoned them to the medieval, aristocratic, and absolutist monarchs, the Hapsburgs. How could he topple the Republic of Venice, they asked, only to deliver it into the hands of a Conservative monarchy? In truth, Napoleon had never really given the matter much thought. The Venetian terra firma was simply the price he paid for peace with Austria. As for Venice, it had angered him. It deserved its fate.

Adding insult to injury, Napoleon ordered his men to confiscate twenty paintings and five hundred rare manuscripts in Venice before departing. The paintings, which included masterpieces such as Veronese's *Wedding Feast at Cana*, were shipped to Paris, where they still hang in the Louvre. But Napoleon meant to claim even more impressive souvenirs. He ordered the four bronze horses of San Marco, a symbol of Venice since their capture in Constantinople in 1204, to be removed from the facade of the church and sent to Paris. On December 13, 1797, amid a grand parade of French soldiers, the deed was done. The ancient bronze horses were lowered by pulleys to the Piazza, crated up, and sent to France. When they arrived in Paris, Napoleon mounted them above his Arc de Triomphe du Carrousel with the caption "Brought from Corinth to Rome and from Rome to Constantinople, from Constantinople to Venice, from Venice to France: they are at last in a free country!"

And that was by no means the end of the looting. The ancient winged lion, which had perched on its column in the Piazzetta since the twelfth century, was taken down, only to follow the horses to Paris. The lion was placed on a column near the Hôpital des Invalides with its tail between its legs. The Arsenale, once the greatest shipbuilding factory in the Western world, was systematically stripped down to the bare walls. A regiment of French soldiers took axes to the lavish bucintoro, a symbol of Venetian pomp and spectacle for centuries. And, of course, there was the famed Treasury of San Marco. Dozens of priceless works of medieval art, including Golden Roses bestowed on Venice for centuries of faithful service to popes, were broken apart for their diamonds, pearls, and precious metals. Astonishingly, the French spared the nine-hundred-year-old Pala d'Oro only because it was thought to have little value.

On January 18, 1798, Austrian general Oliver von Wallis formally took possession of Venice, entering via the Grand Canal. The democrats and Jacobins fled, while the rest of the Venetians dutifully cheered. As a Conservative state, the Hapsburg empire was the mortal enemy of Liberalism. Monarchy and nobility had ruled Europe for centuries. Conservatives believed that Liberalism, while it might sound good on paper, had overturned the old order only to replace it with bloodshed and chaos. The new Austrian masters "restored" the Venetian republic by reimplementing its legal code and placing patricians back into the Great Council, but these changes were merely cosmetic. In fact, Venice was a city-state under Austrian rule. Now shorn of its empire and without tourism or much trade, Venice had very few ways in which to support itself. Its economy quickly declined. Venetians petitioned the Hapsburgs to return Trieste and Dalmatia to them, but without success.

Six years later Venice changed hands again. Napoleon's victories over the Hapsburgs led to the Treaty of Pressburg, in which the Austrian emperor ceded back to France all of the Veneto, Venice, Istria, and Dalmatia. In January 1806 the Austrians evacuated the city and the French once again returned. But there was no return of the Liberty Tree or any proud speeches extolling freedom and democracy. The Venetian supporters of the Municipality had long since fled. Besides, Napoleon had outgrown the rhetoric of his earlier conquest. Having dispensed with the Directory and its constitution, he had become emperor of France—a more absolute ruler than any of the old French kings. Venice was thus incorporated into the new kingdom of Italy, with its capital in Milan. The king of Italy was, of course, Napoleon Bonaparte. His viceroy was his stepson, Eugène de Beauharnais, later given the title Prince of Venice. Napoleon planned to use Venice as a naval base to support his Mediterranean operations. As for the city itself, he meant to treat it as his own property. Venice, Napoleon insisted, was "a country of conquest. How have I obtained it other than by victory? The right of victory established, I will treat it as a good sovereign if they are good subjects." He declared the Ducal Palace the home of the viceroy, although when that proved too small, the "Royal Palace" was moved to the Procuratie Nuove on the south side of the Piazza San Marco.

French revolutionaries had always targeted the Catholic Church, and Napoleon was no exception. He recognized the necessity of the Church—indeed, he was himself a practicing Catholic. But he believed that the Church must be smaller, weaker, and out of his way. In Venice and the islands the new royal government ordered the closure of nearly sixty monasteries and convents. It reduced more than a hundred Venetian parishes to just thirty-four. Large numbers of churches were shuttered, demolished, or converted to other purposes. Sant'Anna, for example, was emptied of its art and transformed into a gymnasium. The monastery of Santa Maria delle Vergini became a military prison. Every year more churches were closed and the artwork warehoused or sent elsewhere—much of it to Paris or Milan. Hundreds of scuole were abolished, their buildings confiscated or destroyed, and their artistic treasures looted. The six Scuole Grandi buildings survived, but they, too, were given more useful occupations. The Scuola Grande di San Marco, for example, was turned into a hospital, as it still remains today. The French government also moved the cathedral of Venice from San Pietro di Castello, where it had been for more than a thousand years, to the church of San Marco. Thus was the doge's chapel transformed into the seat of the patriarch of Venice, as it, too, still remains today.

All these changes had a profound effect on religion and piety in

Venice. Modern Venice is a place where one sees on every *calle* (narrow street) and campo the floppy hats, short pants, and fanny packs of the tourist. For a millennium those areas were filled with religious habits. Priests in cassocks, Dominicans and Franciscans in their distinctive robes, and religious processions could be seen almost everywhere. The bells of Venice's campaniles rang to call the faithful to Mass. They heard and they came. It was the French who began the work of stripping the richly vibrant religious life of Venetians from the fabric of their city. Worship and prayer, once so vital to the life and identity of the Venetian people, had been replaced with a secular devotion to the state.

The emperor/king Napoleon Bonaparte personally visited Venice in 1807, and the French-controlled government spared no expense on welcoming its ruler. The pomp and slavish obsequiousness showered on "the hero of the century" measured beyond anything that republican Venice had ever witnessed. An enormous floating *arc de triomphe* was placed at the north entrance of the Grand Canal to welcome the savior. Napoleon lodged in the Royal Palace (the Procuratie Nuove) and made many sightseeing tours in the city and lagoon. Spectacles such as a regatta, acrobats, and lavish banquets and receptions were held daily. Of course, the emperor also took in an opera at La Fenice, which had to abandon its boxes of democratically equal sizes to make room for the construction of an enormous imperial box at the very center of the theater.

Yet for all the pomp, the city that had transfixed generations of poets and artists left Napoleon cold. It was, he believed, a hodgepodge of old and new without character or discipline. Shortly after his departure, the royal government announced a plan to reform and renew its cityscape. Napoleon wanted to introduce to Venice the modern style of urban planning, which included classical forms, geometric simplicity, manicured public parks, and broad avenues. These were the principles on which Paris was being rebuilt, as were other cities such as

Washington, D.C., across the ocean. In an urban environment as thoroughly built up as Venice, though, this necessarily meant demolitions.

The Riva degli Schiavoni was cleared, widened, and extended all the way to Castello. This provided a pleasant walking area along the Bacino from which the San Marco area could be seen at all times. Today this still remains the most-walked street in Venice, filled with tourists, restaurants, and souvenir carts. The wide Rio di Castello was filled in and paved over to produce a new boulevard, originally named the Via Eugenia (for the prince). It is today called Via Garibaldi. Farther east lay the densely populated Motta di Sant'Antonio, a poor district for fishermen, day laborers, and lace makers. The French cleared the entire area, including several churches. There they built the Giardini Pubblica. Although Venice had (and has) hundreds of gardens, they were private affairs tucked away in courtyards behind large walls. The Giardini were public and visible from anywhere on the Bacino, thus bringing a bit of nature to the artificial world of the common Venetian.

On the north side of Venice, Napoleon had a new gate placed in the Arsenale, giving it direct access to the lagoon. He also insisted on a proper cemetery. The island of San Cristoforo, on which Pietro Lombardo's fifteenth-century church had stood, was cleared for the purpose. The new cemetery filled up quickly, so it was extended onto the adjacent island of San Michele, by which name it is known today.

One place that Napoleon did admire was the magnificent Piazza San Marco. A thousand guidebooks notwithstanding, Napoleon never did call the Piazza "the finest drawing room in Europe." But he still found much to commend it. Like the great squares in Paris and London, the Piazza provided a pleasant area for citizens to meet, promenade, and generally enjoy each other's company. As today, the Caffè Quadri and Caffè Florian did a brisk trade and the orchestras played most of the day and night. It was a pleasant backdrop for the Royal Palace, which had expanded to occupy all of the Procuratie Nuove and the Biblioteca

Marciana, and even reached all the way to the church of San Geminiano, designed by Sansovino in 1557. The church was splendid, of course, but the palace needed a proper entrance, complete with grand staircase. Despite strong protests, San Geminiano was demolished and the "Napoleonic wing," as it is often referred to today, was completed along the west side of the Piazza. The demolition of San Geminiano struck a nerve, for it had always been associated with the center of Venetian civic life. Today one can still see both a commemorative marker of the lost church as well as the stairway that took its place.

To the south of the Royal Palace stood a host of buildings and tents along the waterfront in which commerce was still conducted. Napoleon planned to make this area the new front yard of the palace. The malodorous fish markets were quickly cleared away. So, too, was the grain warehouse, the Granari de Terra Nova, one of the oldest buildings in Venice. In their place was planted the Royal Gardens—a pleasant refuge that, surprisingly, is hardly visited today by the legions of tourists in the nearby Piazzetta. With these last demolitions the Molo had finally ceased to be a commercial location. It had been refashioned as a facade for a city of the French Empire. To underscore that point, on Napoleon's birthday, August 15, 1811, a colossal statue of the emperor, clad as Adonis and carrying an orb signifying his domination of the world, was unveiled on the Molo. Napoleon had thus obtained what no doge, and not even the condottiere Colleoni, could. His statue had been erected in the plaza of the people.

It did not remain there long. In 1812 Napoleon began his disastrous invasion of Russia, culminating in the devastation of his army by the cruel Russian winter. Great Britain, Prussia, Russia, and Austria seized the opportunity, marching on France. Paris fell in March 1814 and the captured Napoleon was exiled to the island of Elba. Venice, the Veneto, Istria, and Dalmatia were returned once more to Austrian rule. No one, not even the Venetians, entertained the idea of restoring the republic. It was, nonetheless, deeply humiliating for a people who prided them-selves on their long history of political stability to be passed back and forth between Europe's grasping powers.

The Austrians returned to Venice in April 1814 and announced their firm intention to restore everything that had been taken by the criminal Bonaparte. They did not, but they made a good start. The horses of San Marco were removed from Napoleon's triumphal arch and shipped back to Venice, where they arrived on December 7, 1815. Greeted by a de-scendant of Doge Enrico Dandolo, they were placed back on the porch of the church of San Marco with much ceremony and celebration. The Austrians also sent back the ancient bronze winged lion for the column on the Molo. Although it was badly damaged in transit, the Venetians worked diligently to repair and replace this symbol of their city, if no longer their state.

The return of the Austrians restored stability to Venice and a mea-sure of self-respect to Venetians, but it only slowed the continued eco-nomic decline of the city. The population had dwindled to fewer than a hundred thousand people, and many of them were poor. Struggling old patrician families started selling off their villas and even renting out their crumbling palazzi to foreigners. The English had stopped coming during the Napoleonic Wars, yet even after Napoleon was safely impris-oned, the extinction of the ridotti, Carnevale, Sensa, and, of course, the prostitutes made Venice a much less desirable stop on the Grand Tour. This is not to say that the English did not return to Venice, but they did so in much fewer numbers and spent considerably less money.

An absence of Englishmen was precisely what Lord Byron sought when he arrived in Venice in 1816. One of England's greatest poets and a giant of the Romantic movement, Byron had come on a self-imposed exile to escape the infamy of his actions back home. Larger than life, he had much in common with Venice's own Casanova. Strikingly attrac-tive, robustly athletic, and extremely intelligent, Byron was also brash, violent, mercurial, and sexually insatiable. There is no doubt that he suffered severe bouts of depression and anxiety, and he may have been bipolar. As his popularity grew, the English public was both scandalized and titillated by his escapades, which included a string of affairs with married women such as Lady Caroline Lamb. In 1815, at the age of twenty-seven, Byron married. But his wealthy wife, Anne Isabella Milbanke, would not abide his infidelities. After one year she took their infant daughter, Ada, and left him. Assisted by a string of Lord Byron's jilted lovers, Lady Byron accused her husband of serial adultery, an affair with his half sister, and homosexuality. And so, the great English lover decided to follow the example of his poem *Childe Harold's Pilgrimage* and seek greener pastures elsewhere.

For the next three years, Lord Byron lived in Venice, becoming just as much a sensation in the lagoon as he had been back home. As a study of decline amid a physical backdrop of greatness, Venice embodied the majestic ruin that the Romantics so loved. The descendants of a great empire, the people of Venice lived amid an imperial beauty that they inherited, but could not maintain. While there he composed the Venice canto of *Childe Harold* as well as *Beppo, Don Juan*, and two plays about medieval Venetian doges: *Marino Faliero* and *The Two Foscari*. In all these works, Byron popularized for the English-speaking world the old myth of Venice as a state that had mixed beauty and culture with intrigue, treachery, and oppression. This Romantic, yet largely false, image was further bolstered by one of Napoleon's former generals, Pierre Darù, who published an extensive history of Venice based on the newly available state archives. Although Venetian scholars strongly rejected Darù's characterization of the republic, it stuck nonetheless. As for Byron, he simply loved it all. The decayed beauty of the city, striving to hold its head up as it sank beneath the waves of history, appealed instantly to his Romantic tastes. He wrote to his publisher, "I like the gloomy gaiety of their gondolas and the silence of their canals. I do not even dislike the evident decay of the city, though I regret the singularity of its vanished costume." It was Byron who coined the name "Bridge of Sighs" for the ornate baroque bridge stretching from the Ducal Palace to the prisons. He imagined, wrongly, that prisoners condemned to death by the Council of Ten crossed the bridge and, having caught their last glimpse of Venice, could not help but sigh.

Byron resided at several places in Venice, but eventually settled in the Palazzo Mocenigo on the Grand Canal. It was a magnificent building with a large and ornate main portal and an entrance with a beautiful, if not always strictly maintained, garden. Its majestic staircase ascended to the *piano nobile* (principal floor) with rich art, stunning mosaics, and a breathtaking view of the Grand Canal. Then, as now, the Palazzo Mocenigo was a fashionable address available for rent to those with the money. Within a few months of his arrival, he began an affair with Marianna, the twenty-two-year-old wife of a Venetian shop owner. "I have passed a great deal of my time with her since my arrival at Venice," he wrote, "and never a twenty-four hours without giving and receiving from one to three (and occasionally an extra or so) pretty unequivocal proofs of mutual good contentment." When not amusing himself with Marianna, Byron studied Armenian with Father Pasquale Aucher on the island of San Lazzaro degli Armeni. Fascinated by Armenian culture, he began learning the language, but did not stick with it long enough to gain proficiency. There were also, of course, the dinners, coffeehouses, salons, and the Rossini operas at La Fenice to amuse Byron.

Because he had a foot deformity that caused him to limp, Byron favored athletic activities that did not require walking or running. He became an expert swimmer, having successfully crossed the Hellespont from Europe to Asia. In Venice he was notorious for jumping out of his gondola fully clothed and swimming home. During a prolonged period of boredom in June 1818, he staged a much-publicized swimming race from the Lido to the Molo. The lone challenger gave up before reaching halfway, while Lord Byron not only swam to San Marco but then the length of the Grand Canal as well.

Byron was also a lover of horseback riding, which he did daily on the Lido—sometimes accompanied by his friend, the poet Percy Shelley. It was on one of these rides that he met his new infatuation, Margarita Cogni, another fiery twenty-two-year-old, this one the wife of a Venetian baker. Margarita "said she had no objection to make love with me, as she was married and all married women did it." He did not, of course, give up his romance with Marianna, but Margarita did not object. She took the fact of Byron's other lovers casually, for, as she put it, "it don't matter—he may have five hundred but he will always come back to me." The same could not be said of Marianna. When she learned of Margarita and confronted her, the latter replied in fierce Venetian: "You are not his wife; I am not his wife. You are his *donna*, and I am his *donna*. Your husband is a cuckold, and mine is another; for the rest, what right have you to reproach me? If he prefers what is mine to what is yours, is it my fault?" Margarita later moved into the Palazzo Mocenigo, but Byron eventually tired of her and asked her to leave. Although she threatened him with a knife, and even drew blood, he refused to change his mind. Like Marianna before her, Margarita was sent back to her husband.

Byron and his proclivities quickly became well known across Venice. Since he had a great deal of money to spend, they were cordially tolerated. He went from woman to woman nightly. "Some of them are countesses," he admitted, "and some of them are cobblers' wives; some noble, some middling, some low, and all whores. . . . I have had them all and thrice as many to boot." Finally, in April 1819, Lord Byron met the nineteen-year-old Contessa Teresa Guicciolo of Ravenna, who was visiting Venice with her fifty-eight-year-old husband. Once again, he fell hopelessly in love. For the remainder of the year in Venice, and for another three years elsewhere, the contessa would be the center of his life. The aged Count Guicciolo soon learned of the love affair, about which

the entire city buzzed. Nevertheless, he largely ignored it and even occasionally boasted of it, happy to have a man with the wealth and connections of Lord Byron as a virtual member of the family. Yet by the end
of 1819 Lord Byron's time in Venice was nearing an end. He would spend
several years elsewhere in Italy, always near Teresa, advocating for Italian independence. In 1823 he left to fight for Greek independence and
died at Missolonghi the following year.

Byron's raucous adventures in Venice came during a low point in
the city's history, although this hardly troubled him. Like all Romantics,
who extolled crumbling ruins and echoes of medieval grandeur, Byron
found Venetian decay quite suitable. But time marched on and the city,
ever so slowly, began to recover. By the 1820s the Industrial Revolution
was in full swing, bringing unprecedented levels of prosperity to parts
of Europe and North America. "Progress" was the new virtue, and would
remain so for the rest of the century. Newly wealthy bourgeois began
turning up in Venice, eager to see the sights that had previously been
reserved exclusively for the gentry. To cater to the new arrivals, Venetian entrepreneurs transformed old palazzi into new hotels. The Palazzo
Dandolo on the Riva degli Schiavoni, for example, was purchased by
Giuseppe Dal Niel and converted into a hotel in 1824. The Hotel Danieli
(named for its new owner) quickly acquired a reputation as the finest
hotel in the city—a reputation it retains to this day.

Tourism, which was still well below its pre-Napoleonic levels, was
insufficient to revive Venice's ailing economy. To its credit, the Austrian
government initiated a number of projects to modernize Venice. During
the 1830s gas lines were run into the city, providing light for the streets
and homes. Thereafter, the Piazza San Marco shone nightly with ninety-
eight gas lamps. The Austrians finally granted Venice free port status
and even built new salt warehouses, the Magazzini del Sale on the
Dogana, not far from the church of Santa Maria della Salute. The most
controversial of the modernization plans, though, was the proposed

railroad bridge connecting Venice to the terra firma. The railroad had revolutionized Western society, making long-distance travel widely available and the transportation of goods much less expensive. The Austrians promoted a plan by Italian businessmen to build a railroad link between Milan and Venice, the two capitals of the Austrian province of Lombardy-Venetia. Milan had profited mightily from the Industrial Revolution, becoming an economic powerhouse in its own right. The hope was that the railroad would bring similar prosperity to Venice.

Most cities longed for a railroad link. In Venice, though, the very idea seemed a dagger to the heart. Venice was founded on the sea. Its history, its identity, its whole raison d'être had been its separation from the mainland. Now the modern industrial world sought to invade its isolation with a mile-and-a-half-long bridge and the steam-belching monster known as the locomotive. Venetians were divided into two factions on the matter: the *pontisti* and the *antipontisti*. The latter insisted that Venice must remain unchanged, for it was only in preservation that it could retain its dignity and continue to attract visitors. This group would establish the principle of *dov'era, com'era* (where it was, as it was) when dealing with restoration and repair of the city. When La Fenice burned down in 1836, for example, it was promptly rebuilt with only minimal alterations. The *pontisti*, on the other hand, insisted that the railroad would bring "blood to the heart" of Venice. The most radical of the *pontisti* wanted the railroad to wind its way through the Giudecca Canal and disgorge its contents right onto the Piazzetta San Marco. In the end, though, a compromise was struck. The bridge, completed in 1846, connected Mestre, on the mainland, with the far northwest corner of Venice—in other words, its back door. The great facade of Venice remained unspoiled by "progress."

Ironically, the railroad killed the ailing Grand Tour, for now a trip to Rome, Florence, or Venice was not the exclusive enjoyment of the elite, but was available to a whole new class of commoners. And, indeed, they came. In the 1840s guidebooks for Venice appeared in a variety of languages, each advising its readers where to stay, eat, and shop. Specialty glassmaking was revived on Murano, thus establishing a new and indispensable class of souvenir for tourists. During the summer months the Piazza San Marco began once again to fill with tourists, who packed into the Florian and the Quadri seeking coffee and ambience. In 1845, just before the railroad opened, the population of Venice equaled the annual number of tourists: about 122,000. The latter number would only increase as the century unfolded.

The railroad had brought something else to Europe, something that would change the world: nationalism. Rapid travel combined with high rates of literacy and instantaneous communications created a new consciousness among national groups. Despite centuries of warfare among themselves, Italians knew that they were different from the French and the Austrians. They longed to forge an independent Italian state. Similar desires motivated nationalists across Europe. Conservatives like Prince Metternich of Austria opposed nationalism just as vehemently as they fought against Liberalism. The Austrian Empire, after all, was a patchwork of ethnicities. Poles, Hungarians, Croats, Czechs, Slovaks, Romanians, and, of course, Italians had awakened in themselves a new identity and a desire for self-government. Nationalism threatened to rend the Austrian Empire to shreds.

Talk of nationalism filled the salons and coffeehouses of Venice. Although Venice was rebounding under Austrian rule, Venetians still chafed under the strict censorship laws of the empire. Some suggested joining Venice to other Italian nationalists in Naples or Piedmont, while others simply wanted the restoration of the Republic of St. Mark. In any case, both groups wanted the Austrians out. The de facto leader of the nationalists in Venice was Daniele Manin, a modest, well-respected lawyer who had been jailed for his efforts to establish an autonomous government answerable only to the Austrian emperor. A quiet, educated man with thick spectacles and an infectious smile, he hardly seemed the sort to inspire a revolution.

In 1848 a cocktail of nationalism, liberalism, and socialism mixed liberally with food shortages and high prices led to violent revolutions across Europe. In Italy, armed rebellions temporarily toppled governments in Naples and Rome. Because Austrian forces in Lombardy-Venetia were numerous, Milan and Venice remained calm. That changed, however, in March when news arrived that Vienna itself was in flames and that the Austrian emperor had fled. Now, it seemed to the revolutionaries, was the time to strike. Crowds of excited Venetians formed, as they had for centuries, in the Piazza San Marco. Sensing the winds of history at their backs, they rushed to the prisons near the Ducal Palace, broke open the doors, and carried Manin out on their shoulders, hailing him as their new leader. The Venetian revolution had begun.

Manin formed a Civil Guard of several thousand men, identified by a simple white sash. On March 22, 1848—a day that would remain hallowed among Venetians—they stormed the Arsenale, which was loaded with Austrian munitions and a few warships. On the same day, King Charles Albert of Piedmont, on the advice of the nationalist Count Camillo Cavour, declared war on Austria and, joining Milan, declared its independence. Badly beaten and uncertain of events back home, Austrian forces retreated, evacuating Venice completely. The city was at last free. In an emotional gathering in the Piazza San Marco, Manin declared the restoration of the Republic of Venice to the cheering crowds. Once again the forbidden chant rose from the people: "*Viva San Marco! Viva San Marco!*"

But the old order was not so easily put away. All of Europe's 1848 revolutions were soon crushed or made irrelevant. Emperor Ferdinand returned to Vienna in June, promising a new constitution and the restoration of order. Among his first acts was to send Austrian troops to restore Lombardy-Venetia. By August the Austrians had secured the countryside and put down the rebellions in the cities, including the one in Milan. Venice alone stood defiant. The new Venetian Assembly voted Manin full powers to deal with the emergency. He organized a wide conscription of Venetian men into the Civil Guard and prepared for the worst. The Austrians planned to starve Venice, setting up a land and sea blockade. But continued unrest in Vienna made the blockade occasionally porous, which in turn allowed the republic to survive. In the Great Council Chamber of the Ducal Palace the assembly announced to the world that "Venice will resist Austria at all costs."

And she did. In January 1849 the new emperor, Francis Joseph, crushed the remnants of rebellion in Vienna and established military rule over rebellious Hungary. His adviser Prince Felix Schwarzenberg meant to put down the Venetian revolution just as quickly. The blockade of the lagoon was tightened, leading to massive food shortages and rationing of almost everything. On May 29 the Austrians began what the French had only threatened: They fired on the city of Venice. Over the next several weeks, round-the-clock bombardment battered the city. And if that was not bad enough, in August a cholera outbreak brought on by *acqua alta* (high water) and the unsanitary conditions of the siege struck the city. Thousands of Venetians died. Conjuring up images of the old plagues, bodies were stacked high in the open grassy campo outside the church of San Pietro di Castello.

The "Year of Revolutions" had ended in Europe, yet only Venice continued to wage its hopeless fight. At last the Venetians realized that it was over for them as well. On August 19 a small boat waving white flags rowed out to the terra firma and surrendered to the Austrians. Daniele Manin and the other republican leaders fled or were exiled. Yet in all other respects the Austrians left Venice unpunished. Although Manin died in Paris, his remains were returned to Venice in 1868 after his dream of independence was finally realized. In an unprecedented move, the Campo San Paternian, where Manin had lived, was renamed in his honor. The campanile and ruined church were demolished and a statue of the hero was erected in their place. It, and the outlines of the old church, are still there.

The bodies had been buried, but Venetian antipathy for the Austrians had not. Austrian military bands that played daily in the Piazza San Marco received only sneers from the Venetians in the coffee shops and never a trace of applause. And yet, although the city remained tense, there was little violence. Slowly the foreign visitors returned, now whisked across the causeway in a matter of minutes rather than the hours of a gondola trip. Among the first to arrive was the English art critic John Ruskin. He had visited the city when he was a young man and was amazed at its ruinous beauty. Now he returned on a mission— to preserve in drawings and daguerreotype (a primitive photographic process) every aspect of Venice's medieval architectural glory. Like most Romantics of his time, Ruskin detested the revival of classical architecture during the Renaissance, and thought the baroque embellishment of it was even worse. What he sought was the beauty of the medieval Gothic—in particular the uniquely Venetian Gothic, a melding of East and West unknown elsewhere. Over the course of several years during the late 1840s and early 1850s Ruskin spent countless hours perched on ladders, balanced on gondolas, and crouched beneath the black cloth of his camera. He meant to record Venice's beauty before it was lost forever.

Like Byron, Ruskin would change the way that the English-speaking world thought about Venice. However, in form, style, and temperament Ruskin was the very opposite of Byron. Thin, sensitive, and a trifle effeminate, Ruskin made no advances on the married women of Venice— indeed, not even on his own wife, Effie. Years later their marriage was annulled on the basis of his "incurable impotency." He denied the charge, but admitted that he found his wife's naked body repugnant and therefore had never consummated their marriage.

In 1851 and 1853, Ruskin published the three volumes of his great work, *The Stones of Venice*. It considered in precise detail the three periods of Venetian architecture: Byzantine, Gothic, and Renaissance. Ruskin provided a selective history of Venice, interspersed among the measurements, drawings, and rhapsodic elegies on form, conforming this history closely to the architectural styles themselves. For Ruskin, Venice rose to power during its Byzantine period and then, after the Serrata of 1297, arrived at the peak of its glory while producing Gothic structures. After the fifteenth century, he believed, the city declined rapidly. Grasping the fad of Renaissance classicism, men like Sansovino and Palladio had marred the face of Venice with bland and soulless reason.

The Stones of Venice is much discussed today, but little read. Although a font of information, it is by modern standards overwritten. Venetian Gothic, for example, is

> prickly independence and frosty fortitude, jutting into crockets and freezing into pinnacles; here starting up into a monster, there germinating into a blossom, anon knitting itself into a branch, alternately thorny, bossy, and bristly, or writhed into every form of nervous entanglement.

And so on. But Ruskin was important not merely because he popularized and catalogued the crumbling city, but because he warned the world of Venice's peril. Loud and clear in *The Stones of Venice* Ruskin sounded the alarm. Unless something was done soon, an irreplaceable jewel would be lost. Venice was "uniquely precious—a miracle that could not be reworked, a dream that could not be redreamt." For Ruskin, the Venetians themselves did not understand the danger. Instead they undertook restorations that were in reality just demolitions. Venice, he believed, was more than the Venetians—indeed, it existed independently of them. Venice was a treasure that belonged to all of humanity.

Ruskin gave voice to a profoundly changed identity of Venice. It had become the physical city of crumbling beauty, a work of art, a world heritage. Those who read Ruskin, including thousands who traveled to Venice on package tours, began to feel that the city truly *did* belong to them, indeed to everyone. And they meant to take care of it. After the unveiling of an extremely poor restoration of San Marco's southern facade in 1875, concerned people in Great Britain formed the St. Mark's Committee of the Society for the Preservation of Ancient Buildings, the first international organization formed to make certain that Venice was preserved just as it was. It would not be the last.

Nationalism in Italy, as everywhere else, continued to erode borders that did not agree with it. In Italy, Giuseppe Garibaldi and his republican fighters waged guerrilla war against the Austrians. To the French under Napoleon III, Garibaldi and his ilk seemed too wild and unstable to form a government on their southern border. Instead, they supported Piedmont and its liberal king, Victor Emmanuel II. In 1861 Garibaldi conquered the medieval kingdom of the Two Sicilies and its capital at Naples. With French help, Victor Emmanuel captured the Austrian territories in Lombardy. On March 17, 1861, the two met and formed a unified Italy. Only Rome—still ruled by the pope and defended by French troops—and Venice remained outside the new Italian state. Five tense years followed, as the Austrians continued to rule the Veneto. Most Venetians wanted unification. The feeling was palpable to tourists, who wrote home about the stigma Venetians attached to even speaking cordially to an Austrian, let alone befriending or marrying one. Arrests were made, bombs exploded, and general unrest occasionally erupted. Finally, in 1866, after the Third Italian War of Independence, Austria ceded Venice and the Veneto to Napoleon III, who in turn ceded it to Italy. On October 19, after ruling the city for more than half a century, the Austrians left Venice. With some cause they felt ill-used by the Venetians. Their empire had sunk enormous resources into Venice in an attempt to restore, modernize, and preserve it. For their efforts, they received only jeers at their backsides as they marched back home.

Ecstatic cheers greeted the Italian forces when they arrived in Venice on October 19. That Venetians could applaud a foreign army—even one that spoke Italian—as liberators only demonstrates how much the world had changed since the days of the republic. The people of Venice celebrated their independence because they were no longer just Venetians. They were Italians. On November 7 they welcomed their new king, Victor Emmanuel, with a ceremony that rivaled any staged before. The Venetians had greeted their French and Austrian conquerors with fanfare, but the celebration of 1866 conveyed true feeling. Indeed, they soon decided to place a bronze equestrian statue of Victor Emmanuel riding triumphantly into the future on the Riva degli Schiavoni. This work of Ettore Ferrari was completed in 1887 and remains there today. Although the main statue is unremarkable, the bronze groups at its base vividly express the feelings Venetians had for their unification with Italy. Behind the king a woman, depicting a weary Venice, bears a broken standard, while the lion of St. Mark lies chained and defeated. Before the king, thanks to the creation of the Italian state, the lion and the woman have awoken and enthusiastically look forward to a bright future.

Much of that future would rely on tourism. With Venice safely part of a united Italy, new waves of foreigners began to arrive in the lagoon. Most came on package tours offered by Cook's tours, Wagons-Lits railroads, and Lloyd Triestino shipping. The end of the American Civil War and the rise of oceangoing steamships had also opened Venice to an increasing number of Americans. Some, like Henry James, brought a new perspective, but one not too unlike that of the elite elsewhere. During his first visit in 1869, James appreciated the beauty of Venice, but was shocked at its poverty and poor condition, writing, "The misery of Venice stands there for all the world to see; it is part of the spectacle." Like millions of tourists after him, he decried the tourists who descended on Venice and noted with displeasure "a horde of savage Germans en- camped in the Piazza," who "treat the place as an orifice in a peep show."

But the starkest meeting between American and Venetian culture must surely have occurred in July 1867, with the arrival of Mark Twain. A Missouri native and former Mississippi riverboat pilot, Twain could not help but have a keen interest in the "Queen of the Adriatic." He was, of course, paid to be irreverent, but his view of Venice from the perspec- tive of the common American was unprecedented. Like James, Twain was struck by the decay of the great city.

> She that in her palmy days commanded the commerce of a
> hemisphere and made the weal or woe of nations with a beck of
> her puissant finger, is become the humblest among the peoples of
> the earth,—a peddler of glass beads for women, and trifling toys
> and trinkets for school-girls and children. The venerable Mother
> of the Republics is scarce a fit subject for flippant speech or the
> idle gossiping of tourists.

Upon arriving in Venice, Twain boarded a hotel gondola. Yet it failed to match his tourist's expectation for grandeur and musical bliss.

> This the famed gondola and this the gorgeous gondolier!—the
> one an inky, rusty old canoe with a sable hearse-body clapped on
> to the middle of it, and the other a mangy, barefooted guttersnipe
> with a portion of his raiment on exhibition which should have
> been sacred from public scrutiny. Presently, as he turned a corner
> and shot his hearse into a dismal ditch between two long rows
> of towering, untenanted buildings, the gay gondolier began to
> sing, true to the tradition of his race. I stood it a little while. Then
> I said: "Now, look here, Roderigo Gonzales Michael Angelo, I'm a

pilgrim, and I'm a stranger, but I am not going to have my feelings lacerated by any such caterwauling as that. If that goes on, one of us has got to take water."

Despite his disappointment in the musical talent of the gondoliers, Twain the boatman found their skill on the water absolutely fascinating. Indeed, he is perhaps the earliest traveler to remark in detail on the gondolier's craft.

[A]nd how in the world he can back and fill, shoot straight ahead, or flirt suddenly around a corner, and make the oar stay in those insignificant notches, is a problem to me and a never diminishing matter of interest. I am afraid I study the gondolier's marvelous skill more than I do the sculptured palaces we glide among. He cuts a corner so closely, now and then, or misses another gondola by such an imperceptible hair-breadth that I feel myself "scrooching," as the children say, just as one does when a buggy wheel grazes his elbow. But he makes all his calculations with the nicest precision, and goes darting in and out among a Broadway confusion of busy craft with the easy confidence of the educated hackman. He never makes a mistake.

Twain, of course, saw all the major sights, including a large number of paintings. He was not, however, as rapturous in his praises of Venetian art as most visitors. "We have seen pictures of martyrs enough, and saints enough, to regenerate the world.... [T]o me it seemed that when I had seen one of these martyrs I had seen them all." Nevertheless, Twain, like almost every other tourist, could not help but be struck by Venice's beauty. For him, the greatest delight was the Redentore celebration, in which people boarded hundreds of gondolas with colored lanterns that floated out on the mirrorlike water to watch the evening fireworks. They were "like a vast garden of many-colored flowers, except that these blossoms were never still; they were ceaselessly gliding in and out. . . . The fete was magnificent. They kept it up the whole night long and I never enjoyed myself better than I did while it lasted."

Along with the tourists came the artists. Venice had become the city that must be painted. Edouard Manet visited in 1875, James McNeill Whistler in 1879, Auguste Renoir in 1881, and Claude Monet in 1908. And these were but the most famous. The growing crowds were eager to purchase paintings from lesser-known practitioners; almost anyone with an easel and a bit of talent could find a ready customer. More tourists meant more business for the growing number of hotels and restaurants. However, for Venice's hundreds of gondoliers, the bonanza was ending. In the 1880s the first steam-powered water buses—the *vaporetti*—were introduced to the city, forever changing the face of Venice. Tourists and common Venetians no longer needed to hire a gondola to get from place to place, but simply loaded aboard the noisy, but speedy, vaporetti. The gondola soon ceased to be a form of transportation and became instead just a ride.

Progress found yet other ways to intrude into late-nineteenth-century Venice. Iron bridges were built across the Grand Canal at two new locations, the Accademia and the train station, thus significantly opening up the city to foot traffic. A cholera outbreak in 1867 led to modifications in water flow so as to allow sewage to more easily be flushed out to sea. Water lines were run into Venice from the Brenta Valley, providing indoor plumbing and bringing to an end the rich culture of campo gossip at the *pozzo*. The Industrial Revolution came to Venice in the form of the Stucky mill on the end of Giudecca. Giovanni Stucky, the son of a Swiss father and a Venetian mother, built the giant flour mill and granary in a classic industrial mode that stylistically defied the city across the canal. The local government only allowed it because the factory provided much-needed jobs for its citizens. A similar kind of monumental building was constructed (by the same architect, Ernst Wullekopf) out on the Lido. The European craze for saltwater bathing fit Venice like a glove and led to the construction of new luxury hotels on the largely empty sandbar facing the Adriatic. Where Byron and Shelley had once raced their horses, the Hotel Excelsior Palace and the Hotel des Bains soon opened their doors.

By the turn of the century the city of Venice had in many ways come full circle. Passed from one foreign power to another, it had at last returned to Italian, if not Venetian, control. Searching for purpose in a modern world, it had come back to the tourism that had sustained it before the fall of the republic. And yet, the tourists who arrived no longer came to see the operas, or the prostitutes, or the ridotti. They came, instead, to see Venice.

CHAPTER 19

WAR, WATER, AND TOURISTS:
VENICE IN THE TWENTIETH
CENTURY AND BEYOND

For Venice, the twentieth century opened with a bang. Literally. The 323-foot Campanile of San Marco, completed in the twelfth century under Doge Domenico Morosini, had developed a significant crack in early July 1902 after some repair work on Sansovino's Loggetta at its base. The worrisome fissure wormed its way upward over the next few days, finally reaching the fifth window. Despite numerous warnings and a great deal of discussion, nothing was done. Tourists even climbed up the stairs of the campanile on the weekend of July 12–13. By Sunday afternoon, though, it was obvious to all that the medieval structure was in trouble. The municipal government forbade music in the Piazza that night, fearing that the vibrations from the orchestra would shake the tower too much.

The next morning at 9:45, a crack rang out across the Piazza San Marco and in a moment the campanile had collapsed in on itself, sending up a great cloud of dust and smoke. Fortunately, the collapse was localized. A few shops and a corner of the Biblioteca Marciana were damaged. The Loggetta, of course, was completely crushed. Yet the nearby church of San Marco and the Ducal Palace remained untouched. Amazingly, no one was physically hurt—only the pride of the Venetians. More than one observer cited the collapse as evidence of Venice's continued ruin, or at least the inability of the Italian government to maintain the great city. In an age of cheap print and newspapers, the image of the San Marco area had become as internationally recognizable as Big Ben or the Eiffel Tower. Laments for the campanile's collapse and calls for its restoration echoed worldwide.

The city government moved quickly. On the day of the collapse it voted unanimously to rebuild the campanile *dov'era, com'era*. The builders, however, decided to interpret *com'era* somewhat loosely. The new campanile, dedicated on the Feast of St. Mark—April 25, 1912—looked precisely the same as the old. Fragments of the Loggetta had been painstakingly collected and reassembled. The golden Angel Gabriel was repaired and replaced at the campanile's peak. Even the bricks of the new tower were fired to look medieval. Beneath its exterior, though, the new Campanile of San Marco was thoroughly modern. Its frame was made of iron and its old stairs (similar to those in the Campanile of Santa Maria Assunta in Torcello) were replaced with a modern elevator.

The modern construction of a medieval building was emblematic of a larger debate that would affect Venice throughout the twentieth century—one between modernists and preservationists. From the international community of tourists that filled the city's streets, a cry arose in favor of the latter. They came, after all, to see Venice's best-known sights—San Marco, Salute, Rialto, and so on. It would not do to overtly tamper with any of those. But what of the rest of the city? Could it not be modernized? At the turn of the century cholera continued to be a serious problem in the poorer areas of Venice, yet attempts at updating housing and sanitation invariably met with concerns over preservation.

"The Collapse of the Campanile." A possibly
doctored photo by Antonio de Paoli, 1902.

Even electricity was resisted, since some feared that artificial illumination would sully Venice's famous moonlight on the canals.

Venetian modernists made the most headway on the periphery of the city, such as with the construction of the Stucky factory on Giudecca. On the barren Lido they were presented with a virtual blank slate. The construction of the Hotel Excelsior Palace and the Hotel des Bains attracted a new clientele of wealthy tourists to these magnificent resorts, and high-end housing and shops quickly filled up the sandbar. Within a decade, the Lido was transformed from an empty breakwater into a posh, modern community within sight of San Marco. The Lido had everything that Venice lacked—automobiles, a tram, and wide, straight tree-lined boulevards.

This stark division between old and new became the inspiration for the twentieth century's most famous work of fiction set in Venice: Thomas Mann's *Death in Venice*. Mann had stayed at the Hotel des Bains in 1911. The novel's main character, Gustav von Aschenbach, is a successful, yet severe author taking a much-needed vacation on the Lido. While staying at the luxurious hotel, he spies a boy from Poland, who is visiting Venice with his family. Aschenbach is unexpectedly overwhelmed with feelings for the young man, whose name is Tadzio. He soon finds himself stalking Tadzio on the beach and in the hotel—so much so that others, including the boy, begin to notice. Mann used the progressive atmosphere of the Lido to suggest an environment of rational modernity, one that Aschenbach leaves behind as he is pulled deeper into his love for Tadzio. Although cholera has broken out in the old city, Aschenbach is still driven to follow Tadzio and his family there, even adorning himself in makeup and hair color in a pitiful attempt to restore his own withered youth. Entranced by the dark mystery of old Venice, Aschenbach remains there all day, finally contracting cholera from a bad strawberry. He dies on the beach of the Lido, still watching his love, Tadzio. Mann's novella, published in German in 1913, was later translated into English in 1924, and became an instant hit, appealing to the growing number of well-educated readers who appreciated its philosophical and emotional tensions told against a backdrop of one of the world's most admired resorts. Mann's story is one of struggle between discipline and freedom, between repressed desires and the expression of forbidden love. At its core, it is not a story about Venice at all. But Mann's decision to set it in Venice was important. The youthful innocence of Tadzio on the bright and new Lido contrasts sharply with the secret desires that led Aschenbach to the disease-ridden old city. Although Venetian officials try to hide the epidemic, Aschenbach knows the truth—a "criminal secret of the city which coincided with his own dark secret." Venice in Mann's work became a symbol of decay and death. The popularity of *Death in Venice* would assure that the association was one that would endure.

In 1914 the outbreak of World War I produced as much anxiety in Venice as anywhere else in Europe. The Italian government joined the Allies against the Austro-Hungarian Empire, Germany, and (later) the Ottoman Empire. For Venetians the Great War may have brought back shades of previous struggles—against their occupiers the Hapsburgs and their longtime enemies the Turks. But this was a new war, fought with new weapons that killed with industrial efficiency. Like millions of other men across Europe, Venetians marched off to war to fight and die in its hellish trenches.

For the Venetian economy, the first casualty of war was tourism. The second was shipping, for Venice remained a minor commercial port. The Austrians, who controlled the Adriatic, quickly blockaded the lagoon. The airplane, invented by the Wright brothers in America just a few years earlier, was quickly pressed into service for the war. Austrian aerial bombardment of strategic targets in Venice, particularly the Arsenale and the railroad station, began in May 1915. But accuracy was poor and shells rained down instead on Santa Maria Formosa and the hospital at SS. Giovanni e Paolo, and even destroyed the Tiepolo ceiling of the Scalzi church. Between 1915 and 1918 more than forty air attacks dropped nearly a thousand bombs on Venice, although many (including those that hit San Marco) failed to explode. The damage would have been worse had the Venetians not prepared for the onslaught. In the months before the attacks the horses of San Marco were taken down and hidden, the statue of Colleoni packed away in a wooden box filled with straw, Titian's *Assumption* carted off to the mainland, and numerous churches filled with padding and old mattresses to protect their treasures. The Venetians even took some measure of revenge when the poet, writer, and early aviation enthusiast Gabriele D'Annunzio flew his plane, emblazoned with the lion of St. Mark, over Vienna dropping insulting leaflets on the Austrians.

The misery that Venice experienced during the war was redeemed by the Italian victory over the Austrians at the Battle of Vittorio Veneto (October 1918) and their subsequent conquest of Trento, Udine, and Trieste. Italian Irredentists, who believed that Austria must return all lands that had ever been Italian, were plentiful in Venice. With the armistice signed, they had high hopes that Venice would be lifted from its state of poverty and restored to the territories it had held under the Most Serene Republic.

That was not to be, yet after the war Venetians and their allies in Rome were able to persuade the Italian government to restore to Venice an industrial and commercial vitality that it had not had for centuries. The heart and soul of the new initiative was the construction of Porto Marghera—a massive, state-of-the-art naval port and industrial zone on the shore of the terra firma, not far from the rail bridge at Mestre. For more than a century Venetians had debated whether the main port of Venice should be moved from its traditional location in the Bacino San Marco. When the area proved to be incapable of servicing large modern vessels, the first new port had been built at Stazione Marittima on Venice's western end. Yet Porto Marghera was something much larger. Built on otherwise unused coastal marshes, Marghera was designed to establish Venice as a modern commercial center for industry and trade. And it was to be Venetian in every way. Rather than mar the grandeur of the world's most beautiful city, Porto Marghera would allow Venice a completely free hand to modernize on the mainland. Large-scale projects of excavation, dredging, and reclamation took place over a period of almost a decade. By 1940 more than sixty factories operated at Marghera, each belching out smoke yet bringing in revenue and jobs. In 1926 the municipal government of Venice grew to encompass Marghera and Mestre, as well as the lagoon islands of Murano and Burano. Venice had at last returned to the mainland.

During the 1920s and 1930s the Fascists, led by Benito Mussolini, took over the Italian government. Although physically Venice lacked a Roman pedigree—always an important component in Fascist rhetoric—it nonetheless benefited from Fascist modernization plans. Industry at Porto Marghera led to a rapid expansion of the city of Mestre. Venetian workers soon found it easier to live there rather than commute across the bridge on trains, which were again crowded with tourists. To allow bus and car traffic between Venice and the mainland, the Fascist government funded another bridge, this one built directly adjacent to the railroad bridge. The Ponte de Littorio (Bridge of Lictors—Roman officers who carried insignia called *fasces*) diverged from the rail line just as it approached Venice and then made its way to the new Piazzale Roma, a square filled with bus stands and a large parking garage. The Piazzale Roma was derided almost immediately as an eyesore. It remains one today, although an extremely busy one nonetheless.

The most powerful man in Fascist-era Venice was Count Giuseppe Volpi. A brilliant businessman and native Venetian, Volpi had made his fortune by bringing electricity to northeast Italy and Venice. In 1912 he negotiated the peace treaty between Italy and the Ottoman Empire, acquiring for his country Libya and Suleiman's prize, the island of Rhodes. Thus by his efforts Italy joined the exclusive club of colonial powers. Volpi was a major proponent of the Porto Marghera, for which he took credit regularly. After establishing the world-famous Gritti Hotel on the Grand Canal, he helped form the Compagnia Italiana dei Grandi Alberghi (CIGA), a luxury hotel chain that included the Lido resorts. In 1925 Mussolini appointed him Italian minister of finance. When in 1930 the Fascist government took over the Biennale, the international art exhibition with pavilions in the Giardini, Volpi was made its president.

In June 1934 Volpi hosted in Venice the first meeting of Mussolini and Adolf Hitler. Hitler's plane landed on the Lido on June 14, and the German leader emerged wearing a simple jacket, tie, and trench coat to meet Mussolini, who was dressed in his magnificent military uniform. It was said that a communication mix-up had led one of them to dress as a civilian and the other as a military officer, but Hitler suspected Mussolini of doing it on purpose so as to make himself look grander on newsreels and in photos. Amid a brass-band welcome, Hitler and Mussolini went to the monumental Villa Pisani, a luxurious estate of Venice's extinct aristocracy, and then returned to Venice for a tour of the Grand Canal and a concert of Verdi and Wagner in the Ducal Palace. On June 15 Hitler was taken to visit the German pavilion of the Biennale. Its Greek style was not quite to his liking. Several years later the German pavilion was revamped in Nazi style. The delicate Ionic columns were replaced with square Teutonic pillars, and an imperial eagle and a swastika were situated prominently over the door. Minus those symbols, the pavilion still remains as it was in 1938, although there are regular demands that it be demolished entirely. In 1993 the German artist Hans Haacke took a jackhammer to the floor on which Hitler and Mussolini had met. The debris-art was called *Without Foundation*.

Although Fascism was resisted elsewhere in northern Italy, the Venetians offered little resistance and less criticism. After all, with a champion like Count Volpi, Venice prospered under Fascist management. Anti-Jewish decrees did begin trickling out of Rome in 1938, but Jews constituted less than 2 percent of the Venetian population. Laws forbidding Jews to conduct business or be served in restaurants in Venice were given lip service, but were just as often ignored.

World War II began without Italy on September 1, 1939. Mussolini continued to waver, entertaining offers from both sides of the conflict. Believing that Germany's rapid victories would bring a quick end to the war, Mussolini finally had Italy declare war on France and Great Britain on June 10, 1940. He hoped to collect something in the expected peace talks. But peace was not on Hitler's mind. His subsequent invasion of the Soviet Union surprised Mussolini as much as Stalin. As a result, Italy prepared for another long and brutal war.

As during World War I, Venetian men left the lagoon to fight. Most of them were sent to Greece or Dalmatia, where the plan was to "restore" those lands to Italian rule. Although Italian forces quickly bogged down in Albania, the offensive proceeded smoothly once the Germans arrived. Dalmatia, the core of Venice's old empire, was quickly conquered and delivered over to Fascist Italy. Crete and the Aegean islands, which had long been Venetian, were occupied by the Nazis.

For Italy, the tide of the war turned rapidly in 1943 when American and British troops invaded Sicily and prepared for the conquest of the peninsula. By July the Fascist party had been thoroughly discredited. King Victor Emmanuel III ordered the arrest of Mussolini, and soon afterward, the Italian government signed an armistice with the Allies. Hitler, however, was not willing to lose Italy so easily. In August a massive invasion of German forces entered Italy from the north to hold the line against the Allies. Although Hitler attempted to prop Mussolini back up, most Italians refused to accept him. And so Germany simply occupied Italy. Hitler ordered the disarmament of all Italians and seized control of local governments.

Nazi troops arrived in Venice on September 8, 1943. There were arrests of some notable anti-Fascists, but not many. Most of Venice's Jews had either fled or hid themselves before the Nazis arrived. Since Jews had not been confined to the Ghetto since 1797, hiding was somewhat easier than it would have otherwise been. The de facto leader of Venice's Jews, Professor Giuseppe Jona, committed suicide rather than obey a Nazi order to turn over lists of Jewish names and addresses. Between December 5, 1943, and late summer 1944 more than two hundred Venetian Jews were arrested and sent to concentration camps—most to

Auschwitz. They included Venice's chief rabbi, Adolfo Ottolenghi. Only eight survived the death camps.

Provided one was not a Jew, Venice was the safest place to be in Italy during the war. Whenever possible, the Allies were determined to preserve historical treasures in Italy, and Venice contained multitudes. As war between the Allies and Germans tore apart the Italian peninsula, those who could escape headed to the beauty and comparative security of the city of the lagoon. Venice was at the eye of a storm that was tearing Europe apart, and like the first Venetians, people found safety in its brackish waters. Some local resistance to the Nazis cropped up in Venice, but not much. Anyone who wished to fight Germans joined the partisans in Padua. Occasionally resisters would be discovered in Venice, and in 1944 seven of them were shot on the Riva dell'Impero in Castello—later renamed the Riva dei Sette Martiri. In 1968 a monument to the women of the Venetian resistance was set on the waterfront there. The bronze statue depicting a dead woman lies on concrete platforms where the tide sometimes hides it and sometimes brings it into view, much like the Venetian resistance itself.

The war did not damage the city of Venice, but its new industrial centers were demolished. Allied bombers targeted Porto Marghera, Mestre, and all rail lines leading to Padua and points north. The Germans responded by sending tankers into Venice itself, where they would unload their contents and place them on smaller vessels heading north via canals and rivers. This tactic led to the only Allied air strike on Venice during the war. On March 21, 1945, British captain George Westlake commanded Operation Bowler to knock out German shipping in Venice. It was what we would today call a surgical attack. The Allied commanders let it be known that anyone who damaged Venice in the strike would be "bowler-hatted," that is, discharged from the military. Westlake led the dive-bombing run, a nearly vertical descent from ten thousand feet, which successfully destroyed the German vessels. Venetians standing on nearby roofs watched the entire operation without receiving so much as a scratch.

By that time, however, the war in Italy was already winding down. U.S. forces under General Eisenhower had captured Rome on June 5, 1944. Henceforth the Germans found it difficult to stop the Allied advance. By April 1945 the U.S. Fifth Army and British Eighth Army had reached the Po Valley and Italian partisans had captured Padua. On April 29, just one day after the execution of Mussolini, Venice was liberated by the British Eighth Army under the command of Major General Bernard Freyberg of the New Zealand Second Division. Before leaving for Trieste, Freyberg "captured" the Hotel Danieli, where he had spent his honeymoon in 1922.

The end of World War II brought a new age in which a devastated Western Europe struggled to rebuild and a victorious United States became its defender against the Soviet Union. The rapid rise of American affluence and the simultaneous development of reliable transatlantic air travel meant that American tourists were no longer an occasional oddity in Venice, but a regular fixture. Indeed, American perspectives on Venice would play a prominent role in shaping the city and its image in the late twentieth and early twenty-first centuries. (One could argue that this history, written by an American scholar, is another brick in that wall.) To name even a few influential Americans in Venice is to leave out thousands. The years immediately following World War II saw, for example, the arrival of Ernest Hemingway, who spent several months there in 1948–49. As with everywhere else that Hemingway frequented, a litany of stories circulated about "Papa" and his stay in Venice. Hemingway was a frequent patron of Harry's Bar, a frequent hangout of the rich and famous, which he went on to popularize in his novel *Across the River and Into the Trees* (1950). Like Mann's *Death in Venice*, Hemingway's story threads together the concepts of death and beauty in Venice. Its main character, American colonel Richard Cantwell, returns to Venice, which he had helped liberate from the Nazis, to take stock of his life at its very end.

Although *Across the River* was not well received by critics, it nonetheless made Harry's Bar an icon for Venetian tourists. Its founder, Giuseppe Cipriani, had been a waiter in the luxurious Hotel Europa when a longtime American patron, Harry Pickering, asked to borrow ten thousand lire. Cipriani loaned him the money and, against all hope, he was repaid four times over. Pickering suggested that Cipriani found his own high-end bar and further suggested that he name it Harry's Bar. It opened in May 1931 and quickly became popular with well-to-do tourists. Hemingway had his own corner table, where he drank more than a few martinis. By the mid-1950s droves of Americans were lining up to get into Harry's Bar and drink a Bellini—the house specialty originally made of Prosecco, pureed white peaches, and a bit of raspberry juice. They still do.

For the upwardly mobile Americans of the 1950s and 1960s, Venice came to rival Paris as the most romantic city in the world. Guidebooks poured out of New York presses advising visitors where to eat, stay, and soak up the local charm. American movies reflected this pervasive image. In the very successful *Three Coins in the Fountain* (1954), American secretary Maria Williams (Maggie McNamara) is swept off her feet by the dashing Prince Dino di Cessi (Louis Jourdan), who whisks her away to Venice in his private plane. One of the first CinemaScope films, *Three Coins in the Fountain* boasted stunning scenes of what its trailers called "fabled, fabulous Italy." Likewise, in the movie *Summertime* (1955) another single American woman, Jane Hudson, played by Katharine Hepburn, is seduced as much by Venice as by the intriguing Renato de Rossi (Rossano Brazzi). *Summertime* was the first mass-market film to use the cityscape of Venice as a crucial element in its story. Jane strolls through the Piazza San Marco, buys Murano glass, shops for fashionable clothes, and visits the brightly colored island of Burano. Yet, like the dark Venice of eighteenth-century myth, the romantic Renato has a terrible secret. He is married. Although Jane suspects that he has simply used her, she nevertheless remains with him until her departure. In these movies, as in works of fiction for three centuries, Venice retained its image as enchanting, mysterious, and decadent. It was a place that powerfully attracted its visitors, who quickly came under its seductive spell.

In *Summertime*'s most famous scene, Katharine Hepburn, while attempting to take a photo, careens backward into a canal near San Barnaba. Director David Lean insisted that Hepburn do the stunt herself—and was not satisfied until the fourth take. Shortly afterward, Hepburn developed a rare eye infection, which would plague her the rest of her life. She blamed it on keeping her eyes open while tumbling into the dirty canal. The canal could have been to blame, although it might also have been the gallons of disinfectant that the film crew poured into the water before each shot.

Hepburn's worries about the health risks of Venice's canals represented a stark change from the earlier widespread belief in the health benefits of swimming in them. At the start of the twentieth century, posh floating bathing stations were moored in the waters off Salute. For decades after, Venetian children regularly dived into the canals to cool off on summer days. The reason for the shift is not simply one of greater standards of hygiene. The waters of the lagoon really were dirtier in the 1950s. Although new agricultural technologies greatly increased crop yields in the Veneto, they had also led to chemical fertilizers and pesticides running off into the rivers that feed the Venetian lagoon. Heavy industry in Porto Marghera dumped its share of chemicals into the water, too. And, of course, the canals of Venice are, as they have always been, the city sewer. Everything that goes down a drain or toilet in Venice is eventually released into the lagoon.

This had never been a problem during the days of the Republic of

Venice. Although the population of the city swelled then to over 150,000, the tides efficiently removed sewage and waste twice daily. Indeed, Venice was the cleanest city in medieval Europe (admittedly, not a high standard). That was no accident. The Venetian government paid close attention to the health of the lagoon, regularly maintaining canals, dredging deepwater channels, and creating breakwaters to facilitate flow. But changes to the city and to the lagoon in the nineteenth century reduced its ability to renew itself. Chief of these was the gradual filling in of dozens of Venice's canals. The wide avenues of Via Garibaldi and Strada Nuova are only the most famous of these. Each new walkway (often called a *rio terà*) had its own reason for construction. Sometimes it was to make an area more accessible to tourists. Sometimes it was an attempt to avoid the smell of a canal at low tide or the cost of maintaining it. And sometimes it was purely aesthetic. In each case, though, the filled canal further restricted the flow of water into and out of the city, putting increased stress on the other waterways. In 1867 Mark Twain described Venice as a place with "no dry land visible any where, and no sidewalks worth mentioning; if you want to go to church, to the theatre, or to the restaurant, you must call a gondola. It must be a paradise for cripples, for verily a man has no use for legs here." By the early twentieth century, Venice had become a pedestrian city.

During the early 1960s an increasing number of voices warned of the dangers to the lagoon. Since solutions were expensive, the only ones seriously considered were those agreeable to the region's two major economic engines—tourism in Venice and heavy industry at Marghera. For some time tourists had complained of massive tankers and barges churning their way through the Giudecca Canal and past the Piazza San Marco on their way between Porto Marghera and the Adriatic Sea. Not only were these industrial behemoths ugly, but many people worried that an accident could cause damage to city buildings or even an oil spill. The route was necessary, though, because Giudecca was the only channel sufficiently wide and deep for these vessels. Visitors to Venice often imagine the lagoon as a watery canvas that is all the same depth. In truth, most of the lagoon is quite shallow—no more than waist-deep. Navigation there has always been confined to clearly marked channels maintained by the authorities. For centuries, Venice stood impregnable because invaders could not navigate those channels, particularly when they were unmarked and filled with debris.

In 1965 and 1966 a new channel was dredged near Malamocco, the ancient capital of the Venetian lagoon. It ran in a straight line through the southern lagoon to the new third industrial zone on the mainland. It was hailed, like Porto Marghera itself, as a way of preserving both the industrial modernization of the region and the touristic beauty of Venice.

But then came the flood.

On November 3, 1966, a powerful storm blew across Italy. Torrential rains and fierce sirocco winds from the south whipped the Adriatic Sea into a churning mass of waves. It was truly the storm of the century. On the morning of November 4 the waves, driven by gale-force winds, forced their way into the Venetian lagoon, increasing the sea level there almost six feet above high tide. Venetians awoke to find their city underwater. Electricity was cut off, heating-oil tanks were swamped, ground floors were submerged, and transportation was almost impossible. Because the winds continued all day, the tide bore nothing out. For almost twenty-four hours the city was paralyzed. When at last the waters receded, the damage left behind was severe. Furniture, garbage, dead animals, and raw sewage lay everywhere. Venice's fragile buildings were damaged not only by the salt water on the lower levels, but also by the wicking of the moisture to the upper levels.

It is difficult to overestimate the effect that the flood of 1966 had on the way people still think about Venice. Today the most common opinion, held even by people who know nothing else about Venice, is that it is sinking. Before 1966 this opinion scarcely existed. The devastating flood had cast Venice in an entirely new light. It had always been a fragile place of exquisite beauty and slow death. It was now an emergency. Venice was descending beneath the all-consuming waves, and something needed to be done—immediately.

Since "immediately" is not a word that one normally associates with Italian government, other organizations and institutions moved boldly ahead. Indeed, it is surprising how quickly the flood ended the debate over how much responsibility the outside world had for the preservation of Venice. The United Nations immediately opened a UNESCO office in Venice and began paying for studies on the flood and the repair of its damage. Affluent private individuals with an abiding love for Venice founded charitable organizations to support the city. The first was organized by the former British ambassador to Italy, Sir Ashley Clarke. Later named Venice in Peril, the organization would grow to become one of the largest of its kind, pouring thousands of pounds into conservation and restoration across the city. In 1971 the well-known British author John Julius Norwich became the chairman of Venice in Peril, a position he held until 1999. Its most successful fund-raising effort was its partnership with the English restaurant chain PizzaExpress, which donated a portion of every sale of its Pizza Veneziana (with red onions, capers, olives, sultanas, and pine nuts) to the preservation of Venice.

Venice in Peril was the first, but by no means the last, of the charitable organizations that responded to the need. Twenty-nine of them in eleven countries were organized into the Association of Private Committees for the Safeguarding of Venice, an NGO that works closely with UNESCO and the municipal government to identify worthy projects. The giant of these organizations, not surprisingly, is American. Save Venice Inc. was founded in New York in 1971 and later added chapters in Los Angeles and Boston. It single-handedly pumps about a million dollars per year into Venetian projects—more than all the other APC members combined. Its major fund-raisers come not from pizza sales, but from gala masked balls and exclusive lectures and tours of Venice for America's wealthiest people. Save Venice is frequently criticized for catering to an extremely affluent elite circle who know nothing and care less about Venice itself. And, of course, it is true that if one wants to dress to the nines for a Carnevale celebration at New York's Plaza Hotel, it really should be for *some* sort of charitable cause. But, at the same time, there is no denying the good work that Save Venice has funded and continues to fund. The extraordinary restoration of the convent church of Santa Maria dei Miracoli was entirely bankrolled by Save Venice. If not all of the partygoers have a firm grasp on where their money is headed, it is nonetheless used for a worthy cause. And many of them do have a firm grasp—to suggest otherwise is simply to engage in a peculiarly American reverse snobbery. Whatever the case, Venice is certainly no stranger to opulent luxury. If some of the fruits of opulence still make their way to the city of the doges, there is something altogether fitting about that.

Not all of foreign largesse since 1966 has gone to physical preservation. Some of the private committees fund art historians seeking better approaches to restoration. The most important organization for the scholarly study of Venice is the Gladys Krieble Delmas Foundation. Founded in 1976 by Delmas and her husband, Jean Paul Delmas, the foundation is primarily devoted to funding all aspects of research into Venetian history and civilization. Although dwarfed by organizations like Save Venice, the Delmas Foundation has made it possible for hundreds of American and British Commonwealth scholars to undertake original and innovative research in the Venetian archives, the Marciana library, and any of the other repositories of Venetian history and culture. It is no exaggeration to say that the Delmas Foundation has made possible an extraordinary flowering of Anglophone scholarship on Venice that continues to this day (indeed, even to this book).

Foreign organizations helped repair some of the damage of the flood, but offered few answers as to how to avoid another one. After some wrangling, the Italian government passed the Special Law of 1973 that guaranteed funds to preserve "the historical, archaeological, and artistic environment of the city of Venice and its lagoon." Just how this was to be accomplished, of course, would remain a source of debate among Venetians and other Italians. The general consensus among lawmakers, as well as political groups such as Italia Nostra, was that Marghera was principally to blame for the flood. Decades of pumping water out of the aquifer for industrial use had, it was argued, lowered the ground level of the lagoon. In addition, the creation of the Malamocca channel and the third industrial area had restricted the lagoon's ability to absorb additional water. To combat these problems local groundwater pumping was prohibited and strict laws on industrial pollution enacted. The Special Law also provided funds to upgrade Venetian residences to natural gas in order to reduce air pollution and the possibility of heating-oil contamination in the lagoon.

Not everyone agreed that Marghera was to blame. The historian Wladimiro Dorigo in his book *Una leggo contro Venezia* (A Law Against Venice) insisted that industrial modernization was the salvation of Venice, and that the Special Law was merely a reactionary attempt to keep the area embalmed in historical stasis. Others pointed to factors not directly connected to Marghera, such as the creation of Tronchetto (an artificial island used for car and tour bus parking) and the building of the car and rail bridges to the mainland. Since 2000 Venice has also become a football in the climate-change debate, as rising sea levels would clearly exacerbate its problems. In truth, however, no consensus yet exists about the real reasons for the flooding. Science quickly became mired in a morass of political and economic agendas, each espousing the preservation of Venice.

There was never any doubt, however, that something was going on.

Although Venice often flooded during the Middle Ages—sometimes, as in 1110 or 1240, even higher than in 1966—it did not do so as often as it has since 1970. *Acqua alta* was occurring more than fifty times a year by 1980 and sometimes much more often. During the winter months, when the winds whip up from the south, sirens warning modern Venetians of the coming *acqua alta* quickly became a common occurrence. At Piazza San Marco, the lowest portion of the city, gangplanks (known as *passerelle*) were provided so that people could cross without wading through the waters. They have since become a permanent fixture of the area.

Just as there was no agreement on what caused *acqua alta*, there were fierce disagreements about what to do about it. Predictably, things moved slowly. It was not until 1994 that the Higher Council of Public Works approved a roughly six-billion-dollar initiative known as the Modulo Sperimentale Elettromeccanico (Experimental Electromechanical Module), or MOSE—a name meant to conjure Moses, the great parter of the waves. When complete, MOSE would consist of networks of submerged gates lying flat on the seafloor beneath the three openings of the lagoon to the Adriatic Sea (Malamocco, Lido, and Chioggia). When the tide rises above 110 centimeters (3.6 feet), the gates would be inflated with air, causing them to elevate to a forty-five-degree angle, thus completely closing off the lagoon. Opponents (and there were many) insisted that MOSE would cause more problems than it solved. If the tides were halted, how would the lagoon refresh itself? It would become like a toilet that cannot flush. Environmentalists insisted that MOSE would upset the fragile ecosystems of the lagoon, causing the disruption of fish and waterbird life cycles and leading to the growth of harmful algae. MOSE proponents countered that the gates would be elevated only for short periods, insufficient to cause any environmental problems. They rejected outright the environmentalists' depiction of the lagoon as a natural sanctuary, countering that it was instead completely artificial. Had nature had its way, Venice would have become as landlocked as Ravenna centuries ago. The lagoon, like MOSE, was man-made.

In the years that followed, MOSE remained highly controversial. Lawsuits, appeals, and demands for additional environmental impact studies slowed its implementation. A host of alternative solutions were presented, ranging from the raising of Venice's pavements, to the erection of barriers along the islands, to the pumping of groundwater back into the aquifer. All were rejected. The question became more bedeviled by the close association between Prime Minister Silvio Berlusconi and MOSE. The prime minister had laid the first stone of the project in 2003 and he remained its strong proponent. Those who opposed Berlusconi and his center-right party tended also to oppose MOSE. Nonetheless, the project continued to move forward. When (or if) it will ever be completed is currently anyone's guess.

Despite the dire warnings, *acqua alta* did nothing to slow Venice's tourist industry—an industry that now produces more than half the area's revenues. Indeed, the waters covering the Piazza San Marco became a tourist draw, yet another reason to visit this most remarkable city. The stunning growth in the number of tourists visiting Venice in the latter half of the twentieth century is directly related to a similar rise of world affluence, particularly in the United States, Japan, and Western Europe. When American audiences watched Katharine Hepburn fall helplessly into the Venetian canal, very few of them could ever hope to visit Venice. That has changed. According to the United Nations World Tourism Organization, there were 25 million international arrivals in 1950. In 2005 that number had skyrocketed to 806 million. In the twenty-first century one need not be rich to see Venice. Indeed, one need not have much money at all.

During the 1950s and 1960s tourism in Venice was largely limited to the summer months, when the package tours would book their groups into Venice's many hotels. Visitors would generally divide their time between the historical center of the city and the beach resorts on the Lido. During the 1970s and 1980s the arrival of budget travelers (many clutching their copies of *Let's Go!*) led to a steady increase in the numbers, but not a corresponding increase in revenue. Before cheap international flights, it had been nearly impossible to get to Venice without money in one's pocket. By the 1970s that was no longer true. Student travelers and others watching their wallets would frequently stay in a low-cost pensione in Padua or Mestre and simply take the train into Venice. These day-trippers wanted to get into Venice, see the major sights, and get out before it was late or they had spent too much money. They crowded the railroad stations, the *calli* between Rialto and San Marco, and the No. 1 vaporetto route running the length of the Grand Canal. They poured into the Piazza San Marco, filled up the church there, crowded onto the Molo to have their pictures taken, and then left behind tons of sandwich wrappers and paper bags. During the 1970s a number of new laws were passed to prohibit sleeping in the campi and train station, sitting in the Piazza San Marco, and generally loafing in such a way that made the city look bad. McDonald's restaurants were even forbidden to offer their food to go.

Venetians also began to think of ways to attract a higher-quality clientele and to spread their visits beyond just the summer months. The idea that they came up with was both old and new: Carnevale.

Extinguished by Napoleon in 1797, Carnevale had made a few reappearances during the nineteenth century, although it never really caught on. Without a ready supply of Grand Tourists, opulent opera houses, dark ridotti, and a legion or two of prostitutes, the famous celebration simply fell flat. But with the return of more affluent travelers, perhaps it was time to try again. In February 1979 a small four-day celebration attracted a handful of tourists, curious about the local festival. Word spread quickly. In 1980 Carnevale was expanded to one week with activities scattered across the city. On Fat Tuesday that year some fifty thousand, mostly Italian, visitors crowded into the Piazza San Marco for a night of music, dancing, and costumed revelry. It was hailed by the *Gazzettino* (a Venetian daily paper) as a beam of light in the otherwise dreary gray Venetian winter.

By the mid-1980s the Carnevale crowds were large enough that hotels and restaurants that used to close for the winter decided to stay open instead. Rapid growth, though, brought its own problems. There is no admission cost to Carnevale, since it theoretically takes place everywhere in Venice. But the city government nevertheless accrued larger and larger expenses for police, garbage collection, and street maintenance during the fair. To pay those expenses, it needed to collect more taxes, which naturally upset Venetians, who thought that shop, hotel, and restaurant owners should pay the cost. The matter became so contested that in 1988 the government approved no funding at all for the event. In effect, Carnevale was canceled. It did not matter. The tourists came anyway—by the thousands. And so, too, did the media, with lights and cameras ready to film the world's best-known party. Although the *Gazzettino* had a good time with the headline "Crowd Gathers Around Nothing," the organizers and officials nevertheless broke down and put up some stage acts for the thousands of people who arrived in Venice expecting *something*.

Carnevale was subsequently extended to almost two weeks before Fat Tuesday. The crowds took up the challenge. In 1994 around 450,000 people came to Venice for Carnevale. In 1995 that number jumped to 600,000 and reached 700,000 by 2000. By 2010 Carnevale was attracting more than a million visitors. Because of the extraordinary expense of dealing with such crowds, the city government began accepting corporate sponsorship. With a million pairs of eyes watching, there was no shortage of takers. Dozens of companies poured money into the event, placing their logos and ads wherever they could. Among the largest sponsors were Volkswagen, which sometimes placed its new models at various locations in the carless city, and Coca-Cola, which placed itself virtually everywhere. Indeed, in 2009 it won a contract to place Coke machines at key locations throughout Venice. Some Venetians complained that their Carnevale had become "privatized," but there was no disputing the revenues generated for Venetian businesses. In 2010 most estimates put gross receipts at approximately a hundred million dollars.

Venice can reasonably handle approximately 20,000 tourists per day before the narrow streets become jammed and the vaporetti fill up. During Carnevale 2010 around 150,000 people descended on the city each day, and it was worse on the days just before Fat Tuesday. As a result, Carnevale has long since ceased having any real Venetian participation. The residents are simply submerged in the flood of foreigners. Instead, Venetians who do not have to work during Carnevale often flee the city to avoid the whole thing. Media pictures of Venice's Carnevale invariably feature the richly dressed revelers with golden masks and elaborate silk costumes. Yet these people are not Venetians. They are, like the crowds taking their photos, visitors. Like everyone else, they have come for the party. It is a party with a Venetian theme, but largely devoid of Venetians.

Not surprisingly, after Fat Tuesday few Carnevale revelers head home to take up their Lenten fasts. Either they remain in Venice or others come to take their place. Because Venice is both small and one of the world's top tourist destinations, the explosion in world tourism since the 1980s has made it a place where foreigners frequently outnumber residents. In 2010 an estimated eighteen million tourists arrived in Venice. The city's population at that time was only about sixty thousand. The summer months, of course, are the worst. That is when the tour buses pull up at Tronchetto or the Piazzale Roma in greater numbers and the trains increase their frequency. There are also the cruise ships, some of which hold three thousand passengers each. These fifteen-story floating hotels, some of which are manufactured at Marghera, dock at the Stazione Marittima on the west side of the city. More than a million tourists come to Venice annually by cruise ship. To get them more efficiently into the city center, a light rail similar to those used in major airports was opened in Venice in April 2010. The futuristic "People Mover" runs on an elevated track between Tronchetto, Marittima, and Piazzale Roma. A new, sleek footbridge—the Ponte della Costituzione—was also built across the Grand Canal between Piazzale Roma and the train station in 2007.

One of the attractions for cruise ship tourists is their vessel's journey through the Giudecca Canal and across the Bacino San Marco before leaving the lagoon. Because of the enormity of these ships, passengers get a splendid view of the entire city. But these floating mountains, of course, spoil the view for everyone else. As a result, there have long been calls for banning cruise ship traffic through Venice's historic center. Opponents of the giant vessels cite the danger to Venetian buildings and waters should an accident occur. These warnings were given greater credence after January 2012 when the cruise liner *Costa Concordia* struck rocks and partially capsized off the coast of Tuscany. Activists insist that something similar could happen in Venice and that the results would be catastrophic. Although plans were subsequently drafted to phase out cruise ship traffic in Venice, whether they are ever implemented is an open question. There is a great deal of money at stake. And the dangers are not quite as dire as the activists suggest. Cruise vessels are tugged through Venice, allowing no possibility for pilot error. Because the deep channels are relatively narrow, any ship drifting off course would only become mired in mud, as occurred in 2004 near San Giorgio Maggiore when the *Mona Lisa* ran aground. It is hard to see how Venice's buildings could be harmed. As with so many other arguments in modern Venice, this one seems to have more to do with aesthetics than practicalities.

The new bridges and light rail were designed to increase traffic flow, and they do but only on the periphery of the city. Deep in the gnarled calli of Venice there is nothing to be done about major bottlenecks. Most tourists follow the ubiquitous yellow signs leading them between the train station, the Rialto Bridge, and San Marco. Routes between San Marco and the Accademia can also become snarled. During peak seasons these streets become so crowded that they simply stop moving. This is naturally irritating to Venetians who are trying to get to work, to an appointment, or simply back home. Venetians, of course, know shortcuts and alternative routes, but at certain points along the way, such as near the Rialto Bridge, they have no choice but to plunge into the flow of people. It is rather like commuting to work on a highway where drivers periodically screech to a halt when they spy an interesting shop or beautiful vista.

For these and many other reasons, Venetians have developed a strong love-hate relationship with tourists. On the one hand, the city of Venice cannot survive without them. It literally has no other industries except tourism and those that service the tourists or the tourism industry. On the other hand, Venetians see their city regularly swarmed by millions of visitors. To add insult to injury, about 75 percent of the tourists are day-trippers, contributing little to the local economy. Indeed, the 25 percent of tourists who stay more than one day are responsible for generating more than 60 percent of the overall tourism income. Since 1990 the city government has attempted various methods to persuade visitors to stay. In 2001 restrictions on bed-and-breakfasts were lifted. Vaporetto ticket prices were also dramatically increased, particularly on the much-touristed No. 1, in an attempt to extract more money from the short-term visitors.

So much tourism in such a small area has led many observers to compare modern Venice to a theme park, with an army of workers that maintain the sights and service the tourists but little else. The exodus of

Venetians for the mainland has led some to conclude that like a Disney resort, Venice has become a fake city in which people work, but do not live. The creation of imitation Venices in Walt Disney World's Epcot Center and at the Venetian in Las Vegas has also led many Venetians to ask what differentiates the theme copies from the original. Indeed, tourists can even experience the real Venice through the eyes of Disney "cast members," with the creation of Adventures by Disney, which began touring the city in 2008.

Of course, there is a fair amount of hyperbole in these comparisons. People do live in Venice. Yet an increasing number of them are "resident tourists." These are the visitors perpetually seeking the "real Venice," away from the crowds—the hidden city that the *New York Times* often features in its Travel section. And despite the frequent complaints, it does exist and can be found. Each year has seen more and more of Venice's residential areas filled with these foreigners. Wealthy resident tourists often purchase second homes in Venice, usually carved out of refurbished palazzi. Because they are vacation homes, they stand empty most of the year. And because they are a limited commodity, their price has skyrocketed since the 1990s. In 2011, for example, two-bedroom apartments near San Marco sold for well over two million dollars each.

The buying up of Venice's residential spaces has had two complementary outcomes: There are fewer homes for Venetians and their cost is much greater. When the other difficulties of living in a city without cars are factored in, a great many Venetians have made the logical choice to move to the mainland. There one can find a home for a fraction of the cost, own a car, and shop at the big-box stores without fighting through waves of tourists. Since 1950 the population of Venice has decreased from approximately 150,000 to around 60,000. Venice is also aging, as schools close and children become rare. Although this is an Italian, not a Venetian, problem (Italian birthrates in 2011 were 9.18 per 1,000 population), it hits Venice particularly hard. Indeed, in 2009 a group of Venetians led a mock funeral procession, bearing a coffin representing the corpse of Venice. They claimed that with the population dipping below 60,000, Venice was no longer a city, but a village. Authorities disputed their figures, contending that 120,000 people live on the other islands. But the protesters' point had been made. Venice was sinking beneath successive waves of both *acqua alta* and tourists.

And that is not all that is upsetting Venice's dwindling population. For many years a general suspicion has grown that municipal leaders are selling Venice to the highest bidder. One example is the infamous Pink Floyd concert in 1989, held on the night of the Redentore festival just before the fireworks show. The popular rock band, which performed from a floating stage in the Bacino, attracted some two hundred thousand rowdy fans who filled the Piazza, Piazzetta, and the entire Riva degli Schiavoni along the water's edge. Thousands climbed onto roofs, where they tore apart roof tiles. When the crowds finally departed the next day, they left behind a wasteland of vandalism and more than a thousand tons of garbage.

Some point also to the gigantic billboards that began appearing in 2009 over the scaffolding used for the restoration of Venice's buildings. These tennis court–size advertisements covered buildings such as the Ducal Palace (Coca-Cola), the Procuratie Nuove (Breitling), and San Simeon Piccolo (Calvin Klein Jeans). The most infamous of all, though, was a billboard that covered the facing corners of the Ducal Palace and the prisons and both sides of the canal between them. Along the canal sides the billboard depicted a panorama of blue skies and white clouds. Tucked securely in the advertisement was the Bridge of Sighs, which had been transformed into a feature in the billboard called *Il Cielo dei Sospiri* (the Sky of Sighs). The billboard was then made available to advertisers such as Coca-Cola and Sisley, among others. Despite numerous protests, Venice's mayor, Giorgio Orsoni, defended the scaffolding billboards scattered across the city as an efficient way to pay for much-needed restorations and repairs to Venice's architectural treasures. Indeed, in 2010 he even allowed the billboards to be lit at night. A letter from the directors of museums worldwide and a protest from Venice in Peril claimed that the advertisements violated Venice's status as a UNESCO World Heritage Site. In March 2011 Italy's newly appointed minister of culture insisted that the "mega-ads" must come down, although the economic tensions that led to them still remain.

The Venetians have a saying: "*Sempre crolla, ma non cade*" (It is always crumbling, but it never falls). Death and Venice have been so conceptually bound together during the last two centuries that it is hard to conceive of them apart. At the beginning of the twenty-first century Venice's demise was blamed on (among other things) global warming, environmental degradation, industrial pollution, greedy corporations, fleeing citizens, and rampaging tourists. It seems that Venice is always just one mistake away from utter destruction. In the popular James Bond movie *Casino Royale* (2006) the exciting climax takes place in a Venetian palazzo on the Grand Canal. The palazzo, like all of Venice in the movie, is floating on enormous air tanks. (After all, if Venice is sinking, does that not suggest that it must be floating?) When gunfire ruptures the tanks, the entire building drops beneath the waves without a trace. In the modern mind, Venice has become so fragile that a well-aimed bullet can sink its most magnificent buildings. It has truly become an endangered species, something that can only survive by means of an international effort to restore its natural habitat.

But is Venice really that fragile? Is it truly dying?

In one respect, Venice is already dead. The Republic of St. Mark, which is the reason that Venice exists at all, died more than two centuries ago. The Ducal Palace is no longer a seat of government. The Most Serene Republic no longer commands the city or the empire that it built. Instead, the buildings are maintained by other people—some the descendants of the republic's citizens, others not. In that respect, then, Venice is indeed a corpse—an exquisitely beautiful corpse, but a corpse nonetheless.

Yet in another, more important, respect, Venice still lives. The spirit of Venice, what made Venice beyond just the Great Council, the Senate, and the republic, is still vigorous and vibrant. Modern Venice faces many challenges, it is true. But what city does not? And for Venice, the challenges are as old as the city itself. The waters of the lagoon threaten the city today, just as they have done since its foundation. As a struggle between man and nature, the Venetian lagoon is perpetually a work in progress.

Foreigners are also nothing new to Venice. It has ever been a city brimming with people from all corners of the world. During the Middle Ages the strangers came to do business or find passage to faraway locales. But they also came there to live. Indeed, the Middle Ages saw large immigrations of foreigners who settled down in Venice and eventually became Venetians themselves. The problem was so acute that one of Doge Enrico Dandolo's first actions in 1192 was to evict all foreigners who had lived in Venice for less than two years. Although Venice's population during the Middle Ages exceeded a hundred thousand people, a good portion of them were foreigners. In fact, DNA tests of Venetians who took part in the "mock funeral" of 2009 proved that two-thirds of them were of European origin, with most of the rest coming from the Balkans or Asia. As the lead scientist, Fabio Carrera of Worcester Polytechnic Institute, concluded, Venice was a "melting pot."

Venetians leaving Venice is also hardly new. During the medieval and early modern centuries the *majority* of Venetians lived outside their city. They were scattered across an empire that reached to the Middle East and across mainland Italy. Some Venetians lived their whole lives and never once visited Venice! The Venetian people, who were the world's most experienced travelers, have always welcomed other world travelers to their home.

They still do—as the millions of foreigners who visit Venice annually attest. This does not mean that relations between visitors and natives always go well—as Dandolo's law suggests. But it does mean that they have continued and for one very important reason: profit. Venetian doges swore to promote the "honor and profit" of Venice. Modern Venice is still true to that promise. For all its challenges, Venice is still a place of majestic beauty and vibrant commerce. The postcards and cheap plastic masks hawked at the vendors' carts may not seem laudable to the sophisticated traveler, but they are profitable. A medieval Venetian merchant would have understood that business model perfectly—and applauded it. That so many people today find modern Venice's commercialism distasteful is not surprising. So did the popes, kings, nobles, knights, and pilgrims who visited the city throughout its long history. It did not, however, stop the Venetians from going about their business.

As a republic in an age of monarchy and a capitalist economy in a time of agrarian feudalism, Venice has always stood apart from the world while simultaneously catering to its needs. In that respect, nothing has changed.

Then, as now, Venice remains a city of honor and profit.

FURTHER READING

Since the opening of the Venetian state archives in the early nineteenth century, legions of scholars have pored through its vast materials and produced thousands of books on the history of Venice. This can be a challenge for the modern English-speaking reader, since most of those books are either highly specialized or not in English (or both). The works listed here are among the best available, and most offer an in-depth treatment of a subject accessible to readers with a basic grasp of Venetian history. They are heavily weighted toward works in English, but I have also included essential books in other languages as well. This is by no means meant to be an exhaustive bibliography of Venetian history (which could easily run as long as this book itself!), but rather a starting place for those interested in learning more about the fascinating and unique history of Venice.

General Histories of Venice

Cessi, Roberto. *Storia della Repubblica di Venezia*. 2 vols. Giuseppe Principato, 1968.

Crouzet-Pavan, Elisabeth. *Venice Triumphant: The Horizons of a Myth*. Johns Hopkins University Press, 2002.

Diehl, Charles. *Venise: Une république patricienne.* Flammarion, 1915.

Horodowich, Elizabeth. *A Brief History of Venice.* Running Press, 2009.

Howard, Deborah. *The Architectural History of Venice.* Yale University Press, 2002.

Kretschmayr, Heinrich. *Geschichte von Venedig.* 3 vols. F. A. Perthes, 1905–34.

Lane, Frederic C. *Venice: A Maritime Republic.* Johns Hopkins University Press, 1973.

Norwich, John Julius. *A History of Venice.* Knopf, 1982.

Romanin, Samuele. *Storia documentata della Repubblica di Venezia.* 3rd ed. 10 vols. Filippi Editore, 1972–75.

———. *Storia di Venezia.* 12 vols. (thus far). Istituto della Enciclopedia Italiana, 1992–.

Zorzi, Alvise. *Venice, 697–1797: A City, A Republic, An Empire.* Overlook, 2001.

EARLY VENICE

Ammerman, A. J., and Charles E. McClennen, eds. *Venice Before San Marco: Recent Studies on the Origins of the City.* Colgate University Press, 2001.

Carile, Antonio, and Giorgio Fedalto. *Le origini di Venezia.* Pàtron, 1978.

Cessi, Roberto. *Le origini del ducato veneziano.* A. Morano, 1951.

Dale, Thomas E. A. *Relics, Prayer, and Politics in Medieval Venetia: Romanesque Painting in the Crypt of Aquileia Cathedral.* Princeton University Press, 1997.

Dorigo, Wladimiro. *Venezia origini: Fondamenti, ipotesi, metodi.* Electa, 1983.

Hodgson, Francis Cotterell. *The Early History of Venice from the Foundation to the Conquest of Constantinople A.D. 1204.* George Allen, 1901.

MIDDLE AGES

Borsari, Silvano. *Il Dominio veneziano a Creta nel XIII secolo.* Fauso Fiorentino, 1963.

Cessi, Roberto. *Venezia Ducale.* 2 vols. Deputazione di Storia Patria per le Venezie, 1963–65.

Crouzet-Pavan, Elisabeth. *"Sopra le acque salse": Espaces, pouvoir et société à Venise à la fin du Moyen Age.* École Française de Rome, 1992.

Fees, Irmgard. *Reichtum und Macht im Mittelalterlichen Venedig: Die Familie Ziani.* Max Niemeyer, 1988.

Fotheringham, John Knight. *Marco Sanudo: Conqueror of the Archipelago.* Clarendon, 1915.

Hodgson, Francis Cotterell. *Venice in the Thirteenth and Fourteenth Centuries.* George Allen and Sons, 1910.

Kedar, Benjamin Z. *Merchants in Crisis: Genoese and Venetian Men of Affairs and the Fourteenth-Century Depression.* Yale University Press, 1976.

Larner, John. *Marco Polo and the Discovery of the World.* Yale University Press, 1999.

Madden, Thomas F. *Enrico Dandolo and the Rise of Venice.* Johns Hopkins University Press, 2003.

Nicol, Donald M. *Byzantium and Venice.* Cambridge University Press, 1988.

———. *The Last Centuries of Byzantium.* Cambridge University Press, 1993.

Ortalli, Gherardo. *Petrus I. Orseolo und seine Zeit.* Centro Tedesco di Studi Veneziani, 1990.

Queller, Donald E., and Thomas F. Madden. *The Fourth Crusade: The Conquest of Constantinople.* University of Pennsylvania Press, 1997.

Rando, Daniela. *Una chiesa di frontiera: Le istitutzioni ecclesiastiche veneziane nei secoli VI–XIII.* Il Mulino, 1994.

Romano, Dennis. *The Likeness of Venice: A Life of Doge Francesco Foscari, 1373–1457.* Yale University Press, 2007.

Rösch, Gerhard. *Venedig und das Reich.* Max Niemeyer, 1982.

Thiriet, Freddy. *La Romanie vénitienne au Moyen Age.* E. de Boccard, 1959.

RENAISSANCE VENICE

Bouwsma, William J. *Venice and the Defense of Republican Liberty.* University of California Press, 1968.

Chambers, David S. *The Imperial Age of Venice, 1380–1850.* Harcourt Brace Jovanovich, 1970.

Chojnacki, Stanley. *Women and Men in Renaissance Venice: Twelve Essays on Patrician Society.* Johns Hopkins University Press, 2000.

Davis, Robert C. *Shipbuilders of the Venetian Arsenal: Workers and Workplace in the Preindustrial City.* Johns Hopkins University Press, 1991.

———. *The War of the Fists: Popular Culture and Public Violence in Late Renaissance Venice.* Oxford University Press, 1994.

Eglin, John. *Venice Transfigured: The Myth of Venice in British Culture, 1660–1797.* Palgrave, 2001.

Finlay, Robert. *Politics in Renaissance Venice.* Rutgers University Press, 1980.

Geanakoplos, Deno. *Greek Scholars in Venice.* Harvard University Press, 1962.

Gilbert, Felix. *The Pope, His Banker, and Venice.* Harvard University Press, 1980.

Hale, J. R. *Renaissance Venice.* Faber and Faber, 1973.

King, Margaret. *The Death of the Child Valerio Marcello*. University of Chicago Press, 1994.

———. *Venetian Humanism in an Age of Patrician Dominance*. Princeton University Press, 1986.

Labalme, Patricia. *Bernardo Giustiniani: A Venetian of the Quattrocento*. Edizioni di Storia e Letteratura, 1969.

Lane, Frederic C. *Venetian Ships and Shipbuilders of the Renaissance*. Johns Hopkins University Press, 1934.

Lowry, Martin. *The World of Aldus Manutius: Business and Scholarship in Renaissance Venice*. Cornell University Press, 1979.

Muir, Edward. *Civic Ritual in Renaissance Venice*. Princeton University Press, 1981.

Pullan, Brian. *Rich and Poor in Renaissance Venice: The Social Institutions of a Catholic State*. Harvard University Press, 1971.

Queller, Donald E. *The Venetian Patriciate: Reality Versus Myth*. University of Illinois Press, 1986.

Redford, Bruce. *Venice and the Grand Tour*. Yale University Press, 1996.

Rosenthal, Margaret F. *The Honest Courtesan: Veronica Franco, Citizen and Writer in Sixteenth-Century Venice*. University of Chicago Press, 1992.

ART, MUSIC, AND ARCHITECTURE

Bellavitis, Giorgio. *L'Arsenale di Venezia*. Marsilio, 1983.

———, and Giandomenico Romanelli. *Venezia*. Laterza, 1985.

Brown, Patricia Fortini. *Art and Life in Renaissance Venice*. Prentice Hall, 1997.

———. *Private Lives in Renaissance Venice: Art, Architecture, and the Family*. Yale University Press, 2004.

———. *Venetian Narrative Painting in the Age of Carpaccio*. Yale University Press, 1988.

———. *Venice and Antiquity: The Venetian Sense of the Past*. Yale University Press, 1996.

Cessi, Roberto, and Annibale Alberti. *Rialto*. Nicola Zanichelli, 1934.

Concina, Ennio. *L'Arsenale della Repubblica di Venezia*. Electa, 1984.

———. *A History of Venetian Architecture*. Cambridge University Press, 1998.

Cooper, Tracy. *Palladio's Venice: Architecture and Society in a Renaissance Republic*. Yale University Press, 2005.

Demus, Otto. *The Mosaics of San Marco*. University of Chicago Press, 1984.

Denker, Eric. *Whistler and His Circle in Venice*. Merrell, 2003.

Glixon, Jonathan. *Honoring God and the City: Music at the Venetian Confraternities, 1260–1806.* Oxford University Press, 2003.

Goy, Richard J. *The House of Gold: Building a Palace in Medieval Venice.* Cambridge University Press, 1993.

———. *Venice: The City and Its Architecture.* Phaidon, 1997.

Hocquet, Jean-Claude. *Venise: Guide culturel d'une ville d'art, de la Renaissance à nos jours.* Les Belles Lettres, 2010.

Howard, Deborah. *Jacopo Sansovino: Architecture and Patronage in Renaissance Venice.* Yale University Press, 1975.

———. *Venice and the East: The Impact of the Islamic World on Venetian Architecture, 1100–1500.* Yale University Press, 2002.

Huse, Norbert, and Wolfgang Wolters. *The Art of Renaissance Venice.* University of Chicago Press, 1990.

Lorenzetti, Giulio. *Venezia e il suo estuario.* Bestetti & Tumminelli, 1926.

Muratori, Saverio. *Studi per una operante storia urbana di Venezia.* Istituto Poligrafico dello Stato, 1959.

Pincus, Debra. *The Tombs of the Doges of Venice.* Cambridge University Press, 1999.

Rosand, David. *Painting in Cinquecento Venice: Titian, Veronese, Tintoretto.* Yale University Press, 1986.

———. *Titian, His World and His Legacy.* Columbia University Press, 1982.

Rosand, Ellen. *Opera in Seventeenth-Century Venice: The Creation of a Genre.* University of California Press, 1991.

Schulz, Juergen. *The New Palaces of Medieval Venice.* Pennsylvania State University Press, 2004.

———. *Venetian Painted Ceilings of the Renaissance.* University of California Press, 1968.

Tassini, Giuseppe. *Curiosità Veneziane.* 9th ed. Filippi Editore, 1988.

Wolters, Wolfgang. *Der Bilderschmuck des Dogenpalastes.* Franz Steiner, 1983.

ECONOMIC HISTORY

Borsari, Silvano. *Venezia e Bisanzio nel XII secolo. I rapporti economici.* Deputazione di Storia Patria per le Venezie, 1988.

Heynen, Reinhard. *Zur Entstehung des Kapitalismus in Venedig.* Union Deutsche, 1905.

Hocquet, Jean-Claude. *Le sel et la fortune à Venise.* 2 vols. Lille, 1978–79.

Lane, Frederic C. *Andrea Barbarigo, Merchant of Venice, 1418–1449.* Johns Hopkins University Press, 1944.

———, and Reinhold C. Mueller. *Money and Banking in Medieval and Renaissance Venice*. Johns Hopkins University Press, 1985.

Luzzatto, Gino. *Storia economica di Venezia del XI al XVI secolo*. Venice, 1961.

MacKenney, Richard. *Tradesmen and Traders: The World of the Guilds in Venice and Europe*. Routledge, 1990.

Mueller, Reinhold C. *The Venetian Money Market: Banks, Panics, and the Public Debt, 1200–1500*. Johns Hopkins University Press, 1997.

Rapp, Richard T. *Industry and Economic Decline in Seventeenth-Century Venice*. Harvard University Press, 1976.

Stahl, Alan M. *Zecca: The Mint of Venice in the Middle Ages*. Johns Hopkins University Press, 2000.

MODERN VENICE (SINCE 1797)

Berendt, John. *The City of Falling Angels*. Penguin, 2005.

Cipriani, Arrigo. *Harry's Bar: The Life and Times of the Legendary Venice Landmark*. Arcade, 2011.

Davis, Robert C., and Garry R. Marvin. *Venice, the Tourist Maze: A Cultural Critique of the World's Most Touristed City*. University of California Press, 2004.

Del Negro, Piero, and Federica Ambrosini. *L'aquila e il leone: I contatti diplomatici per un accordo commerciale fra gli Stati Uniti d'America e la Repubblica Veneta, 1783–1797*. Programma e 1+1 Editore, 1989.

Fletcher, Caroline, and Jane Da Masto. *The Science of Saving Venice*. Paul Holberton, 2005.

Gianfranco, Pertot. *Venice: Extraordinary Maintenance*. Paul Holberton, 2005.

Ginsborg, Paul. *Daniele Manin and the Venetian Revolution of 1848–49*. Cambridge University Press, 1979.

Keahey, John. *Venice Against the Sea: A City Besieged*. St. Martin's Press, 2002.

Norwich, John Julius. *Paradise of Cities: Venice in the 19th Century*. Doubleday, 2003.

Pemble, John. *Venice Rediscovered*. Oxford University Press, 1995.

Plant, Margaret. *Venice, Fragile City: 1797–1997*. Yale University Press, 2002.

Preto, Paolo. *Il Veneto austriaco, 1814–1866*. Fondazione Cassamarca, 2000.

INDEX